Building a Housewife's Paradise

Gender, Politics, and American Grocery Stores

Building a Housewife's

TRACEY DEUTSCH

THE UNIVERSITY OF NORTH CAROLINA PRESS
CHAPEL HILL

in the Twentieth Century

Paradise

This book was published with the assistance of the
Thornton H. Brooks Fund of the University of North Carolina Press.

Designed by Kimberly Bryant and set in Whitman and Stone Sans by Achorn International, Inc. Manufactured in the United States of America. The paper in this book meets the guidelines for permanence and durability of the Committee on Production Guidelines for Book Longevity of the Council on Library Resources. The University of North Carolina Press has been a member of the Green Press Initiative since 2003.

Library of Congress Cataloging-in-Publication Data
Deutsch, Tracey.
Building a housewife's paradise : gender, politics, and American grocery stores in the twentieth century / Tracey Deutsch.
   p. cm.
Includes bibliographical references and index.
ISBN 978-0-8078-3327-8 (cloth : alk. paper)
1. Supermarkets—United States—History—20th century. 2. Grocery trade—Social aspects—United States—History—20th century. 3. Grocery shopping—Social aspects—United States—History—20th century. 4. Women consumers—United States—History—20th century. I. Title.
HF5469.23.U62D48 2010
381.456413009730904—dc22   2009039274

cloth   14 13 12 11 10   5 4 3 2 1

Contents

Figures and Tables

Building a Housewife's Paradise

Introduction

In the fall of 1932, Chicago was in the throes of the worst economic depression in American history: nearly one of every four employable adults was without a job. Bread lines stretched for blocks on end. City officials warned of the potential for riots. The city's economy, political culture, and basic social structures seemed poised to change dramatically, and no one knew what directions those changes would take.

While many businesses closed their doors for good in the early years of the depression, the National Tea Company—one of Chicago's oldest and largest chain grocery firms—took a different tack: it dramatically remodeled 250 of its stores. Robert Rassmussen, a member of the company's board of directors, described the gleaming new refrigerators, state-of-the-art lighting, and impressive arrays of meats, produce, canned goods, delicatessen items, and staples. The new "super-food stores" were, he said, a "housewife's paradise."[1]

When Rassmussen made this assertion, he was reflecting his own hopes—he did not actually know what women shoppers would have called a "paradise." Indeed, the very design and structure of these new stores made it hard to determine what individual women wanted, let alone to offer them the personal attention or services that might have adapted the store to their needs. Yet over the next few decades, Rassmussen's claim came to undergird widely accepted ideas about grocery stores, women, and consumer society.

This book asks how and why a certain vision of what women wanted became so important to the National Tea Company, to women's experiences of food shopping, and to mass retail generally. In so doing, it argues for a more complicated view of the emergence of supermarkets than that offered by Rassmussen. The large, standardized supermarkets that dominated the post–World War II retail landscape depended on an enormous transformation in the ways in which women sought to feed their families. For much of the nineteenth and early twentieth centuries, women shoppers had been expected to

seek out bargains—to haggle with, threaten, praise, cajole, or shame the grocer, as circumstances warranted. Indeed, the workings of food shopping were
premised on women's claim to authority in negotiations with retailers. This
premise had begun to fade in the decades before World War II, however, and
by the post–World War II period women were expected simply to choose from
the grocers' offerings and to value low prices and peaceful anonymity above
full service and personal attention. By the late 1960s, when this study ends, the
woman supermarket shopper had become an emblem of the troubling political
disengagement and dissatisfaction fostered by middle-class life.

How did supermarkets, and the top-down, passive model of shopping that
they sustained, come to dominate food retailing and consumer society—and
ideas about both—in the postwar era? Conventional wisdom holds that supermarkets won shoppers by offering low prices and other features, such as large
parking lots, that matched shoppers' preferences.[2] In this telling, the needs of
consumers for low prices or efficiency guided economic actions.

But this explanation falls short when examined in light of the long history of women's reputation as difficult and demanding customers. Why, for
example, did the low prices of supermarkets displace women's expectations
of personal attention and service—if, in fact, they did? How did it ever seem
plausible that grocery stores would make shopping a passive experience rather
than active work? How and why did business owners decide to operate large,
top-down stores in the first place? And how could a single model of food retailing be, at least rhetorically, malleable enough to serve as a symbol of the
benefits of consumer society as well as its pitfalls? In other words, how did
supermarkets emerge, why did they come to seem so stunningly important,
and what does that importance tell us about women's history and the workings
of mass retailing and consumption in the United States?

This book answers those questions by embedding stores and retailing in the
gender relations, social politics, and political economies that shaped them. Supermarkets and the model of mass retailing that they epitomized emerged not
from straightforward consumer demand, but from a more complicated set of
causes: federal efforts to administer policy through stores from the late 1930s
onward, women's struggles for autonomy in the 1930s and 1940s, consumer activists' unwillingness to allow housewives any visible authority, the emergence
and embellishment of an ideology of the conservative female shopper in the
1940s and 1950s, as well as retailers' long-standing strategies to impose order
on their stores and achieve economies of scale.

At the heart of these efforts was control over the shop floor and women's
problematic assertion of their individual needs. Federal policy and capitalist

impulses toward mass retailing required that retailers and the state be able to impose policy. Neither government programs nor industrial standardization had any hope of working if women continued to expect and to assert control over store operations. The question of women's authority was inseparable from the question of how food would be sold.

I argue that politics (of many kinds) must frame any understanding of grocery stores and of shopping more generally. In groceries, the formal rules of governments (for example, collection of the sales tax) intersect with less-formal power relations of social life (for example, grocers' conversations with customers). Sometimes ethereal ideas about how women ought to behave took on material, economic, and structural importance in the spaces of stores and in the policies they imposed. Finally, grocery stores were sites not only for the purchase of food but also for the operations of the mid-twentieth-century state and its increased dependence on top-down, standardized, and predictable consumption. Despite the frequent claim that supermarket shopping was a depoliticizing experience premised on individualistic satisfaction-seeking, supermarkets and other grocery stores were deeply political.

GROCERY STORES MATTERED for many reasons. First and foremost, food and the stores that sold it were basic to physical survival throughout twentieth-century urban America. Grocery stores provided daily foodstuffs, as well as socialization and ties to neighbors and to traditions. They were spaces where ethnic loyalties, gender identities, and race relations were negotiated, reconfigured, and troubled. Even when grocery stores were not there, they mattered; the absence of grocery stores epitomized the decline and difficulty of life in urban "ghettos" in the late 1960s and the 1970s. Grocery stores make clear that consumption was as much about daily necessities and daily struggles as it was about commercial pleasures.

Food buying was also an important aspect of local and national economies. Grocery stores were by far the largest retail sector, in terms of both sales and numbers of stores, for most of the twentieth century.[3] Chicago, where I locate this study, had thousands of grocery stores.[4] These were scattered along business arteries that ran from neighborhood to neighborhood and were owned by firms of various types: national chains like A&P, local firms that operated only in the city and adjacent suburbs, huge independent firms that ran supermarket-type stores, and a healthy representation of consumer cooperatives. Grocery stores thus offer a window onto the complicated and sizable business of retail.

Finally, grocery stores foreshadowed changes that would come to virtually all retail sectors. It was in food stores that mass retailing took hold most suddenly, first with the rise of chain stores in the 1920s and then with the sudden increase in popularity of supermarkets in the later 1930s and 1940s. Both proponents and critics of mass retailing closely watched changes in grocery stores for evidence of the risks and challenges of new retail strategies. In the years following the emergence of chain store firms and supermarkets in the food industry, retailers in other fields began to borrow from and sometimes to improve upon the strategies of such firms, building very large stores, often on the fringes of cities and suburbs, that offered self-service and easy access to an enormous range of goods. Supermarkets became a model for how all retailers, not just grocers, might sell larger amounts of goods at lower prices than they had thought possible. This history, then, traces the story of big business coming to the grocery store, of grocery stores coming to epitomize mass retailing, and of the role of social relations in that process.

Putting Stores in Their Place

This history of supermarkets centers on Chicago. My approach departs from that of most stories of mass consumption and consumer society, which focus on changes at the national level.[5] Mass retailing, of course, affected how people shopped and how food was distributed in every region of the country, and it relied on broad networks of suppliers and stores. Even the names of firms (Atlantic and Pacific Tea Company, National Tea Company) suggest the scope of the enterprises that dominated food selling in the new era.

Nonetheless, supermarkets and the large systems that they undergirded ultimately operated in particular settings and must be studied in those settings. A local study has the virtue of demonstrating the simultaneous operation of different levels of political economy and corporate structures. It also makes clear the intersection of these institutional systems with less bureaucratic but equally significant social systems and cultural ideologies. In other words, studying stores in the spaces in which they operated complicates, in extremely useful ways, the stories we tell about modern economies and the ways people buy things in them.

Even the largest systems of exchange are embedded in and constrained by local spaces, as recent studies of globalization have demonstrated. Large firms negotiate local social networks in hiring workers, confront local environmental laws in choosing where to harvest, and almost never impose their original vision without encountering resistance. Laws and regulations initially regarded as unrelated to the product turn out to matter very much, while other policies, developed in national capitals or corporate offices far away from worksites, turn out to be difficult to enforce.[6] These studies of global flows of capital document the constant refiguring and strategizing that go on between people who seem to have a lot of power—like firm owners—and people who seem to have very little.

Studies that demonstrate the contingencies of globalization have implications for studies of large businesses generally, even ones that operate only domestically. Viewing stores in local contexts makes it clear that grocers cared not only about low prices and efficiencies of large-scale systems but also about social relations in individual stores, local politics, and many other issues. Moreover, the size of a firm does not always indicate its importance in provisioning people. Despite the importance of grocery stores, Chicagoans obtained their food from a complicated patchwork of enterprises, some of which were very small. Public markets, peddlers' wagons, small family operations, large national chains, and consumer cooperatives all have a part in this story, as they did in the lives of Chicagoans buying food. Studying the local efforts of large grocers muddies the clear-cut narratives that so often emphasize efficiencies and rationality, and thus easily explain the domination of the marketplace by large firms.

A local approach also complicates the neat categories into which stores are typically divided. Terms like "chain" or "independent" obscure overlaps in strategies and internal organization. Independently owned stores could be quite large, both physically and in terms of sales. Some very small, family-owned stores adapted the standardization of large corporate chains, and sometimes large chain firms found themselves forced by local language or dietary preferences to move away from the rigid standardization that they had envisioned when planning store operations. Chain stores offered a compelling vision of a new way of selling food, one that promised women both new freedoms and lower prices; but their strategies worked only in fits and starts, failing as often as they succeeded. As much as the operators of grocery stores aspired to particular models of retail, centralization and systematization proved extraordinarily difficult to implement in everyday life.

Furthermore, a local study also suggests the demographic limits on the "mass" market. Although chain stores and supermarkets operated in virtually every city in America by the end of the 1940s, they did not operate in every neighborhood. What now is referred to as "segmentation"—limiting target markets based on social variables—was always present. Race, class, and gender lie at the core of these spatial politics of retail.

Finally, just as a local study tests the workings of large firms, it can also test the meaning of trends in national and state laws. It is one thing to pass a law.

It is quite another to enforce and administer it in a local context. Laws often had unintended consequences that proved enormously important to retailers, but that may be missed if viewed only from the perspective of U.S. senators and representatives. Although often overlooked in discussions of twentieth-century political economy, municipal laws proved enormously important to the everyday work of grocers. A bottom-up study makes clear the impact that extralocal legislation, often credited with putting consumption at the center of American life, actually had.

Chicago offers particular advantages for a study of retail. It contained a variety of firms that operated on many scales—from tiny corner stores to networks of hundreds of stores throughout the country—and ranged in complexity of organization from sole proprietorships to large bureaucratic corporations. Moreover, the city's diverse demographic groups revealed the ways in which mass retailing created distinctions among people, as well as the common ground of national brands and chain stores. Finally, the city's vibrant local politics is a vivid reminder of the ongoing importance of municipal-level political economies. Studying stores in Chicago makes it impossible to overlook the ways in which mass retailers, however grand their scale or ambition, existed in small places and were constrained by the frictions of everyday life.

This book forwards a complicated understanding of consumption. Food shopping was never a straightforward way of satisfying needs—not for shoppers, but also not for retailers, who could not always consider consumers' needs and desires if they were also to fulfill the imperatives of turning a profit and observing a host of laws and regulations. Store buildings in the pre- and postwar periods encompassed not only spacious aisles of artfully arranged products but also careful navigation of changing government regulations, familial responsibilities, ideologies of masculinity and femininity, and economic realities. Seen in this way, the supermarket, that icon of postwar American life, emerged not from a straightforward attempt to satisfy consumer demand but through retailers' sometimes contradictory efforts to administer government regulations, achieve financial success, and control the shop floor and also through women customers' negotiation of budgets, familial needs, ethnic loyalties, political desires, and ideologies of domesticity. Supermarkets, and the food they supplied to so many Americans, emerged through politically minded and socially embedded calculations made by many players.

THE STORY OF MASS RETAIL and modern food shopping begins long before the first supermarkets emerged. Chapter 1 establishes the context for subsequent analyses of the business of food shopping. Through the 1910s, food shopping was conducted much as it had been for decades: women bought food in small-scale enterprises that were also settings for neighborhood politics. Women negotiated the busy stalls of public markets, bargained with neighborhood peddlers, and sought personalized attention at small grocery stores. This was difficult and time-consuming work, and it was recognized as such. Local newspapers, advice columns, and records of city government all remarked that women's work of shopping required careful negotiations with sellers and attention to community standards. This work and its place in political and cultural debate became increasingly visible in crowded urban districts and in the context of ethnic and racial tensions.

Chapter 2 focuses on the emergence of chain stores in Chicago and across the country. In the 1910s and 1920s, chain stores spread across cities and suburbs. They encroached on mainstays of urban commercial life, like hotels and candy stores, and came close to total domination of some retail sectors, like variety and cigar stores. Chain grocery stores, especially, captured the public imagination and the attention of politicians. The sudden growth of the chains, however, did not guarantee them stability; even their proponents worried that the explosion of chains would not last. They feared that women's "natural" demands for personal attention would add to the already high costs of renting and administering so many stores and so eventually would undermine chains' success.

The next two chapters turn to the emerging and still unsettled political economy of consumption. The future of grocery stores looked even less certain in the 1920s and 1930s, when it became clear that the political environment could dramatically alter competition among stores—a process narrated in Chapter 3. Grocers always had to contend with some government regulation, mostly municipal. Now, however, a state-level anti-chain movement, the state sales tax, relief policies, and the federal government's National Recovery Administration restructured grocers' interactions with their customers. To grocers in the 1930s, these government policies and the debates over them made the future of mass retailing unclear. What was quite clear, however, was that consumption, consumers, and women (those consummate consumers) were now crucial to government and would remain crucial to the future of food retailing.

In the interwar years, Americans, especially women, sought more equitable distribution of goods and broader economic and political change. Chapter 4 focuses on the ways in which grassroots protest figured into the political economy of consumption. These years witnessed an increasing number of boycotts, the growth of an organized consumer movement, and the new organizational

7

sophistication and success of consumer cooperatives. Grocers' concern with political economy was heightened by this new activism. Policymakers, meanwhile, feared that women consumers might disrupt such important policy efforts as the National Recovery Administration or state-level sales taxes simply by refusing to abide by them. Many Americans imagined that women, organized as consumers, might also demand and receive new authority over stores and over the state.

Chapter 5 explores how in the late 1930s and the 1940s, a conservative, middle-class model of femininity and women's authority informed the re-creation of supermarkets and of women's shopping. Chain store firms, independently operated stores, and consumer cooperatives now all built modern supermarkets—large, centrally managed stores that limited personal attention. This change was favored by regulations that gave political advantages to supermarkets, yet most store operators used the language of gender and femininity to explain it. They argued that women liked the convenience of larger stores, but even more so they needed the refinement of clean, well-lit, and orderly stores. Even consumer cooperatives adopted more conservative gender ideology and further undermined individual women's autonomy as they expanded into chains and larger-sized stores.

During World War II, the focus of Chapter 6, concerns about women's authority informed even the most progressive prescriptions for grocery stores. As the war intensified tensions surrounding food shopping, women confronted complicated government programs and family demands while they searched for food that was in shorter and shorter supply. The war also heightened the question of whether and how women would wield new political power because of their role as shoppers. On the one hand, women could and did use price control and rationing programs to report violations and to threaten uncooperative grocers. Officials, however, feared that women would put their own interests above those of the nation to sidestep wartime regulations, and they retreated from policies that allowed individual consumers significant influence over local retailers. Large, centrally managed chain store firms and the supermarkets that they operated proved best able to enforce rationing and price controls because their structure effectively prevented women customers from demanding personal exceptions to store policy.

In the postwar years, even as women continued to engage in the careful calculations required for grocery shopping, the labor, contingency, and everyday strains of food shopping were becoming muted by the top-down structures and celebratory rhetoric of cold war supermarkets. Chapter 7 explores the long-term importance of supermarkets. Both structurally and symbolically, supermarkets stood at the heart of the emerging consumer economy. By the 1950s and 1960s, access to large supermarkets was a real benefit of American life and was marketed as such both in domestic advice literature and in cold war–era anticommunist efforts abroad. In all these texts, women's demand was seen as central, while other factors that had shaped supermarkets—as well as constraints on what women could demand, and how they could demand it—were erased. The parallel case of hardware stores suggests the importance of the discourse of apolitical female consumers. Although certain mass retailing strategies encroached on the retail hardware sector, the stores remained small and continued to offer personalized attention to male do-it-yourselfers. Accordingly, although men shopping in hardware stores were also crucial to postwar consumption and the normative domesticity that it celebrated, they were featured neither in critiques nor in celebrations of the new mass-consuming society. Women, however, were invoked in depictions of the bounty of the postwar world, in explanations for the emergence of large, top-down supermarkets, and, increasingly, in critiques of postwar materialism and excess. Both discursively and structurally, women's satisfied and apolitical shopping was central to mass retail and the world it undergirded.

Writing about Consumption

This study is part of a new appreciation—in many fields—of the broad significance of exchange and consumption to power relations in modern life. Recent and important work has focused on the ways in which mass consumption and consumer society undergirded U.S. politics for much of the twentieth century. Lizabeth Cohen, Meg Jacobs, and Charles McGovern document and analyze the growing centrality of consumption to understandings of what it meant to be American in the twentieth century.[7] Much of this work highlights the conservatizing rhetoric and politics associated with consumer society, which ultimately encouraged Americans to view the purchase of products as an end in itself, unconnected to broader rights or responsibilities.

For all the attention to consumer politics, there has been relatively little work on the spaces in which purchases happen. This book shifts the focus back to stores themselves and to the retail contexts in which people encountered, negotiated, and ultimately sustained consumer society. Seen in this way, new variables in the study of consumer society emerge.

Because women were the primary focus of grocers' efforts, this history draws heavily from the literature on women and consumption. Although women's experience of consumption varied enormously across time and place, female responsibility for family meals remained a near ubiquitous norm.

9

Procuring food, or at least determining what was procured (what Marjorie DeVault has called "the invisible work of coordination"), fell squarely into their laps.[8] While early second-wave feminists' work on housework has pointed to the economic importance of women's reproductive labors more broadly, scholars still know very little about the commercial underpinnings of unpaid domestic work, the mechanisms through which everyday purchases were made, and their historical meaning in women's lives.[9] Such insights are especially needed, because some scholarship suggests that consumption and consumer goods offered important venues and catalysts for women's claims to public power.[10] A narrative of food shopping extends this work by highlighting women's everyday negotiations with grocers and demonstrating that stores offered a public sphere in which women tested their political and economic authority.[11] Women, therefore, might challenge the tenets of mass retail even as they embraced the benefits of particular stores.

Literature on business and economics suggests that such practices had economic importance. Recent work on particular firms and businesses has argued that social networks and political systems are crucial to firms' success. Successful manufacturers worked closely with retailers to obtain knowledge about shoppers and to build products that they would buy. Moreover, firms were themselves constituted by social networks that drew in, or excluded, potential managers and workers.[12] Decisions to expand or, alternatively, the ability to succeed as nodes in small-scale local networks, often reflected the laws and regulatory environment in which the firms operated.[13] Meanwhile, work on topics as varied as housework, imperialism, and U.S. slavery, has used capitalism—and the social relations it encompassed—as a framework for analyses of trade, labor, and exchange in the modern United States.[14] Although recent work has neither consistently acknowledged the centrality of gender and sexuality to exchange nor treated twentieth-century retail, it offers exciting and accurate visions of the significance of commercial structures.

Food retailing offers important opportunities for bringing these literatures together. Grocery stores were as much about capitalism as they were about gender. Indeed, they helpfully illuminate the connections between the two. For instance, although the middle decades of the twentieth century are often seen as a low point in women's activism in the United States, a close look at women's food shopping demonstrates both that consumption remained a sphere in which women claimed authority in the 1920s, 1930s, and 1940s and that women's challenges to store operation continued in the postwar period. Similarly, a close look at supermarket operations suggests the contingencies of their growth and the work of social relations that was crucial to everyday operations. Seen in this way, women's everyday resistance to and accommodation of store policy become crucial variables in the story of mass retail.

Taken as a whole, work on the social and institutional nature of enterprise suggests a need to explain rather than to assume the workings of consumer society. The seemingly stable liberal consensus of the cold war period tells only part of the story. Mass consumption was far less steady than policymakers had hoped it would be, and its everyday operations far less secure. The story told in this book reveals the work of maintaining it.

The "Politics" of Supermarkets

Much of the story centers on questions of authority and structure. Its focus on politics and power, on the many choices available to grocers and their many experiments, may seem to overlook the benefits and enjoyments found in the sorts of orderly, large-sized stores that ultimately became known as supermarkets; to discount the possibility that supermarkets succeeded because, simply put, they sold what consumers—or at least the women who were responsible for so much of food purchasing—wanted. It is certainly likely that many female shoppers found such stores satisfying. It seems unlikely, however, that their satisfaction is a useful concept in explaining stores' success.

Even the many women who embraced the possibilities of mass retailing did not always enjoy all aspects of food shopping. Their organized boycotts and their individualized demands and circumstances disrupted mass retailers' dreams of overarching standardization, as well as the policies of smaller neighborhood stores. A focus on women's attempts to procure food suggests the ways in which mass retailing was never quite as all-encompassing or as satisfying as its proponents have contended. And certainly grocers' frequent claims that such stores satisfied the collectivity of "women" cannot stand up to empirical review. Differences of class, status, preference, race, and so on, render profoundly misguided any attempts to generalize about women's wants.

Finally, both the context of capitalism and that of large, hierarchical chain stores make it impossible to know what customers of any demographic type really wanted. In an ideal world, many people might have wanted their food to be free, or at least much more affordable, or delivered fresh every day, or available in smaller quantities, or provided by members of their own race, class, religion, or ethnicity. We do not even have to imagine such radical alterations of food distribution to understand why demand was so difficult for grocers to meet or even to understand. The institutional context of stores shaped what customers could and did demand. Retailers' understanding of what people wanted was constrained by the limits of what they could realistically offer in a profit-oriented system of private business. That is, customers could "ask" only for certain things, and even then, retailers offered only some of them. My hope is that this book will complicate the category of "consumer" and the ways in which scholars so often ascribe both the successes and the problems of modern consumer societies to their intransigent desires.

The arguments presented here about political economy, social politics, and grocery stores extend the lesson that so many have drawn from Claude Lévi-Strauss's famous observation that food is "good to think [with]" by contending that the spaces in which food is sold are also "good to think."[15] In particular, such spaces help us think about the ways in which capitalism and its attendant power relations happen in everyday social encounters, in the most mundane of spaces, and in the most basic purchases. Rather than make capitalism seem pernicious and all-encompassing, this analysis reveals its contingencies and the enormous importance of an ordinary trip to the grocery store.

Women and the
Social Politics of Food Procurement

For much of the nineteenth century and the first decades of the twentieth, urban Americans bought food from peddlers, public markets, and local grocers, and picked produce from their own gardens. They bartered, negotiated, demanded personal attention, and submitted themselves to the canny gaze of food sellers—when they were not scavenging or stealing. Too important to be done thoughtlessly or according to anyone else's standards, food shopping in its everyday enactments was a complicated pursuit, which made it difficult to think of women as a unified group or of food selling as a peaceful procedure.

This chapter argues that urban food shopping in the late nineteenth and early twentieth centuries was—and was understood to be—difficult, time-consuming, and important work. The narrative uncovers the central components of that work, focusing on the gendered division of labor that assigned food shopping to women, the weighty social and cultural role of food, the geographic density of food retailers, the diversity of retail formats, and the legacy of personal assertiveness that surrounded food marketing in this period.

The social context of food shopping helps explain why it was such difficult work and why women took it so seriously. Following Marjorie DeVault's conclusion that the difficult labor of food preparation is part of a larger "care-giving" project for which women are primarily responsible, I embed food procurement in broader ideological and social contexts.[1] The chapter investigates particularly the gender norms, communal ties, religious identities, and familial loyalties that were at stake in food work during the late nineteenth and early twentieth centuries. In endless negotiations over the price and quality of goods, grocers and customers scrutinized each other's personalities and habits, as well as racial and ethnic loyalties. Small independent grocery stores, market stalls, and peddlers' wagons—although often romanticized in our own time—were places of discord and debate as well as friendship and community.[2]

The chapter also reveals the structural implications of these social politics, demonstrating that the commercial spaces in which food was sold were shaped by grocers' expectations that women customers would demand significant authority over the terms of purchase. Personalized interactions and attention seemed both problematic and inevitable to most retailers.

Ultimately, the social tensions that permeated stores and women's food shopping motivated grocers to move toward the top-down, standardized aesthetics of supermarkets and mass retailing. Thus, the way in which women shopped had enormous implications for political economy and the workings of capitalist exchange over time. The world of personal transactions described in this chapter stands in contrast to and helps explain the origins of the streamlined world of supermarkets and mass retail described later in the book.

Shopping and Social Relationships

At the heart of shopping for food was the effort to win individual attention. Indeed, this remained a constant refrain of Chicagoans for nearly forty years. A personalized interaction, steeped in mutual skepticism and canniness, required work on the part of sellers as well as buyers. "Marketing," noted one observer in 1911, "is still a question of beating down the tradesman from an outrageous price to a reasonable one."[3] One letter writer in 1913 urged her comrades to avoid shopping in the afternoon, when clerks were too busy to pay attention to individuals. In the mornings, she observed, "you have the pick of the market . . . instead of stale leftovers."[4] Sometimes, this expectation of individual attention resulted in requests that required remarkable levels of trust and personalized service from sellers. Marion Harland advised readers of her housekeeping column in the *Chicago Tribune* to have "a little forethought" and ask butchers to save cheaper cuts of meat until they could come in and purchase them.[5]

Women might ask for these services, but there was no guarantee that retailers would comply or that they would do so readily. Not surprisingly, when Chicagoans talked about stores, it was often to complain about their shortcomings: "As every housekeeper knows," wrote a Chicago journalist in August 1896, "one of the most exacting demands of housekeeping is marketing." The author went on to decry the options available to women. Placing orders with stores, either via delivery boys or over the telephone, could lead to subpar foods arriving at one's doorstep. If one "sallied forth" oneself, the well-meaning housewife found "the task of spending money scarcely less laborious than the task of earning it." Such a job required a shopper to be able to leave home just after breakfast or risk limited selection and long lines later in the day. "Then," she continued, "there is the friction of discussing the demerit of items previously delivered . . . and the often fruitless effort to secure just what is desired." Even women who had time for this face-to-face bargaining found it "weariness to the flesh."[6]

Shoppers' frustrations speak to the institutional effects of this mode of shopping and to the difficult business of distributing food. The inescapable individualism of shoppers was credited with causing spectacular bottlenecks all along the distribution chain. One anonymous observer of grocery stores pointed out that efforts to guess at what women wanted and therefore to standardize and minimize service would surely end in failure: "About the only thing upon which housewives are agreed," they lamented, "is that prices are too high."[7]

Similarly, the authors of a 1926 study on Chicago's South Water Market explained the difficulty of streamlining produce distribution as an inevitable result of selling to individual women. Quoting from a contemporaneous study of markets in New York, the authors asserted: "Partly because she cannot find the room to store perishables in a city apartment and partly because she prefers to see what is new at the vegetable market each day, the modern housekeeper pursues a hand-to-mouth purchasing policy . . . . The consumer wants a head of lettuce or a half-dozen oranges today and a grapefruit and two ounces of mushrooms tomorrow. The retail grocer or vegetable man tries to carry a little bit of everything and consequently not much of any one variety." The result, they concluded, was enormous congestion at produce markets as large lots were broken into very small quantities.[8] A frustrated housewife summed up her own perspective on the matter succinctly: "Individuality is greatly discouraged by those who serve her," she noted, "as they deem it an inroad on the even tenor of their way."[9] The need to serve women as individuals was both fundamental to and a problem for the operation of grocery stores.

As these accounts of shopping attest, food buying in the first decades of the twentieth century was an intensely, indeed uncomfortably, social encounter. The exchange was neither abstract nor impersonal, but took place through relentlessly messy social relations. Indeed, these social relations made exchange possible and, in the minds of retailers, they were an inevitable part of doing business.[10] Understanding how these relations mattered to stores themselves requires exploring food shopping in the lives and work of women who so often undertook this task. To appreciate the social relations in stores, one must appreciate what food buying meant outside stores.

Shopping in the Context of Housekeeping

Food shopping was difficult, in large measure, because it had to be accomplished around so much other work. Evidence from early Anglo America describes women's responsibility for most tasks associated with home life. In the antebellum United States, in the words of Jeanne Boydston, "housework remained the personal responsibility and defining labor of women."[11] Although the particular tasks, standards, and technologies changed over time, "women's work" conjured up images of cooking, cleaning, and caretaking through the later nineteenth and twentieth centuries.[12] Even amid the astonishing changes in women's tasks during the extension of industrial production and market relations in the early nineteenth century, women continued to answer for the cleanliness of their homes and continued to oversee the procurement of needed items, to process the raw materials of food and cloth into meals and clothing, and to perform the bulk of the child care in their households. Things had not changed by the end of the century: "There is the whole house to put in order and keep in order," wrote the pseudonymous "Aunt Hannah" in 1897, "the marketing, etc., sewing for the whole family, mending and darning and necessary attention to the laundrying. The children must be kept clean and clothed, fed and nursed through all of those dread forty children's diseases and brought up in the way they should go." "The life of a housewife," she concluded, "is an extremely busy one."[13]

What we know of household technology and housework shores up Aunt Hannah's claim. In the late nineteenth and early twentieth centuries, women did perform and oversee an enormous number of tasks. Some took up whole days (washing, for instance), but most were intermittent. Into this category went meal preparation, sweeping and mopping, and tending fires and lamps. The poorer the household, the more difficult daily maintenance could be. Crowded tenements were more difficult to keep clean than were less densely populated middle-class homes. Food was more difficult to come by for the poor than for the better off. And in working-class neighborhoods, water was more likely to require long hauling than to be available in backyard pumps or indoor taps.[14]

Finally, ideological pressures and tensions contributed to the difficulty, rewards, and significance of housework generally and of food shopping spe-

FIGURE 1.1. *Catharine Beecher's kitchen. Catharine Beecher and Harriet Beecher Stowe, plan of sink and cooking form, 1869. (Catharine Beecher and Harriet Beecher Stowe.* The American Woman's Home. *1869. (Reprint, Hartford: Stowe-Day Foundation, 1975.)*

cifically. Food, and its preparation and serving, figured prominently in the ideology of domesticity and its classed nature.[15] Beginning at least in the antebellum period with the publication of women's housekeeping guides, cooking and serving were celebrated as the stage on which women could best enact the work of efficiency and of generosity—work that would maintain familial coherence. Meals were the vehicle for love, nutrition, the reinforcement of religious and communal norms, the education of children, and displays of skill— for all the ways that women might convey their affection, nurturance, and fitness.[16] Prescriptions for cooking and eating changed over time but nearly always posited meals as central moments in families' lives. Catharine Beecher's famous sketch of the ideal kitchen points both to the work of cooking and to its importance in the vision of middle-class domesticity. Later iterations of the ideology of domesticity continued to place enormous emphasis on women's work around food. By the turn of the twentieth century, the emerging "science" of home economics encouraged women to see food and its preparation as a framework for their performance of efficiency and careful attention to family's health. (This emphasis on mealtime has not ended; in the early twenty-first century, researchers suggested that home-cooked family dinners would prevent everything from premarital sex to obesity to drug use.)[17] The ideology of domesticity emphasized the "work" done by meals and firmly assigned responsibility for those meals to women.

Over time, food purchasing became a marker of gender normativity for women. Even novelists reflected this broad discourse, which regarded failure to shop as failure to perform one's duties as a wife and mother. In *Sister Carrie*, Theodore Dreiser uses the male protagonist Hurstwood's assumption of food shopping as a mark of his declining fortunes and the dissolution of his and Carrie's relationship.[18] This ideological context made women's food procurement a social and cultural necessity as well as a physical one.

Commerce, Food, and Shopping as Women's Work

For all of the celebration of cooking as a bulwark against the dangers and exhaustions of work, and therefore as a duty particularly appropriate for women, the ingredients that cooks used and the technology with which those ingredients were prepared often required enormous physical labor. Experts at the turn of the century estimated that the work of tending stoves for a little under a week could easily require the cook to lift 292 pounds of coal.[19] Nor were tasks such as preserving fruit, baking bread, or plucking chickens for the faint of heart. For these reasons, servants sometimes did much of the work of cooking in middle-class homes, although this practice was less common by the early decades of the twentieth century. Even in families that employed a maid or cook, the employer was supposed to oversee techniques, meal choices, and ingredients.[20] Thus, employing a servant complicated but did not preclude a middle-class woman's taking credit for feeding her family.

Perhaps the most important contradiction that food-work revealed in the ideology of domesticity was the involvement of commerce and money in housework. By the turn of the twentieth century, food was increasingly obtained through marketplace transactions.[21] Food was one of the first commodities encompassed by a burgeoning system of mass distribution, so that by the turn of the century, many women could purchase glassed and canned soups and jellies, preserved vegetables, crackers, cereals, and nationally or regionally branded flour and cornmeal. All these products eased the work of cooking and introduced more variety in the diets of those families who could afford them. Other changes also increased the variety of food purchased. As transportation and refrigerated shipping became more feasible, urban markets also offered an impressive and much-appreciated selection of fresh fruits and vegetables, meat, and dairy.[22] According to one estimate, Water Street Market in Chicago, an important distribution point for both local and regional produce, saw fifty-three different varieties of produce move through on an average day.[23] While not all families could afford to purchase exotic goods, access to markets allowed many to make occasional forays into more extensive and varied diets—and to lessen some of the work of meal preparation.

There are many reasons why Americans regularly purchased their food. Some reflected sheer practicality: the increasing numbers of Americans who lived in cities encountered enormous difficulty in trying to produce and preserve food in small urban lots. Also, the rudimentary refrigeration of the era necessitated daily purchases, since food bought one day might not last until the next.[24]

Frequent food purchases, however, also reflected changing cultural standards and diets. As Jeanne Boydston has observed, the ability to enjoy variety in diet and in personal possessions had become a marker of respectable middle-class status.[25] That variety could be obtained only by access to nonlocal—and often canned, processed, or preserved—foods. From a limited presence on family's tables, canned goods had become common features of household larders by the late 1800s. By 1910, production of canned goods accounted for roughly 20 percent of U.S. manufacturing output and more than 3 billion cans of food.[26] As Glenna Matthews has documented, chemical leavening agents (for example, baking soda and cream of tartar) furthered Americans' use of processed ingredients.[27] By the late nineteenth century, even the most self-sufficient of lives had come to require goods obtained on the market. Most urban people purchased significant amounts of their food.

Food Shopping as Women's Work

Even if food and technology required market purchases, they had not always required women to make those purchases. That women obtained these food-stuffs for their own household use in the early twentieth century was in fact a historical shift. Ann Smart Martin has speculated that it was relatively common for women in the colonial and early national periods to go to markets and stores themselves.[28] By the antebellum period and into the mid-nineteenth century, however, responsibility for food shopping had become an open question. European and some domestic observers reported with alarm that men often shopped for food on their way home from work. Middle- and upper-class women employed female servants to go to markets or to order from the grocers and peddlers who rang the doorbell.[29] Catharine Beecher, the famous codifier of domestic advice for the nation's aspiring middle class, did not feel the need to add a chapter on shopping until 1873.[30]

Beginning in the late nineteenth century, however, procuring food came again to be the responsibility of women among all social classes. As an integral component of meal planning and preparation, food shopping emerged as a task appropriate even for middle-class women. Critics warned that the alternatives—sending servants or purchasing over the telephone—resulted in the delivery of lower-quality goods.[31] "[M]any a good dish and many a good temper . . . have been ruined by a carelessly given, carelessly received, carelessly filled telephone order," sternly advised one domestic economy expert.[32] This advice extended even to women who did not expect to carry goods home with them: "The wise woman is the one who resists the habit, picks up her market basket and her courage, and meets the potatoes and the apples face to face before she orders them sent to her home."[33] In this way, middle-class women claimed marketplaces as spaces for the performance of distinctively domestic tasks.

Because food was a daily necessity, regardless of the class of the consumer, its frugal purchase figured prominently in the financial strategies overseen by (and financial responsibilities borne by) many women. Economizing on food figures strongly not only in the accounts of working-class women but also in virtually all historical accounts of food shopping from the nineteenth and twentieth centuries. Indeed, it is a dominant theme of both prescriptive literature and women's autobiographical writing. For instance, Martha Coffin Wright's careful accounting in her private journal reveals that her shopping saved the family $60 to $70 annually on food purchases. Describing the industrializing landscape in the post–Civil War years, the anonymous author of *Six Hundred Dollars a Year* credited her ability to live comfortably on a mechanic's salary to her careful gardening. Particular commodities also loomed large in her advice to those who wished to emulate her success. "Butter," she helpfully noted, "appears to be a great stumbling-block in the way of every thrifty housewife."[34]

Chicagoans fully participated in these national trends. From the middle of the nineteenth century through the first decades of the twentieth, amid profound changes in politics, urban life, and material culture, the *Chicago Tribune* regularly featured articles alerting housewives to which fruits, vegetables, and types of meat could be had at especially good prices in city markets. Addressing a middle-class audience, the paper's editors and writers embraced the notion that class status required thoughtful expenditures around food. "There never was a time when a man drawing a salary and watching the expenses had the chance to enjoy luxuries as he has at present: A dollar will buy nearly twice as much as has been the rule in previous years. It is the chance of a generation to live on the top notch for a small outlay."[35]

Concern with food prices emerged from real financial constraints that continued to be felt by many, if not most, urban families in the early twentieth century. Researching the budgets of Chicago households, the economist Paul Douglas found that "maintenance" for a family of five was about $800 annually. However, the average family of that size earned only $560 in 1905 and $670 in 1915.[36] Studying working-class Chicagoans in the 1920s, Florence Nesbitt estimated that impoverished families spent about 50 percent of their monthly income on food.[37]

Even middle-class women conveyed a sense of economic duress in discussing their food shopping. For instance, a series of letters in the *Chicago Tribune* between 1912 and 1913 described how families coped with the "high cost of living" and focused on corners cut in food purchases.[38] One writer explained that she had "solved the problem of living within their income" through "marketing." All of her examples were drawn from careful planning of food purchases, often substituting her own labor for more processed goods—buying cheap cuts of meat and grinding them up or doing her own baking, for instance. Another wrote, more succinctly, "I think the main trouble in fighting the high cost of living is in marketing."[39] Other letters excruciatingly detailed the work of carrying one's own containers to the store and being sure one was getting a full measure of goods.[40] Another woman proudly recounted the ways in which she had structured her world around saving money on food. "We live near good markets and grocery stores," she explained. That, however, was not enough. In addition, "I can fruit in season, buying sugar at lowest price to be ready for canning time. Buy potatoes for winter from peddler and store in basement . . . . Buy flour at 'sale' prices by 25 pound sack. Do all own baking."[41] The ability to economize on food was important both to these women's daily labors and to their understandings of their contributions to household life.

Slowly, careful purchasing became a marker of class identity and a justification for public authority. One woman letter writer to the *Chicago Tribune* declared: "The less choice [goods] can be . . . sent to those 'real ladies' and 'social butterflies' who have neither time nor inclination for the details of household economies."[42] Economical food buying justified—indeed required—women's hard work and assertiveness. Its successful completion was a mark of responsible housewifery.

Food shopping was one of a number of women's tasks that involved complicated financial strategies. One woman's recounting of how she made ends meet eloquently illustrates the inextricable entwining of commerce, domesticity, and pride. A letter writer to the Chicago Tribune who shared a home with her brother and his son took pride in their healthful living (including "plenty of nice milk and cookies for my boys") and in her family's savings account, meant to pay the boys' college tuition. Yet, these accomplishments had a cost. She explained that they made do by eating meat only twice a week and by her baking all the family's bread. Moreover, she relied on a complicated combination of in-kind and cash exchanges to make ends meet. "One neighbor is glad to do my washing and cleaning for a little help with her sewing and fitting, which takes but little of my time. During the school year I give Saturday afternoons and evenings to helping high school pupils in algebra and often during the week from 7 to 9 eighth grade pupils come in for help. For this work I get 20 cents per hour. I work fine buttonholes for 25 cents per dozen, and do fine darning on torn garments and lace. I am often needed as extra help in the stores."[43] The impressive accomplishments of this unnamed author attest to the melding of market and home, to the amount of work required even to keep up middle-class households, and to the meaning of shopping as skilled labor.

A successful dinner, a savvy purchase, an opportunity to exercise authority over tradespeople or to perform culinary and economic skills for other women—all of these could result from satisfying shopping. But it was precisely the transient and fleeting nature of these rewards that made food shopping so important and so difficult. Food purchases, perhaps the purchases over which women exercised the most control, were also the one commodity in which prices paid and choices made were most open to question. Every transaction represented labor saved (for instance, by purchasing processed food) or precious cash wasted (for instance, by purchasing processed food of poor quality or that family members would not eat). Every transaction meant a choice—buying in bulk and preserving produce or buying in smaller quantities to be sure that food did not go bad. Indeed, for all of economists' frequent admonitions that demand for food is inelastic, food choices felt (and I would suggest continue to feel) elastic, variable, adaptable, uncertain—and extremely weighty. Women's food shopping was, for all these reasons, difficult and important labor.

A Diversity of Retailers: Shopping in
the Industrious Landscape, c. 1900–1920

Food retailing was a net that could keep families safe from the pervasive risks of urban life—and from which, as many housekeepers would have reported, it was all too easy to tumble. This net was woven of many distinctive ropes. Indeed, food businesses represented a coherent retail sector—and food buyers a coherent market—only in the broadest sense of the terms; the spaces in which food was bought and sold were made up of many different kinds of food retailers and infinite variations in familial structures, resources, and needs. Food shopping was, in other words, a complicated business. The spaces in which women bought food were busy, steeped in racial and ethnic tensions, and embedded in very local political economies. It was in these busy peddlers' cars, market stalls, and grocers' counters that the notion of women customers as demanding, assertive, and political was most powerfully forged. Here, the work and public authority claimed by women shoppers was both visible and unavoidable. Indeed, it was asserted in the discourse and reinforced by the institutional structures of early twentieth-century food retailers. These small enterprises left a legacy of expectations of disorder and disruptive personal encounters in the spaces of food buying.

Although stores lie at the center of this narrative, an understanding of the history of food shopping requires a look at other retail formats as well. The most famous sources for Chicago's food at the turn of the twentieth century were the city's busy public markets. Although historians have often pointed to the city as a site for the emergence of mass retail in the form of department stores and mail order firms in the late nineteenth and early twentieth centuries, public markets remained vital sources of food, clothing, and supplies for many Chicagoans.[44] (Chicago's most famous public market—the Maxwell Street Market—was not officially created until 1912, though merchants had made the district a de facto open-air market long before that.)[45] Chicago markets were concentrated in the Near West Side and along the railroad terminals near downtown, as the city served as a national hub for the transportation of western and southern meat, grain, and produce to the more urban northern and eastern parts of the United States. Although many of these markets were dominated by wholesalers (the city never seems to have seriously tried to keep nonproducers from selling at the market site), individual shoppers were also welcome. In places like Maxwell Street, Fulton Street, Kinzie, and the South Water Markets, Chicagoans looked for low-cost seasonal goods as well as items that could not be grown locally. Food came from nearby farms as well as from far-away orchards and commercial processors. Fruit, vegetables, meat, eggs, and dairy arrived and left on trains, wagons, pushcarts, and trucks of all sizes.

Public markets took on ideological as well as practical importance. Observers then and now have pointed to them as spaces of "civic life" offering public spectacles through which people from all classes might mix on relatively equal ground. A reporter describing the opening of one neighborhood public market in 1914 noted, "Democracy and cosmopolitanism in Chicago seldom assumes such an unusual and picturesque guise."[46] A bemused journalist describing opening day at a different market reported, "The vegetables were carried away in vehicles of all sorts, from the family baby carriage to the limousine."[47]

Precisely because of their appeal to people of many backgrounds, public markets could be congested and confusing places. Chicago's public markets were known for the great numbers of people brought together and transactions concluded in relatively small quarters. South Water, the city's largest public market, was a national point of distribution of fruits and vegetables.[48] Never a model of efficient planning, the market's notorious congestion only grew as more trucks and fewer wagons used its space and as farmers' production increased. Passageways were so narrow that a single truck making a delivery to a stall could back up traffic for hours. Movement was only slightly easier at the Randolph Street (aka the Haymarket—produce) and Fulton (meat and fish) markets and at the egg markets further west on Kinzie Street. All told, for the first decades of the twentieth century, the bulk of the produce needs of Chicago, its metropolitan area, and the shippers and wholesalers that it served, were handled in a two-square-mile section of the city.[49]

The busyness of these spaces made them daunting.[50] That reputation was reinforced by much of the writing about markets, in which their sheer congestion and the consequent dangers they posed to outsiders were regular tropes. In her novel about suburban truck farmers attempting to sell in Chicago, Edna Ferber described Chicago's Haymarket Square as "a tangle of horses, carts, men."[51] Contemporary journalists offered similar descriptions. One reporter reprinted at length a South Water Market worker's description of a maze of "barrels and boxes and gory calves, and chicken-coops, redolent with the unmistakable odor of the badly kept country barnyard and huge piles of sacked potatoes, and egg-cases, squashes, barrels of cider, and hogs cold and stiff in death." The author went on to note that if these sights were not enough to dissuade would-be shoppers, there was always the threat of being run into by a "red-faced Hercules propelling a two-wheeled truck."[52] While going to public

FIGURE 1.2. *The city's central site for produce distribution, South Water Market was famously crowded. This image shows the horses, carts, and people, as well as the newly constructed elevated train. (Chicago History Museum, DN-0000891, 1904, photographer unknown)*

markets could save money, these were, he warned would-be buyers, unsettling spaces.

Much of the physical congestion and intensity of these spaces was understood by observers as being representative of racial and ethnic otherness, only problematically accessed by "white" people. These qualities were ascribed to public markets in general, not only to those in Chicago. One Chicago journalist describing a market in Manila articulated directly concerns about the disquieting "foreignness" of the space in terms of physical revulsion: "The smells of the Chinese market and the sight of the half-naked Chinos who act as merchants there is enough to destroy a healthy appetite for a week."[53] The American sociologist Louis Wirth used a more detached tone in his description of Chicago's Maxwell Street Market but harbored similar suspicions. Maxwell Street, he wrote, was "full of color, action, shouts, odors, and dirt. It resembles a medieval European fair more than the market of a great city today. Its origins are in the traditions of the Jews, whose occupations in the Old World differed little from what they are here. To these traditions correspond also the traditions of other national groups who form their clientele."[54]

Of course, the accounts of actual Jews and of immigrants generally told a different story. Hilda Satt Polachek, a Jewish immigrant from Poland, wrote one of her first English-language essays on the unhygienic state of food stores in Maxwell Street Market. Her critique of the practices there problematized Wirth's claim that they reflected long-standing traditions and current desires of its immigrant clientele. Polachek noted chicken and fish being wrapped in "dilapidated newspaper," waste pipes that emptied directly onto the floors of shops and stalls, and cakes covered in masses of black flies. In a question that reflected both middle-class norms of sanitation and her own well-grounded fears of the spread of typhus and other diseases, Polachek demanded, "Why should this class of people who work harder than any other be compelled to eat inferior food when they might be supplied with good food for the same money?"[55]

For all their suspicions, Chicagoans looked with hope toward public markets. A small-scale market emerged at the corners of State and Lake streets in the central business district soon after the city's founding, and citizens soon began demanding markets closer to their homes.[56] Indeed, the notorious crowding of markets was itself an indication of their success. When new markets opened in the 1910s, they were stunningly popular. A neighborhood public market on Irving Park Road in 1918 saw nearly twelve thousand people despite having only recently opened, and it hosted as many as forty thousand people on its peak days.[57]

The weighty hopes and fears surrounding Chicago's markets were reflected in the immense set of municipal rules under which they operated. Public markets were designed to bring farmers and shoppers into direct contact, to keep prices low, and to make towns attractive destinations for foodstuffs. Thus, the earliest public markets almost always prohibited "forestalling"—the purchase of large stocks of commodities for resale at a later time. (In Chicago, rules about forestalling were more complicated; neighborhood markets preserved spaces for farmers and often succeeded in luring neighborhood consumers, while wholesalers quickly came to dominate the large downtown markets.)[58] In all cases, sellers were required to purchase licenses from the city. Market masters oversaw everyday operations and exercised significant police powers over buyers and sellers. Their responsibilities included everything from checking the accuracy of sellers' weights and measures to preventing the sale of rotten meat and produce—for example, by ensuring that dealers were not hiding spoiled fruit under opaque gauze.[59] Market masters were also responsible for assuring the orderliness of these spaces—even deciding whether swearing was to be allowed.[60] Sometimes, the significance of public markets in the body politic was made palpable, as when the young city of Chicago installed a public market on the first floor of its brand-new city hall in 1848.[61]

Skepticism swirled around markets, both because and in spite of the hopes placed in them. Over and over, Chicagoans bemoaned the difficulty of getting a fair deal from sellers. When plans to expand the city's public market first surfaced in the late 1850s, the *Chicago Tribune* editorialized that merchants at public markets were "hucksters" who joined forces to "adopt a high scale of profit" and forced up overall prices of food in the city.[62] Another editorial prompted by the same expansion effort expressed fears that municipal overseers had little real interest in preventing forestalling and that the markets would not give shoppers access to farmers (and thus, presumably, would not lower costs).[63] More than fifty years later, the suspicion was just as sharp. A housekeeping adviser described sellers as "a class of dealers with the ugliest of social qualities, who hold food for a price while it wilts or deteriorates or spoils."[64] Distrust was a constant feature of market life.

Middle-class women were understood to incur particular risks in these disorderly spaces. One article noted that young women entered the market under the watchful eye of their teacher, "their silk-lined skirts swinging clear of the sawdust-covered floor, and drawn carefully aside from contact with greasy tubs and unsightly vessels."[65] A housekeeping expert advised her audience of middle-class readers to study wholesale prices for days before making a foray into one of Chicago's markets or else risk being taken advantage of by a merchant.[66] A later article suggested that this advice had not proven helpful: "Many women go to the market once," noted one observer, "and never go again because they saved nothing by the trip."[67] This last comment suggests an emerging and critical failing of public markets in Chicago. Put bluntly, the trip was becoming longer and longer for most residents. As the population expanded beyond the central downtown area and the Near South and West Sides, shopping at downtown central markets began to seem overly burdensome. The markets' distance from residential areas forced shoppers to carry large parcels of food home on public transportation—or to pay extra for their delivery; markets were increasingly busy and inhospitable places for retail customers, even as they became crucial nodes for local and national food distribution. Public markets seem not to have loomed large on the everyday retail landscape of most Chicagoans by the turn of the twentieth century. Although they continued to provide most of the food that people ate, it was by way of wholesalers and peddlers rather than by direct sales. As the city stopped building new markets and as existing ones became less and less accessible to the bulk of the city's population, Chicagoans found other sources from which to obtain foodstuffs.

For people unable or unwilling to travel to markets, peddlers brought food from public markets to their streets and neighborhoods. As in the markets, buyers still made aggressive demands on purveyors. These food purchases were grounded in the politics and social relations of neighborhood life. As with sellers at markets, the city tried to exercise authority over the potentially disruptive politics of commerce by closely regulating peddlers.

The role of peddlers as conduits from the central markets to the neighborhoods is borne out in studies of sales at the city's South Water Market. Although analysts claimed that retail grocers ought to be the primary buyers, they could not ignore the fact that peddlers' buying habits influenced the movement of foodstuffs throughout the city.[68] By 1923, nearly a third of all goods purchased there were sold to "alley peddlers" (who sold directly to consumers) or to "jobber peddlers" (who purchased in small lots and sold to individual peddlers or very small retailers). In addition, peddlers purchased the equivalent of 56,166 wagonloads directly from railroad cars every year.[69] The significance of peddlers was even clearer at smaller markets that sold to a more local clientele. During a roughly contemporaneous period at the Randolph Street Market, 42 percent of all goods sold were bought by street vendors.[70] In 1906, one observer counted a thousand fruit and vegetable peddlers alone. In Chicago, according to one historian, an "army of peddlers" paraded past residents' homes.[71]

Peddlers offered particular advantages. They sold in very small amounts—a crucial feature for women who were struggling to balance limited cash with daily needs. They also fit well in the physical spaces of working-class neighborhoods. In spite of the density of the population, buildings were rarely more than three stories high, and front streets alternated with alleys. The low buildings gave peddlers easy access to women who were home during the day, and the alleys allowed them to set up shop on a given block while customers came to them.[72]

Peddlers also offered services important to families who had more comfortable finances. Their willingness to sell in small amounts allowed people to purchase only what they needed for that day and thus to save space in iceboxes (as well as the money that ice would have cost). Moreover, peddlers' neighborhood routes eased the cramped schedules of women who were busy watching young children, performing time-consuming housework, or performing paid work in others' homes. For many people, peddlers were absolutely essential to everyday financial and physical tasks.

It is not surprising, then, that peddlers and their offerings permeated the daily life of neighborhoods. Their cries alerted residents to the produce, ice, wood, dairy goods, prepared foods (like hot peas or bagels), clothing, or rags they had for sale.[73] Years later, the children of Italian immigrants remembered peddlers who offered strawberries, fresh fish (imported from Boston), grapes (for eating and for winemaking), roasted pumpkin seeds, and pizza.[74] Peddlers provided "a constant supply of fresh food" to vast numbers of urbanites and supplemented working-class neighborhoods' restaurants, taverns, bakeries, and delicatessens in supplying processed or precooked food.[75]

Both despite and because of the important position of peddlers, transactions with them were not straightforward; indeed, the culture of street buying was one of loud, public negotiation. One woman recalled that as late as the 1930s, fruit peddlers made alleys into temporary markets: "Peddling . . . took place in the streets, the gangways and alleyways of our neighborhood. 'Watermalone, watermalone,' the fruit peddler shouted in this special way. From my porch, I could see the mothers streaming out of their back doors. Soon they filled the alley, crowded around the peddler's truck, arms waving, voices lifted to get the peddler's attention, as he carved out a red pyramid of sweet watermelon and held it up for the ladies' approval."[76] Residents also remembered the "constant verbal exchange" of bargaining between housewives in apartments and peddlers who were calling out their wares in the street. This exchange could become lengthy and complicated; it was not uncommon for peddlers to halt for as long as an hour while women inspected and chose fish or produce.[77]

Peddlers had to be willing to work extremely hard—close to sixty hours per week at the turn of the century. Much of this time was spent in the predawn hours, as many sought out the best bargains at public markets or loaded wagons with fresh bread or dairy goods. They then faced the prospect of walking outside regardless of the weather—no easy task in the face of Chicago's famously difficult climate.[78] While peddlers often hoped to save enough to open a storefront, average profits were not high.[79] One urban reformer in Chicago claimed that Greek immigrant men who became peddlers earned an average of $10 per week in 1909 and paid $30 per month for a stall for their horse and a room above the stall for themselves.[80] Contemporaries estimated peddlers' wages, nationally, at between $3.30 and $7.50 per week. An observer wrote in 1905 that peddlers "are very poor, hard working, and earn a precarious living."[81]

The work of peddlers in Chicago was compounded by the complicated social and legal context in which they operated, more particularly the anti-Semitic and anti-immigrant sentiments of many Chicagoans. Ethnic hostilities, of course, had swirled around the public markets as well, but they took on new meanings for peddlers in the neighborhoods. In Chicago in the late nineteenth century, peddlers consisted largely of recent Jewish, Greek, and Italian immigrants.[82] Peddlers' status as recent immigrants made them particularly tempting targets for Irish and native-born street gangs.[83] Because so many peddlers were Jewish, an entrenched anti-Semitism both informed the language and justified the viciousness of physical attacks on them. News of European pogroms, for instance, often sparked attacks by Polish immigrants on Jewish peddlers.[84] Similarly, in the wake of Russia's defeat at the hands of Germany, a Polish-language newspaper warned its readers about the dangers of patronizing peddlers, who were presumably Jewish: "So we looked upon with loathsomeness how these vermins [sic] how these parasites brought up on our bread, in the heart of the Polish quarter were gushing upon us with slanders and lies. Remember, brothers, continue feeding and breeding this vermin, buy from them, and you will get the same as Russia."[85]

Of course, anti-Semitic and nativist discourses circulated among middle-class readers as well. Edna Ferber's fictionalized portrait of the intimidating Haymarket used the stereotype of the peddler to convey the difficulty of doing business there: "Peddlers and small grocers swarmed in at four—Greeks, Italians, Jews. They bought shrewdly, craftily, often dishonestly. They sold their wares to the housewives. Their tricks were many. They would change a box of tomatoes while your back was turned; filch a head of cauliflower."[86] For many readers, images of crafty Jews, unamericanized immigrants, and outright criminals were conflated in the discourse around peddlers.

Peddlers' social ostracism was not the product solely of outside racism, however. With a reputation as recent and impoverished immigrants, unschooled in American ways, they evoked suspicion from more established middle-class members of their own ethnic groups. The German Jewish newspaper the *Occident*, for instance, called upon its readers to refuse to assist recent Russian Jews who threatened to "over-run our city with peddlers." The editors explained that this concentration of Jewish peddlers would "simply be a disgrace to us."[87] Similarly, Chicago's Greek-language newspaper referred to Greek peddlers as "ignorant" and decried them for their rudeness.[88]

This general disapproval, filtered through classist, nativist, and anti-Semitic sentiments, was reified in legal barriers to peddlers' work. Many of these regulations were lobbied for by competitors of peddlers. For instance, Chicago's newspapers in the late nineteenth and early twentieth centuries were filled with accounts of local grocers organizing to demand punitively high licensing fees and even garish badges to distinguish peddlers on the sidewalk.[89] Retailers also complained that peddlers could sell cheaply because they often operated as unlicensed businesses. In one instance, the local trade association described peddlers as "parasites of the trade."[90]

Chicago's city government responded to this combination of racist sentiment and business rivalry with heavy regulations designed to put peddlers at a disadvantage. For instance, the city council passed measures that dramatically limited the hours during which peddlers could operate, the neighborhoods through which they could walk, and their ability to call out their wares and alert housekeepers to their presence.[91] License fees for peddlers were much higher than those for conventional grocers. The city responded to pressure from native-born restaurateurs by temporarily forbidding the sale of food by peddlers on city streets.[92] Council members even considered an ordinance to restrict licenses to native-born peddlers.[93] Indeed, Chicago famously had some of the "strongest anti-peddler laws in the nation," although cities like Omaha, Milwaukee, and New York passed similar laws.[94]

Peddlers, it was true, did not always follow the letter of the law; but the bevy of municipal regulations meant that the threat of government harassment attended their daily operations. The city's uneven enforcement of food safety regulations was but the clearest example. Inspectors of weights and measures seem to have targeted peddlers in particular.[95] Also, both officials and progressive reformers regularly claimed that peddlers sold unsafe or improperly packaged food—"generally low-grade and overripe commodities" as one analyst put it.[96] As late as 1926, city health inspectors focused their inspections of meat on "wagon peddlers," proudly noting, "In many cases the food was condemned as unwholesome and the peddlers arrested and fined."[97] City officials expressed similar glee in announcing the success of their ad-hoc fruit auctions, held in the wake of an inflationary boom in the summer of 1922. City council members crowed that they had been able to cut off customers from "fruit peddlers who heretofore have been able to rob the public in inferior and oftentimes decayed fruit."[98] Peddling represented precisely the sort of ungovernable commerce that city officials resisted.

As had been the case with public markets, however, these new regulations rarely succeeded in bringing order to the work of food selling. Peddlers continued to ply their trade in Chicago and in other cities, even as officials tried to contain and regulate them.[99] Neither anti-immigrant sentiment nor fears of unsafe food nor city regulations stopped peddlers from claiming their place in the retail landscape. In New York City, for instance, one study found that although only four thousand licenses had been issued, between fourteen and fifteen thousand peddlers were operating in the city. Small-scale corruption of local police, mayoral permits allowing peddlers to bypass regulatory mechanisms, and the sheer difficulty of reigning in people who were both mobile and needed proved to be too much for local officials to overcome.[100] Peddlers' own creativity also explained their resilience; despite attempts to give Chicagoans direct access to wholesalers and producers via public markets, so many peddlers made their rounds in and around markets that they crowded out other kinds of businesses.[101] A plaintive note from a 1933 city council session bears vivid testimony to the inability of the city to effectively contain peddlers. In an order passed by the entire council, the commissioner of compensation was directed to "remove the peddler from the corner of Melrose Street and Lincoln Avenue."[102]

Eventually, of course, peddlers did become less prevalent. This decline, however, seems to have been the result of a combination of decreased immigration after the 1920s, the restriction of peddlers to special peddler "markets" (usually only a few square blocks), and prohibitions on buying or selling in urban residential neighborhoods rather than an expression of consumer demand. Indeed, there are indications that people would have preferred to continue to use peddlers. For all the suspicion heaped on them, peddlers were important resources in daily struggles to organize time and to make ends meet.[103]

Conventional Food Shopping before Chain Stores: A World of Personal Negotiation

By the early years of the twentieth century, public markets and peddlers shared the work of distribution with an enormous number of small grocery stores. As Chicago's population boomed in the late nineteenth century, these sorts of stores became vital sources of food supplies. Transactions in these stores, too, reflected the charged nature of exchange with peddlers and in public markets. It was these small neighborhood grocery stores that supplied most Chicagoans' food through the middle decades of the twentieth century. And it was the proprietors of these stores who articulated the notions that personal attention given to women and women's traditions of personal assertion were both inescapable and problematic.

Grocery stores in the 1920s were very small enterprises, both in terms of physical size and in terms of sales. Even the "model" grocery store of the era's prescriptive trade literature occupied only 1,134 square feet; the first chains, designed for efficiency and rapid stock turnover, often occupied only 500 or 600 square feet (approximately a 20' by 25' room).[104] Moreover, sales were notoriously low in most grocery stores. Average annual sales for an independent grocery in Chicago in 1929 were only $13,285.[105] Business was so limited that grocers could keep close track of changing habits. The son of one Chicago grocer remembered, "If my dad had 50 customers, that's all he had, 50. If he got 51 one day, it would be an odd thing. Somebody from the next block was passing by or got mad at his butcher that day."[106]

In these small neighborhood stores, customers developed more personal relationships with their grocers than they might have with transient peddlers or nonlocal market stall sellers. Grocers offered a range of services that could include letter writing or translating for customers who did not speak English, advice about which foods would keep well, and information about neighborhood goings-on.[107] One 1931 Chicago sociology student described the way in which a neighborhood grocer was drawn into personal relationships with his customers: "He knows their family troubles and family joys. He knows when a child is born, when a boy or girl has married. He is often solicited to help influence certain relatives who also patronize the store." Reflecting on this level of intimacy, she characterized these relationships as being of "primary contact."[108] A University of Chicago sociologist categorized such grocery stores as a "town and unit store." In these sorts of businesses, he reported, "the relationship between the store proprietor and the customers is very intimate."[109]

Close personal relationships, of course, did not guarantee smooth interactions in grocery stores, just as they did not in other retail formats. Buying and selling were still the result of bargaining and haggling. These were "service stores." Customers approached clerks or proprietors about what they wanted to buy, and staff helped customers choose from the goods that were kept behind the counter or in a back room. Clerks then retrieved items from storerooms and inaccessible shelving. Because prices were not posted, clerks also determined how much customers paid. Finally, grocers and their employees also filled phone orders for delivery later that day.

Familiarity may have enabled trust, but the dependence on store staff also bred suspicion among customers. Because proprietors and employees presented customers with the items from which they might choose, shoppers often held them responsible for the quality of goods sold. Bad flour might mean that the clerk had simply refused to get the good flour from the back room or tried to foist onto unsuspecting customers goods they knew were substandard. Similarly, because prices were negotiable, shoppers were never sure that they were not being made to pay more than other customers. One *Chicago Tribune* reporter found that even stores under the same local management charged wildly varying prices across the city.[110]

Phone orders were a special source of concern. Ordering via telephone was a relatively recent variation on the long-standing practice of making purchases by sending children or, for the better-off, servants. Critiques of women who used the telephone echoed those of women who did not do their own shopping; they depended far too much on staff to fill their orders accurately and to substitute high-quality goods if a particular brand were unavailable. Indeed, the danger of ordering over the telephone became a near truism among home economists and among middle-class women themselves. One columnist referred to placing orders by telephone as an "insidious habit" while another referred to "this class of buying" as "an outlet for the merchant to dispose of unsalable goods."[111] An embittered letter writer used even harsher language: "Careless and incompetency in the housewife show themselves mostly in the reckless abandon with which she places her order with the trades people over the telephone or from the kitchen door. Needless to say, the clerk who takes her order puts it up with no more care and attention than she has given it. . . . Rarely will your grocerman tell you over the telephone that lettuce which is selling at 10 and 15 cents a head is not choice today, but that leaf lettuce at two bunches for 5 cents is just as good. Nor will he tell you that the oranges are small and not worth the price. He will not select the corn, the tomatoes, and the cantaloupes as carefully as if you were there in person."[112] In this emerging discourse, *not* traveling to stores was a sign of poor housekeeping skills.[113]

Even face-to-face negotiation was no guarantee of obtaining the best deal. Clerks and proprietors used their knowledge of the customer—and of their own bottom line—to advise would-be purchasers. Both employees and firm owners frequently pushed certain goods and steered customers away from others. Indeed, grocers and clerks so influenced customers' ultimate purchases that early distributors of branded foods considered small, independent grocers crucial allies in winning customers over to their brands.[114]

Even as clerks tried to shape customers' purchases, however, customers demanded equitable treatment, low prices, and high-quality merchandise that fit their needs. Home economist and business consultant Christine Frederick explained that grocers would have to resign themselves to what she believed was women's natural and long-standing proclivity to distrust and bargain with them: "Watch the average woman shopper as she goes about shopping. . . . She perhaps likes to haggle a bit, or ask questions, or just rid herself of a few irritations over some piece of merchandise that wasn't just right, or which she

FIGURE 1.3. *This photograph of the wealthy widow Bertha Bauer was meant to demonstrate her attention to the details of everyday life. It also suggests the intricate give-and-take that characterized encounters in grocery stores. Note the high shelves of goods behind the counter.* (Chicago History Museum, DN-0080838, 1926, source: Chicago Daily News)

had no luck in cooking."[115] A middle-class observer of one working-class Italian grocery described the scene more vividly: "The counter is often a scene of bargaining and haggling. Often a visitor feels that the grocer and customer are most unfriendly to one another, as this bargaining goes on. It is with great surprise that the stranger observes the very intimate conversation between the grocer and his bargaining customer after the haggling has been dispensed with."[116] In small stores, the act of shopping was enmeshed in personal interactions and shaped by never-ending negotiation within the context of ongoing relationships. Social pressure was as much a part of these businesses as was the food that they sold.

Bargaining and haggling required shoppers to acknowledge that they might be taken advantage of—and to have the social resources to resist grocers' attempts to foist inferior goods on them. This aspect of food shopping had particular implications for Chicago's African Americans, who sometimes hesitated to engage in overt challenges to grocers. One 1934 article in the African American newspaper the *Chicago Defender* criticized black shoppers who simply took what grocers and butchers wrapped for them: "A foolish pride leads too many Race people not to question the fairness of a price or to walk out on what they consider an unfair price for the class or merchandise offered." The article continued by pointing to the special reasons that Chicago's blacks had for complaint: "It is a known fact that inferior merchandise at high prices is the rule in neighborhoods largely populated by Race people. A casual survey of display windows in nearby store areas, where the population is not predominantly of the Race, will quickly confirm this."[117]

Personal credit was a special catalyst for the negotiation. Credit bound grocers and customers to each other, whether they liked it or not. Small retailers made many of their sales on credit—anywhere from one-half to two-thirds according to a 1928 government survey.[118] That statistic, however, does not reveal the marginal finances and emotional tensions that lay behind many extensions of credit—particularly to working-class families. In hard times, customers could be desperate, and grocers frequently granted credit even when it was not financially wise. A University of Chicago student reported that grocers in the working-class neighborhood of Bridgeport granted credit during strikes and layoffs, knowing full well that they would, most likely, never see their money. One woman grocer recalled that in the early 1930s, "They come, kneel down . . . just like to the Lord, you know. Please give me. My children are starving. . . . So we gave."[119]

Both in spite of and because of the difficulty of getting paid back, grocers pressured customers to honor their debts. One indication of the intensity of their efforts is their resistance to giving up on collections; in the late 1920s, analysts estimated that grocers typically wrote off between 10 percent and less than one-half of 1 percent of the money owed them. This low rate of account closure among small grocers was not a reflection of customers' prompt repayment. In fact, collection rates were dramatically lower in the smallest businesses, the ones in which grocers could least risk alienating customers. A store with annual sales of under $10,000 collected, on average, only 34.3 percent of the debts due it every month.[120] The pages of trade journals were filled with advice about how to collect on debt, and editors often advised grocers to limit the credit they offered.[121]

Despite this concern over the dangers of extending credit, grocers frequently refused to cut off customers, maintaining that it was only by offering credit that they could ensure regular purchases. And customers, though they complained about the terms and resented the embarrassment of need-ing credit, continued to make use of it.[122] However many problems it caused, credit allowed customers to continue to buy food through hard times and tight budgets, and it was crucial in grocers' attempts to win customers. The messy account books of grocers were testaments to the complex social encounters in their stores.[123]

THESE EVERYDAY QUARRELS OVER PRICE, quality, and credit were structural features of food retailing, reflecting a long history of women's food procure-ment and the dense network of businesses in which they shopped. Evidence from grocery stores suggests, however, that bickering over the terms of pur-chase was also often an expression of animosity arising from other sources, especially from ethnic or racial rifts. Like peddlers, grocers did not always share the ethnicity, race, or religion of their customers. Even when they did, many community leaders complained that shoppers did not show them proper support. Group solidarity, popular prejudice, and a desire for economic au-tonomy played out in food stores, complicating shopping and raising the stakes of transactions.

Social tension characterized the food shopping practices of African Ameri-cans in particular. Two facts made grocery stores in African American neigh-borhoods especially politicized. First, African Americans owned very few retail businesses. Second, the firms that they did own tended to be grocery stores. These stores, then, were both an important source of capital for African Ameri-cans and one of the most common kinds of businesses through which con-sumers could support a program of economic autonomy for blacks.[124] Resent-ment of white entrepreneurs who lived outside of black neighborhoods but did business within them, as well as calls for racial solidarity, often centered on food shopping. African Americans' attempts to organize around the point of consumption illuminate the ways in which food stores became arenas for racial tensions and social change.

As in most other cities, the vast majority of businesses that operated in Chicago's African American neighborhoods were not owned by African Ameri-cans.[125] But Chicago also seemed to many to contain the ingredients for suc-cessful black entrepreneurship. Chicago's "Black Belt" boasted some of the na-tion's most important black-owned businesses and a highly concentrated and rapidly growing population. Binga's Bank lent money, African American insur-ance companies granted policies, and African American–owned stores sold daily necessities. The city also had a noticeable, if still small, African American middle class. Although certainly poorer than their white counterparts, African

American railroad porters, clerks, door-to-door salesmen, and teachers, together with working-class day laborers, domestics, and industrial workers, patronized busy "Black Belt" business districts, most notably along Thirty-first and Forty-seventh streets on the city's South Side. The highly concentrated black population and the presence of at least limited capital suggested that if black owned retail could flourish anywhere, it would be in Chicago.[126]

The urban uprisings of the summer of 1919 marked a watershed in the racial politics of the city—including the politics of retailing. Between May and July, a series of increasingly violent encounters between African Americans and whites marked rising anger and frustrations on both sides of the color line. The violence climaxed with a wave of looting, attacks, and disorder in African American and working-class white neighborhoods in late July and early August. For days on end, stores in black neighborhoods were closed, and African Americans were told to stay home from work because it was too dangerous for them to travel through white neighborhoods to their jobs. The riot crippled the city and made its ugly racism clear to the country.[127]

It also demonstrated that stores were places in which racial tensions played themselves out. In the wake of the riot, and in the course of assessing the financial costs of the physical damage, the city council interrupted its proceedings to pass a resolution requiring retailers to mark prices clearly. Only a few days later, many of the Jewish retailers doing business along African American sections of State Street stopped repairing damage to their stores long enough to form a "protective association" to support each other if another insurrection occurred.[128]

Over the long term, the riots sparked a new era of consumer organizing among African Americans. The newly articulated collective outrage of many African Americans, coupled with a general faith in entrepreneurship in the 1920s, reenergized community leaders' long-standing campaigns to organize support for black-owned businesses. The Chicago Whip, a militant African American newspaper that had begun publishing just before the riots, frequently called on its readers to shop only in black-owned businesses.[129] Both the Whip and its more mainstream competitor, the Chicago Defender, went on to organize boycotts of white-owned stores throughout the early 1920s.[130] In that decade, they were joined by numerous national organizations that also began encouraging African Americans to support African American businesses. Marcus Garvey's Universal Negro Improvement Association (UNIA) had as one of its primary goals economic self-reliance and urged members to support UNIA-owned Universal stores and laundries. The Colored Merchants' Association, a national trade group begun in 1928, tried to stir up support for its members by organizing "Housewives' Leagues" to drum up support for CMA businesses.[131] In food shopping as in other arenas of consumption, Chicago's African Americans confronted and resisted the meanings of racial inequality.

Of course, the politics of communal loyalty and of racial and ethnic hostility also played themselves out in predominantly white neighborhoods. Indeed, African Americans' efforts to organize consumer support for black-owned businesses were mirrored, albeit less extensively, by similar campaigns in many of Chicago's white ethnic communities. Foreign-language newspapers kept constant pressure on readers to shop in stores owned by members of their respective ethnic groups. One Slovakian paper noted that Slovak-owned stores were especially likely to help their own during hard times and to give good advice about which foods to buy. More important, supporting Slovakian stores would help the community in general. "Our patronage," the paper maintained, "helps their business to grow and consequently our ideals become a reality."[132] Similarly, an article in a Lithuanian publication celebrated and perhaps intended to foster ethnic loyalty: "The time has gone when the Jews or Germans could carry on a thriving business among the Lithuanians of America: our people like to buy from Lithuanians."[133]

Just as grocers from within a community were portrayed as helping consumers, customers were warned away from "outsiders." Rhetoric about supporting one's own community often shaded into negative portrayals of other ethnic groups. The same article that urged readers to support Slovak stores menacingly pointed out that non-Slovaks "may be your enemy."[134] Most Chicagoans were more specific about the ethnic and religious identities of potential enemies. In 1934, the secretary of the Yugoslavian Woman's Club claimed that Yugoslavians resented Jews "because the Jewish people don't patronize Jugoslavian stores when the Jugoslavians still patronize their store." Jewish merchants were especially resented, the author claimed, for their unethical practices. "Jugoslav businessmen know the Jewish merchants steal on the weight, therefore, charge a little less to make more business," she observed.[135]

Native-born European Americans, of course, also articulated racial and ethnic prejudice. Writing in 1925, the home economist and business consultant Christine Frederick described one reason why she was so ready to welcome chain stores: "To be perfectly blunt, the independent merchant is often a dirty, illiterate, short-sighted, half-Americanized foreigner; or a sleepy, narrow-minded, dead-from-the-neck-up American. It irritates and annoys me to trade with such people."[136]

Ethnic and racial animosities, then, exacerbated the always-present contentiousness of food shopping. Simply getting credit or quality goods required intense personal negotiation. Distrust and resentment by grocers and customers could make the negotiation that much more difficult. But there were other reasons, beyond race and ethnicity, for the rise of chain store firms. Behind all the tensions surrounding grocery stores were contests over gender norms and gender relations. In grocery stores, the issues of women's loyalties and their normativity were particularly charged.

Gender and the Politics of Shopping

The gendered division of labor that made shopping women's work continued through the twentieth century. Although many families' schedules and workloads did not allow for full-time housewives, women's responsibilities for cooking and food shopping remained a powerful norm across lines of class, race, and ethnicity. Wives and mothers were much more likely than husbands and fathers to take responsibility for the everyday work of food cooking and preparation, and consequently women were the most common customers in food stores.[137] Indeed, male customers were so rare that trade journals occasionally urged grocers to make men more comfortable in their stores and to try and expand their business by selling to them.[138] It was women who often controlled their families' foods, women who were the focus of grocer's policies, and, in grocers' minds, women who were the source of their problems.

Thus, the bargaining, conversation, and negotiation that marked grocery stores were often explained as natural reflections of women's most basic qualities. In discourse among grocers, gender figured prominently. Customers pushed grocers to their limits, but women customers did so especially.

The centrality of gender relations to grocery stores is especially clear in grocers' discussions of personal service. Trade journals and advice literature frequently mentioned the dangers of alienating women customers. A Commerce Department study warned small grocers against attempting to limit the personal attention they bestowed on women: "[Grocers] will not wisely attempt to control the time, and consequently the cost, of the service. This lies within the province of the customer only, and she may resent any evident effort to hurry her."[139] Similarly, a monthly column in the trade journal *Progressive Grocer* advised small grocers to accede to women who asked for donations to neighborhood organizations. The motivation was not altruistic, but purely practical. Women would not be satisfied with rational arguments about shopkeepers' costs and might well organize their peers to boycott a store. "When women get together and pass resolutions," the article reminded grocers, "reason and logic sink through the floor."[140]

Individual grocers in Chicago also keenly felt that women customers were too demanding. One grocer signing himself "the Hebrew slave" complained in a newspaper editorial that Jewish women would not allow their grocers to close the store for the Sabbath. Suggesting that force be met with force, he encouraged his retail colleagues to join together and "demand" that women observe posted opening and closing hours.[141] Not surprisingly, when Jewish grocers did attempt to unite and close early (though on Sunday, not on the Jewish Sabbath), they felt compelled to address women specifically. "We request that all women do their shopping early, and permit dealers a few hours of rest," read the notice in a local Yiddish-language newspaper.[142]

A store serving a very different market shared similar concerns about women, even if its methods were more genteel. The owners of Hoyt & Sauer, a store serving the upper-class, native-born community of Morgan Park, explained a recent remodeling by referring to the ongoing need to please women. They wrote, "Our beauty-conscious women now do 85 percent of the food buying. No longer can we afford to arrange a food store to suit the whims or fancy of some one man—it must have the open display arrangement, pleasing color, beauty, and the charm that appeal to the American woman."[143] The depression of the early 1920s evoked similar concerns over women's ability to disrupt grocer's sales. Chicago's Retail Grocers Association published numerous full-page ads in the women's section of the *Chicago Tribune* to assure their customers that grocers were working to lower prices.[144] Throughout the city, grocers shared the belief that store operations could be, and often were, altered by the preferences or resentments of just a few female customers.

Community leaders (both male and female) also saw women as responsible for what happened in grocery stores. Spokespeople of all races, sexes, religions, and ethnicities, middle-class and working-class shoppers, and leaders in churches and in the city council all looked to women to resolve the problems and the limits of ethnic and racial solidarity. In neighborhood grocery stores, the loyalties and skills of women were particularly scrutinized.

Chicagoans regularly urged women to use their shopping to further the struggle for autonomy. A Yugoslavian community leader explained that Jewish merchants were able to fool customers into thinking they were saving money because "more of the buyers—women—are quite ignorant."[145] Similarly, African American merchants often looked to women, in particular, to support their stores. "I would say without fear of contradiction that Negro women are responsible for the success or failure of Negroes in business," asserted one confident merchant.[146] Echoing his suggestion that African Americans were responsible for the demise of locally owned stores, one woman explained, "I try to spend as much as I can with Negro stores, but most of them don't have what you want, or they are too high. That may be our fault for not trading with them more, but we are too poor and have to count pennies."[147] Women were regarded as both the cause of and the solution to difficult social and economic problems.

ALL PLAYERS IN THE FOOD DISTRIBUTION chain understood that food selling was difficult business. Food buying stood at the center of complicated and unstable social systems, the moment in which gender might be made or unraveled, in which families might remain healthy or purchase dangerous food, in which a local business owner might succeed or offer credit one too many times.

In this way, the haggling and bargaining, the hard work of traveling to the market, and the busy jockeying for position at public markets, were moments in which autonomy, excitement, and appetite mixed with suspicion, exhaustion, and performance. Eventually, however, spaces for food shopping changed dramatically in size and in tone—coming to seem spaces of relaxation and leisure rather than work and politics. This story begins with the dramatic expansion of chain grocery firms in the 1910s and 1920s and the ways in which a legacy of women's assertiveness shaped the new world of mass distribution.

Small Stores, Big Business

The Rise of Chain Store Groceries, 1914–1933

In the years surrounding World War I, chain grocery stores remade Chicago's retail landscape. It is difficult to overestimate the rapidity or the scale of this change. Neighborhoods once dominated by small, locally owned and operated stores were transformed into strongholds of national and regional chains. The singsong rhythms of peddlers hawking their wares and the raucous sounds of crowded public markets grew quieter. Names like "A&P," "National Tea," and "Piggly Wiggly" now marked the signage and the store windows of neighborhood shopping districts. "Voluntary" chains of independent grocers also sprang up, adopting the standardized aesthetic and foods of "private" chains. Not all neighborhoods saw the same levels of chain store concentration, but all Chicagoans felt the impact of the new way of selling food.

What explains the sudden and dramatic growth of chains? The answer is both rational (that is, chains' success reflected customers' calculations of economic interest and chain store firms' ability to offer low prices) and social. Although chain stores are conventionally understood as marketing themselves on overt price appeals, a closer look reveals a more complicated story, one in which firms also succeeded because of their promises of modernity, independence, and equality for women shoppers.[1]

In spite of—indeed, because of—their success, chain stores highlighted alarming new possibilities in gender relations. In this new world of shopping, women might use stores and their consumption in them to claim new authority and to upset social structures. Indeed, women's use of consumption as a realm in which to challenge the political and social order, and especially to challenge conventional gender norms, had come to seem an eminently modern thing to do.

In chain stores, economic efficiencies were inseparable from social change.

Chain stores were as much social institutions as they were economic ones. They remade retailing not through numerical domination or their insistence on structural efficiencies or their celebration of low prices, but through their linking of these things to notions of women's autonomy, independence, and lives unencumbered by prejudice or inequality. It was these social promises that made mass retailing meaningful, as opposed to merely less expensive. Indeed, chain stores unleashed questions about the authority and power that women wanted, and the sort that they *should* want, that would haunt mass retailers for decades to come.

The Unsettledness of Chains

Chain stores, especially chain grocery stores, offered a radically new model of food shopping in which small stores were sites of big business—where efficient bureaucracies, large investments of capital, and clear lines of authority replaced the literal and figurative messiness of conventional grocery stores. This was a dramatic alternative to usual models of food shopping and usual understandings of the needs of the women who did it. It borrowed more from the mass production of manufactured goods than it did from conventional models of grocery selling. For instance, unlike independently operated stores embedded in neighborhoods and dependent on a small but steady demand for groceries, chain stores were designed to work in coordination with each other, efficiently overseen not by local proprietors but by nonlocal branch, regional, and national management.

On the face of it, this new model of retailing seemed foolhardy. Regional and national chain store firms invested large amounts of money in elaborate enterprises whose success depended on a very complicated set of factors falling into place: Women would need (1) to choose chain stores rather than their accustomed, neighborhood grocer (2) in large enough numbers to achieve the massive sales that headquarters required (3) to pay off the significant overhead of running large numbers of stores that firms needed (4) to achieve the economies of scale required by their low prices. For this to work, women would need to relinquish the authority and personal attention they had been used to in stores, to be willing to adhere to store policy, and to take on many tasks (like transporting goods from stores to homes) that stores had previously offered.

Rarely, if ever, did all of those factors come together. As a result, firms borrowed, experimented, retreated from, and modified an enormous range of policies. "Independent" stores might be operated by proprietors who owned three or four stores scattered throughout the city. Chain stores, as the term was used in the business press, could denote firms as small as five stores or as large as a thousand. Similarly, standardization—the hallmark of chains—was also used by many individual proprietors when they allied with "voluntary chains."

Sometimes this structural unsettledness is evident in the language I employ. In this chapter, I use the vocabulary of "chain" and "independent" but also describe stores more precisely: for instance, "proprietors" denotes the operators of relatively small enterprises—people who controlled the capital and determined the strategies of those firms. "Managers" or "administrators" or "executives" worked within the large bureaucratic organizations that operated chains of stores. Thus, this chapter also pays close attention to firm strategy, that is, to the policies and programs that firms actually deployed in the stores, and distinguishes firm strategy from firm type.

This linguistic variation reinforces the possibilities for operating grocery stores in the 1910s and 1920s. The fluidity of terminology (as many arguments that follow will point out) speaks to the experimentation and borrowing that characterized the grocery business and mass retailing itself in this period.

Women and the Politics of Price during and after World War I

Post–World War I inflation sharpened the long-standing resentments that swirled around grocery stores and deepened the antagonism between grocers and customers. In this context, price became more than simply one factor among others; rising food costs became the object of collective action, governmental inquiry, and public discussion. Inflation intensified the long-standing politics of food stores, exacerbating preexisting social tensions in a way that made chains' promises of low prices especially meaningful. First a personal frustration, then a political problem, the "high cost of living" (or "HCL," as it was often abbreviated) sparked anger and creative solutions to the shortcomings of conventional distribution via small neighborhood grocery stores.

The cost of living was undeniably high. Americans paid twice as much for rent, food, clothing, and other living expenses in 1920 as in 1913—on *average*.[2] The prices of certain commodities—butter, eggs, meat, milk, sugar—drove the point home. The cost of potatoes, for instance, rose 147 percent in the ten years between 1913 and 1923.[3] In Chicago, still home to the nation's largest meat-packing houses and food wholesalers, the food price index doubled between 1914 and 1920—one of the highest rates of inflation in the country.[4]

The "anti-high-cost-of-living" movement of the late 1910s and early 1920s, as it emerged in Chicago, exemplified both the impact of this inflationary burst and women's frustrations with conventional food distribution. Concern over rapid inflation, especially of food prices, was a catalyst for government action.

In 1919, the federal government extended its wartime powers to create a High Cost of Living Division and distributed surplus foods at below-market prices in Chicago and other large cities across the country.[5] Municipal governments also felt compelled to respond to citizens' complaints. Chicago's mayor issued a "food shortage warning" and made the high cost of living an issue in the upcoming mayoral election.[6] The issue continued to have political resonance; between 1919 and 1926, members of the city council created several committees to deal with the problem of high prices.[7]

In the face of popular outrage, the federal government and municipal officials worked to short-circuit the conventional food distribution network. For instance, Chicago aldermen spearheaded a number of creative efforts to disrupt retailing as usual and to lower food bills. Projects ranged from a mail-order arrangement between dairy farmers and people the alderman called "housewives" to investigations into whether perishables were being held off of the market in order to create false shortages.[8] As these efforts suggest, both the federal government and municipal officials felt pressured to address the problem.

One of the most common responses to inflation was to look beyond conventional grocery stores to older forms of retail, especially farmers' markets. Unlike the city's other public markets, predominately serving wholesalers, these producer-dominated retail forums would, in theory, reduce the profits going to middlemen (that is, wholesalers and grocers) and thus reduce food costs to the consumer. Women's clubs and city officials alike called for the establishment of such markets.[9] At various times, such markets operated in working-class and lower-middle-class neighborhoods on the city's Near West, Near South, Far South, and Near North Sides.[10] Even the relatively tony suburb of Evanston attempted to open a public market as a way to limit inflationary price gouging.[11] In opening these sorts of markets, Chicagoans adopted the same tactics employed by reformers in cities across the country.[12]

In the short run, some of these markets were remarkably effective, attracting large numbers of Chicagoans and significant public attention.[13] However, the same problems that plagued other large public markets (racial and ethnic tension, crowded conditions, suspicion of merchants) appeared there as well. For instance, one angry letter to the *Chicago Tribune* charged that the new Irving Park Market was home to more peddlers than farmers and that it was operated by "jews and greeks" who bought at South Water and sold items at a profit.[14] The Evanston farmers' market witnessed a fistfight between its operator and a man who claimed to have leased the land on which it stood for a parking lot.[15] The opening of one market proposed for the South Side of the city was delayed for years because the building had been constructed without elevators, so that it was nearly impossible to get produce up to second-floor stalls.[16] A general fear of government-operated stores during the post–World War I red scare also hampered the spread of municipal markets.[17] Finally, in Chicago as elsewhere, shoppers regularly decried the quality of goods available in markets. One writer charged that the new generation of public markets in Chicago had failed because "the food put up for sale was the poorest stuff, as a collection, I have ever seen in the poorest stores in the world."[18]

Neither the Markets Commission nor the city's other efforts to constrain high food costs lasted long. Shoppers' suspicions, the postwar red scare, and feuds among city council members about oversight of the potentially lucrative public markets combined to bring an end to the projects. The dramatic failure of government efforts did not go unnoticed by Chicagoans. In 1917, a Polish-language paper reported that "the people of Chicago are suffering as a result of the exorbitant prices of foodstuffs. . . . Investigations by the municipal, county and Federal authorities in the matter of the high cost of living have produced so far no results at all." The *Chicago Jewish Courier* put the matter succinctly: "Democracy apparently sometimes defeats the will of the majority."[19]

Instead of blaming the government, however, shoppers in Chicago and elsewhere saw inflation in deeply personal terms. Angry urban residents launched violent attacks on peddlers and grocers in New York and Boston. In European cities, protests, riots, and upheaval were even more dramatic. Indeed, postwar inflation heightened preexisting class tensions and sparked anti-immigrant and racial riots across the world, including the 1919 race riot in Chicago.[20]

The fury over high prices is epitomized in the rhetoric of the high-cost-of-living journalism that appeared in newspapers of the time. Writers from a broad span of class and ethnic backgrounds regularly portrayed neighborhood grocers not as community pillars but as extortionists and profiteers. In 1917, a Slovak paper asked, "Of what use is it if we raise vegetables in our back yards to help agricultural production—of what use are all the appeals to the public to support our food administration, if the war profiteers, unconscionable speculators, and other parasites hoard food, only to let it rot rather than accept lower prices?"[21] The mainstream press followed suit. In one dramatic but not atypical presentation, the *Chicago Tribune* put an editorial cartoon on the subject of high prices on its front page. The cartoon featured carloads of young couples being held up at gunpoint. All of the victims made it clear that they had already given all of their money to the grocer or butcher.[22]

Women shoppers, too, were blamed for high prices. In the spring of 1922, the *Chicago Jewish Courier* had warned its readers not to expect much from the

FIGURE 2.1. *"The Harvest Moon." This cartoon by popular cartoonist John McCutcheon appeared on the front page of the* Chicago Tribune *at the height of post–World War I public alarm at rising food prices. (Bill Loughman Collection, The Ohio State University Cartoon Library and Museum)*

city's Committee on the High Cost of Living. Instead, women themselves were to take up new burdens. In stark language, the newspaper warned, "There is only one way to fight the high cost of bread and that is, the housewife must do her own baking. If the Jewish women would begin to bake their own bread, they would get good nourishing bread at small cost and they would help reduce the price of bread at the stores."[23] Later that same month, another Yiddish-language paper, the *Forward*, urged Jewish women to join the Mothers' League, an organization dedicated to uniting women around issues of consumption: "Women speak singularly, they are dissatisfied, they criticize the landlord, the butcher, the baker, the laundry collector, but, as an organized body of united working women, they do nothing. This is the main task of the Mother's League.

It tries to unite all the working women in an organization, through which the scattered minds of individual working women shall be united. Through instruction and education, they will become a force, a factor, in the social, economic, and political life of modern society."[24]

More middle-class women's organizations, although less incendiary in their rhetoric, shared similar views of women's responsibilities to keep watchful eyes on grocers. The newly organized Housewives' League and the "housewifely thrift committee" of the Chicago Women's Club met regularly throughout the early 1920s.[25] Even Russell Poole, head of the city's Committee on the High Cost of Living, looked to women for answers to high prices. For instance, when turkey prices rose just before Thanksgiving 1922, Poole urged women to wait until Christmas to buy turkeys and thus force the price down.[26] Years earlier, the city sealer (in charge of inspecting the accuracy of merchants' weights and measures) and the secretary of the city's Markets Commission issued a list of guidelines for women to use in their shopping. Tips included traveling to the store themselves, carrying goods home with them, and refraining from "gossiping" while shopping.[27] Echoing this logic, speakers at a local men's club blamed high living costs on "extravagant" housewives. One offered as an example: "She telephones for this and that and has it sent to the house. All involves extra expenses."[28]

These were local expressions of a national trend toward blaming women for high costs. Even organizations established (ostensibly) to empower women echoed the discourse of housewifely laziness as the root cause of inflation. Mrs. Julian Heath, the president of the National Housewives' League, warned readers of the *Ladies' Home Journal* that women's ignorance of market conditions, their naïve trust of grocers, and sheer laziness resulted in wasted food dollars. Heath advanced the contradictory but increasingly common advice that women should adopt men's business practices for home maintenance (for example, keeping accounts, as men presumably did in their business firms) while also adhering to particularly feminine concerns with domesticity. "With the high cost of living one of the most pressing questions of the day . . . with men spending thousands of dollars making their business methods more efficient, the average American housewife is sitting complacently by, absolutely indifferent to the serious situation that confronts her," Heath charged.[29] A reporter paraphrased the former president of the United Master Butchers' Association of America as telling attendees at the organization's 1924 convention, "The passing of the market basket and the waning of that day when wives delighted in frugal marketing for their family table is to blame largely for the high prices of food. . . . The lazy housewife who will not study a cook book to learn how to prepare all kinds of meats in all kinds of ways is to blame for the high prices of meat."[30]

As these examples make clear, women stood at the nexus of social change in the conventional discourse of food shopping. Their choices were responsible not only for the well-being of their families, but also for the struggles of their communities and indeed for broad changes in price.

In the fall of 1917, as food prices soared, Nevada Davis Hitchcock, a national home economics journalist sympathetic to women's problems, summed up her frustrations with the new wave of interest in high food prices. "There is no problem in which the public is more interested than that of food," she wrote. "And I may add, no problem in which the public is inclined to do less except to give advice." For Hitchcock, as for many other Americans, the problems in food distribution had come to seem far outside the control of individual women. "The housewife, equipped with such weapons as 'how to use left-overs' and a market basket, has about as much chance of lowering the high cost of living as a baby armed with a powder puff has of frightening a burglar,"[31] she bitterly noted. Instead, Hitchcock proposed an array of structural changes—the establishment of neighborhood public markets, better enforcement of antihoarding provisions at both local and national levels, and cooperative associations that would use produce grown by members of agricultural cooperatives.[32] But running through her long list of suggestions was the sense that the problem of high prices was structural—a result of inefficient modes of distribution that themselves needed to change.

The Chain Store as an Alternative Food Store

Although Hitchcock did not suggest chain stores as a solution to high prices, they emerged as one at about the time that her essay was published. Chain stores and their administrators were responding to the social and economic tensions that surrounded food shopping—particularly the sense that high prices were beyond individuals' control. As chains of stores expanded, they appealed to women with promises of low prices, trustworthy foods, and freedom to choose products themselves rather than depend on clerks. The success of these stores did not mean, however, that women who shopped there intended to give up their expectations about service or individuality. Even as chains grew, their owners worried about their ability to link their promises of modern aesthetics and shopper autonomy to their strategies of limited service and less personal attention.

Early chain store firms in Chicago took advantage of Chicagoans' frustrations with local independent grocers. In fact, some were the direct results of that frustration. Drawing support from the labor movement and the wave of working-class peoples' activism that immediately followed World War I, the Cooperative Society of America (csa) operated nearly two hundred stores in Chicago at its height in 1922. At that point, it was not only the largest cooperative but also the largest chain in the city.[33] The csa promised its working-class members a share of the profits made by the stores and a way of keeping their earnings from going to the pejoratively called "capitalist" class.[34] The firm was phenomenally successful despite later accusations by labor unions that its finances were unsound. When the csa was eventually forced into receivership, angry shareholders (most of them women) stormed the chambers of the presiding judge, yelling such slogans as "We want justice."[35]

The Cooperative Society of America may have been the most successful working-class chain in Chicago, but it was not the only one. Similar promises of economic autonomy were held out by Lithuanian community leaders, who worked to persuade would-be entrepreneurs to establish a Lithuanian-owned chain of stores,[36] and African Americans, who worked through the Colored Merchants' Association to create collective purchasing agreements for African American–owned stores.[37] Although these overtly politicized chain stores did not succeed (the Cooperative Society of America dissolved in 1923, and there was never a successful national chain of Lithuanian- or African American–owned stores), the fact that they were even proposed suggests the hopes that working-class Americans had for the chain store system. Although many analysts, then as now, believed that chains undermine community, in the 1920s many Chicagoans also saw the structure of centrally controlled chains of stores as a tool for making their communities stronger.[38]

Perhaps because of these associations, but also because of their organizational innovations, even the corporate chains that came to dominate food retailing—firms like Kroger, a&p, and the National Tea Company—often retained the aura of being somehow progressive. On one level, their emphasis on efficiency, low prices, and standardization was "progressive," as contemporary business analysts and executives used the term. But implicit in their business model was the possibility of a different form of progress—the possibility that chains could eliminate the high costs, personal scrutiny, and cross-cultural tensions that pervaded conventional grocery stores. Even the most conventionally organized chain store firms, owned and operated by far-off corporations, addressed at least one of the concerns that drove many shoppers to look for alternatives to local stores. They did this by promising, advertising, and seemingly delivering lower prices. This was their most obvious difference from smaller independents, which often did not even post prices, let alone compete on the basis of price. Chains lowered prices by taking advantage of economies of scale, an idea long practiced in manufacturing. Producing goods on a grand scale made it possible to lower production costs per item. Large retail chains adapted this strategy by buying items in very large lots and, ideally, selling those items quickly through as many stores as possible. Chains were able to lower their per-item cost by negotiating discounts from processors and suppliers and by operating their own processing and wholesale subsidiaries. It is impossible to estimate how much the average family saved by shopping at the chains, but virtually every study of large chain grocery firms' stores and small grocery firms (those operating only one or two stores) in the 1920s and early 1930s found significant differences in prices.[39] A 1930 study of Chicago grocery stores found that self-service chains had lower prices on nationally branded items than did full-service and self-service independent stores. Investigators concluded that chains undersold independents by anywhere from 8.82 percent to 11.54 percent.[40]

Chains also defused many sources of tension in food stores by sharply limiting specialized goods and services and personalized attention. Chains sold standardized, often mass-produced goods. Such goods were sold in standardized settings—sometimes down to store fixtures and layout. That uniformity allowed one central office to oversee vast networks of stores in much the same way that one foreman could oversee a long assembly line. Other strategies simply eliminated policies over which customers and clerks formerly had bargained and negotiated. Employees in chain stores generally were not authorized to grant credit, thus eliminating a notoriously expensive and time-consuming part of grocery store operations. Moreover, prices were set by district or regional authorities and posted in stores, so that customers and clerks no longer bargained over the price of goods.[41] A manager of the Piggly Wiggly chain celebrated and cataloged the areas of standardization when he wrote, "Uniformity is the first principle of Piggly Wiggly. Every store must do everything in exactly the same manner, and to my mind this is one of the greatest advantages of our systems. Clerks, goods, fixtures are interchangeable."[42] By excising many services and fixing prices, chain store administrators also limited the degree to which personal animosities could interfere with customers' experiences in stores.

The very nature of these large firms also defused the racially and ethnically charged atmospheres of food stores and conventional food shopping. Lizabeth Cohen has documented the willingness of African Americans to shop in chains,[43] an attitude shared by many first- and second-generation European Americans as well. Of course, chain owners were as likely to differ from customers in terms of race and ethnicity as were owners of independent stores. Chain store owners, however, were far removed from the daily operations of chains and from the neighborhoods in which they were located. Moreover, the standardization that limited individual service also discouraged discrimination in the form of variable treatment of customers in and across stores or variable quality of goods in stores in different neighborhoods. Also, unlike family-run independents, chains needed outside workers. They were willing to hire African Americans (and white immigrants) to fill positions, especially when the stores were in African American or white ethnic neighborhoods.[44] This is not to say that African Americans or recent immigrants experienced equality in chain stores, either as workers or as customers.[45] But this structure did offer new possibilities for avoiding and undermining local expressions of racism. However indirectly, wary Chicagoans could see chains as supporting an ethnic or racial community.

At the very least, centrally managed chains offered respite from the communal norms and tensions that permeated neighborhood grocery stores. Neighbors were simply not as likely to know what a newly married woman served her in-laws or whether a family paid its bills on time if shopping was done in chain stores rather than neighborhood independents. At the most, chains allowed people to meet family budgets while not shopping in or using credit from the stores of people who, as the Slovakian paper put it, "may be your enemy." Since these stores were less personalized, their profits did not directly benefit rival racial or ethnic groups. They allowed people to avoid the guilt of supporting outsiders.

In addition to central management, low prices, and uniform offerings, chain stores deployed another innovation—self-service. Efforts to impose this model of retailing stood at the center of the stores' financial and social strategies. Rather than ask a clerk to wait on them, customers chose goods themselves from open shelves and carried the goods to the clerk's counter, where they paid. Self-service stood in stark contrast to older forms of selling, in which a clerk waited on each customer. Self-service had enormous implications for grocery stores—cutting down on the time customers waited (and therefore chatted with each other), requiring the purchase of specialized store fixtures (for example, open shelving that customers could reach), and encouraging more attention to the design of stores and packages. Most important, self-service cut down on stores' labor costs because they could now employ fewer clerks while selling the same (or even greater) amounts of stock more quickly than ever before.[46]

Self-service was almost never discussed as a cost saver, however, and rarely as a challenge to store design and infrastructure, although it certainly was both these things. Store executives and analysts treated it—at least publicly—as a kind of marketing device: one perfectly fit for women customers. Chain store proponents noted that self-service (and limited interaction with clerks) was especially attractive to women shoppers. Their claim was based on the idea that women wanted to make choices about products without the close supervision of store staff. Under a self-service model, shoppers could purchase whichever brand or item they wanted, free from the pressure that a clerk might exert. "A woman does not like to run a gauntlet of clerks looking her over when she enters a store. This is sometimes the case in stores where the clerks are not busy and loll over the counter sizing up the ladies," noted one Piggly Wiggly manager. He went on to assert, "In Piggly Wiggly stores, this cannot happen for no one but the checker is in front and his back is usually to the door."[47] Although this system went against the conventions of personalized advice and service, grocers promised that it would lead to more, not less, satisfied customers.

Gender, the Female Consumer, and the Marketing of Chain Stores

The manager who celebrated the anonymity offered by Piggly Wiggly stores was participating in a new discourse surrounding women's consumption, one whose strategies reinforced a widespread sense that consumption offered autonomy and independence to young, modern-minded women in the interwar years. In the years just preceding the rise of chain groceries, women had begun to adopt a rhetoric of liberation, equality, sexual freedom, and modernity in new institutions of commercial culture—institutions that seemed far removed from neighborhood grocery stores. In dance halls, jazz clubs, movie theaters, and department stores, women celebrated strong peer cultures, new fashions, open socializing with men, and other possibilities for expressing themselves away from the careful eye of family and community. Through the first two decades of the twentieth century, while male and female progressive reformers and conservative critics worried about the morality of heterosocial amusements and the lure of department store wares, more and more women were claiming their right to inhabit and enjoy public space. Women asserted their independence not only in cultural terms—with shorter haircuts and hemlines—but also in material ways—through their attempts to support themselves, to live apart from family, and to pursue professional careers. Many of these new jobs were in the garment factories, offices, stores, film studios, and newspaper bureaus that supplied the commodities at the center of new commercial culture. The promise of consumer society, then, stood at the heart of women's new work opportunities and the new images of women. It was what many women worked for, both literally (given the consumer industries in which they labored) and figuratively (given its promises of fulfillment).[48]

At the same time, much of contemporary politics seemed set to undermine male privilege and female dependence. Women's political activism had grown enormously in previous decades. Campaigns for such contradictory goals as equal wages and women's right to vote, on the one hand, and protective labor legislation and the institution of voting requirements that limited suffrage, on the other, drew on women's energies and vocal participation. A slew of Progressive Era reforms, ranging from child labor laws to housing codes, also grew out of women's organized lobbying. The most vocal reformers tended to be middle-class white women, but women also peopled the religious and reform-minded political and cultural institutions that blossomed in immigrant and African American neighborhoods in the first decades of the twentieth century. In addition, working-class women made it an era of unprecedented labor activism. Factory women formed tight social ties with each other, engaged in strikes, and pressured both their unions and their employers to accommodate their demands. Women's struggles, and their occasional successes, threatened the authority of male peers, politicians, and supervisors.[49]

Moreover, the spread of commercial culture sometimes facilitated political activism. Suffragists used advertising, pageants, buttons, and souvenirs to "sell" suffrage to American women. Shared participation in new styles and leisure activities fomented a strong peer culture among working-class women, which in turn shaped their political activism in regions as far removed from each other as North Carolina and New York City.[50] Finally, participation in commercial culture was used by working-class and middle-class women to argue for changes in political and economic structures. Both suffragists and strikers argued that women's shopping and their adoption of modern styles entitled them to new respect and gave them new political and economic influence.[51]

The image of the "new woman" came to encapsulate the possibilities of commercial capitalism for women. Women's political activism of the 1900s and 1910s did not continue into the 1920s, in part because achievement of suffrage seemed to end the need for widespread politicization, in part because of a growing social conservatism after World War I, and in part because of generational differences. Women's hopes for autonomy and individuality did continue, however, and became the mainstays of this symbol of modern womanhood.

The "new woman" rejected many of the qualities of conventional femininity and, especially through her purchase of new products, worked to inculcate and display qualities that had seemed the sole domain of men—decisiveness, sexual promiscuity, and vocal participation in businesses. Describing this change in women and in society, the journalist Frederick Lewis Allen explained, "Women were bent on freedom—freedom to work and to play without the trammels that had bound them heretofore to lives of comparative inactivity."[52] Scholars have often criticized this ideology as effectively undercutting women's political and economic gains, hurting support for previously powerful women-only organizations, and playing on deeply classist images of what a woman should be. That analysis is borne out in the decline in working- and middle-class feminist organizations and the simultaneous decline in the rhetoric of women's rights that such groups had popularized.[53] In important ways, the emphasis on "gender sameness" proved limited and limiting, as many scholars have shown.[54] The discourse was, nonetheless, enormously powerful in the 1920s. Articulated most clearly by women, it offered a compelling vision of a world without the constraints of gender.[55]

The possibilities of gender sameness reshaped the vocabulary, images, and tools used to sell to women customers. Mass marketers all over the country worked to attract women to their products with the claim that they could exercise autonomy through their choices in the marketplace. New products promised less drudgery, more time for pursuits outside the home, access to exciting urban amusements, and help with the scientific work of modern housekeeping.[56] The historian Roland Marchand described advertisers' new comparison of women to business executives as a direct outgrowth of the emphasis on gender sameness as a route to equality: "To view the home . . . as a business concern and the housewife as a business executive seemed, in a business-minded age, to banish the archaic aura of the home. As purchasing agents, women could command respect for exhibiting qualities previously honored primarily in men—capacities for planning, efficiency, and expert decision-making."[57]

Although women all came to their own understandings of what the modern world might give them, working and middle-class, African American and Euro-American women saw exciting possibilities in the new stores, leisure activities, and styles associated with the new century. There is no denying that with participation in this consumer culture came financial and social costs that could increase women's dependence on men. Certainly, women's participation in this culture was limited by a host of factors, including age, ethnicity, and class. Nonetheless, in the late 1910s and 1920s, commercial culture seemed to many observers—men and women, black and white, progressive and conservative, rich, poor, and in-between—to be a modern and liberating experience for women.

THE PROMISE OF INDEPENDENCE for women via modern-minded purchases became an important trope for processors and retailers of groceries. This was true in spite of, and perhaps also because of, the connections between the most conventional aspects of feminine caregiving and food. Kellogg, Nabisco, and Campbell's published ads that compared purchase of their products with women's right to vote.[58] According to historian Katherine Parkin, "Advertisers took the progressive ideals of the era and suggested that one purchase would guarantee these ideals in women's homes."[59]

Similarly, the marketing staffs of grocery chain store firms quite consciously tapped into the discourse of new womanhood. An emphasis on autonomy and respect for women ran through national chains' early advertising. Many of these ads explicitly reminded both women and men of women's important role in the family and explained that chains supplied women with the "scientific" information required for modern-minded housekeeping. A&P, for instance, ran a series of ads in the *Saturday Evening Post* designed to convince men that their wives' difficulties with shopping were as challenging as the problems they encountered in the workplace. "Daily the wife must purchase the family food needs. Countless brands, grades, and prices are confusing, yet she must decide. And she does, wisely and profitably. Give her credit," advised the caption of one advertisement. Other ads in the campaign portrayed the brands that chain stores stocked as an aid to the woman seeking high-quality foods with which to impress her husband's boss.[60]

So profound was chain store firms' anxiety to seem modern and empowering that even when they clearly meant to sell to women, they did not mention gender explicitly in their ads. For instance, chains in Chicago ran ads in the evening newspapers that targeted women readers (morning papers, by contrast, targeted male workers), and the national trade press made it clear that chains wanted to win women's patronage in particular.[61] Nonetheless, many early ads were simple, straightforward lists of items and prices. Even some institutional advertisements of chain grocery firms promised equality without mentioning women's special interest in this endeavor. A 1922 advertisement for the Piggly Wiggly chain in the *Chicago Tribune* extolled the independence and the acumen customers could exercise in the firm's stores: "Piggly Wiggly fosters the spirit of independence—the Soul of Democratic Institutions, teaching men, women and children to do for themselves." The advertisement went on to make an implicit comparison between Piggly Wiggly's self-service stores and their stocks of national brands, and what customers could expect at small-er, independent stores: "In Piggly Wiggly stores you will find only well-known, established brands of unquestionable quality, and there will be no one there to try to get you to buy 'something just as good.' "[62] Again, although executives and advertising writers knew that they were speaking to women, they sought to attract them by downplaying distinctive gender characteristics and playing up women's rights to be taken seriously as citizens and rational economic ac-tors. Chains' promises of autonomy were entirely in line with the moves being made by other mass retailers; indeed, easier food shopping might make more real mass retailing's promises of liberation.

Chain Store Firms' Successes

Chains grew quickly in the 1920s and 1930s, as a result of the popularity of many of their methods among customers and business owners alike. The rapid expansion of chain stores and of chain stores' sales came through clearly in the country's first business census of retailers and wholesalers. In 1923, according to Lizabeth Cohen's calculations, chains operated only 18 percent of all Chi-cago grocery stores. Just six years later, the census reported that chains (de-fined as firms controlling four or more stores) were making 50 percent of all grocery sales in the city and operating nearly a quarter of all grocery stores.[63]

This growth in Chicago echoed a national trend; throughout the country, national food retailing firms managed ever-larger chains of stores in the 1920s. In 1920, Kroger Grocery and Baking Company operated 799 stores. By the end of the decade, Kroger commanded 5,575 stores. Safeway owned 2,020 stores, most on the East and West coasts and virtually all of them acquired since 1914.[64] National Tea Company, a relatively modest regional chain centered in Chicago and the upper Midwest, owned 1,627 stores by the end of 1929, a dramatic increase from the 143 stores that it had owned when the decade began.[65] These large firms were dwarfed, however, by the stunning growth of A&P, which expanded its national chain from 4,600 stores in 1919 to 15,000 stores in 1929.[66] Over the course of those ten years, it had become the first retailer to have more than $1 billion in annual sales[67] and the fifth-largest industrial corporation in the United States.[68]

Although overshadowed by more famous national and regional firms, small, locally owned chains were an important indication of the appeal and impor-tance of chain stores in Chicago. E. G. Shinner and Company, of Chicago, operated forty Shinner Markets and thirty Brownie Meat Shops in Illinois, Indiana, Wisconsin, and Ohio. Their annual sales (about $4 million in 1928) were tiny in comparison to the sales of larger firms, but the company's growth was nonetheless indicative of the widespread appeal of chain stores.[69] Smaller chains spread throughout the city. The six stores operated by Anderson Bros. Stores on the city's southeast side; the eight stores operated by the Central Produce Company on the North Side; and the sixteen Grogan Brothers stores on the Far South Side[70] were all part of the same impetus toward consolidation and standardization in food retailing.

The popularity of consolidation and standardization reflected general trends in business organization in the 1920s and a new emphasis on "progressive efficiency."[71] The techniques of mass production, publicized most famously by Henry Ford in the mid-1910s, depended on interchangeable (that is, standardized) parts used together in large-scale production, which was overseen by trained members of management, with the goal of increasing efficiency so as to lower cost per unit.[72] By the late 1910s and 1920s, these precepts had spread through business schools, the popular press, and federal agencies to the executives controlling some of the country's largest firms.[73] Some degree of mass production had already crept into the consumer goods industries, and particularly into food marketing and sales. Manufacturers and, increasingly, distributors and retailers seized on these techniques and, as Marina Moskowitz perceptively argues, on the very idea of standardization of consumer goods and aesthetics to a new degree in the 1910s and 1920s.[74]

If standardization and rationalization were the goals of big business (including chain grocery store firms), acquisition of other firms was often the mechanism by which the requisite "bigness" was achieved. The 1920s saw a wave of mergers among businesses, and chain stores were no exception. Indeed, many of the largest firms grew exponentially by buying up other companies that oversaw relatively small groups of stores. These firms completed mergers that are dramatic even by the standards of later merger crazes.

The National Tea Company, a longtime presence among Chicago-area grocery stores, is a good example of this method of growth. Between 1920 and 1923, the firm more than quadrupled the number of stores that it operated in Chicago and its environs (from 120 to 598) as it swallowed up smaller groups of stores operated by firms like the Cooperative Society of America, the Piggly Wiggly stores, and a small chain run by the John R. Thompson Company. The firm's size and influence grew still greater when in 1925 it was listed on the New York Stock Exchange. By the end of the decade, the firm operated more than sixteen hundred stores in four states.[75]

Other large firms also worked hard to become larger. Kroger Grocery and

Baking Company, for example, was already an important midwestern grocery chain when it entered the Chicago market with a dramatic takeover of the Consumers Sanitary Coffee and Butter Stores, itself an extensive network of 339 stores.[76] A&P, already the largest grocery chain in the country in 1920, more than tripled the number of stores that it owned over the course of the decade.[77]

Operating large chains of stores was crucial to firms' ability to compete and was a point of pride with executives. In a weekly advertisement of its sale items in 1922, Piggly Wiggly included a want ad for "50 new store locations."[78] Similarly, the Green Front stores, a smaller local chain, began featuring "The Week's New Store" in its ads.[79] When Loblaw Groceterias, which already owned numerous stores in Toronto and western New York, expanded into Chicago in the late 1920s, it felt compelled to open several stores at once. The president of the firm explained that in addition to making a psychological impression, "the simultaneous opening of a number of stores in a city is economical from the point of view of advertising expense."[80] Expansion was so crucial to the chains' strategies that when sales per store began falling at A&P in the mid-1920s, the firm maintained overall profits not by closing stores, but by opening more.[81]

The stock market was crucial to the discourse and the development of large chain store firms. Analysts regularly encouraged investments in chain store stocks, alerting customers to the possibilities of reaping profits from the very stores that they patronized.[82] The size of these firms, analysts promised, was itself an indication of their soundness. One 1928 review of trading activity in chain store securities noted that consolidation among chain stores was all for the good: the larger a chain was, the lower its margins and its prices could be.[83] An executive with the investment firm of Merrill Lynch argued that large chains were able to expand more economically than small chains because they already had the administrative capacity to operate new stores without having to add new personnel. More consolidations would, he assured chain store administrators, only make chains into better investments and sounder firms.[84]

Analysts' overheated rhetoric, which touted size as a vital feature of firms, paid off for chains in very literal ways. Virtually every national firm relied on issuances of common stock for the infusions of cash needed to acquire ever-larger numbers of stores. National Tea Company, which experienced its greatest period of growth in the mid-1920s, exemplified this trend, acquiring stores in Illinois, Minnesota, and Wisconsin by issuing a hundred thousand new shares of stock throughout 1924 and 1925.[85] Similarly, when Safeway groceries began expanding aggressively on the West Coast, it also relied on stock issues. According to historian Edwin J. Perkins, efforts to buy up other chains often "involved the swap of stock certificates, with little cash changing hands." Charles Merrill, who maintained a controlling interest in Safeway throughout the 1920s while also continuing to operate the investment firm Merrill Lynch, felt that the sheer size of chain stores gave them automatic advantages over smaller firms.[86]

The promise of stock-financed expansion motivated local firms, as well as regional and national ones. The charter for the local chain Consumers Sanitary Coffee and Butter Company (before its purchase by Kroger) allowed the firm to issue $12,000 worth of common stock in 1917; ten years later, after a series of nearly annual revisions to the charter to increase the amount of capital that could be raised through stock offerings, company executives had the authority to raise up to $2.75 million.[87] In all these cases, brokers' and directors' celebration of the greater efficiencies of large firms demonstrates how cultural faith in economies of scale has very material effects; stock sales led to ever-larger mergers, which encouraged analysts to push chain stocks even harder, which encouraged more mergers, and so on.

The spread of chain grocery stores was made dramatically visible through their concentration along the busy streets of many Chicago neighborhoods. In some areas, it was difficult to walk a single block without passing a national or regional chain grocery store. Along Lake Park Avenue in the university community of Hyde Park, A&P had a store on every corner—in one case it had two stores across the street from each other.[88] There was a similar concentration of chain stores along Madison Avenue, which stretched from Chicago's poverty-stricken West Side immigrant neighborhoods to the middle-class suburbs of Oak Park and River Forest.[89]

THE REAL SUCCESS OF CHAIN STORE firms was measured not by the number of stores they operated, but by the influence of their practices, policies, and aesthetics on independent proprietors of smaller grocery store firms. Throughout the 1920s, owners of small grocery firms often mimicked or adapted the techniques of the larger chains. By the end of the decade, the strategies of chain store firms had come to define mass retailing and in the process had redefined the nature of all food retailing.

Throughout the 1920s, proprietors of smaller independent stores were under increasing pressure to join the chains in adopting what were becoming the fixtures of mass retailing: limiting the credit and services offered, buying efficiently (that is, in large quantities), moving toward self-service, and emphasizing fixed low prices. Even the Department of Commerce urged small-scale independent grocers to use chain store techniques. Julius Klein of the department's Bureau of Foreign and Domestic Commerce assured small merchants that they could succeed in the new world of mass retailing as long as they had "a willingness to work, to utilize new methods, and to take advantage of new conditions."[90] In a similar vein, wholesalers and the trade press urged independents to mark prices on items and to price uniformly.[91]

Operators of small stores, who typically identified themselves as independent grocers, saw self-service and the independence that it promised as important factors in attracting women customers. Although smaller grocers could not always eliminate credit or personal attention, they joined the chains in moving toward self-service operations. *Progressive Grocer*, a popular trade journal aimed at proprietors of single stores, described the success of shopkeepers who made the transition to self-service. The editors assured their readers that "every grocer . . . reports that his customers commend him on the change, and the fact is well established that women prefer to shop at a store arranged with open stock and display—and a large number of them prefer to wait on themselves."[92] When the Department of Commerce and the staff of *Progressive Grocer* worked together to build a model grocery store, the editor explained that "the store was so planned that every item sold in the store can be seen by the shopper, without the assistance of the clerk" and so took advantage of women's "highly developed shopping instinct."[93]

Independent grocers also worked to achieve their own economies of scale. For the most part, this was accomplished through membership in a "voluntary chain." These associations of independently owned stores agreed to buy from the same wholesaler and often operated under the same name and imposed similar policies on customers. In other words, these associations sought to adapt the standardization and mass buying power of chains to the needs of small, neighborhood stores. By the end of the 1920s, nearly 60,000 stores across the country—3,151 of them in Illinois—operated as members of voluntary chains.[94]

Stores could join relatively loosely organized voluntary chains, which required little from members beyond an agreement to purchase from the same supplier,[95] slightly more demanding associations—like the Independent Grocers Alliance (IGA)—or highly standardized and demanding voluntary chains, which differed little from private chain store firms except that the people engaged in the everyday operation of individual stores (unlike the managers of chain stores) often owned the store fixtures and goods. Royal Blue Stores, an example of the last type, were explicitly modeled on chain stores. Royal Blue was an especially successful voluntary chain, operating close to a hundred stores in the city by the end of the 1920s.[96] Member stores had to buy standard Royal Blue equipment and purchase through the central wholesaler. Royal Blue stores were identified through a standard blue-and-white sign and through their stock—40 percent of which carried the "Royal Blue" label. Every week, every Royal Blue store featured the same "price leaders" and presumably charged the same prices for them. The central office not only offered advertising copy and display advice, as was common in many voluntary chains, but also went so far as to help independent grocers negotiate their leases.[97] In at least one case, and in spite of public claims that it never assumed financial responsibility for its individual members, the firm even cosigned the lease with a new store's proprietor.[98]

As the chains grew, and as independent proprietors adopted and adapted chain techniques, the public bravado of many chain store proponents reached new heights. Analysts declared that the continued expansion of chain stores was inevitable, despite the financial risks that chains were incurring. "Those executives who place their business on a firm financial foundation," noted one securities broker, "cannot fail to show a profit for themselves and the original investors as well as to the public in general."[99] At a public debate about the soundness of chains, Godfrey Lebhar, longtime editor of *Progressive Grocer*, declared that the public should not worry about the danger of concentration or monopoly but instead should feel satisfied by chains' many benefits: "The engineer at the throttle of the Twentieth Century [a popular passenger train], tearing along at sixty miles an hour, has the power to send a thousand lives crashing into eternity, but who gives that remote possibility even a passing thought? . . . If mass distribution is worth having, the slight element of risk involved in the possibility that great power may be abused is a small price to pay for it."[100]

Urban Real Estate and the Spatial Politics of Class:
The High Cost of Chain Store Firms' Strategies

As chain store operators knew all too well, continued success was not inevitable. It depended on a series of strategies—constant expansion, adequate financing, and the success of standardized stores and management methods. At the heart of these strategies were new ways of seeing both food and women customers. A look at the high costs of operating a chain suggests the vulnerabilities of chain store firms at the moment of their most dramatic growth.

63

Rapid expansion left the chains little room for error. Large numbers of people had to come through their doors, or their entire strategy, based on rapid turnover of low-priced items, would fail. Thus, chains carefully picked where they located and whom they targeted. Rather than adapt to local conditions and to a truly mass market, chain store firms had to find populations likely to agree to their predetermined terms. Selling to particular segments of consumers, a phenomenon that flourished in the 1950s and thereafter, had its roots in the very origins of mass retailing.

Not all neighborhoods, or even all local business strips, saw increasing numbers of chain groceries. Chains were famous in Chicago and elsewhere for choosing locations "scientifically"—developing complicated formulae and devoting significant resources to picking sites. Chain stores went so far as to establish a rating system for potential sites, labeling the best spots "100 % locations."[101] The operators of chain groceries were especially interested in intersections of important thoroughfares or transit hubs where there would be a lot of traffic (that is, people), but they also took into account such variables as the ethnicity of surrounding populations, the number of families living nearby, and the number of other chains nearby (a sign that people were used to chain store methods).[102] Youth, too, mattered to chain executives. As one hopeful grocer put it, "We think the younger generation of women appreciate the full value of buying from a store, for cash. The older ones probably still feel a longing for the old days when cash was not king, but . . . we feel sure that [younger women] will be enthusiastic about a store that sells for cash, and is proud of it."[103] More than anything, it was this openness to change, to new ways of choosing and buying food, that chains needed in their customers.

All of these variables meant that areas of recent urban development—for instance, areas reached by newly expanded streetcar lines or commuter trains, or in which new apartment houses were going up—were especially desirable. Thus, middle-class neighborhoods of native-born Americans and areas of second settlement for immigrants tended to house chain stores.[104] Unlikely to be home either to the city's poorest populations or to its wealthiest, these "good or middle class apartment areas" were, according to one analyst, "chain store communities" from the first.[105] Chains located stores there, hoping to attract young, budget-minded, forward-thinking families willing and able to leave behind traditional neighborhoods and to participate in mainstream commercial culture. If the new woman seeking independence and autonomy existed anywhere, chain executives reasoned, she existed in these neighborhoods.

The transformation of local shopping districts took place in similar ways throughout the city and suburbs. Chain stores moved into Uptown (along the

FIGURE 2.2. *A&P store, c. 1920. The prominent advertising of prices, the store's location in an area of new construction, and its relatively small size were typical of early chain grocery stores. (Chicago History Museum, ICHi-21059, photographer unknown)*

lake on the city's North Side) in the wake of a housing boom, the extension of several commuter train lines, and the subsequent development of "amusement centers" (there were two nearby beaches and several theaters).[106] Similarly, when the suburb of Berwyn finally paved its streets and began to change from a "peaceful, outlying village" to a "semi-urban center," its stores changed as well. One resident writing in 1933 described the transformation that had occurred during the previous decade in this way: "Even ten or twelve years ago this urban encroachment could scarcely be detected. The stores were still primarily home-owned and managed and were the old-fashioned type with sawdust covered floors. . . . [After the street paving] chain stores, with their modern, efficient, impersonal methods, began to crowd out the independent owners. Windsor Avenue became a busy, crowded street with brightly lighted, attractive looking stores."[107]

Chain operators, in those years, began to see immigrants—especially those who demonstrated a willingness to move beyond initial ethnic enclaves—as potential clients. A report on Humboldt Park, an area of second settlement for many eastern European immigrants, noted that four different chain grocery firms competed for the neighborhood's business and were steadily cutting into the sales of independently owned groceries.[108]

It was not only a youthful population that made for a good location. Chain grocers, like all grocers, understood their primary market to be women, and that factor weighed heavily in the answer to the most basic question—where to open a store. Safeway stores in California sought out locations that were easily accessible to mothers who walked to the store with young children.[109] A University of Chicago sociologist reported that chains often chose blocks that had other "women's stores," like clothing shops.[110]

In their fevered search for the perfect location to attract precisely the right sort of customers, chains helped create real estate booms. In neighborhoods that seemed ripe for chain store development, land prices soared.[111] Real estate prices had been on the rise in Chicago since the 1910s, but in the 1920s, inflation and fierce competition for prime locations exacerbated the problem. Prices rose most dramatically in outlying neighborhood business districts— precisely the sort of neighborhoods most desirable to chains. In these areas, the average value per frontage foot increased by 1,000 percent between 1915 and 1928. The value of one frontage foot at the intersection of Wilson and Sheridan in the popular Uptown district was $150 in 1910. By 1929, it was $5,500.[112]

The problem of expensive real estate gave rise to extraordinary business practices. Chain firms sometimes sublet desirable locations to independent grocers until they had developed enough business to justify taking over the store.[113] Chain store executives also tried to limit their costs and guarantee their locations by signing very long leases, pledging themselves to pay ever-increasing rents for anywhere from three to fifteen years.[114] One such executive wrote to a trade journal that firms now had to sign leases years before they actually wanted the property, just to keep competitors from getting it. Casting about for some reason that chains continued to sign under such terms, he resigned himself to the hope that customers' patronage would justify the expense: "The only salvation for the chain store . . . is to make the best deal he can on as long a lease as possible and be optimistic enough to sell himself the idea that business conditions will expand and improve and he will feel satisfied that the volume of business he is doing is more than compensating him for the rental he is paying."[115]

The high costs of rentals, and of expansion more generally, threatened chain store firms' much-vaunted economies of scale. One study of grocer's costs by the Harvard Business School warned readers away from "the notion frequently held that an expanding industry necessarily obtains economies in operating expense."[116] Chains were incurring significant costs by following the very precepts designed to lower cost per unit.

Women, Gender, and the Shortcomings of Chain Stores

It is easy to see executives' endless search for the perfect location as reflecting their focus on middle-class customers. However, the actual model used by many real estate analysts at the time was more complicated.

Many retailers saw desirable customers—and, by extension, desirable class—in terms of gender. The goal for chain store owners was the sort of stable homemaker who was willing to give up some service for the sake of low prices and autonomy in choice. It was this focus on a very particular sort of "modern" shopper—young, married, independent-minded (but not to the extent of challenging firm policies), needing to economize, but also willing and able to purchase for cash—that distinguished large chain store firms' profiled customers.

Securing the loyalty of these model customers was not easy, however. Many executives worried that their promises of modernity and independence had not ended women's demands for personal attention. The very women that chain firms sought out, it seemed, were the ones who might be least willing to accept the new regime.

Chain stores' emphasis on price, ostensibly their most compelling feature, also carried a suggestion of cheapness that respectable women might seek to avoid. Chain stores were often associated with working-class and lower-middle-class shoppers. Describing Woodlawn's recent changes, one longtime resident linked a troubling demographic change to the arrival of chain stores: "At the present time Woodlawn seems to be filling with the typical rooming-house class and a rather low class it seems to be. Take for example 63rd street. Formerly the street was considered 'smart' for an average middle-class residential community in Chicago." Now, however, the old furniture and clothing stores were being replaced by "chain store millinaries [sic] . . . chain store dress shops . . . chain grocery stores; and ten cent stores, ten cent stores, and ten cent stores."[117] Chains' willingness to open in densely populated urban neighborhoods and their emphasis on prices encouraged analysts to see them as being best suited to people for whom cheapness, rather than class status or pride, was a priority.

Christine Frederick, a professional home economist who generally saw chains as a good thing, warned executives that they would never get the business of middle- and upper-class women until they better understood the female desire for personal attention and service. Working-class women, she

67

suggested, shopped at chains only because they had no choice but to sacrifice their inner desires for the sake of their budgets.[118] The president of Jewel Tea Company, which had long used traveling salesmen to sell and deliver dry groceries to customers' homes, took a similar stance. He noted that chain stores did best in "crowded apartment districts" where most residents (including women) worked during the day and bought only in small amounts. He proudly observed that Jewel's techniques "suit best the community where you always find someone at home and where the service and quality count more than small price savings." The company's salesmen, therefore, avoided urban neighborhoods, "which are populated largely by light-housekeepers, transients and the like."[119]

The self-service model was a particular problem. Chain store operators had long vaunted the independence and anonymity that it offered women. Many analysts pointed out, however, that the same plan eliminated opportunities for advice, conversation, and help from store staff. Frederick rather sternly argued that businesses were alienating women by promoting self-serve stores and limiting the accommodations they made to individuals: "A large corporation doing business with women simply dare not ignore this problem, for there is no denying that women have a strong personal attitude in their buying habits."[120] Julian Heath, a New York City home economist famous for her support of mass distributors of groceries, argued that women did not want to be kept waiting in line and that chains needed to accommodate their busy schedules and sense of importance.[121] Critic after critic warned chains that low prices were not enough to keep customers because women—at least the sort of women so coveted by chains—wanted more.

Chain store executives themselves began to take up the cry that a single-minded dedication to self-service and low prices was self-defeating; women who thought only of price were disloyal customers and probably not the women that the chains were really after. As early as 1926, a well-known advertising executive explained that chains should move away from an emphasis on price as they sought to secure customers. He argued that "instead of depending entirely on price she [the customer] might be influenced to buy from a given chain all of the time because of their policies and methods which have been sold to her through institutional copy. . . . The future of the chain store lies in service."[122] The featured speaker at a 1928 convention of grocery chains encouraged his audience to offer service and personal attention because prices were no longer enough to attract financially stable customers.[123] One worried chain store analyst wrote, "Right now there are some women in any town who think it beneath their dignity to walk home from a store with even a small sack of goods in their hand."[124] One woman shopper echoed just these concerns, even as she celebrated the benefits of self-service by asking rhetorically, "Isn't it worth it now and then to pocket one's pride?"[125]

In this context, chain store firms' standardization began to break down across the country. Middle-class customers seem to have won concessions from even the largest firms. A&P, for instance, went after "the better type of trade" with service stores in desirable neighborhoods.[126] Similarly, in 1928, the owner of Acme stores explained that an emphasis on service helped them win women customers: "These things impress women you sell to, without anyone having to bother to put them into words."[127]

, Similar accommodations were made in Chicago. Grocery stores that sold fruit and vegetables often retained a clerk to help customers choose, weigh, and wrap produce.[128] Through the mid-1930s, National Tea continued to employ clerks who obtained items for customers in many of its upscale stores. Proponents of the practice argued that some women simply would not shop at self-service stores.[129] The failure of self-service in the 1920s and 1930s was not always the result of the search for well-off customers. Firms that served recent immigrants, for instance, had to make certain accommodations to local situations—for instance, by opening packages for customers unfamiliar with a product or by hiring clerks who spoke foreign languages.[130] As late as 1936, only one of Chicago's large chains operated all of its stores as self-service units.[131] For all of chain store firms' claims that limited service was appealing to women customers and important for keeping prices low, they were not able to institute rigid self-service and standardization.

One other topic makes clear the limits of mass marketing. The growth of chains paralleled and built on the growth of mass-processed foods. As numerous scholars have documented, food was one of the first commodities to be processed at large factories and sold through far-flung distribution networks. By the 1910s, such national brands as Campbell's soup, Nabisco crackers, and Kellogg cereals were mainstays of American diets.[132] Advertisements encouraged customers to ask for goods by brand names, thus short-circuiting the authority of local merchants and store clerks. The promise of branded goods was, like the promise of chains, that all customers would get the same product, in the same amount, with little room for individual treatment or discrimination. Even the standardized, colorful packages themselves—designed to entice customers visually and to stack neatly—dovetailed with a move to self-service, standard-sized store shelving, and aesthetic interiors.[133]

And yet, these mass-produced goods did not always fit neatly into chain stores. The stores' insistence on lowering prices on national brands was a

FIGURE 2.3. *Self-service. Even in the self-service layout of this recently updated store, shoppers needed clerks to procure goods from high shelves and to weigh and wrap goods. (Chicago History Museum, DN-0086026, 1928, source:* Chicago Daily News)

source of antagonism between these firms and mass producers and proces-sors. Manufacturers worked to enforce higher retail prices on their goods (and thus increase the prices that they could charge to wholesalers and distributors) and resented retailers' attempts to lower the wholesale prices of the goods. Pro-ducers of branded foods also resented chain stores because they sold so many private label goods—that is, house brands produced solely for their stores and often sold for lower prices than parallel products from national brands. For this reason, chains and mass retailers often had antagonistic relationships with mass producers and mass processors, despite their shared reliance on similar business strategies (high throughput, economies of scale, and so on).[134]

Other features of mass-processed goods also worked against the efforts of chain store firms to substitute packaging and manufacturer advertising for store clerks. Numerous exposés of adulterated mass-processed foods and con-sequent lawsuits against national firms provided further reasons to distrust promises of standard sizes and quality. Packages did not always deliver on the promise to provide all needed information. As generations of activists attested, packaged food often had misleading—and sometimes outright false—labeling, with little information about ingredients. Packages were sized to suggest far larger quantities of food than they actually contained.[135] For all of these reasons, customers continued to rely on store personnel for information, and they continued to view packaged merchandise through a skeptical lens.

The same skepticism extended to chain stores. The appeal of self-service, standardization, and clean, bright interiors, was real—but qualified. Of course, chain groceries were enormously popular in the 1920s and 1930s, and many Americans found it worth the effort to shop there. Moreover, many women—working-class women in particular—expressed a clear preference for chains' self-service features. In 1936, for instance, a University of Chicago student found that poorer women were sometimes the least likely to want full-service stores. Instead, these women claimed that self-service was often the best way to buy.

This was not, however, because shopping at these stores was an entirely straightforward experience for these women, many of whom also said they needed assistance in deciphering English-language packaging and expressed concerns about low-quality products being foisted on them.[136] Indeed, what emerges from this study of chain store firms is that neither customers nor retailers were fully satisfied. The same study found that more than 71 percent of the women who shopped in local chain stores listed self-service as a reason for their choice of store. However, when asked what their ideal was, only 37 percent favored complete self-service, and most preferred some service and help in the store.[137] In chain stores, as in independent stores, women negotiated the terrain of retailing, pressuring for change when they could and making do with what was offered when they could not.

IT IS IMPORTANT TO REMEMBER that chain stores' explosive growth in the 1920s suggests the limits of mass retailing as much as its dominance. Chain stores' roots were shallow, their financial health able to be undone by women's insistence that they deserved actual authority in stores, by the debts firms incurred as they navigated the unexpectedly high overhead costs of mass retailing, or by popular resistance to their method. Firms constantly recalibrated, developing new strategies of standardization only to limit or abandon them in the face of customer resistance and localized political or economic vagaries. The uncertainty that marked the rise of chain stores in the 1920s is akin to the uncertainty that dogged the attempts of all grocery stores to assert authority over customers.

This struggle for authority over the shop floor illuminates the ways in which social concerns—racial solidarity, femininity, women's duties as wives and mothers, and communal obligation—permeated everyday buying and selling in the 1910s and 1920s. It is not difficult to see these social politics in small, independent, neighborhood stores. But it is also important to see socially weighty encounters, although the debates were more muted. The decision to shop in a chain indicated a rejection of communal scrutiny and of local grocers. Certainly, chain grocers played on the social politics of women's desire for autonomy in their advertising and marketing. Moreover, even when chains' attempts to profit from new gender relations did not work—when women demanded personal attention or when chain proprietors feared the damage they were doing to femininity by not offering this attention—social relations were at the heart of the grocery store. Price was an important variable, but not the only one at play in the creation of mass retailing. Women's actions and ideas about women continued to undermine chain stores' efforts to fully impose standardization and streamlined efficiency.

The Changing Politics of
Mass Consumption, 1910–1940

In the 1920s, the emergence of chain store firms, executives' attempts to standardize stores and limit personal treatment of customers, popular protests against high prices, a new rhetoric of modern, independent women, and attempts by working-class whites and African Americans to capture some of the profits of retail for their own communities led to new questions about the social politics and, therefore, the organizational structure of grocery stores.

There soon emerged yet another source of uncertainty about the social politics and organizational future of groceries—the new wave of state and federal policies directed at, and often administered by, grocery stores. In the 1930s, policymakers increased their attention to grocery stores, and to consumption and retail sales generally, through a number of policies—anti–chain store taxes (designed to ease the competitive burden on independent grocers), relief and welfare programs, new sales taxes, and, by the mid-1930s, attempts to regain business prosperity via the National Recovery Administration (NRA). Although many of the lasting policies tended to confer advantages on larger firms, that outcome was not at all obvious when these rules were created. Indeed, for much of the 1930s, the only clear message that retailers received was that government programs and regulations would be increasingly important to their operations.

These government initiatives shifted the ground on which grocers and food shoppers operated, reshaping power relations and the experience of consumption more directly than better-known Keynesian-inspired efforts, which encouraged consumer spending in the aggregate. Although scholars have effectively demonstrated that concern with consumption shaped government policy for much of the twentieth century, the opposite was also true—concern with government policy shaped consumption.[1] Thus, this chapter demonstrates

73

how grocery stores and food shopping were political in the most conventional sense of the term—they were permeated by government edicts, laws, regulations, and guidelines. The perspective of local retailers who contended with local and state laws, along with federal-level politics, reveals that government shaped the structure as well as the discourse of consumer society.

The chapter also acknowledges that another sort of politics underlay this formal policy regime—the social politics between grocers and their customers. The policies discussed here, however unintentionally, reshaped those personal relations. Thus, a close examination of the everyday administration of new laws explains why the issue of women's authority as consumers was so difficult and so important to the emerging political economy of mass consumption.

Municipal Government and the Personal Politics of Grocery Stores

Grocers, like the public markets and peddlers discussed in Chapter 1, had never operated outside government control. Before 1930, however, most of that control came from the city, not from state or federal governments. Thus, despite the focus of much of the literature on federal-level changes, the political environment in which stores operated and in which chain stores first evolved was based on more local political culture and local institutions.[2]

In the case of Chicago, store owners had to confront what can only be called an infamous political machine. The 1920s were a time of notable political corruption, even for Chicago. Laws were created, enforced, or ignored as a result of highly personalized negotiation with local aldermen and mayoral representatives. In this political climate, the fortunes of a grocery store depended as much on the proprietor's relationship with local officials as on its internal structure.[3] No single type of store was at an advantage, though all had to spend time (and probably money) negotiating the city's complicated local political scene.

What is most striking about municipal-level regulations is their personal nature. Zoning, licensing, and a host of other regulations made city government a palpable presence in the operations of virtually all urban retailers. But that did not mean that retailers were faced with the task of navigating a bureaucracy. Instead, it meant that retailers often engaged in regular negotiations with the mayor's office and with city officials. Institutional structure (whether national chain or local independent) and store policy (its strategy for expansion) mattered less than the retailers' personal relationships with city officials.

THE CITY HAD A LONG HISTORY of regulating weights and measures, setting health and sanitation standards, and devising codes for commercial buildings.[4]

The 1922 municipal code, for instance, required inspections of grocers' refrigerators, their scales, and the ways in which they bundled produce.[5] Not only did the city require these inspections; store owners themselves had to pay for them. The health department, which conducted the inspections and licensed retailers, charged inspection fees (ranging from $25 to $400, depending on the number of employees) as well as a fee for the license (a minimum of $5, increasing if the store sold meat in addition to dry groceries, if there were more than two employees, or if there were a delivery wagon). Weight inspectors, notoriously corrupt, were prohibited from collecting fees from business owners more than once a year—unless, of course, the inspector had found a violation in that shop in the previous year.[6]

Throughout the 1920s, the city council continued to influence the daily operations of grocery stores and to pass new regulations on food retailing. The Committee on the High Cost of Living, a city council committee created in the wake of World War I to rectify high food costs, was only one example of the municipal government's attempts to assert control over grocery stores and food prices. In addition, local officials also expanded the range of allowable weights for loaves of bread, hoping to make available lower-priced versions of this daily necessity.[7] Other agencies also revamped regulations covering grocers in the 1920s. In 1925, weights and measures inspectors were declared "special policemen" by the city council and given the power to arrest violators.[8] That same year, the council passed an ordinance prohibiting meat sales on Sundays.[9] The municipal government even threatened retailers by periodically opening municipally owned produce stores.[10]

Perhaps the farthest-reaching extension of the city's authority over retailers came through the zoning ordinance, enabled by the state government in 1919 and implemented by the city in 1923.[11] The act itself was lengthy, complicated, and broad. It brought about the creation of one of the city's most powerful agencies, the Zoning Appeals Board, and the implementation of some of the city's most extensive regulations.[12] Theoretically, dividing the city into zones allowed for cleaner, healthier, and more aesthetically pleasing neighborhoods. Residences would no longer be scattered among noisy and polluting businesses, and commercial districts would be clearly designated.[13]

Because the ordinance was not made retroactive (that is, existing firms did not have to move if they were located in the wrong sort of zone), it was difficult to see any immediate results on city streets. But property owners, including grocers, quickly saw one important change. The new regulations provided the city with authority over a remarkable range of store activities. The city could approve (or prohibit) changes to store exteriors—in particular, the construction

75

of additions. It could approve or prohibit the construction of a sign. It could tell retailers whether they could open a new store in a particular neighborhood.[14] And, perhaps most important, the city could grant exemptions to its own regulations. Zoning legislation was another way (often underappreciated by historians) in which municipal authority touched retailers' lives—and the lives of all Chicagoans—in the 1920s.

That these ordinances were passed, however, did not mean that they were enforced. Chicago's system of governance was characterized by personally negotiated exceptions to rules. For instance, the city council allowed the mayor to circumvent the licensing department and to issue licenses himself. Moreover, he could grant individual exemptions to certain provisions of the law; for instance, he could waive the licensing fees normally charged.[15] So common were exceptions that the city council entertained several proposals to force city departments to collect the licensing fees required of retailers.[16]

The Zoning Appeals Board exemplified the sort of practices that marked municipal governance. For instance, between January 1 and October 1, 1925, the board heard 561 cases. Although the official tally counted only 181 of these appeals as having been granted, the board's own figures showed that another 168 had been partially granted—so that more than two-thirds of all appeals met with measurable success. A year later, the zoning ordinance was still enforced only sporadically. The report of the exasperated, reform-minded Mayor Dever noted, "One of the principal difficulties encountered in the enforcement of [the zoning] ordinance is the tenacious refusal of certain retail merchants to vacate stores located in new and existing buildings in residence zones. These violations can only be eradicated by persistent prosecutions."[17] These prosecutions, however, were not forthcoming.

Aldermen were just as complicit as the mayor and zoning board members in permitting lax enforcement. The records of special orders passed by the council show large chains, as well as very small stores, demanding refunds of license fees, asking permission to build driveways over city property, and requesting exemptions from laws restricting the size and nature of store signs. The usual pattern was for an individual alderman, generally the council member for the ward in which the business was located, to introduce the petitions, which seem to have been granted in most cases.[18] Winning politicians' support was crucial for negotiating municipal regulations.

The city showed little interest in the large-scale changes that were transforming the retail sector in this period. With the exception of somewhat higher licensing fees, the city did not apply any special sanctions to large businesses or to chain store firms.[19] Individual relationships, not business strategies, were most important in negotiating municipal policy.

Municipal government, in other words, was a force in the world of retailing, in everything from store location to signage to costs. Whereas scholars have often thought of municipal government as losing importance during and after the Progressive Era, a look at retailing suggests its ongoing importance. In its attention to personal relations and in its focus on the mundane aspects of commerce, municipal government continued to shape the everyday work of grocers and the choices available to their customers.

New Regulations by State Governments: Anti-chain Legislation

Slowly, over the course of the 1920s and 1930s, extralocal governing bodies became increasingly interested in what happened in grocery stores, and that interest marked the beginning of a new era in grocery retailing as well as in state and federal political economies. Grocers had more cause for concern over what state and federal laws were passed because these laws were more likely to be enforced in a straightforward manner.

Extralocal governments were first drawn into the world of grocery stores through the efforts of small, independently owned stores and their suppliers to halt the advance of large chain store operations. Protective legislation for small business was not a new concept; legislators had a history of considering protective legislation for small, local businesses that claimed to be victimized by larger competitors.[20] But this was the first time that such attention had been extended to grocers, and it made the scope of mass retailing clear. Moreover, and in the end more tellingly, it was in anti-chain debates that the power of policy to determine the shape of mass retailing, and not just of individual businesses, was most clearly articulated. It is helpful to view the anti-chain phenomenon nationally, before returning to its local manifestations in Illinois and in Chicago, in particular.

One of the first indications of extralocal interest in grocery stores came in the late 1920s, in Herbert Hoover's Department of Commerce. The department produced several studies and a raft of prescriptive literature designed to help small firms compete with larger chain store operations. Most of the information encouraged proprietors of smaller stores to adopt the chains' efficiency and careful accounting.[21] This was hardly overt regulation, however. Whatever the sympathies of the federal government and policymakers, there were few national laws or organized efforts to slow the growth of chains in the late 1920s and early 1930s.

Formalized group efforts to slow chains' growth, however, did become important in various state legislatures. The "anti-chain movement" was a catalyst for state-level regulation of grocery stores, and it marked the beginning of a new interest by state governments in retailing and in consumption.

State legislatures had entertained anti-chain bills throughout the 1920s.[22] But the number of such bills introduced—as well as the likelihood of passage—increased dramatically when, in May 1931, the U.S. Supreme Court declared graduated taxes based on the number of stores a firm owned entirely legal.[23] In 1931 alone, forty-four states debated more than a hundred anti-chain bills in their respective legislatures.[24] Even before the court's decision, the editors of *Chain Store Age* were referring to the bills as an "epidemic"; after the decision (and even in the face of falling prices and devastating financial losses), the president of Kroger identified the anti-chain movement as the single biggest problem then confronting chains.[25]

Chain store firm executives feared that a burgeoning social movement stood behind the legislation. Thus, at both the national and the local levels, these firms devoted significant resources to improving their public images and defusing any resentment they had engendered. Their efforts ensured that in the halls of legislatures, the pages of magazines, and the everyday shopping choices made by Americans, the implications of chain retailing for neighborhoods and communities were hotly debated.

Although the most vocal participants in anti-chain campaigns were independent grocers and wholesalers, consumer opinion was clearly the most important variable. Over the course of the next two years, Kroger, A&P, and the National Tea Company instituted public relations campaigns to combat charges that chains were monopolies that undermined the prosperity of communities. Kroger advertised its contributions to local economies and increased managers' autonomy so that they could participate in local trade associations and buy from local firms.[26] The president of the National Tea Company gave public speeches defending chains and eventually became head of the national trade association for grocery chains. Even A&P, which at first had denied the threat of anti-chain laws, eventually acknowledged the movement's strength by hiring an outside public relations firm and mounting an all-out campaign to win over farmers and shoppers.[27]

Scholars have typically framed the anti-chain movement as having rural and small-town origins, particularly in the South and West. However, support for the anti-chain movement was less geographically contained. As Cory Sparks has pointed out, grassroots buy-at-home movements were as likely to be urban as rural. Indeed, some of the greatest difficulties chains encountered came from well-organized urban retailers' campaigns.[28] In Detroit, New York City, and Minneapolis, anti-chain activists had a sizable presence.[29]

Although Chicago was known as a city receptive to chains,[30] by July 1933 it was also home to a full-time anti-chain activist, Winfield Caslow, who had a daily editorial on station wjjo, published a weekly newsletter, and spoke to both businessmen's clubs and their ladies' auxiliaries. The blue-collar northwest side of the city was home to particularly active "Shop at Home" campaigns, and in the 1931 mayoral elections, one enterprising politician ran as the candidate of the "Anti-Chain" Party.[31] Chicagoans testified in favor of anti-chain bills being debated in the state legislature, and state senators and assembly members voted in favor of passage.[32] This spate of anti-chain activity left few archival sources, but the few anecdotes that we have—as well as the experience of other cities—suggest that the rhetoric of anti-chain activism was a palpable presence in the city's lively political scene. Even cities that were usually strongholds of chains seemed only partially won over in the early 1930s.

Chicago's vulnerability to anti-chain legislation was heightened by its location within the state of Illinois. The Illinois legislature had debated anti-chain bills periodically since 1927.[33] After the 1931 U.S. Supreme Court decision legalizing such bills, the state assembly began considering the most punitive anti-chain bill in the country, with rates running as high as $1,000 annually for the biggest stores.[34] Four months later, in February 1932, chain store owners were concerned enough to sponsor the first state-level chain store firm trade association—the Illinois Chain Store Association.[35] Only a year later, legislators introduced five different anti-chain bills in a single legislative session, with vocal support from associations of independent retailers.[36]

Typically, anti-chain bills in Illinois were formulated as licensing measures. Sometimes firms that owned only one or two stores paid no licensing fee at all, and sometimes the fee was minimal (rarely more than $5). But for firms that owned many stores, the fees could be astronomical—anywhere from $200 to $1,000 per store.[37] The first bills often simply empowered (and ordered) local officials to collect and distribute licensing proceeds; later bills established state-level offices and a Chain Store Tax Fund. Otherwise there was very little difference among the bills.

Although many stores failed to fit neatly into these categories (very small chains of two or three stores, for instance), the dichotomy of "chain" versus "independent" nonetheless became entrenched in the heated rhetoric of these campaigns. Opponents of chain stores often argued that chains bled communities dry by taking out revenue and never putting any back; as local monopolies, they simply could not be trusted to keep people's best interests at heart. "The net profits made by the National Tea Company store in your community goes into HEADQUARTERS! And that's all the prosperity that the National Tea Company is supposed to answer for in your community," read a typical critique by Chicago's tireless anti-chain activist, Winfield Caslow.[38]

Proponents countered that chains provided goods at prices lower than those most independents could match and so lowered the cost of living and improved people's lives. National Tea was so concerned by Caslow's attack the company ran a response in the city's major dailies: "The savings created by National Tea Company's modern economical food distributing methods bring to you and your community the advantages of a higher standard of living. . . . [F]urther with these savings you have additional money to spend with others in your community."[39] It was a typical response; many argued that chains should be allowed to beat out inefficient, higher-priced independents because in the final analysis, low-priced merchandise was the best guarantor of a family's well-being. In a 1931 address to chain store owners, Albert Morrill, president of Kroger, described chains as having a social responsibility to continue their work: "From a broad economic viewpoint, this is not so much our fight as it is the public's fight. As is not unusual, however, the great mass of people have no clear perception or understanding of precisely where their best interests lie."[40]

Grocers interpreted subsequent policies in terms of the "chain question," even if those policies were silent on the issue—and no matter how inadequate the categories themselves became as firms' strategies changed over time. Throughout the 1930s, retailers frequently expressed concern that the government was unfairly favoring (or punishing) one type of store. Session after session of the Illinois legislature saw new chain-taxation bills introduced and considered. So common were these debates, and so pervasive were retailers' concerns, that many began to monitor state government bills and policies, regardless of whether the legislation explicitly punished chain stores.

New Regulations by State Governments and New Resistance
from Shoppers: Relief Policies and the Sales Tax

Two new programs, the sales tax and public relief, seemed to favor chain stores. Large chain stores better fulfilled new government guidelines and were easier to regulate than were smaller, more autonomous, and less organized independent stores. Independent grocers, using uncharacteristically gender-neutral language, frequently charged that government edicts complicated both their operations and their efforts to keep customers' goodwill. Whereas much scholarship has described World War II as a turning point in the state's preference for working with large stores and businesses, the examples of the sales tax and New Deal relief reperiodize that history and point to important relationships established in the prewar years, especially the 1930s.[41]

The implication of independent grocers' complaints goes beyond the rivalry between chains and independents. In establishing both relief programs and the new sales tax, government policymakers had to confront the possibility that shoppers simply would not cooperate with store staff and would prevent them from carrying out government directives, thus crippling the new programs. Consumers could exercise significant political and economic muscle simply by refusing to cooperate with government policies in their daily shopping. How far Americans would go in politicizing their shopping and how much authority they would win in this new political economy emerged as unsettling questions for grocers and for policymakers.

TRADITIONALLY, PEOPLE ON RELIEF had received either in-kind assistance or vouchers for supplies from local merchants. Most retailers were used to working with local churches, mutual-aid societies, and other private organizations. But the scale of poverty in the 1930s overwhelmed these traditional sources of temporary aid. As Lizabeth Cohen has ably documented, small charitable societies had to turn away needy applicants; fraternal societies sometimes had to shut their doors entirely.[42] In Illinois, as elsewhere, the city and county stepped in. But even then, the massive numbers of unemployed and destitute Chicagoans overwhelmed the already-strapped municipal and state governments. Politicians feared riots, and social workers warned of mass malnutrition.[43] Neither the $45 million provided by the Reconstruction Finance Corporation nor the $15 million raised by private citizens in two successive campaigns could meet the growing need in the city and county.[44]

In the winter of 1933, the federal government took a more active role through the creation of the Federal Emergency Relief Administration (FERA), the precursor to the Works Progress Administration. FERA oversaw both public works projects and nonwork relief. It established an administrative structure that became a pattern for other federal programs during the New Deal, distributing federal dollars through state- and county-level agencies. The Illinois Emergency Relief Commission (IERC) and its designated subsidiary agencies quickly became important forces in the distribution of relief.[45]

Food figured prominently in relief operations. Relief recipients regularly complained about food, and critics of relief often grounded their claims of either inadequate or overly generous benefits in examples of the food provided to clients.

But food was also important in the most basic financial terms. It was at the center of what grocers came to call "the relief business." The profits food purveyors stood to make from sales to relief clients were potentially enormous. In the winter of 1932–33, about 80 percent of monthly relief funds used for clients were used to purchase food for them—coming to approximately $2.7 million per month.[46] These funds were especially important to grocers in the tight times of the 1930s.

The creation of FERA and its use of state-level counterparts for administration of federal relief programs brought the state squarely into the ongoing competition among grocery stores. Administrators of the IERC determined which grocers the state would do business with and signed contracts for supplies of in-kind aid (generally boxes of staple foods). Social workers employed by the IERC or its designated agencies set the basic household budgets of relief clients and so determined the aggregate amount spent by and on behalf of relief recipients. They also determined the distribution of aid—how much a client would receive in vouchers, in cash, or in-kind assistance. Finally, social workers and relief recipients themselves wrote up the vouchers in the names of individual retailers and so ultimately determined which merchants would receive the government's business. In other words, relief highlighted government involvement in the most everyday aspects of food retailing.

In-kind aid (often called "ration boxes") and grocery vouchers were always controversial, in part because of individual corruption by officials and store staff and in part because of the generalized suspicions of wary Chicagoans.[47] For instance, when the National Tea Company was the only acceptable bidder on the first IERC rations contract, there was a massive public outcry and accusations that the bidding process had been fixed.[48] In one particularly illustrative moment, the former head of fraud investigation for the IERC "denied that he had in his possession secret affidavits purporting to show that relief employees have been guests of large wholesale grocery concerns on liquor parties, or affidavits in which irregularities involving food orders were disclosed."[49] There does seem to have been extensive corruption; the IERC estimated that it had been defrauded of more than $800,000 by late 1936.[50]

Graft and suspicious coincidences came as little surprise to most Chicagoans, however. It was systematic policies rather than the corruption of individuals that made the vouchers and ration boxes controversial.

Among the most controversial policies was the provision of in-kind aid, such as ration boxes of staple foods—flour, canned goods, and so on. The state purchased these goods in bulk, theoretically at prices lower than clients would have paid had they bought them individually. Providing this in-kind aid not only had economic benefits but also encouraged clients to cook and eat foods deemed nutritious and economical by relief agencies.[51]

The voucher system was another attempt to shape the behavior of clients, although the goals of the program were more covert. Relief clients received vouchers for the purchase of foods not included in their ration boxes—meats, fruits, cheeses, and some dry groceries. These vouchers worked like checks; clients could take them to a store and make purchases for the amount of the voucher. Unlike personal checks, however, the vouchers were not blank—social workers made them out to particular grocers. Theoretically, the client chose the grocer; making out the voucher in advance simply facilitated the state's payment to the grocer and ensured that relief money was spent on food.[52] In practice, however, the system curtailed the choices available to relief recipients, because it was very difficult to make changes in vouchers once they were issued and because only certain grocers were eligible to work with the IERC and fill relief clients' orders.[53] Grocers and clients tried to work around these restrictions. For instance, they substituted desirable goods for those relief officials had expected them to provide.[54]

Small independent grocers complained long and loud about the state's use of ration boxes and vouchers. In particular, they accused the IERC of favoring large stores and chains at the expense of small local merchants. The Retail Meat Dealers of Chicago, a particularly vocal group, complained throughout the spring of 1933 that they were not receiving as much business from relief clients as they should. They demanded that social workers remind clients that they could have separate vouchers made out for meat purchases and so, for instance, could patronize a butcher shop that did not sell dry groceries.[55] Small merchants repeatedly charged that social workers guided clients toward chains.[56]

In response to these charges of favoritism, officials worked at the state level to assist the small neighborhood stores that were so important to the wards they represented. As early as September 1932, the Subcommittee of the Illinois Commission on Taxation and Expenditures, which included several representatives from Chicago, recommended that the IERC purchase from "neighborhood merchants" whenever it was "practicable."[57] In addition, Chicago mayor Edward Kelly, representatives of Chicago department stores, and the Chicago Association of Commerce asked the IERC to make its purchases from Illinois concerns and from small retailers whenever possible.[58] The city council itself launched several investigations into small retailers' allegations that they were being denied the "charity business."[59] There was, noted the Cook County director of public relief, "constant criticism that the client's choice has been influenced."[60]

Were small retailers right to be concerned? Despite constant denials by the director of public relief, Joseph Moss, there is substantial evidence that relief officials favored chains and sometimes pressured clients to shop at them. While some social workers in downstate counties routinely prevented clients from shopping in chain stores, it was more common for them to favor the low prices and efficiencies of chains.[61] In Cook County, both relief recipients and small business owners presented frequent anecdotal evidence of favoritism toward chain stores. Moreover, a suspiciously high number of relief orders were placed at chains—more than 60 percent according to the director of the Cook County Bureau of Public Welfare.[62]

The clearest evidence of favoritism toward chains at the expense of other stores comes from more consistent and systemic policies. The IERC much preferred doing business with well-organized, centrally managed chains to contending with the informal practices of small grocery stores. As early as March 1932, it issued specific instructions on how grocers were to be repaid for relief orders. The instructions noted that grocers without their own stationery could be repaid but made it clear that the agency preferred dealing with grocers who submitted bills on letterhead.[63] One grocer recalled that the advent of relief finally persuaded her to record individual sales: "The only time we filed is when they were taking those what were charity tickets, you know . . . . They [customers] would take from the store, like on credit, and every month we had to go and file whatever they took . . . each customer, and then the city or the county would pay back, and it had to be just so because if you were a penny short or a penny over, then they would send the whole thing back to you. So, I did."[64]

It was not only formal billing procedures that gave larger, more bureaucratized stores an advantage. The IERC spent millions of dollars on ration boxes. Ideally, these boxes were to be furnished by wholesalers who submitted quarterly bids to the commission. But the National Tea Company, one of Chicago's largest retail grocery chains, also had the capital, warehouses, equipment, and staff to supply ration boxes; unlike small stores, National Tea Company could compete with wholesale firms. Occasionally, it even won. Contracts worth anywhere from $1 million to $2 million were often divided between the National Tea Company and one of Chicago's wholesale firms. Winning these contracts had special importance for National Tea because its contracts, unlike those of the wholesale houses, specified that clients must come into their stores to pick up the boxes. Even as this system lowered costs for the relief commission, it also afforded chain store firms opportunities to win new sales from people who now had to come into their stores.[65]

Independent grocers regularly charged that other features of the relief system also put them at a disadvantage. For instance, several hundred retail grocers held a meeting at the Hotel Sherman in downtown Chicago claiming that the prices that they were allowed to charge relief recipients did not cover their costs.[66]

Relief clients themselves seem to have understood the problem in different terms. They complained not about chains per se, but about systematic constraints on their individual choices and the poor treatment they received as a result of their lack of choice. They did not necessarily desire the demise of chains or the success of neighborhood stores, but the ability to determine for themselves where they shopped.

The voucher system was a frequent target of complaints for precisely this reason. Many clients complained of being told where to shop by social workers rather than being able to choose freely.[67] Moreover, the likelihood of making changes to vouchers was so minimal that it was difficult for relief clients to threaten not to patronize a store once its name had been inscribed on the voucher. As one woman put it, some grocers "are pretty nasty to you when they no [sic] you got to trade with them."[68]

Ration boxes were a similar source of dismay. Clients and relief officials both recognized that standardized rations, even when they were differentiated by ethnic group, as they were in Chicago, could not possibly satisfy every individual recipient.[69] As one FERA researcher reported after a trip to Chicago, "Negroes did not like things that the Italians liked and the Jews would not eat things given to them, yet the things were common to all boxes."[70] In addition, clients claimed, what they did receive was often spoiled and unusable—food that suppliers had been waiting to dump on people who had no other choice. Outside reviews supported this claim; one newspaper investigation of the contents of relief baskets found that every carton of eggs swarmed with maggots.[71]

Relief clients' desire for choice was often articulated in demands for cash relief and for more adequate relief funds. Throughout the 1930s, relief recipients joined "unemployed councils" and pressured state and federal authorities to replace in-kind aid and vouchers with cash payments.[72] Massive protests occurred throughout 1932; in November of that year, fifty thousand people marched through Chicago's downtown to protest cuts in grocery rations and vouchers.[73] "What the unemployed want is cash relief, as they feel competent to handle their own affairs without the aid of a social worker," declared a representative from the Workers' Committee on Unemployment.[74] In January 1933, relief clients drove their point home in a more graphic way, dumping the moldy, wormy food that they had received in ration boxes outside IERC offices.[75] When the federal government took over much of the funding for relief in 1933, protests continued. Members of organizations of the unemployed appeared before the commission regularly, demanding better food and more autonomy in choosing it.[76] Relief recipients pressured the IERC both to increase their leverage over grocers and to allow them to shop when and where they pleased.

Cash relief appealed to local civic leaders as well, though not always for the same reasons. Many leaders in nutrition and social work believed that cash relief would "educate" women as housewives and provide them with a sense of personal accountability. Representatives of two of Chicago's largest settlement houses (Chicago Commons and Hull House) argued that providing goods "deprived the housewife of the privilege of shopping and in a sense destroyed their responsibility as housewives."[77] A nutrition expert for the state of Illinois, although suspicious of relief clients' ability to spend wisely, nonetheless admitted, "The intelligent housewife certainly could do better with cash."[78] This gendered division of labor, in which women did all food shopping, shaped support for cash relief.

City and county officials, meanwhile, were also favorably disposed toward clients' requests for cash relief. Pressure from an enormous array of constituents, including chain store firms and small grocers (each of whom felt that the switch would increase clients' willingness to shop with them), social workers, and even conservative opponents of relief spending (who felt that the switch would lower the administrative costs of distributing relief) argued their cases on a grand scale.[79]

In spite of this protest, relief officials were slow to make the change. In January 1933, Walter LaBuy, a member of the Cook County Board of Commissioners, asked that the IERC make it easier to switch grocers—and was denied.[80] LaBuy was apparently so frustrated with the IERC's intransigence that he began changing the names of grocers on clients' vouchers himself.[81] On September 15, 1933, the Cook County director of public relief formally requested that the state authorize a system of cash relief or at least make it easier to switch grocers once a voucher had been written. The request was rejected.[82] Finally, in September 1935, following yet another presentation by Chicago's unemployed council, the Cook County administrator of public relief recommended to the IERC that clients receive cash, though his stated reason was that relief rolls were changing too quickly for grocery orders to be practicable.[83] After years of pressure from local officials and relief clients themselves, the plan for cash relief was approved. By December 1935, all of Cook County was on cash relief.[84]

Once the new system was finally put in place, relief officials celebrated its ability to quell clients' unrest and anger. Pronouncing the experiment in cash relief "astonishingly successful for so short a trial," the county administrator produced story after story of relief recipients who were far happier with cash relief than with the voucher and ration system. "I feel like a different person when I can hand money over the counter instead of using a disbursing order," said one woman. In Union Park, a working-class neighborhood near the stockyards, clients claimed that they were able to get better fruits and vegetables from peddlers than from the chain stores at which they previously had been forced to shop. Relief recipients all over the city echoed the sentiment that they were able to purchase better-quality goods for less money once they were allowed to shop around. Even grocers welcomed the lowered bookkeeping costs of cash relief.[85] By mid-December, when Cook County's experiment had been in place for only a few weeks, the governor was pressuring the IERC to move the whole state to cash relief.[86] Indeed, so popular was the system of cash relief that when the city ran into cash-flow problems the following summer and temporarily began paying with vouchers, "hundreds of protests [were] made by relief clients who declare they can buy more cheaply with cash," according to the *Chicago Tribune*. Within three weeks of having left cash relief, the city promised that it would return to cash distributions by September 1.[87]

As the story of relief suggests, in the 1930s, consumption became politically important for several reasons. Politicians increasingly celebrated "the consumer" in their rhetoric. Also, federal officials became increasingly interested in Keynesian thinking and its emphasis on consumer spending. However, consumption also became significant in a structural way. Spaces of consumption occupied new importance in the everyday workings of the modern state. In its efforts to administer relief, the state of Illinois also administered buying habits and behavior in stores and, indeed, shaped the fortunes of retailers.

The story of the sales tax reinforces this, even as it tells a slightly different tale about political economy. The sales tax makes clear the importance of consumption to state governments' fiscal stability and illuminates the growing importance of consumers who were willing to adhere to store policy.

The sales tax affected all stores and all shoppers, and it made the state a participant in all retail transactions. Although the issue of chain stores versus independents suffused the debate over the sales tax, the more immediate question was how stores could compel consumers' cooperation. In tough times, could grocers exert enough pressure on clients to make them pay an extra few cents on every purchase? To a greater degree than any other single piece of legislation, the sales tax placed the state firmly in the center of mass consumption and hence firmly in the path of shoppers.[88]

The sales tax was the result of both national trends and local conditions. State governments all over the country faced fiscal crises in the early 1930s, the result of an economic one-two punch. On the one hand, state governments were being pressured to fund relief programs. On the other, state revenues, traditionally based on property taxes, were rapidly declining.[89] Nor was there any immediate improvement in sight. As popular resentment of property taxes reached new heights, raising the tax rate to obtain the needed revenues seemed politically impossible.[90] Federal-level assistance, in the form of loans and direct grants, was both temporary and inadequate.[91]

The first public discussion of sales taxes took place in the early 1920s during the postwar recession.[92] Support for a sales tax quickly faded, but by the 1930s, general taxation of retail sales seemed the only politically viable solution left. Proponents argued that consumer purchasing would never entirely disappear, that prices did not fall as quickly for consumer goods as they did for industrial goods, and that sales taxes would not spark the sort of resentment engendered by property taxes.[93] Thus, sales taxes promised steady sources of revenue even amid falling prices.

Beginning in 1932 with the Mississippi sales tax, in what was generally acknowledged to be a move of desperation, numerous states instituted sales taxes. In 1933, Illinois was one of eleven states to establish a sales tax.[94] By 1937, sales taxes were in place in twenty-six states, New York City, and the District of Columbia.[95] A year later—and still with only half of all states levying a sales tax—it was supplying 14 percent of all states' revenues: more than such mainstays as income, estate, inheritance, liquor, tobacco, and motor vehicle taxes and fees.[96] Neil Jacoby, a professor of finance at the University of Chicago School of Business and a specialist in business-government relations, called sales taxes "the most spectacular and fiscally important revenue development in the field of state taxation during the present decade."[97]

Support for the sales tax resulted from the failure and inadequacy of other funding sources. In the 1931–32 fiscal year, property tax receipts dropped 50 percent, and the state revenue fund declined by 30 percent. All too aware of the need for additional revenue, Chicago mayor Anton Cermak asked the state legislature to find revenue from sources other than the property tax.[98] Unfortunately, federal sources did not pick up the slack; in 1932, the state of Illinois received the very first loan made by the Reconstruction Finance Corporation, but the $45 million was exhausted within eight months.[99]

At this point, city officials saw the sales tax as the next best option for funding state aid to the city. In 1932, the Chicago city council considered a resolution urging that a special session of the state legislature be convened to institute a sales tax.[100] When the state supreme court declared the first sales tax unconstitutional, the council demanded that the state enact a sales tax, calling it "the most equitable and least painful of all forms of taxation, . . . [and] the most modern way of raising revenue."[101]

As the city council's unqualified support for a sales tax suggests, the city of Chicago had a special interest in avoiding reliance on other sources of revenue. Chicago had been particularly hard-hit by property tax protests. Complaints had begun with the 1927 quadrennial assessment, and in 1928, two Cook County courts had declared part of the rolls fraudulent, and the tax commission had ordered that all real estate be reassessed.[102] While the reassessment was completed, tax collection ceased.[103] But Chicago's fiscal problems did not end when property tax collection resumed in 1930. A widespread tax strike, catalyzed by suspicions of local government corruption and resentment of taxation generally, crippled local finances. During the 1931–32 fiscal year, 53.4 percent of all property taxes billed by the county and state went uncollected.[104] The city desperately needed to defuse popular resentment of the property tax and to increase its revenues.

The sales tax seemed the perfect solution. It offered a way of decreasing the state's reliance on property taxes while lowering Chicagoans' annual tax bills. It also was passed with the understanding that the state would funnel new revenues to help the financially embattled city's relief funds—a provision crucial to gaining the support of progressive organizations. For these reasons, the tax received broad support among Chicago-area businessmen and in the Chicago press. Even retailers, who at first had opposed the tax, came to support it publicly.[105]

One other factor pushed Illinois toward adopting the sales tax. The only viable alternative—an income tax—was both unconstitutional and unpopular.[106] Tax reformers had often proposed a graduated income tax as a progressive alternative to flat-rate taxes, like property and sales taxes.[107] Teachers and social workers were among the proponents of such a tax in Illinois, but their voices were not strong enough to force a constitutional amendment.[108] In November 1930, Illinois voters defeated a constitutional amendment that would have allowed a graduated state income tax. In February 1932, the governor signed into law an act establishing an income tax, but it was declared unconstitutional. The state supreme court called the law a violation of the state constitution's "uniformity clause," which provided that items in the same category had to be taxed at the same rate.[109] Finally, in March 1933, facing rising unemployment, the state passed its first sales tax.

Proceeds from the sales tax fulfilled all expectations. As promised, the tax provided a steady source of revenue, even amid falling prices. In December 1933, as hoped, the state announced that it would cease to levy any part of the property tax.[110] By the 1933–34 fiscal year, the sales tax had become the single largest component of the state's revenue—23.9 percent.[111] In the 1937–38 fiscal year, it made up 42.8 percent.[112]

The sales tax marked the state's dependence on continued, stable consumer spending. Stores and consumers were now crucial players in the state's ability to function, and as a result, both received special attention in the crafting of sales tax legislation.

The sales tax was nominally a tax on retailers. Indeed, its official title was the "retailer's occupation tax"—a tax on the "privilege" (to use the law's term) of engaging in retailing. In titling the law in this way, policymakers hoped to suggest that store owners would pay the tax and thus to allay their constituents' concerns that individual citizens ultimately would pay more. But in Illinois, just as in states that did not attempt this linguistic sleight-of-hand, the difficult questions remained. How would the state effectively enforce collection on thousands of scattered storekeepers, many of them unaccustomed to keeping any records at all? Would store owners, or shoppers, ultimately pay the tax?

The state immediately and aggressively tackled the difficulties of enforcement by requiring all retailers to engage in extensive record keeping. Retailers had to send in monthly returns listing their total sales for the previous month,[113] accompanied by payment of the tax due—3 percent of sales under the first, only briefly enforced act; 2 percent under the second, permanent act.[114] In 1935, the state extended its enforcement powers by requiring all retailers to register with the Department of Finance and to display a certificate of registration. If retailers did not pay the tax or keep adequate records, the registration could be revoked.[115]

The sales tax extended the principle, demonstrated as early as nineteenth-century railroad regulations, that record keeping was crucial to the governance of modern states.[116] The amount that each retailer owed and the proof that the firm had paid were determined by the business's own records. Thus, the state now required retailers to keep extensive records and to allow state inspectors to see those records upon demand.[117] Not only did proprietors have to document sales, but they also had to retain "invoices, bills of lading . . . copies of bills of sale and other pertinent papers and documents."[118] The original legislation had required such records to be kept for two years; a 1939 change increased the retention time to three years.[119]

Retailers had strong incentives to keep accurate records; if a store owner's data were missing or inaccurate, the courts presumed that the state inspector's assessment of what was due was correct.[120] Nor were penalties for withholding taxes easy to overlook. In addition to paying taxes that were due, retailers could be forced to pay an additional 25 percent of the total taxes due.[121] The authors of a comprehensive study of sales taxes in the United States noted that in Illinois, "The powers of the department of finance relating to the inspection of taxpayers' books are broad, and the penalties imposed are fairly severe."[122]

If the law was clear about the records to be kept, it was much less clear about how tax collection would actually work. The precedent set by other states and the financial hardships of many retailers suggested that the tax would be tacked onto the price of goods and collected from shoppers. In resolving the dilemma of how the tax was to be collected, both grocers and policymakers came to understand the advantages held by stores that could allow them to limit the personal attention, and exceptions, granted to customers.

No state politician wanted to take responsibility for increasing the tax burden on citizens. Thus, the second, permanent law clearly stated that the tax was a tax on retailers, not consumers: "The tax imposed by this Act is an occupation tax upon retailers and is not a tax upon consumers. . . . He [the store owner] is neither required nor authorized to collect the tax as a tax from his customers."[123] The state finance director reiterated the state's position—that retailers were responsible for the tax—on the day that the tax went into effect.[124]

The specific provisions of the law, however, qualified and softened the impact of the state's insistence that storekeepers bear the brunt of the tax. Much of the law suggested that retailers were to consider the tax as part of their overhead—a thing that could be either fully absorbed or added to the price of goods. "In fixing the price of his products the retailer may consider the tax to be paid by him under this Act as one of the elements of cost in the conduct of his business and may include the amount of such tax in fixing such price in the same manner as rent, general taxes and other general overhead expenses are taken into consideration," the legislation advised. In other sections, policymakers made it clear that they fully expected retailers to charge customers for the tax. For instance, the law warned retailers not to use the tax in attempts to gouge customers by raising prices more than was necessary to pay the tax. "He should not misrepresent the amount of the tax imposed by the Act nor engage in profiteering under the guise of collecting such tax from purchasers," it stated tersely.[125]

The state's indirect acknowledgment of the fact that retailers would include the tax in their prices did not fully satisfy storekeepers. If the tax was treated as simply one more cost of doing business, then, like other costs, it would remain invisible to customers. Many retailers argued that an already cutthroat competitive atmosphere would become only worse as storekeepers struggled to shave prices and absorbed the cost of the tax themselves. Prosperous and large retailers might well use the tax as a marketing campaign, letting it be known that they would save customers some or all of the additional cost. Small retailers, their advocates warned, would be unable to do so and would be forced out of business. In the fierce price competition of the early 1930s, an added cause of lower profit margins was a horrifying possibility. Better, many merchants argued, that all retailers be required to tack the full tax on to the purchase price of all goods. Then the tax could not be a basis of competition.[126]

The struggle to make the tax visible to (and borne by) customers began almost immediately. Store owners created schedules that displayed for customers the amount added to their bills.[127] Theoretically, these would facilitate tax collection and allow customers to see exactly how much they were being charged. In Chicago, merchants' attempts to tack on the tax as a separate item were also part of a broader strategy to provoke antitax feelings among the public and thus to do away with the tax entirely. On June 27, 1933, just before the sales tax went into effect, the Illinois Chamber of Commerce put the matter succinctly: "If your city merely meets the tax by raising prices [and not by producing a schedule], the result will probably be the same except for the fact that the consumer public will not know it is paying a tax, will not become 'tax-conscious' and will be lukewarm to any future efforts to take the tax off the books."[128]

Schedules also had a practical advantage. Simply put, it was difficult to collect fractional cents. Under Illinois's 2 percent tax, sales that did not amount to even dollars or half dollars had to be rounded up or down; the tax on an item that cost 76 cents, for instance, had to be charged either at the amount for a 50 cent item or at the amount for a $1.00 item.[129] In the first scenario, the consumer came out ahead; in the second, the retailer did. A set schedule made clear to the customer how much tax was to be collected on any given price and, ideally, minimized the amount of rounding up to which consumers were subjected.

The schedules set by most stores, however, did not live up to that ideal. Under the original 3 percent tax in Illinois, many retailers adopted schedules that allowed them to round up on almost all purchases—that is, to recoup more than the cost of the tax on many items. The schedule developed by members of the State Street Merchants Association[130] charged a full cent for all goods at 33 cents and under, 2 cents for all goods between 34 and 66 cents, and 3 cents for all goods between 67 cents and a dollar.[131] Under this schedule, taxes on goods at the lower end of any bracket were dramatically overcharged. The schedule provoked the anger of individual shoppers and the articulate wrath of organized labor.[132]

At first, Chicago-area merchants used the schedules frequently, publicizing them in general newspapers and in the trade press. After only a few months, however, schedules fell into disuse, victims of their own questionable legality, customers' suspicions, and stores' desire to undersell each other. By October 1933, even the State Street Merchants Association announced that it would no longer ask its members to adhere to the schedule. Researchers found that such cooperation among competitors could not be maintained in the face of "the combined pressure of resentment expressed by consumers, and displeasure expressed by the [state] administration."[133]

Without even the power of collectively administered schedules, stores were left to their own devices. Many firms began collecting the tax only with great difficulty. One gas station owner pointed out that he could hardly force customers to pony up the extra 2 percent once the gas was already pumped and in their tanks.[134] Even sellers who might have had more leverage over consumers frequently absorbed the cost themselves, approaching their customers with great trepidation. One milkman regularly budgeted an extra $1.50 into his costs to cover customers who refused to pay the tax.[135] Similarly, grocers publicized their promise to collect the tax by folding it into the price but then assured customers that they would increase only the prices of items not already "subject to frequent market fluctuations."[136] By adding the cost into prices and assuring customers that competitive goods would not be subject to the tax, grocers hoped to ease customers' resistance to paying the tax.

One shopper's protests suggest the wisdom of grocers who tried to obscure their tax collection efforts. This letter to the editor of the *Chicago Tribune*, written more than two years since the tax had first gone into effect, asked whether the customer was actually legally obligated to pay the tax. "For instance," the unnamed author wrote, "when shopping in a chain store where they take the money before they wrap up your groceries, if you refuse to pay the sales tax . . . can they refuse to give you your groceries?"[137] The question suggests the sort of shop floor confrontations that grocers feared—having to publicly force a customer to pay the tax and thereby risking the loss of the sale as well as alienating other customers.

The letter also implies that a chain store actually did try to force the writer to pay the tax. This suggestion is in line with what seems to have been a greater willingness (and ability) among larger stores to collect the tax from customers. In these stores, "shifting" (adding the tax as separate item on customers' bills), was relatively common. In small stores, by contrast, shifting was difficult. One 1934 study of retailers in Chicago found that only 19 percent of firms with less than $5,000 in annual sales shifted all of the tax to customers—another 8 percent were able to shift part of the tax. In contrast, 92 percent of firms with annual sales above $100,000 shifted all or part of the tax to customers.[138] The same study found that "customer resentment" was the reason most commonly given by retailers that did not shift the tax.[139] These statistics confirm what many merchants had earlier suggested—it was difficult for small retailers, dependent on their customer base and already competing with lower-priced chains, to pass on the cost of the sales tax.[140]

Smaller stores experienced difficulty with another feature of the sales tax as well: the extensive record keeping that the state now required was often beyond their capacity. At that time, small retailers and grocers were only beginning to use monthly sales accounts and invoices. In 1934, for example, only 3 percent of all retailers making less than $5,000 a year employed a bookkeeper; 98 percent of all retailers making more than $100,000 did. Small retailers' accounting systems were "at best rudimentary," observed sales tax analyst Neil Jacoby, resulting in consistent underpayment of taxes and making it difficult to prove whether the error was intentional.[141]

Because of their size, their relatively depersonalized relationship with customers, and their superior record-keeping techniques, large retailers had an easier time paying the sales tax and so became more important than small stores to state fiscal health. State investigations bore out the fact that large firms were a more important source of tax revenue than were smaller ones. For instance, during an enforcement drive in the late 1930s, the state filed charges against nearly forty firms in a single day—none of which was part of a chain.[142] The average shortfall was less than $1,000.

The low shortfall suggests another way in which the sales tax reshaped the politics of retail. Large firms owed more tax, and so their success became more important to state government finances. More than 80 percent of the tax collected in 1937 came from only 14 percent of the retailers in Illinois, a fact that researchers ascribed to "the presence of mail order houses and many chains in this state."[143]

Over time, opposition to the sales tax increased. When the tax was renewed (and raised) in 1935, independent grocers, liberal commentators and groups representing unemployed workers voiced their opposition to this regressive tax. By the end of the decade, Republican candidates for the state legislature and governorship were seeking to capitalize on frustration with the tax by promising to reduce or eliminate it. Despite these outcries, the sales tax remained. Those antitax efforts that did continue seem to have been individual moments of resistance. For instance, efforts to sell "mille tokens" (fractional cents) to pay the tax failed. Customers, it seemed, would just as soon fight out that issue with individual retailers or accept being over- or undercharged a few cents rather than exchange real cash for a kind of parallel currency. The failure of the mille tokens speaks to the degree to which the tax had become an established fact of life by the late 1930s and early 1940s. Consumers tolerated the idea of the tax even as they did their best to negotiate the terms of collection, complaining of overcharges and the tax's regressive nature.[144] In a few years, the sales tax had become a central feature of state finance. In the midst of the Great Depression, when Americans perhaps had the least disposable income, consumer spending became tied in a structural way to state fiscal stability.

The implications of the state government's experience with relief policies and the sales tax were clear. The state needed to regulate people's shopping and purchasing, and it looked to stores to do that regulating. This meant, on the one hand, that stores worked as part of the state, in part by compelling behavior from consumers. But it also meant that Americans who organized at the point of consumption had more potential power, for good or for ill. They might demand changes and, as in the case of the relief system, bring about those changes via government action. Or sheer individual resistance might prevent the smooth functioning of tax collection efforts and subject stores to government censure. There was no quick resolution to the ongoing struggle between chains and independents, but it was increasingly clear that government policy and consumers' own political authority would matter to that competition. A full view of the state's interest in consumption in the 1930s must acknowledge not only policymakers' well-documented interest in furthering spending but also the less obvious and less explicit, but no less important, array of policies that came to center on stores and, by extension, on the question of authority in them.

The National Recovery Administration, the Hopes of Consumers and Retailers, and the Problem of Gender

Women were mostly absent, at least as a rhetorical category, from debates on the sales tax, relief, and even anti-chain legislation. Neither policymakers nor grocers regularly marshaled the rhetoric of housewives' frustrations or of women's communal responsibilities when making their arguments. There were exceptions. Occasionally political movements around these issues singled out women. For instance, in the spring of 1940, Richard Lyons, a candidate for the Republican nomination for governor, made the elimination of the sales tax a centerpiece of his campaign promises. Women mobilized by the Cook County Republican Central Committee distributed shopping bags printed with slogans decrying the sales tax and mounted anti–sales tax rallies on his behalf.[145] These efforts were sporadic, however, and stand in stark contrast to the prominence of women in actual stores and in the marketing of food.

There are many possible explanations for the absence of gender from these discussions. One reason was the recognition that, whatever the normative gender division of labor, men still sometimes shopped for households' food and, probably more importantly in the minds of politicians and grocers, made decisions about where food shopping occurred. Also, although the events discussed here occurred after women had won the right to vote, few political movements of the 1920s and 1930s confronted issues of gender or mentioned women's particular stake in their efforts.

These hypotheses, however, point to another reason for women's rhetorical absence—one that became increasingly relevant in subsequent years: a widespread ambivalence about women's influence over government and particular discomfort with the idea that people who performed unpaid reproductive labor should wield state-sanctioned authority over businesses and the economy as a result of that labor.[146]

The everyday acts of negotiating, haggling, and selling had never granted women, as a group, national or even regional political importance. The state's increased investment in consumption, however, made this possibility quite real.

THAT POSSIBILITY, AND THE CONCERNS that it occasioned, emerged in another contemporaneous consumption-related policy, this one at the federal level. The complicated history of the short-lived National Recovery Administration and the burgeoning consumer movement demonstrate how politicized consumption in the 1930s raised disturbing questions of women's political power. An overview of the NRA and a discussion of the issues that it raised for grocers and their customers serve as a fitting end point to a survey of the new, consumption-oriented, and still unsettled political economy. It made palpable the power of the federal government to affect the future of grocery stores, the futures of all businesses, and consumers' political influence.

Consumption mattered to the NRA first and foremost as a tool for recovery. During the depression, many legislators and policymakers argued for relief or work programs, not only to help the impoverished but also to boost spending and bring about recovery. Thus, the NRA was created at least in part to raise wages and, by extension, to increase consumer spending. Franklin Roosevelt himself explained, "The aim of this whole effort is to restore our rich domestic market by raising its vast consuming capacity."[147] Although neither Roosevelt nor most New Deal politicians ever accepted the Keynesian emphasis on deficit (countercyclical) spending, they did bring about a crucial change in thinking about federal economic policy: fostering purchasing power would now be as important as fostering production.

The NRA reflected both the new emphasis on consumption and the older policy goal of easing competition among large firms.[148] It was arguably the federal government's most ambitious regulatory plan. The industry codes that the NRA administered theoretically governed businesses and covered a broad range of operations. In the case of retail stores, that meant prices, the number of hours the store was open, the claims made in advertisements, and of course employee wages and hours. These codes were meant, ideally, to decrease destructive competition among firms—and, in particular, to keep wages high and to prevent firms from suicidally underbidding each other. The codes also reified the emerging consumer identity. Through the Consumer Advisory Board, which advised the NRA before an industry's code could be approved, and through participation in public hearings required for code approval, self-described representatives of consumers had the potential to wield power over businesses with the federal government's blessing—a new situation in the history of federal regulation.[149]

The enforcement mechanism for the NRA left the door open to the development of a more complicated consumer politics. The power of the NRA hinged on popular support expressed through people's everyday shopping. Although the program could not be legally enforced (the government could neither fine nor sue violators), the general public, and women in particular, were expected and encouraged to boycott firms that did not adhere to the codes and to shop instead in stores that displayed the blue eagle symbol of the NRA. The NRA's Women's Division was responsible for much of the effort to censure businesses

FIGURE 3.1.
The NRA's famous
"blue eagle," meant to
be displayed in stores
that adhered to the
retail code. (Courtesy
FDR Library)

that failed to observe NRA codes; indeed, its primary goal seems to have been to channel and shape women's shopping habits toward the ends desired by the government. It was this politically aware shopping that stood at the heart of the NRA's enforcement mechanism. Ultimately, all that the code authorities could do was withdraw a firm's right to display the blue eagle logo. But individual Americans, through their consumption patterns, could drive a firm out of business.[150]

Because of the NRA's wide-ranging nature, its indication of a dramatic change in federal policy (particularly a new openness to government-facilitated, industrywide cooperation and coordination), and the dire economic circumstances of many retailers when the plan was announced, many store proprietors attached enormous importance to the codes. In the words of one chain store analyst, the NRA represented "a new industrial revolution."[151]

Small, independent grocers had high hopes for the new program, particularly in the early days of the codes. In Chicago, independent grocers even housed an office of the local retail code authority in the headquarters of their citywide trade association.[152] They clearly looked to the codes' minimum prices and outlawing of below-cost selling as ways of reducing price competition.[153] Independents had to have a 6 percent markup over their wholesale price, while chains had to maintain an 8 percent markup. This provision, at least in theory, would handicap the chains and make it easier for independents to match their prices.[154]

Independents' hopes were based in part on other signs of support from policymakers. One Chicago NRA official expressed sympathy toward local, small independents, wondering how they ever did any business when they had to compete against large chains like the National Tea Company.[155] Franklin Roosevelt himself made concessions to independent grocers when he exempted stores in very small communities from the provisions of the code. And the Roosevelt administration also supported the independents' long struggles to outlaw "loss leaders"—goods sold below cost to attract customers into the store. Hugh Johnson, head of the NRA, explained the agency's censure of below-cost selling as a measure to protect small—and presumably independently operated—stores: "The little fellow cannot afford this. . . . In the last four years, 400,000 small retailers have been driven out of business and it is bitterly complained that this "loss leader" was partly to blame."[156]

Chain grocery firms, too, supported the NRA and indeed were among its earliest and most vocal proponents—chains, like independents, wanted to see their interests reflected in the Retail Food and Grocery Code.[157] In particular, executives of chain store firms hoped that the codes would restore prices and financial stability to the grocery trade, and they were willing to absorb increased wage costs to that end. Like many other grocers, these retailers also wanted a resolution to the depression. Their suspicions of New Deal politicians notwithstanding, chain grocers felt that the NRA represented their best hope for recovery. "While full cooperation with NRA may seem to endanger profits, *without* such cooperation there will be *no* profits to endanger," noted one trade journalist.[158]

But chains also hoped that their support for the codes would win them popular and political support. As anti-chain bills continued to come before state legislatures, executives hoped to offset any federal-level anti-chain activity by demonstrating their value to New Deal priorities. The trade press urged chains to raise wages even before the codes were officially in place and celebrated the fact that grocers were the first industry to have their temporary code approved.[159] Implicitly acknowledging the importance of winning public support, individual retailers not only publicized their support of the NRA but also cast their remodeling campaigns as efforts to create jobs.[160] Political support was as important as, and indeed would be key to, economic stability.

The hopes of the chain store firms proved more realistic than those of independents. Both in Chicago and nationally, chain grocery stores proved far more adept at observing the codes than did small independent stores. NRA officials often noted the marked difference between the behavior of chains and independents. The authors of one report for Region 6, which included Chicago, Detroit, and the upper Midwest, noted that compliance rose with the size of business. Firms with more than a hundred employees had, according to the report's authors, "excellent" compliance, while firms with fewer than ten employees had "very poor" compliance.[161] A report on the compliance levels of Chicago grocery stores noted that large chain stores were very supportive of the NRA and wanted to continue following the industry's code even after the act itself had been declared unconstitutional. The officials went on to report that chains had rarely ran afoul of the code; what violations occurred were usually the work of very small chains or of managers overstepping their bounds.[162] Centralized, concentrated authority, it seemed, was crucial to adherence to the codes.

The same analysts who praised the chain stores noted that the complaints their office did receive came from "small stores in poor Negro and Italian sections of the City [sic]" whose owners had overworked and underpaid their night watchmen.[163] The surviving records of the state NRA office back up this anecdote. Small stores do seem to have been particularly frequent violators of the code, and most of their violations centered on the requirements for minimum wages and maximum hours. Of the twenty-three grocery stores called to appear before the state NRA authority between January and May 1935, none were chain stores, and nearly all were cited for violations of wages and hours provisions.[164] That section of the code had been written by—and some said for—very large chains and was an especially difficult provision for the often marginally profitable sole proprietor to observe.[165]

One of these cases provides a window into the operations of very modestly scaled stores and their less-than-scientific management. In January 1934, George Ostrihon was employed at a grocery store owned by Henry Svihla in a working-class neighborhood on the city's southwest side. Ostrihon charged his employer with violating the wages and hours provisions of the Retail Food and Grocery Code. Investigators found that Svihla had paid his employee less than the code specified and had forced him to work more hours than were allowed. Despite these prima facie violations of the code, they also decided to close the case. Upon examination, it became clear that the grocer had provided Ostrihon with all of his meals, presumably out of the store's stock.[166] Other cases involved circumstances that were difficult to adjudicate—for example, proprietors who had only one official employee but who relied on the voluntary labor of family members. Small firms raised questions that NRA officials had difficulty answering.

Independents' violations of the NRA codes were mooted after the enabling law itself was declared unconstitutional. The U.S. Supreme Court's *Schechter* decision in May 1935 quickly brought about the end of the code authorities and of both chains' and independents' hopes for permanent solutions to the problem of price-based competition.[167]

The NRA was not mourned by many Americans. By the time it was abandoned, most observers thought of the NRA as an unsuccessful experiment in a planned economy. The codes had succeeded only in creating complicated new regulations, not in bringing about economic recovery. Firms blatantly had broken the NRA's regulations, and the shopping public had done little to censure them. The lack of sufficient public support for the NRA stemmed in part from the fact that the codes were designed to keep prices high at a time when poverty was endemic. Americans worried about how to pay their bills were unsympathetic toward a program designed to prop up retail prices. Even the *Chicago Defender*, an African American newspaper whose editors were erstwhile supporters of the Roosevelt administration, eventually agreed that the program made no sense: "We are unable either to understand or appreciate a national program which increases the cost of every necessity."[168]

Organized consumers also criticized the NRA. They argued that the codes' attempts to maintain prices in the face of consumer resistance was symptomatic of the fundamental problem—the lack of authority and outright disrespect with which the Consumer Advisory Board (CAB) had to contend. The CAB had no vote on the codes and was generally ignored at hearings and code authority meetings. Chronically underfunded, the CAB was unable to garner much public support or to achieve concrete results. Members of the board accused representatives of business and labor of blithely ignoring the very people who could ensure their codes' success. Critics charged that the federal government had left organized consumers without support, without funding, and without meaningful authority.[169]

The activism facilitated by the NRA, and particularly that by local consumers councils established under its aegis, remained even after the NRA lost momentum and disappeared.[170] Indeed, in much the same way that the Wagner Act encouraged workers to pursue long-standing efforts to unionize, the NRA had provided American consumers, and women in particular, with federal recognition and encouragement to organize in the face of daily frustrations in procuring goods for their households.

Many calls made in the name of consumers focused on the need for more information and education. This was the case with the best-known example of the new consumer movement—the work of Stuart Chase and Frederick Schlink.[171] The former accountant and the engineer galvanized public frustrations with their first book, *Your Money's Worth*, which cataloged the many ways in which consumers suffered because of businesses' waste, inefficiency, and willfully misleading marketing.[172] They charged that the bewildering array of sizes, qualities, and items coupled with alluring but inaccurate advertisements left would-be purchasers vulnerable to manipulation and unable to determine which goods best met their needs. The answer, they felt, was not direct political authority over stores, but better-educated consumers. Calling for clearer labeling and packaging, objective grading of goods, and impartial testing of advertiser claims, Chase, Schlink, and the editors of popular journals and newsletters argued that consumers' problems stemmed from their lack of knowledge about the products they bought.

The book and the two resulting organizations—Consumers' Research (CR) and Consumers Union (CU)—proved enormously popular. *Your Money's Worth* was a huge commercial success. Named a Book-of-the-Month Club selection, it sold more than a hundred thousand copies between 1927 and 1937.[173] It also prompted the publication of similar exposés.[174] These books and the work of CR and CU exploited consumers' suspicions of big business and of advertisers and expressed the latent frustrations of many American shoppers. Middle-class professionals proved especially dedicated to the cause of closer regulation of consumer goods. Teachers, engineers, and other professionals—of both sexes—were at the forefront of demands for consumer education, the testing and grading of consumer goods, and an end to misleading advertising.

This concern with consumer education, however, does not fully characterize the extent of women's activism around issues of consumption in the 1930s or its links to the state. Women continued to work toward federally supported authority that would enable them to address their concerns with retailers. One example of this activism is the letter that Alicia B. Gibson, of Chicago, wrote in 1936 to the Consumer's Project—one of the only remaining vestiges of consumer agencies organized under the NRA. She explained that her neighborhood Mother's Club wanted to change its name and become a "Consumer Club, as we will have a better chance to grow in membership." Could the government, she wondered, put her in touch with other like-minded organizations in the city and help them form such a club?[175] Others supported politicized consumption in more dramatic displays. In Detroit, for instance, more than seven thousand angry women confronted visiting politicians and demanded that President Roosevelt grant them an interview to discuss meat prices.[176] Clearly, the NRA had catalyzed something that the state could not fully contain. By 1939, the editors of *Business Week* expressed genuine surprise and concern at the new effectiveness of women politicized as consumers. "Until recent years," they noted somewhat wistfully, "the consumer movement was supposed to be nothing but a lot of ladies' bridge clubs meeting every Thursday and setting up committees between rubbers to heckle the local advertisers and merchants."[177]

Business Week's characterization of the consumer movement is telling. At the heart of retailers' fears was profound uncertainty about the role of women—still assumed to be families' primary purchasers. The new political importance of consumers led to uncomfortable questions about the future of retailing and about women's role in it. What would become of the new woman of the 1920s—modern, efficient, upwardly mobile—in the depression and social unrest of the 1930s? Would she accede to the new policies of stores and the state? Would the state recognize and institutionalize women's power as consumers? Would women shoppers resent chains' lack of community involvement and return en masse to more personalized and service-oriented independents? Did women want—did they deserve—political power now that consumption was at the center of crucial new economic policies? Would they organize and demand that grocers give them direct power over stores?

Examined as a whole, the years from 1928 to 1935 highlight the new severity of an old condition—grocers were dependent on vagaries of government policy. But the new activism of state and federal governments and the new demands by organized women for more equitable treatment as consumers marked the transformation of an old system of locally policed food shopping. Now state and federal authorities, as well as local ones, could be looked to for assistance with the everyday work of food shopping. The very gender relations that had suffused grocer-customer bargaining were now liable to state intervention—for instance, by the requirement that grocers adhere to food orders, collect food stamps, and pay the sales tax. Retailers confronted not only new laws but also the very real possibility that whole systems of distribution— from chain stores that incurred popular wrath to small independents that could not keep records—would lose their viability. The spaces of grocery stores expose the fundamental dependence of formal political economy on the unpredictable power relations of everyday life.

Moments of Rebellion

The Consumer Movement and Consumer
Cooperatives, 1930–1950

In the fall of 1944, a columnist writing in a cooperative newsletter described the attractions that consumer cooperatives held for women consumers:

> I think most women have moments of rebellion against household tameness when they'd like to go out and weld bombers or paint houses or manage stores or do *something* more spectacularly of service for (and with) their fellow human beings. . . . And, then along comes the co-operative movement with its message that a new world can be made by consumers. . . . It raises shopping into an adventure when you know that with your dollars you can buy either monopoly or democratic business. Your dollars can buy you not only government graded canned goods for your family but also a stake in the economic system.[1]

This column suggests several things about the nature of food retailing in the 1930s and 1940s. The first and foremost is that organized resistance both to new mass retailing and to older, conventional marketing and distribution was on the rise. The newsletter and the cooperative store and society whose membership supported it were part of a broader network of liberal (though not necessarily leftist) Chicagoans who voiced their frustrations via groups primarily organized around consumption. The problem was not only poor treatment in individual instances, but an entire marketing and selling system devoted to fleecing and misleading shoppers.

Moreover, as this anecdote makes clear, it was women (in this case, middle-class women) whose dissatisfaction and labor lay at the center of this critique. The very people considered central to the emergence of chain stores and to the preservation of local grocery stores—and the very people central to discourses of housewifery and separate spheres—were now threatening both systems.[2] This was not a problem that could be easily fixed.

This chapter explores Americans', and especially Chicagoans', participation in consumer protests in the 1930s and early 1940s, the surge in consumer co-operatives, and the place of gender and of women in these movements. A close look at the growth of cooperatives suggests the unsettled nature of distribution, consumer protest, and gender relations in the 1930s.

Previous chapters have detailed how changes in business and government practices challenged the usual ways of buying and selling food. This chapter explores another source of change: widespread resistance from consumers. The consumer cooperatives detailed here were worrisome to other retailers not so much for the sales that they took away, but for what the (remarkable) growth rate of their sales and their stores, and the interest of New Dealers in them, suggested: that consumers—mostly, but not entirely, middle-class—would not be satisfied by anything less than democratization of distribution and direct control over the stores in which they shopped.

The Long History of Consumer Protests

Consumer protests have recently received important attention from scholars. Most studies have tended to focus on the national level and to evaluate the protests in terms of their impact on federal policy. This national context highlights the shortcomings of these groups and the limited, often temporary, nature of their successes.[3] Consumer protests, however, are especially meaningful when viewed in their local context and through a feminist lens. Studying such protests in Chicago illuminates the ways in which consumer politics spread through networks of activists, energizing new political actors and forging connections among old ones along the way. In the organizations activists created, the alliances they built, the large populations they mobilized, and the local institutions they targeted and changed, the movement's significance becomes clearer.

Positioning gender as a factor in the fortunes of these movements also recasts their histories and suggests that a certain ambivalence toward women's authority was inherent in the emerging politics of consumption. In these groups, women's labor was central, but the politics of gender were obscured. This ambivalence, therefore, offers one reason for the limited success (and agendas) of consumer groups.

Americans had lodged protests at the point of consumption long before the 1930s consumer movement emerged as such. Women were often, though not always, at the forefront of this very localized and often unorganized consumer activism. Historians have documented the importance of women in food riots in both the United States and Europe throughout the eighteenth, nineteenth, and early twentieth centuries.[4] Indeed, American women's responsibility for household shopping made them especially important players in collective protests waged at the point of consumption. In the Progressive Era, the National Consumers' League (NCL) took advantage of middle-class women's willingness to shop with politics in mind. NCL activists mobilized support for better working conditions by reaching out to the middle-class women who bought the products of working-class women's labor. NCL leaders composed a white list of manufacturers and stores that the leaders felt treated women workers with respect and dignity and that limited the use of child labor. NCL members were asked to spend as much as they could with these labor-friendly businesses. The NCL's grassroots campaigns were remarkably successful, earning the group national recognition and a decades-long influence over labor reform. The group's success also testifies to women's willingness to use their consumption for political ends and illuminates the power that they could wield when they did so.[5]

World War I spurred new activism by women at the point of consumption. Americans' responses to high prices and shortages were less violent than those of Europeans, but female-led protests, riots, and organized resistance to high prices forced investigations by the federal government and sparked organized protests in cities across the country.[6] Unions urged their members and their members' families to patronize union-owned or at least labor-friendly establishments. A more radical precursor to the "union label" campaigns later in the century, these efforts centered on creating a kind of parallel economy in which workers' wages ultimately benefited the labor movement.[7] This interest in directing consumption reshaped organized labor's methods in the early 1920s, forcing unions to reach out to the wives and mothers of their male members and to give women new authority over union tactics.

Organized Grassroots Activism in Chicago

Protest at the point of, and around the issues of, distribution became much more prevalent in the 1930s as a range of voices competed to speak for "the consumer." Some of these were long-standing groups—often women's organizations—like the General Federation of Women's Clubs and the American Association of University Women. Others were new, self-identified consumer groups that included men as well as women—like Consumers Union. Labor unions, African American organizations, and even the Communist Party expressed concern for the plight of "the consumer" and argued that new activism was needed to offset the economic influence of business. Connecting these disparate groups were shared concerns with misleading packaging, with fraudulent claims by processors, retailers, and marketers, and with the general difficulty of intelligently choosing among the bewildering array of items that crowded retailers' shelves.

"Consumer politics," however, was not confined to issues of distribution. Interest in the consumer was also grounded in new activism by Americans in spaces of consumption as well as around consumer goods themselves. Lizabeth Cohen has referred to this activism as a discourse of the "citizen-consumer"—the notion that citizens ought to use their shopping to assert political claims. This turn of phrase aptly characterizes the uses that Americans made of consumption for causes as varied as supporting American businesses (Hearst's "Buy American" campaigns), avoiding chains (small business owners' "Shop at Home" efforts), and boycotting German-made products (in the early 1930s after Hitler's rise to power).[8] Over the course of the 1930s and 1940s, wherever one stood on the political spectrum, consumer protests and boycotts seemed like useful tools for furthering one's aims.

Like the anti-chain activism and relief protests of the same time period, few of these efforts focused on women in particular—though women were, of course, the implied audience. In limited ways, some self-proclaimed consumer groups of the 1930s, like Consumers' Research and Consumers Union, did try to tap into women's frustrations and to acknowledge their importance as consumers. Consumers' Research, for instance, ran exposés of *Good Housekeeping* magazine's Good Housekeeping Institute and its Good Housekeeping Seal of Approval in efforts to appeal to women who had relied on the institute's ratings of household products. Consumers Union, for its part, employed a female home economist to speak exclusively to women's groups.[9]

More often, however, both critics and leaders of the consumer movement denigrated women's activism as consumers. Popular journalists poked fun at politicians who were intimidated by "housewives."[10] Even people and institutions avowedly supportive of female activists' goals proved unable and unwilling to take seriously their desires to make their shopping a basis for political action and authority. The Communist Party (CP), for instance, provided only tentative support to members' efforts to organize women around the issues of high food prices and high rents. The party pulled its funding for "housewives' councils" in 1937.[11] Similarly, Consumers' Research systematically distanced women from discussions of power. The group's publications used female pronouns and addressed women only when they were relaying cautionary tales of consumers' naïveté.[12] Hazel Kyrk, a leading home economist and an early proponent of consumers' political rights, recognized women's importance to retail purchasing but addressed neither gender nor women when she called on consumers to become politically active.[13] There was, notes historian Annelise Orleck, a "strong visceral resistance to the idea that housewives could assert political leadership."[14]

And yet, women's energies catalyzed much activism around issues of consumption. A prime example is the spectacular (in its use of elaborate public expressions of support) boycott of Japanese silk. Japan's 1931 invasion of Manchuria led China and Chinese emigrants to organize an international boycott of Japanese-made goods. In the United States, the boycott was endorsed by virtually all liberal media and became a kind of *cause célèbre*. The progressive journal the *Nation* and such Hollywood legends as Anna May Wong and Frances Farmer promoted the boycott. One of the most dramatic and popular acts of protest was a refusal to wear silk stockings. At anti-Japan rallies, women of all nationalities vowed to give up their silk garments. In especially risqué moments, they even stripped off their stockings and threw them into bonfires.[15]

Chicagoans were part of the expanding consumer protests in the 1930s. In the city, as elsewhere, issues of distribution were often part of broader agendas for economic change and social justice and hence figured into a panoply of local social movements.

Complaints over unfair treatment by stores, for example, resonated particularly in African American communities. "Double duty dollars"—spending that procured needed goods and also went to black-owned businesses—had long been a theme of sermons, editorials, and daily conversation.[16] This movement reached a kind of fever pitch in the 1930s when street preachers, churches, and numerous local newspapers organized "Don't Buy Where You Can't Work" campaigns. As in other consumer boycotts, women assumed particular importance, providing both organizational and financial support.[17] Chicago was the site of some of the most effective of these campaigns.[18] As the *Chicago Defender* eloquently put it, both large national chains, like Woolworth's, and smaller locally owned stores "began to hire from the ranks of those that supported them."[19]

The frustrations of African Americans were not only about who worked where, however. The same *Chicago Defender* article that recounted the "Don't Buy Where You Can't Work" campaign claimed that retailers resisted employing blacks not only out of racism but also because black employees would reveal to black shoppers the many ways in which they were being cheated. Scales that had weights hidden underneath so that customers were charged for more than they actually purchased, grocers who substituted old chickens for fresh ones, and tricky math that resulted in customers' paying more for the sales tax than they should have—all these practices were decried in the *Defender*'s pages.[20] The editors articulated an analysis in which the personal indignities of shopping motivated organized efforts for economic justice. As Devarian Baldwin has shown for other arenas of mass culture, food shopping was a basis for broad-minded collective action even as it was also a stark reminder of African Americans' inequality.[21]

Local African American women's groups eagerly took up the cause of fair treatment and supported the effort to secure jobs.[22] The Illinois Housewives Association, for instance, expanded its agenda from housekeeping advice to politically minded investigations of stores that treated customers unfairly, that offered shoddy goods, or that engaged in misleading advertising.[23] Their efforts resulted in a wave of municipal prosecutions of South Side merchants who cheated their customers. Such efforts also made it clear that individual indignities related to shopping could be countered via organized effort. One letter to the *Chicago Defender* credited the group with "making it possible for women to know what they should rightly expect by way of fair treatment, and how to go about demanding that fair treatment."[24]

By the 1930s, the city's whites were also embracing the potential of organized activism to better working conditions in stores and to increase the availability of goods that workers could purchase. For instance, a meat boycott in the summer of 1935 in Detroit brought out loud and raucous neighborhood pickets. Packers referred to it as "the most powerful consumers' boycott in the history of the packing industry" and credited it with a plunge in wholesale meat prices. When protesters from Detroit traveled to Chicago to confront the packers, they shared their know-how and analyses with eager audiences. Perhaps because the city was at the heart of meat processing, Chicagoans' enthusiasm for activism around meat prices was a particular "new worry for the [meatpacking] trade."[25]

The meatpackers were right to worry; the organization that spread the boycott—the United Conference against the High Cost of Living (UCHCL)—coordinated an array of effective strategies to bring down meat prices. These ranged from pickets and petitions to public confrontations with stockyard officials and even to setting wholesalers' hoarded meat on fire. The organization also joined in a delegation with other angry "housewives" and forced Secretary of Agriculture Henry Wallace to meet with them. This meeting, covered by a number of bemused journalists, highlighted some of the contradictions inherent in New Deal policy. The meeting ended when Wallace hastily excused himself rather than answer a direct question about why meat was being held back from the market.[26]

Whereas previous protests against meat prices had been local and event-specific, this boycott was national, and offered systemic critiques. It proved to be the beginning rather than the end of a wave of consumer protest. The United Conference against the High Cost of Living established chapters across the Midwest and in working-class neighborhoods and cities on the East Coast. Over the next few years, it established an identity as a "militant consumers' organization" articulating a broad analysis of the issues and claiming economics and politics as the rightful concern of working-class housewives and their supporters.[27] In Chicago, the group took on everything from meat prices to milk availability, the need for affordable natural gas, and public transportation. When prices began to rise again in the late 1930s and 1940s, members of the Chicago chapter joined delegates from other organizations in protesting to government officials, resurrecting a strategy that had worked well in the past.[28]

These issues were grounded in an overt class- and gender-consciousness. A flyer distributed in wake of the local gas utility's request for higher rates explained, "If we, the consumers, should allow the gas rate increases to go into effect, while living costs are skyrocketing, this will be an added burden on the average wage earning family and small business man."[29] Openly acknowledging the influence of both organized labor *and* women's domesticity, the president of the Chicago chapters, a self-described "carpenter's wife," explained to a congressional committee that the labor movement had been her model for the group: "It dawned on me," she said, "my husband being a union man, why couldn't we housewives have an organization similar, a homemaker's union?"[30] For this woman, as for others, 1930s consumer activism drew on class and gender analyses.

Such analyses also informed some new and creative consumer organizations among the middle class. The League of Women Shoppers (LWS), for example, shared with "innumerable women's organizations" an interest in issues of distribution but distinguished itself through concern for "the conditions under which goods were produced." The president of the Chicago chapter, Jessie Lloyd O'Connor, described the organization's members as being of the "comfortable class," and the group found itself repeating programs at later times "for the convenience of professional women."[31] Members used their class identities and spending power as leverage in their efforts to secure better working conditions for store employees and to force employers to accept workers' unions.

Over time, they also turned their attention to issues of inequitable pricing and misleading packaging and marketing. Urged to "use [their] buying power for justice," members employed an array of tactics to turn their active consumption into a basis for consumer activism. For instance, Chicago members were offered calling cards to be left with grocers who did not carry union-made products.[32] Another common protest strategy was the "mink coat brigade." Members wore their most stylish fur coats and capes while picketing high-end department stores to demand changes in the retailers' labor policies.[33] So influential were these shoppers that when one member asked the high-end department store Marshall Field and Company to refrain from advertising in Hearst-owned newspapers, the company's head of advertising called her to discuss the matter.[34] As Field's labor woes dragged on, women were also invited to attend mediation sessions between workers and management.[35] While the Chicago chapter never seems to have been especially large (attendance at meetings was generally twenty-five to thirty women), their class status gave them particular visibility and efficacy.

It did not, however, afford them political protection. The LWS, like many other consumer groups, was regularly accused of being, in the delicate phrasing of one officer, "inimical to the best interest of the government."[36] In plainer language, members of the league, like supporters of the UCHCL and other organizations, were often accused of being communist fronts.[37]

But there is no evidence that the LWS, or any other mainstream consumer organization, was being directed from abroad or that its leaders were party members. The records of FBI investigations as well as those kept by the groups themselves point to a different source of inspiration: the cross-pollination that occurred so often in the late 1930s among moderate, liberal, and radical women activists.[38] The groups outlined here worked with each other and in networks of progressive (though not necessarily leftist) organizations, all interested in the possibilities of organized consumption. For instance, the LWS held joint meetings with the UCHCL, as well as the YWCA and various labor unions.[39] Local LWS officer Jessie Lloyd O'Connor lived and worked at Hull House. Another Hull House associate, Alice Belester, led the local chapter of the UCHCL.[40] The UCHCL had chapters all over the country and was a member of the Consumers National Federation, a nationwide association that organized federal lobbying by the many recently formed consumer groups.[41] These activists knew

FIGURE 4.1.
*This card was
distributed to members
of the League of Women
Shoppers for use
during the 1942 holiday
season. (Sophia Smith
Collection, Smith
College Archives,
League of Women
Shoppers Records,
artist unknown)*

each other, worked together, and operated locally powerful networks that made consumption both a site for and a catalyst to political action.

By the 1930s, consumer activism was spreading, as exemplified by the growth of the UCHCL. The UCHCL was an organization of organizations—that is, it coordinated the efforts of the many groups that found themselves with interests in issues of price, fairness, dishonesty, and in gaining more authority and control over distribution. In Chicago, this included "churches, fraternal, trade-union, civic and women's clubs" as well as the UCHCL's own network of neighborhood clubs.[42] Thus, although powered by women's labor, the group included mixed-sex and predominantly male organizations as well.

Activism around consumer issues could serve as a basis for interracial coalition-building among Chicagoans. For instance, issues discussed at a city-wide meeting of local chapters of the UCHCL in the summer of 1935 included "allegations . . . that foods of inferior grade were sold on the [increasingly African American] South Side at higher prices and that the three per cent sales tax actually amounts to seven and eight per cent in most cases."[43] Similarly, a 1940 meeting of the UCHCL featured a speaker from the Northern District Colored

Women's Federation on "consumer problems of the negro housewife" and a representative from the Illinois Housewives' Association invited to discuss the group's successful confrontations of "chiseling grocers."[44] In one particularly dramatic incident, the UCHCL refused to leave its downtown offices when the landlord tried to evict the group for having hired a "negro" clerk. In an effort closely watched by African American groups, the organization won its court case against the landlord, keeping both its offices and its identity as a group that, in the words of the *Chicago Defender*, made "no distinction as to race in its organizational set-up."[45]

An antiprofiteering conference that was held during the first days of World War II encapsulates the depth and breadth of consumption-related activism. By late 1939, when the conference was held, concern with issues of distribution stood at the center of the New Deal coalition that brought together white workers, African Americans, and progressive-minded members of the white middle class. Even the site of the conference, Hull House (a well-known center for social reform and social activism on the West Side of Chicago), suggested the ways in which consumer activism had become a part of mainstream liberalism by this point. The 352 attendees began proceedings by singing "The Star-Spangled Banner," then launched into far-reaching discussions of such matters as the gas company's efforts to raise rates, campaigns to repeal the sales tax, and the benefits of a subscription to *Consumer Reports*, the newsletter of Consumers Union. Speakers at the conference included representatives from the Packinghouse Workers' Organizing Committee, six unemployed groups, sixteen "nationality groups," a farm group, unions and auxiliaries, a businessman's organization, several civic and fraternal organizations, and local Parent-Teacher Associations. Organizers estimated that these groups represented a total membership of more than a hundred thousand.[46]

Chicagoans who used the language of consumerism to claim economic and political rights brought with them widely varying histories, class positions, and, often, long-term goals. Nonetheless, by the late 1930s, they had come to appreciate and sometimes to articulate similar calls for lower prices, for more equitable treatment from retailers, and for trustworthy advertisements. These seemingly disparate groups—middle-class and working-class, white and African American, women's and mixed-sex—embraced the possibilities of harnessing consumption to bring about broader social change. Members of all these groups appear to have been eager to access commercial goods and services, but they also used their consumption as a platform from which to seek both local and systemic changes in the emerging network of distribution. As one 1938 flyer optimistically claimed, "the consumer" was now "the ultimate master of the business world."[47]

Consumer Cooperatives: A Case Study of the New Consumers' Movement

Virtually every participant in Chicago's burgeoning consumer movement shared an interest in consumer cooperatives. For instance, a "cooperative consumers' group" meeting held in Chicago on October 19, 1938, was organized by LWS, the UCHCL, and a local chapter of Consumers Union. Earlier that month, another LWS meeting had been held in the YWCA offices and also had featured a speaker on cooperatives.[48] The *Chicago Defender*, perhaps the most important African American newspaper in the country, frequently published articles encouraging its readers to consider cooperation. Even Baptist Sunday school and youth groups devoted part of their 1936 annual convention to a panel on consumer cooperatives.[49]

Consumer cooperatives were a relatively old retail format with roots in working-class Britain. They were particularly strong in Scandinavia, and immigrants from this region often operated such stores in areas of Danish, Finnish, Norwegian, and Swedish settlement in the upper Midwest.[50] Until the 1920s, however, most Americans encountered cooperatives only in the form of worker-owned factories or farmer-owned granaries and market exchanges, not as consumer organizations.

Popular interest in labor-friendly or worker-owned consumer cooperatives boomed in the late 1910s and early 1920s, reflecting both rising prices and new strategies adopted by unions. Although historians have devoted only limited attention to this wave of activism, these co-ops were fleeting but important presences in many communities. In the mining towns of central and southern Illinois, in the industrial districts of Seattle, and in working-class neighborhoods of Chicago, activists and entrepreneurs established ambitious cooperative ventures.[51] Few succeeded, and most fell victim to poor management, limited capital, or, as in Chicago, outright fraud.[52]

Nonetheless, in the 1930s, co-ops again came to occupy a central place in the hopes of frustrated American consumers. These new co-ops shared two important qualities with their 1920s-era predecessors: a reliance on women shoppers and a promise of more authority for their members. They differed from the earlier models in several important ways, however. They were less likely to target working-class neighborhoods or to consist of foreign-born members; indeed, some of the largest new societies were formed by native-born middle-class Americans. These stores were also more democratic in their organization and operation than the early societies had been. Finally, unlike many older consumer cooperative societies, the consumer co-ops of the 1930s sought to advance the goals of the organized consumer movement.

The dramatic growth in the numbers, sizes, and sales of consumer co-ops in the 1930s and 1940s is startling. Some 45 percent of the co-ops operating in 1936 had been formed since the stock market crash of 1929.[53] This growth, a veteran analyst concluded, indicated a new seriousness of purpose among cooperators and a new viability for cooperative stores.[54] Expansion continued through 1937 and, with the exception of a slight pause during the 1937–38 recession, remained strong through the mid-1940s. By 1944, more than 1.5 million people nationwide belonged to "retail distributive consumer cooperatives," generally grocery stores and petroleum distribution centers. Although it was a small portion of the American population, that number represented an increase of more than 800 percent from 1929. Stores and buying clubs reported that membership increased 28.8 percent in 1941, 30.8 percent in 1942, and 25.6 percent in 1943.[55] Just as important, cooperatives had improved their long-term viability by developing an intricate network of regional and national wholesalers, many of which ordered from a cooperatively controlled manufacturer, National Cooperatives, Inc.[56] Consumer cooperatives proved their popularity and their willingness to act in concert to create a new, more democratic version of mass retailing.

Cooperatives often allied themselves with consumer groups and were often dedicated proponents of the same goals articulated by more moderate groups like Consumers Union. The Cooperative League of the USA (CLUSA), for instance, was one of the first organizations to call for a federal-level department of the consumer.[57] Chains and smaller independents tried to portray themselves as friends of consumers, but cooperatives could back up their claims by pointing to the frequent testing of products by individual societies and their suppliers, to the grading scale used on all goods produced under the "Co-op" label, and to the display of government grades on canned goods two years before chain store firms had adopted them.[58]

As the organized consumer movement won new governmental support, so too did co-ops. Franklin Roosevelt, for example, exempted co-ops from certain provisions of the industry codes produced under the National Recovery Administration. Moreover, Roosevelt acknowledged the antipathy with which other retailers greeted cooperatives when he issued an executive order prohibiting any local code authority from outlawing consumer cooperatives.[59]

The most dramatic sign of Roosevelt's interest in co-ops—and the most worrisome for co-ops' opponents—was his Commission for the Study of European Cooperatives. This move was particularly threatening because cooperatives had a long history in Europe and were a significant presence in distribution there.[60] Both proponents and critics of co-ops took note of the president's openness.

Roosevelt announced that he was forming the commission in June 1936. By July, the commission had begun touring European cooperatives, and its movements were the topic of newspaper stories and public debate all over the country.[61] Almost immediately, retailers and wholesalers spoke out against the inquiry. The editor of *Chain Store Age* called co-ops "un-American," while J. Frank Grimes, president of the Independent Grocers Alliance (a very large purchasing association of independent grocers), accused cooperatives of destroying "individual initiative" and of being a greater threat to independent retailers than chain stores.[62] The Chicago Retail Grocers' and Butchers' Association urged its fifteen hundred members to speak out against the study, warning them that otherwise, "they will find their businesses destroyed by competitors financed with tax dollars which the merchants themselves contribute."[63] In the face of such outspoken criticism, and no doubt influenced by the upcoming 1936 election, Roosevelt backed off from his earlier enthusiasm. He reminded Americans that the commission had traveled to Europe to study co-ops, not to import them. Roosevelt in the end showed little public interest in the report, releasing it only after much prodding from commission members.[64]

Roosevelt's ambivalence was not, however, indicative of the mood of other New Dealers: some cabinet members proved to be even stronger supporters than Roosevelt had been. Secretary of Agriculture Wallace, long a promoter of farmers' producer co-ops, declared cooperatives to be democracy's sole hope. "If democracy is to be saved from Communist or Fascist dictatorship," he warned, "free competition must be abandoned in this country in favor of cooperatives of consumers, of producers, and ultimately of industries."[65] Rexford Tugwell's Resettlement Administration provided the most tangible and dramatic show of federal support for co-ops. Tugwell invited the Council for Cooperative Development, an advisory and educational group, to organize consumer cooperatives in government-built "Greenbelt cities." These stores proved profitable almost immediately. Within a few years of its creation, the grocery in Greenbelt, Maryland, was doing a healthy volume of $2,800 a week, and the trade publication *Business Week* was worriedly analyzing its prospects. "The present population includes 200 persons with some college education and apparently is much more interested in consumer problems than birth

FIGURE 4.2. *One mark of the widespread visibility of consumer cooperatives in the early 1940s: Vice President Henry Wallace visits the Ida B. Wells Consumers' Co-operative in Chicago. (Cover,* Consumers' Cooperation, *October 1943)*

control," the magazine explained, noting that more than half of the nearly 950 children were below school age.[66] The problem, the authors implied, was multiplying.

Cooperatives in Chicago: The Popularity of Politicized Consumption

In Chicago, support for consumer cooperatives proceeded slowly at first. By 1930, several labor organizations and farmers' associations had joined with the regional co-op association to gauge the amount of interest Chicagoans had in consumer cooperatives.[67] In 1933, a cooperative library was formed in the city.[68] Such measures were, however, tentative.

The situation had changed remarkably by the middle of the decade. In April 1934, the Central States Cooperative League (CSCL)—a midwestern association of consumer cooperatives—held its annual meeting in Chicago. Attendance set records as Chicagoans curious about the possibilities of cooperatives flocked to the meeting. Interest in cooperation had grown to such an extent that CSCL organizers approved plans for a local-level co-op association, the Chicago Cooperative Council. More tellingly, they announced they would move the regional organization's headquarters from Bloomington, Illinois, the center of the state's cooperative movement in the 1920s, to newly energized Chicago.[69] In 1936, a regional wholesaler specializing in midwestern urban co-ops, Cooperative Wholesale, opened in Chicago.[70] In 1937, the Department of Labor noted that cooperatives in the city were emerging so quickly that it was difficult to paint a complete picture of the movement.[71] While co-ops in the city were still small in terms of absolute numbers, they were growing at a tremendous rate—the number of societies had increased by 61 percent in 1936 alone, and sales had risen 36 percent from 1935 in spite of the relatively stagnant economy.[72] Nearly four thousand Chicagoans belonged to thirty-five local co-ops as of December 31, 1936.[73] In 1937, the national cooperative wholesaler, copying the move made earlier by the CSCL, relocated its headquarters from Indianapolis to Chicago, and the powerful national co-op association, the Cooperative League of the United States of America, followed it to the city in 1939.[74] In 1943, CLUSA's journal noted that Chicago had "been rightly termed 'The National Cooperative Center.'"[75]

Co-ops in Chicago continued to grow through the 1940s, as stores regularly expanded, remodeled, and added new product lines and services. This growth occurred across the city, as cooperatives attracted white and black Chicagoans alike. The Ida B. Wells Consumers' Co-operative, an African American–operated cooperative based in a housing project, moved into new quarters in June 1943 and outgrew them within six months. The Hyde Park Cooperative Society, located in the upper-middle-class white community surrounding the University of Chicago, opened a four-thousand-square-foot supermarket in 1943 (complete with bakery, meat, and produce sections) in a storefront abandoned by A&P.[76] In that same period, seven new buying clubs (groups that ordered food collectively while gathering funds to open a store) began operations.[77] In August 1945, Chicago Consumers' Cooperative, Inc. (CCC), announced plans to open a chain of ten cooperative grocery stores in the city.[78] The first store in the CCC chain opened the next year, claiming 350 members before its first day of operations. In April 1947, secure in its new home, Hyde Park Co-op celebrated record sales of $250,000 in a six-month period. It still did not have the highest sales figure among Chicago co-ops, however. That spot went to the Altgeld Gardens Consumers' Cooperative, a thriving African American co-op that had just opened its own three-thousand-square-foot store, including a cafeteria.[79]

These societies shared some basic organizational features. The key feature of most consumer cooperatives in Chicago and elsewhere in the 1930s and 1940s was a set of operating guidelines called the Rochdale principles. The principles themselves were quite old, having been established by a group of unemployed British weavers in 1844. Rochdale co-ops were premised on the idea that consumers were the true owners of stores and that they were entitled to a portion of the stores' profits. But unlike the more conventional, top-down structures followed by other kinds of cooperatives and by most privately owned stores, the Rochdale principles stood out for their emphasis on democratic management. Individual members received only one vote, regardless of the number of shares they bought. Thus, increased investment brought increased returns, but it did not bring increased influence. Moreover, membership was open; anyone could purchase shares and become a full member. Most important, Rochdale cooperatives strove for active consumer ownership. Consumer members were responsible for setting and implementing store policy and for financing store growth.[80]

In practice, this meant that boards of directors and member-run committees operated most cooperatives. Typically, directors and officeholders were elected; committee members might be elected or recruited, depending on the number of people who wanted to serve. These active members could determine everything from what stores sold to how to recruit new members and what stand to take on such controversial issues of the day as racial integration. Large and successful co-ops often hired a manager to run their stores on a daily basis, but small cooperative societies depended on volunteer labor of members and on advice from members of older co-ops.

Co-ops experienced the usual problems of volunteer-run organizations. The people who used the co-op did not always become members; members were not always active; and even active members often participated in rival organizations (for example, by shopping at competing stores).[81] Nonetheless, the democratic, committee-run structure of cooperatives created new spaces in which shoppers fought for more and better service in stores and linked their demands to agendas for social change. In consumer cooperatives, more than in other small retailers in the city, shoppers asserted authority over the stores in which they shopped.

Cooperators' desire for direct authority was evident in the ways in which cooperatives radicalized the rhetoric of consumer protest and of mass retailing. Cooperators and cooperatives did not want mere promises that businesses would grade and label their goods; the women and men who sustained co-ops wanted to control the grading and labeling themselves. The Hyde Park Cooperative Society was known throughout the city for its "testing parties," when members would gather in each others' homes and check the quality, size, and value of any number of items.[82] So important were grading and labeling that some cooperators wrote these requirements into their corporate charters. Founding members of the Ida B. Wells Consumers' Co-operative listed as one of their purposes "the performance of services of various kinds for the members in the most economical way, including research into quality, quantity, packing, and labeling of goods of superior quality at lower prices."[83] New cooperatives even pressured the wholesalers from which they bought to stock more graded goods and to perform more tests.[84] Nor did coops want to wield control only at the point of consumption. At their most ambitious, cooperative organizations worked to secure what they termed "a cooperative economy," in which production, processing, distribution, and selling of goods were controlled by consumer-run entities. In 1934, CLUSA adopted a telling new principle: "continuous expansion." This addition to the classic Rochdale principles was meant to express the belief that even already successful co-ops ought to work to create a cooperative economy by expanding into new lines of business (by adding fresh meats, for instance) or new stages in production (for example, by supporting cooperative wholesalers).[85]

In the heady days of the 1930s and 1940s, it seemed entirely possible that consumer co-ops and their members might gain control over wholesalers, manufacturers, and even their own sources of capital, finally realizing significant economies of scale and becoming serious competitors as mass retailers. By the mid-1930s, Chicago-area co-ops could buy from wholesalers and factories that were run for cooperatives and that graded their merchandise according to the specifications that were so important to co-op members.[86] These wholesalers and manufacturers adhered to cooperative principles and promised that ultimate control rested with consumers themselves.[87] Throughout the 1930s and 1940s, more and more Chicago-area stores became Rochdale cooperatives, joining CSCL and CLUSA and supporting citywide co-op events.[88] Slowly but surely, co-ops began to gain access to the same sorts of distribution networks that buoyed independent and chain store firms.

Cooperatives as Mass Retailers

The business press—magazines like *Business Week*, *Chain Store Age*, and *Printers' Ink*—closely tracked the speed with which consumer cooperatives were taking on the trappings of conventional firms. Centralized distribution, sophisticated marketing, and even collective lobbying of the federal government in the late 1930s and 1940s—all these activities suggested that consumer cooperatives might well become a permanent part of the retailing landscape.[89]

"Consumer cooperation is here to stay," wrote one dejected critic in 1944. "Its continued growth despite formidable opposition has been steady, and in recent years spectacular."[90]

It was the very similarities of consumer cooperatives to other businesses that most alarmed private mass retailers. Over the course of the 1930s and 1940s, consumer cooperatives continued to expand in Chicago and elsewhere. In doing so, they used many of the same strategies that mass retailers were pursuing. Even the most conservative chain store firms tried to win over shoppers with promises of quality, to sell in large quantities, and to control their own sources of supply. Although cooperatives challenged the legitimacy of private retailers, they did not challenge the *idea* of mass retailing itself.

A 1938 *Business Week* article put the concerns of mass retailers succinctly. The author anxiously informed his audience that CLUSA was overseeing the "adoption of practical business and management methods and the throwing overboard of a lot of the idealistic stuff."[91]

Businesses' concern about the future of these upstart stores only intensified when co-ops won crucial legal rights in the early 1940s.[92] In 1940, CLUSA secured a long-sought general incorporation act for consumer cooperatives from the federal government. The law allowed consumer co-ops to incorporate in the District of Columbia regardless of where they were physically located, and it defined their controversial patronage refunds (the proportion of purchases returned to members) as "savings" not taxable as business profits.[93] A group of lumber, petroleum, and food trade associations organized as the National Tax Equality Association (NTEA) to attack the tax-exempt status of patronage refunds. Despite its fiery rhetoric (members argued that consumer co-ops threatened "the entire free-enterprise system"), the NTEA lost its case in U.S. Tax Court in 1944.[94]

That same year, co-ops won another important battle against CBS and NBC, which had refused to air a promotional special on cooperatives. After a nationwide letter-writing campaign and threats of a congressional inquiry, the networks agreed to broadcast the program and to allow co-ops to purchase air time to discuss the principles and potential of consumers' cooperation.[95] Consumer cooperatives seemed to have overcome resistance and to have secured a place among other types of retailers.

Creating a Cooperative World

Even as cooperatives grew, they continued to reflect both their members' desire for better goods and their hopes for other, broader changes. Co-ops operated on the premise that members wanted to make a better world, one with greater racial tolerance, greater equality, and greater economic justice. At their best, one proud cooperator noted, members were able to "[carry] on the duties of a society as well as those of a store."[96] In these ways, cooperatives fostered the most socially progressive impulses of the consumer movement as well the most dramatic possibilities for an economic alternative to conventional mass retailing.

One example of this blending of goals was cooperatives' emphasis on social activities that would build ties among members and inculcate egalitarian values. Folk dances, a popular feature of many co-ops, established a level playing field where people of different backgrounds might mix.[97] Other activities encouraged members to reach out to the communities in which they lived. In the fall of 1944, for example, the fledgling ABC Co-op was trying to gain a following in the neighborhood surrounding Hull House on Chicago's working-class Near West Side. One of its first activities was to begin distributing a newsletter, described as a "village newspaper" featuring "news of real groups and families and reports [of] the comings and goings of visitors . . . births and deaths and so on."[98] The Morgan Park Co-op, in an interracial, middle-class community on Chicago's Far South Side, boasted of a remodeling job on its store in 1942 and used this marketing opportunity to embed itself in local happenings. One observer noted that the co-op intended to "organize neighborhood activities around the co-op in a spirit of fellowship and cooperation."[99]

Perhaps the most dramatic example of Chicago-area co-ops' investment in egalitarian values—and especially in erasing class and race inequality—was the creation of a camp that was run and financed by midwestern consumer co-ops. In 1938, the Central States Cooperative League began leasing part of an old Works Progress Administration camp from the government. The CSCL dubbed the camp "Circle Pines" in honor of the international logo of consumer co-ops—two pine trees in a circle. The camp served co-op members and trained future leaders through an extensive series of workshops and regional and national conferences. It also offered more leisure-oriented sessions for young families.[100] One enthusiastic observer described Circle Pines as "a camp operated by the people . . . at a cost available to the working people, where elbows could be rubbed with people of all races, creeds, and stations of life, where 'learning by doing' was the watch-word, and cooperative living the goal." The camp left no doubt that "the cooperative way of life means more than activity in the field of economics."[101]

Many Chicago cooperatives demonstrated their support for this holistic "cooperative way of life" through their use of space. The site of the Circle Pines camp, originally rented, was eventually purchased by the regional co-op society and became the site of additions to its now-cramped quarters.[102] Also, by the early 1940s, the pages of Chicago co-op newsletters were filled with notices of folk dances, social clubs, and youth auxiliaries.[103] Prosperous co-ops often built or expanded clubrooms for social events when they enlarged their stores.[104] The Hyde Park Co-op, for instance, had a separate clubroom in its store and published its own weekly newsletter.[105] Altgeld Gardens, though still in temporary headquarters in December 1944, planned to open a lunch cafeteria and a "teenage canteen" in addition to a community credit union.[106] The Rochdale Trading Association hosted folk dancing and a fair in October 1941 and remodeled its social hall early the next year.[107]

Women were especially important to this social aspect of co-op programs. Co-op leaders, both male and female, considered women especially well-suited for and especially important to educational work—recruitment, social events, and other efforts to build up community. As early as 1926, a Cana-dian speaker at a national convention noted that every successful cooperative needed a woman's guild to "look after the social feature of a society and raise funds for educational purposes."[108] In 1929, the Northern States' Co-operative League resolved that "the women can be invaluable in aiding the educational committees of the co-operative societies" and went on record as supporting the creation of separate women's guilds. The league's association of women's guilds continued to report on educational and social activities through the 1930s.[109] This firm sense of women's particular fitness for this work persisted into the 1940s, when leaders reported that women members "appear to be more concerned with education generally than with any other one subject, but publicity, recreation and community service activities come in for their share of support."[110]

Yet, these education and social programs reveal a more complicated reality. For instance, despite the frequent suggestions that educational work was espe-cially women's concern, in practice, men and women oversaw these programs together. At the Brotherhood Co-op (founded by the women's auxiliary of the Brotherhood of Sleeping Car Porters) and the Altgeld Gardens Co-op, both men and women worked on door-to-door recruitment efforts and mailings.[111] Many co-ops prided themselves on the *mixed-sex* folk dancing and dinners that they offered.[112]

Leaders' repeated return to the idea that education was properly the work of women suggests a particular discomfort with breakdowns in conventional gender divisions. Consumer cooperatives highlight the ways in which more democratic models of distribution seemed to require women to gain control over economic institutions and assume authority conventionally claimed by and ascribed to men—and the challenge that posed to conventional gender relations.

Gender, Race, and Equality in a Cooperative World

The question of separate cooperative guilds for women forced a discussion of the proper place of women, literally and figuratively. A 1922 speaker at the national cooperative convention noted somewhat hesitantly that women's guilds were not necessarily the best way to include women in cooperative organizations. "There is a feeling that possibly our own women will do more for co-operation by working with the men, becoming officers and directors, taking their places on committees, and insisting upon an equal voice in all the business affairs of the society," she explained.[113] However, the potential for women's equality remained difficult to implement in many cooperatives. Twenty years later, cooperators still were struggling over the need for separate organizations for women. The leader of a regional organization of women's guilds, acknowledging that many women would prefer to join cooperatives on an equal basis with men and forgo a separate club for women, announced that local women's guilds might simply join forces with local education committees. Opponents of this measure, however, worried that such a wholesale migration would mean that women simply disappeared from cooperative management rather than achieving equal footing, "since few women have paid positions in the movement."[114] When the Hyde Park Cooperative Society opened a meeting space in a men's dormitory, one angry woman member pointedly reminded the board, "Its inaccessibility is not compensated for by the fact that it is called a cooperative."[115] As these accounts suggest, few activists doubted that behind enthusiastic proclamations in the name of "the consumer" stood the actual work of women, energized by age-old concerns with procuring high-quality and affordable goods for their families and now claiming a right to participate in new institutions.

Women's organized presence proved a problem for groups that wanted to argue that the consumer agenda was everyone's agenda and that cooperatives could overcome the problems that had forced housewives to become so demanding, so assertive, and so insistent on their particular standards and needs. The last thing that the movement needed was women who continued to be so difficult.

As a result, open discussions of gender imbalances stand out in the documents produced by cooperatives. Male and female cooperators, like most other consumer activists, rarely discussed openly women's struggles for political authority. Instead, the rhetoric of women's limited intellectual and political ambitions permeated the literature of co-ops. In this discourse, women's hard work of locating acceptable food, their efforts to force firms to accede to their standards, and their imposition of their politics onto retail spaces came to be cast as a problem.

For instance, cooperative organizers were endlessly frustrated with women's attention to the details of price and brand. In 1926, speakers at the annual CLUSA convention advised co-ops to appeal to women as bargain hunters rather than via high-minded ideals and calls for justice.[116] Only a few years later, cooperators lamented the related problem of persuading women to buy according to cooperative standards: "We have tried it and find that if you want to progress you must sell the housewife just what she wants and not try to talk her into buying a brand of merchandise she is not familiar with."[117]

The notion that women could best be reached by appeals to their desire for particular goods and the construction of that desire as opposition to cooperatives' emphasis on equality and justice continued through the 1930s. When Oscar Cooley Jr., a frequent spokesperson for and proponent of consumer cooperatives, titled a 1933 article "What Does Cooperation Mean to Women?" he focused on only the most immediate of concerns: the assurance that the grocer would not take advantage of customers' gullibility or mark up the price of goods unnecessarily.[118] That article sparked an angry response from the director of the National Committee of Women's Guilds, who suggested that a better question might be "What do women mean to cooperation?"[119] Tellingly, later articles that portrayed women in even less flattering terms sparked no such critique. The limited expectations of women went unquestioned.

In the late 1930s, as cooperative societies produced ever-more-elaborate forums for educating their members and creating social networks, the discourse of women as narrow-minded shoppers continued. A play that CLUSA urged cooperators to perform for their members portrayed women shoppers as hapless and gullible customers, frequently buying substandard brands or being cheated by grocers until cooperators introduced them to the wonders of consumer cooperation.[120] Similarly, the 1939 runs of the *Co-operator*, a newsletter of a co-op in Evanston, Illinois, carried a regular column by "Lulu," a naïve and daffy housewife who regularly touted the benefits of cooperation even when she did not fully understand them.[121] Over and over, the work of food shopping was posited as a distraction from a more high-minded concern with the structures through which foods was distributed.

The image of the inept female consumer was especially problematic for cooperatives because women regularly assumed authority in their structures. For instance, cooperative societies recognized their dependence on women's shopping and worked assiduously to recruit women as members.[122] Moreover, women frequently oversaw co-ops. The Women's Guild of the Morgan Park Co-op, for instance, managed the store when employees were ill or in short supply.[123] In 1933, the Workmen's Co-op unceremoniously reported that three women had been elected to its board of directors. A woman director of the Evanston Consumer Cooperative led its recruitment efforts.[124] Women often outnumbered men on the Management Committee of the Hyde Park Co-op, and the society's constitution required members to nominate at least two women for board of directors' seats at every election.[125] Women's managerial authority was especially common in African American co-ops, such as the Ida B. Wells and Brotherhood co-ops, which often boasted entirely or predominantly female boards of directors.[126] In cooperatives, men and women often shared decision-making power to a degree that was unmatched in other kinds of firms.

This fact of everyday life underscored the ways in which women's labor as shoppers was a spur to political activism and not, as prescriptive literature would have it, a distraction. Running a cooperative entailed new gender relations and depended on the very dynamic that leaders so often denied—the move from women's insistence on getting affordable and acceptable foods to their claims on political and economic systems. Women's seemingly limited concerns with price and quality were often, in the space of cooperatives, the springboards to more demanding and assertive activities—to leadership positions, to management work and to demands that men acknowledge, respect, support, and assist their efforts to sustain cooperative societies. Proponents of cooperatives' promise of economic authority were hesitant, however, to acknowledge that women might want basic satisfactions as well. Instead, societies and larger trade associations put forward a new model of the consumer—female, self-interested, often confused, and utterly dependent.

Cooperatives' silence on gender bias and inequality stands in sharp contrast to their embrace of a discourse of racial justice. African American and many white cooperators openly pursued racial equality. Both the national and regional trade associations, dominated by white staff, assisted African American co-ops by providing training, educational manuals, and encouragement.[127] Indeed, they took such collaboration as a point of pride. A report on the Central States Cooperative League's 1934 convention noted that the unprecedented number of African Americans in attendance was an "outstanding highlight" of the meeting.[128] Ten years later, the African American press celebrated the 1944 "centennial congress" (also held in Chicago) as a showpiece of racial integration. Both mixed-race and African American choirs sang, the cast of a pageant was composed of African and Euro-Americans in equal numbers, and one ambitious African American speaker even attempted to lead the entire audience in a "negro spiritual."[129] These symbolic efforts reinforced the expansive potential of the cooperative movement as a catalyst for social as well as economic equality.

Co-ops also provided crucial financial support for African Americans' forays into cooperation. For instance, the very prosperous Cooperative Trading Company of Waukegan provided critical assistance to the African American–run Consumers' Cooperative Trading Company in nearby Gary, Indiana. Later, both the Waukegan cooperative and the Hyde Park Cooperative Society provided start-up capital to the largely African American Altgeld Gardens co-op.[130] The newly organized citywide Council for Cooperative Development trained staff for this and other African American co-ops in the immediate postwar years.[131] Both black and white co-ops joined together against anti-Asian sentiment in the United States. Members frequently welcomed speakers from Japan (which had a long-standing tradition of consumer cooperation). More strikingly, Chicago-area cooperators facilitated citywide efforts to employ Japanese Americans from the West Coast during World War II.[132]

More than most co-ops, the Hyde Park Cooperative Society confronted racial fears. A mostly white neighborhood, Hyde Park was surrounded by areas of the city that were home to more and more African Americans. In response to what many members saw as a neighborhood about to succumb to "white flight," the society wrestled with questions of how members might resist the temptation to flee and how to preserve the cooperative vision of a just and integrated society. The group publicized community meetings on restrictive covenants, mobilized members in support of fair-hiring movements, and considered financial support for an interracial housing co-op in nearby Kenwood.[133] Cora Alderton, a member of the co-op, urged other women to join the Chicago Urban League's boycott of downtown department stores that refused to hire African Americans.[134]

Cooperatives did not always adopt progressive positions. The Hyde Park Cooperative Society voted against wholesale condemnation of restrictive covenants, for instance. When its education committee endorsed the recent hiring of a "Negro employee," board members curtly answered that they had not set out to hire an African American and were against any favoritism; the board resisted lending its name to the Urban League's campaign to secure employment for African Americans in downtown department stores.[135]

In spite of some individual white cooperators' wavering support for equality, cooperatives remained especially compelling for African American men and women. Black cooperators generally combined their desire for better goods with their desire for economic equality more broadly. The People's Cooperative Union proclaimed that its object was "to unite our best talents, intelligence and capital in order to foster, encourage and train Negro citizens to improve their economic status as a race through friendly cooperation."[136] Started by civil servants in the 1930s, the co-op provided volunteer labor, advice, and occasional capital for other African American cooperatives in the 1940s.[137] Two of Chicago's most ambitious cooperatives, the Ida B. Wells Co-op and the Altgeld Gardens Co-op, were organized and supported largely by African Americans inspired by the example of People's Co-op and frustrated by the lack of high-quality grocery stores near wartime housing projects.[138]

For many blacks, cooperatives provided a viable alternative to what seemed endless exploitation and inequality in many stores. J. L. Reddix, founder of the country's largest African American co-op (which was also one of the largest African American–owned businesses in the United States), gave eloquent voice to the frustrations felt by many African Americans in the 1930s: "The capitalist system has been benevolent to the Negro. It has given him YMCAs, schools, and education. It has given him his dole during business depressions and has left him poor for the next one."[139] George Schuyler, the founder of the Young Negro's Cooperative League, echoed the words of other African Americans who had noted the tremendous potential of organized, politically aware purchasing. "The white man invented the color line, we didn't," Schuyler said, "but we are going to take advantage of it in organizing this vast army of working people."[140] Similarly, the president of the Brotherhood Cooperative, operated by the Ladies' Auxiliary of the Brotherhood of Sleeping Car Porters, wrote to prospective cooperators that co-ops might "keep within the Negro race the huge sums that are now being spent in other places. Once the Negro develops his economic strength by keeping his money within the race he will be a power to be reckoned with and the Consumers Movement represents an ideal step in that direction."[141] These and other black activists gave voice to the anticapitalist nature of cooperation.

Cooperatives nurtured civil rights activism. Ella Baker, founder of the Student Nonviolent Coordinating Committee (SNCC), had her first training in democratic organizing in consumer cooperatives. She served as president of the Young Negro's Cooperative League and remained a proponent of consumer cooperation through the 1940s.[142] W. E. B. Du Bois spoke about cooperatives to audiences in Chicago and elsewhere, as he came to embrace economic autonomy as the key to African Americans' freedoms.[143] A. Philip Randolph, a prominent union leader at the forefront of the struggle to secure equal employment rights for African Americans, was a vocal supporter of co-ops. At a rally for African American–run consumer co-ops in Chicago, he referred to co-ops as "the best mechanism yet devised to bring about economic democracy."[144]

RANDOLPH'S HOPES FOR CO-OPS and the consumer movement proved to be misplaced. Neither emerged as a tool for economic democracy, although civil rights and other African American activists continued to mobilize protests at the point of consumption.[145] If anything, self-proclaimed "consumer protest" grew more conservative over time. Some reasons for that conservatism were political, a reflection of the stultifying effects of McCarthyism and anticommunism on American progressive organizations.

But some other reasons had been present from the beginning. An examination of women and gender in consumer cooperatives clearly illustrates the limitations of both cooperatives and the consumer movement. Cooperators offered, at best, a limited gender analysis. Their embrace of the idea that women shoppers were daffy and narrowly focused on their own individual preferences made it difficult to argue that consumers could be trusted with control of economic systems like distribution. It made it nearly impossible to claim that cooperatives offered a viable alternative to conventional retail.[146]

If the predominant consumers were women concerned about obtaining trustworthy goods for their families (and few Americans questioned that proposition in the 1930s), then giving consumers political authority meant giving women—even women who were engaged in the everyday work of shopping—important new power. It meant acknowledging that even work that was clearly women's purview could be a basis for citizenship and political authority. The political nature of women's housework and the gendered nature of consumer politics unsettled "consumer" activists and critics alike. In this way, the limitations of cooperatives suggest the pervasiveness of a discourse of women's apolitical nature and the ways in which it framed the politics of distribution.

No story better captures the changing nature and problems of organized consumer protest in the 1930s than that of the National Consumers League (NCL). The NCL, dedicated to consumption as women's tool of protest, became increasingly alienated from the self-proclaimed "consumer movement" of the 1930s. Members found themselves having to justify their support for high wages and organized labor. Their broad agenda and female membership made participation in the government's consumer agencies especially tricky. Although policymakers recruited members for positions as publicity workers and as administrators of consumer agencies (for instance, in the Women's Division of the National Recovery Administration), NCL members smelled a rat. Many suspected that they were being categorized as a "woman's" organization and shunted into relatively weak programs. Lucy Mason, the NCL's leader, declined an offer to publicize the NRA because, she said, it would keep her from criticizing the agency and pushing for progressive changes. Although individual leaders often supported consumer cooperatives and participated in the movement for grading and labeling and although the NCL remained an important player in New Deal labor reforms, it lost both influence and status as a consumer organization, retaining its identity primarily as a Progressive Era association of labor reformers. By the 1940s, the league was having to defend women's right to participate in regulatory agencies at all. Its politically minded consumption and constituency of broad-minded middle-class women shoppers simply had no place in the emerging discourse of the consumer protest movement.[147]

The story of consumer protest in the 1920s, 1930s, and 1940s helps explain the limited efficacy of the consumer movement. Unless they challenged gender relations, consumer organizations could not challenge the power relations at the heart of mass retailing and at the heart of the emerging political economy of mass consumption. In the course of the unsettled 1930s and 1940s, consumption came to seem, to many Americans, best reformed from above, not from below. A close exploration of the success of consumer protest in the 1930s and early 1940s demonstrates the ongoing efforts by women to claim power over stores, as well as the roots of a new kind of mass retailing in which women's purchases were crucial but their claims for power were obscured.

The next chapter explores the implications of the emergent system of mass retailing and its use of the discourse of women as aimless shoppers and stores as the places that provided order to their work. Slowly, both protesters and their critics came to share very similar ideas about what women wanted—and what women should want—from the stores in which they shopped.

Grocery Stores Trade Up

The Politics of Supermarkets and the Making
of a Mass Market, 1930–1945

The landscape of food retailing in the 1930s was, to put it mildly, unsettled. Chain stores continued to work toward dominance but struggled to fully standardize their policies; by the mid-1930s, they were losing market share. Firms and proprietorships operating only one or two stores continued to call on neighborhood loyalty and their promise of service to woo customers, even as they worked through voluntary chains to reap some of the rewards of mass retail. Finally, as the last chapter documented, consumer cooperatives offered yet another way of selling food, one that seemed especially appealing to the tantalizing demographic of middle-class professionals.

One other possibility emerged in this period. Very large "independents" often discarded the notion of small neighborhood stores entirely, building instead massive supermarkets in abandoned warehouses and factories. Like those operated by national chain store firms, these stores featured self-service, limited personal attention, large arrays of goods, and promises of low prices. But they were much larger than even chain grocery stores and were often located away from residential neighborhoods. Marketing included such public spectacles as concerts, celebrity visits, and towering displays of canned goods. These publicity stunts, together with the sheer enormity of the stores, encouraged an air of festive chaos that ran counter to the social order that many chains assured customers they would find in their stores.

This sense of unsettledness lasted through the 1940s, when a much beleaguered John Hartford, faced with an ongoing antitrust investigation of A&P, reportedly threatened to "convert the whole business into the biggest consumer cooperative you ever saw" if the government won its case.[1] Although it's not clear whether anyone took this threat seriously at the time, it does speak to the new—and, for many grocers, quite disturbing—possibilities of this era.

By 1950, however, much of that unsettledness had disappeared. Indeed, sharply delineated retail strategies, in which gender ideology and women's authority had differed enormously, had all but vanished. All over the country, grocery stores came to look more like each other and to operate according to shared understandings of what customers wanted. Small mom-and-pop stores that had offered individual attention, cooperatives that had offered member-customers a chance to control store policy, and large supermarkets that had seemed to outdo chain grocers' promises of low prices and broad choices, lost their distinctive elements. The strategies that firms employed and the stores that they operated achieved remarkable convergence in later years.

Why did grocery stores, once so diverse, begin to adopt such similar policies? To answer this question, this chapter tracks firms' move toward building both strategies and new supermarkets around middle-class women and their normative desires. Just as chain food store firms had established the discourse and model of mass retailing in the 1920s, they did so again in the 1930s. This time, however, they refocused their efforts on middle- and upper-class populations and promised respectability and service, not simply low prices. Gender ideologies and women customers remained crucial to their strategies, but now stores offered glamour and convenience—not autonomy or authority.

One other change in strategy was crucial. Although chain store firms continued to operate many individual stores in order to exploit the advantages of economies of scale, they aimed to operate fewer, but larger, stores.[2] These new "super markets" would come to define mass retailing as their strategies were adopted by consumer cooperatives, by individually owned stores, and eventually by nonfood retail firms as well.[3] This chapter describes the social, political, and economic dynamics that undergirded grocers' slow but sure transition to supermarkets.[4] These stores proved workable not only because they offered low prices but also because they offered proprietors new advantages over unpredictable government policy and reflected a new gender system.

The Perils of Mass Retailing in the 1930s

That chain stores would come to dominate the market was far from clear in the early days of the depression. In those years, chain stores, and especially chain store groceries, demonstrated all too clearly the vulnerabilities of mass retailing.

Many chain store boosters at first discounted the danger posed by the depression. At a December 1930 meeting of business leaders, William H. Albers, the president of the National Chain Store Association and of the Kroger Grocery and Baking Company, reassured President Herbert Hoover that chains bought and sold "'essential' rather than 'luxury' items" and that they therefore would undoubtedly continue to sustain the economy throughout the current crisis.[5] As late as January 1931, as most chains were already seeing their sales fall, the editors of *Chain Store Age* happily reported, "Thousands of people throughout the country have patronized chain stores this past year who never before felt is [*sic*] necessary to test the economies they claimed to offer."[6]

Chains had good reason to feel secure in the early 1930s. They had gone from marginal features of urban life to central institutions, wielding enormous capital and enormous influence over the food that many Americans ate. A&P owned more than 15,000 stores nationally and purveyed one-tenth of all food that was sold at retail in the United States.[7] Kroger controlled 5,575 stores by the close of the 1920s—the largest number of stores that had ever been part of the Kroger chain.[8] National Tea, one of the largest Chicago chains, also expanded over the course of the 1920s; their profits increased from just over $300,000 in 1919 to nearly 3 million dollars in 1929.[9]

Slowly, however, it became clear that chains were facing serious problems. Even the healthiest chain store firm was hurt by the slowing economy of the 1930s; the seemingly impregnable A&P, for example, saw its sales decline steadily through the first few years of the 1930s.[10] Moreover, a rapid deflationary spiral meant that profits were especially difficult to come by, even when sales did not fall. Kroger's profits tumbled even as it moved more goods in the first six months of 1930 than it had the previous year.[11] National Tea experienced a similar phenomenon that same year, when profits fell far faster than sales.

The stock market, on which virtually all large national and regional chains had depended for capital, could no longer sustain chain expansion.[12] Over the course of 1930, for instance, Kroger common stock dropped from $120 per share to $36⅛ per share; by May 1932, the high was only $18⅞.[13] Indeed, chain grocery stocks, the darlings of so many 1920s analysts, were particularly hardhit by the stock market drop. Whereas the New York Stock Exchange as a whole lost 41 percent of its value over the course of the fall of 1929, chain groceries lost 64 percent of theirs.[14] In March 1931, the common stocks of the twelve leading grocery chains cost only one-third of what they had cost at their 1929 highs.[15]

In Chicago, one firm exemplified the mortality of chains—Loblaw's Groceterias. A Canadian firm, Loblaw's had launched its expansion into the United States with the simultaneous opening of dozens of stores across the city of

Chicago in 1928, the heyday of chain expansion. The owner explained that such a large opening itself reflected the logic of chains' preeminent claim to fame—economies of scale. By opening several stores at once, a single, enormous, and (presumably) efficient marketing campaign could be conducted.[16] These stores seemed to exemplify what was best about chains—self-service, clean and bright interiors, and low prices.[17]

By 1932, however, Loblaw's celebrated stores were in dire straits. Customers had not flocked to them in the numbers that Loblaw executives had hoped for. Moreover, the firm was forced to pay exceptionally high rents. Eventually, the company gratefully sold its entire chain to Jewel Food Company, a long-standing operator of wagon routes that was diversifying into stores. Jewel renegotiated all its leases and closed stores rather than relying on scale alone as a strategy. That was not enough, however. Jewel struggled to boost sales and profits at the stores through the 1930s; the stores did not make up a significant part of the firm's profits until after World War II and did not become more profitable than the firm's door-to-door operations until the 1950s.[18] As the sad tale of Loblaw/Jewel suggests, chain grocery stores were as likely to be a liability as a safe investment.

FAILING STORES WERE BAD ENOUGH, but the chains' problems extended beyond falling profits and a lack of capital. Consumers themselves were changing in the early years of the depression, and it seemed to many executives and analysts that lower prices, centralized control, and standardized products— the hallmarks of mass retailing—might prove unworkable in the face of popular and governmental antagonism. Politics, as well as economics, gave mass retailers pause.

Large chain grocers fought anti-chain legislation throughout the 1930s. The anti-chain taxes and costly licensing fees debated in state legislatures paled in comparison to some of the federal-level taxation and regulatory bills under consideration later in the decade. A 1928 Federal Trade Commission (FTC) investigation into chain store practices had paved the way for a series of reports on the "chain store question."[19] Although the FTC concluded that most chains' profits could be ascribed to practices that were entirely legal and ethical (internal efficiencies and volume discounts), numerous legislators were suspicious that chains might also be pressuring their suppliers into granting them lower prices. The Robinson-Patman Act, passed in 1936, prohibited any rebates or price concessions not directly attributable to a supplier's savings.[20] The new law did not ultimately impede the growth of large national and regional chains, but that outcome was not clear in the 1930s.[21] Indeed, the act preceded even more threatening activity from Congress—another lengthy FTC investigation, an eventual suit against A&P when the firm resisted provisions of the Robinson-Patman Act, and the introduction of Wright Patman's anti-chain bill in 1939. This bill carried penalties so high that it was nicknamed the "Chain Store Death Sentence Bill."[22]

One feature common to most anti-chain laws proved especially important to the growth of supermarkets. Anti-chain laws generally taxed firms based on the number of stores they owned. A typical bill introduced into the Illinois state legislature, for instance, would have levied an impost of $5 for the first store owned by one firm, $10 per store for the second through the fifth, $25 per store for the sixth through the tenth, $50 for the eleventh through the twentieth, $100 for the twenty-first through the thirtieth, $200 for the thirty-first through the fortieth, and $400 for each store over forty.[23] Stores were not, however, taxed on sales per store. Indeed, graduated sales taxes were unconstitutional in Illinois, and high flat-rate taxes would have punished independents along with larger chains.[24] Thus firms wishing to avoid actual or threatened (as in Illinois) anti-chain taxes and licensing laws had clear incentives to expand the volume at existing stores rather than to open more stores.

The structure of anti-chain licensing and taxation laws and the economic pressures on retailers help explain the appeal of larger stores but not another change—chains' move to upscale and openly feminized stores. Falling sales and anti-chain measures were only one part of the pressures on chains.

Chain store executives and advocates worried about another possibility: that consumers and newly sympathetic New Deal policymakers were suspicious of businesses in general. As Chapter 4 demonstrated, the organized consumer movement had grown in both size and ambition through the late 1920s and 1930s. Joined by women's organizations like the American Association of University Women and the Parent-Teacher Association, self-proclaimed consumer groups demanded increased government oversight of the quality and marketing of foods, consumer education, the creation of grading and labeling requirements, and consumer representation in the policymaking process. Even more unsettling, many urban residents were showing an interest in rejecting private enterprise altogether and in forming consumer cooperatives. Meanwhile, policymakers were demonstrating unsettling sympathy for the complaints of organized consumers and a new willingness to experiment with a government-administered economy. The combination of alienated shoppers, sympathetic policymakers, and federal interest in a planned economy spelled danger to chain store executives. An editorial in the major chain store trade journal worried aloud, "It is quite possible that the attempts at regulation of distribution under the NRA [National Recovery Administration] codes, if not wisely administered, will give just the impetus needed to start a rapid development of consumers' co-operatives in this country."[25] This rhetoric of anxiety and suspicion stood in stark contrast to the celebratory proclamations that had marked chains' trade journals in the 1920s.

Grocers' concerns quickly came to focus once more on women customers. As one speaker succinctly put it at an annual convention, "You and I are in the business of understanding women."[26] In their view, the problem with the depression was a problem with women's purchasing. Recovery would come, retailers assured themselves, and "once again the housewife will shop as though she meant it."[27]

Solutions to Economic Problems

Before tackling the problem of stubborn women customers, chain store operators first focused on extricating themselves from their immediate financial straits. After a decade of remarkable sales and profits, chain store firms faced hard times. They responded by closing stores, reversing the expansion that had seemed so important to their growth and to stock market support in the 1920s. Rather than continue to try to sell more goods and to rely on economies of scale (as A&P had done when sales fell in the 1920s), chains simply closed down unprofitable stores.[28] Kroger was among the most dedicated to the store-closing strategy, even hiring a "real estate manager" in 1931 to oversee the program.[29] By the end of 1931, Kroger had closed seven hundred stores nationally.[30] Other retailers followed suit. National Tea closed more than two hundred of its sixteen hundred stores between December 1930 and December 1932.[31] Even A&P closed more than three hundred of its nearly sixteen thousand stores during 1930 and 1931.[32]

Chains also renegotiated their leases, pressuring landlords to sign shorter leases and to base rents on a proportion of annual sales rather than a flat rate. By 1933, A&P was happy to report that more than 90 percent of its leases were for only one year and that the firm would refrain from making any new real estate investments.[33] National Tea worked valiantly to sign new leases and, when that failed, to renegotiate the terms of old leases. By January 1933, the firm reported that it had gotten "downward adjustments" on nearly one-third of its pre-1931 leases.[34] Short leases based on a percentage of sales seem to have been especially popular in Chicago, where a controversial reassessment of property values made for an especially unsettled real estate market.[35] Jewel Food Stores, which bought seventy Loblaw Groceterias in Chicago in 1932, appears to have renegotiated the long-term leases that Loblaw had signed in the 1920s as a matter of course and as a condition on its purchase of the older chain.[36]

Closing stores and securing investments in remaining stores were only part of chain store strategies in the 1930s. Dramatic change also came to the stores that were kept and the new ones that were opened. Firms operated bigger stores and sold a larger range of goods. They also sought out middle- and upper-class customers more aggressively than they had in the 1920s.

Many chains responded directly to the threat of the consumer movement and cooperatives, especially demands for testing and grading and for consumer education. However, chain store executives and managers rarely acknowledged it. Instead, they centered their expansion and new marketing campaigns on a middle-class and upper-middle-class market of "housewives." In seeking out richer customers, in responding to demands of the consumer movement, and in explaining the changes as a simple reflection of women's feminine nature and their needs as wives and mothers, chains implicitly defined "women" as middle- and upper-class people who wanted short-term, immediate changes in stores rather than power over stores themselves. This appeal to femininity as a way of keeping order in stores was central to the chains' strategies when they expanded the size of their stores in the 1930s.

Chain stores of the 1920s had been very small, like most grocery stores of the period, and their small size reflected their efforts to sell efficiently and in a streamlined manner. They also tended to focus on packaged and easily handled goods—canned vegetables and meats, bulk staples (like flour and sugar), and other prepackaged commodities. Meats and produce—which required the services of skilled employees and were not prepackaged—generally were not sold at chain groceries. This basic orientation changed radically in the late 1920s and 1930s.

Chain store firms' new strategy had its roots in an older retailing format—the combination store. These stores were slightly larger than standard grocery stores, and they sold meat along with dry groceries. Independents had opened the first combination stores in the mid- and late 1920s, often simply by knocking down walls between neighboring butchers and grocers.[37] Chains, however, had resisted the move toward bigger stores and more product lines until the exigencies of the 1930s forced them to rethink their strategy of constant expansion and stripped-down stores.[38] By 1930, the National Chain Store Association was reporting that larger and better-stocked stores were "the outstanding constructive feature" of chains.[39] Two years later, *Chain Store Age* published a special issue on "modernization" and noted, "Within the past few months, several important chains which had resisted the trend as long as they could and would have nothing to do with meat-marketing have finally succumbed." Nearly 13 percent of all store units had been remodeled during the previous year alone, the journal reported.[40] The depression had made remodeling cheap, and combination stores quickly became all the rage among chains. By the mid-1930s, virtually all the national and regional grocery chains had some combination stores. Analysts estimated that these firms had spent $33 million on store remodeling in 1933, an amount that grossly underestimated the total spent on upgrades: more than one-third of all chains reported that the landlords from whom they rented had borne the whole cost of massive remodeling and modernization campaigns.[41]

Chicago-area food chains exemplified the move to combination stores. One 1932 article noted that in Chicago, "a decided change in the attitude of the chain grocers is . . . establishing larger units and discontinuing the small type of store, which has been their standard for years."[42] The data back up that observation: combination stores represented 4.9 percent of all Chicago chain stores in 1929, but 27.5 percent by 1935.[43]

Indeed, many firms that were closing stores to cut back on expenses were simultaneously remodeling and expanding others. Between 1929 and 1932, the National Tea Company doubled the proportion of its combination stores by closing small stores and expanding remaining ones. By the end of 1932, nearly 20 percent of its stores were combination stores.[44] Not to be outdone, Kroger announced in 1932 that it would open 250 "large" stores in its Chicago district alone.[45] It is unclear whether Kroger actually opened that many new store units in the city, but it is clear that the firm was committed to a strategy of operating fewer, larger, and more elaborate stores.

The combination stores not only were larger than the older chain store units; they were also often fitted out far more elaborately and geared toward a higher-class market. For instance, a Kroger executive explained that the expanded range of products in the firm's newer and larger Chicago-area stores was designed to boost profit margins: "A proportionately large number of luxury items helps these stores show larger percentage profit."[46] The emphasis on luxury was in line with strategies that Kroger used elsewhere; its showpiece store in downtown Cincinnati featured fountain service, a lunch counter, a hostess, a doorman to take orders from drivers at the curb, and such midwestern rarities as avocados and artichokes.[47] National Tea, while not as dedicated to luxury as Kroger, also modernized and embellished its combination stores. The company celebrated its massive remodeling and expansion of a store in the upper-class South Shore neighborhood by noting that the only original pieces of equipment left in the store were the shelving units along the walls.[48]

TABLE 5.1. National Tea Company Combination Stores, 1927–1936

Year	Overall Number of Stores	Number of Combination Stores	Proportion of Combination Stores to Total Stores (%)
1927	1,237	0	0
1928	1,600	0	0
1929	1,627	95	5.8
1930	1,600	264	16.5
1931	1,512	301	19.9
1932	1,389	302	21.7
1933	1,299	372	28.6
1934	1,245	450	36.1
1935	1,224	467	38.1
1936	1,221	477	39

Source: National Tea Company, Annual Reports, 1927–36

As chains built higher-end stores, they also refocused their energies around upper-class customers. Over the course of the 1930s, chain stores regularly moved out of poor and even middle-income neighborhoods and into higher-income areas. In 1930, for instance, the National Tea Company had stores in thirty-seven neighborhoods in which residents were at or below the average income level and in thirteen neighborhoods in which residents had above-average incomes. In 1940, the firm was in only sixteen neighborhoods of average or below-average income but in twenty-nine communities of above-average income. Numbers of stores tell an even more dramatic story. In 1928 and 1929, the city directory listed 533 National Tea stores in the city, of which slightly more than half (275 stores) were in areas of average or below-average income. In 1940, the city phone book listed 219 National Tea stores, of which only 42 (19.2 percent) were in areas of low or average income and 177 (80.8 percent) were in areas of above-average income. The stories of other mass retailers are similar. The distribution of Loblaw stores (later Jewel Food Stores) initially was split about evenly between middle- or low-income areas, and upper-income areas: the firm had 30 stores in upper-income areas in 1930 and 26 in middle- or low-income neighborhoods. In 1940, however, there were 66 Jewel stores in higher-income areas (84 percent) and only 13 (16 percent) in areas of lower or average income. High-Low, a new chain that opened only supermarkets, had 18 of its 20 stores in areas of above-average income in 1940.[49] (See table 5.2.)

Finally, chains' new strategy of focusing on upper-class customers was

TABLE 5.2. Chain Grocery Firms' Concentration in Chicago Neighborhoods, by Income of Neighborhood, 1928–1930 and 1940

	1928–30		1939–40	
	Stores in Areas of Average or Below-Average Income	Stores in Areas of Above-Average Income	Stores in Areas of Average or Below-Average income	Stores in Areas of Above-Average Income
National Tea	275 (51.5%)	258 (48.5%)	42 (19.2%)	177 (80.8%)
Loblaw/Jewel	26 (46.4%)	30 (53.6%)	13 (16.5%)	66 (83.5%)
High-Low	N/A	N/A	2 (10%)	18 (90%)

Source: Numbers of stores are from the 1930 and 1940 Chicago Telephone Directory, Classified Pages, and the 1928/9 City Directory. Demographic characteristics of neighborhoods and neighborhood boundaries are taken from the Local Community Fact Book for Chicago, 1950 *(Chicago: Chicago Community Inventory, University of Chicago, 1953).*

Note: There are no direct data on income for these years because the U.S. Census did not ask about income before the 1950 census. Therefore, I have used the median rental for an area as a proxy for income—the method that social scientists regularly use. See Cohen, Making a New Deal, *108–10 and 404n27.*

reflected in their increasing ambivalence toward selling to relief clients. Chicago chain stores were intimate partners in the state's administration of relief, both as providers of in-kind aid and as recipients of relief clients' vouchers. A manager of a Jewel Food Store in one working-class district recalled that the vast majority of the store's clients paid with the scrip issued by relief offices; indeed, so many customers used these vouchers in the early 1930s that often there was not enough cash in the store to pay employees at the end of the week.[50] While the state was increasingly important to chain store profits, however, working-class customers, in and of themselves, were not. Chain groceries made few, if any, direct overtures to this demographic group. Jewel and National Tea stores (probably the biggest beneficiary of welfare clients' dollars), regularly filled orders of cash customers before those of customers using vouchers.[51] Chains in working-class neighborhoods often carried lower grades and cheaper brands of goods and offered fewer services than the same firm did in middle- and upper-class neighborhoods.[52] To the extent that chains built ties with working-class customers, they were working through and with the state, not out of their own attempts to reach this population.

The Gendered and Classed Nature of Mass Retailing

The move to larger stores and to upper-class customers was built on a gender ideology already present in the 1920s—that chains needed to serve women and that new services and embellishments were there to please these most important customers. Chains regularly justified their larger and better-equipped stores by explaining that they could better reach "housewives." This attention to women was reflected in any number of areas of store operation—from the height of shelves to the hiring of home economists.

Women's authority and their needs as family cooks and shoppers—in the context of hierarchical structures that actually undermined their individual authority in stores—were central themes of chain marketing in this period. Beginning in the early 1930s, chain stores reemphasized their commitment to providing safe, trustworthy products and to advising women customers. Kroger, for example, opened the Kroger Food Foundation in 1930. Its staff of home economists and food chemists would, the firm promised, provide ever more useful and trustworthy products to Kroger's female customers.[53] The foundation also sent its home economists around the country to conduct "cooking schools"—demonstrations of new appliances and products.[54] A&P began publishing and distributing *Women's Day*, a magazine that featured homemaking tips and news and served as a new outlet for marketing A&P's private-label goods.[55] At the National Tea Company, virtually every change in marketing and design was ascribed to the desire to attract women. Managers lowered the height of shelves in new stores so that "the average woman" could more easily reach merchandise, and the firm also began distributing recipes to customers.[56] As a director of the firm explained, "In construction, layout and decoration we planned with one idea in mind—what will the housewife like best?"[57]

The story of Jewel Food Stores offers an especially dramatic case study of this trend toward celebrating women's supposed influence over stores. The Jewel Tea Company had been steadily losing money on its new venture into chain stores in the early 1930s. In 1934, the company took drastic measures. In the spring of that year, it launched a door-to-door survey of potential customers identified as "housewives" living near their stores. In May, it began a new marketing campaign, advertising that the firm had made precisely the changes for which women had asked. "18,389 Women Planned This Store," crowed Jewel ads.[58] From a new store color (white) to new emphases on cleanliness, courtesy, the merits of self-service, and the availability of national brands, the company promised that customers would find what they wanted in its stores.

In remaking its stores and in advertising women's input, Jewel embodied many firms' efforts to preempt women's demands for power while also reaching a middle- and upper-class market. Jewel sought new markets not by expanding into poorer neighborhoods, where residents might have appreciated the firm's lower prices, but by adding touches of glamour and luxury to the stores that it already operated. Fully 87 percent of these were located middle- and upper-income neighborhoods.[59]

Nowhere did large chains' commitment to the new, gendered, upmarket strategy appear more clearly than in their early reactions to the advent of supermarkets. As had been the case with combination stores, chains built on strategies pioneered by independent grocers and adapted them for mass retailing, especially by focusing explicitly on upper- and middle-class women customers. Both their early antagonism toward and their eventual adoption of supermarkets revealed the ways in which gender, class, and social order were crucial to chain grocers' reinvention of themselves in the 1930s.

Growth of Supermarkets: A New Threat and an Emerging Consensus

To understand why supermarkets developed as they did, one must move away from chain store firms and look at the innovations of independent grocers. It was these firms that developed the first true "super markets."[60] These early supermarket operators employed the strategies of mass retailing (selling large quantities of goods in standardized settings), and the more successful sometimes even operated several store units. But they also drastically altered the direction of mass retailing. Rather than the small-sized stores of chains, these were massive stores, often housed in abandoned warehouses or factories. Also, although their primary focus was food sales, these early supermarkets often sold a wide range of goods and services—everything from candy to shoe repair and hair-styling salons. They expanded both the scale and the scope of mass retailing in the grocery sector.

These first supermarkets differed from the smaller stores operated by chain firms in another way, as well. Autonomous proprietors, not a large, bureaucratized staff, often ran the separate departments.[61] The "owner" of the supermarket might be little more than a glorified landlord who leased departments to outside firms and entrepreneurs; or the store might operate as a kind of cooperative partnership of individual grocers, butchers, bakery owners, and other specialized retailers. Indeed, one of the earliest and most famous supermarkets exemplified this unorthodox method of organization. The first Big Bear store was little more than a conglomeration of individual retailers working under a group of partners who pooled their renters' resources and leased space in an old auto factory in Elizabeth, New Jersey.[62] The success of these stores suggested that the highly bureaucratized and hierarchical features of chain store firms were unnecessary in mass retailing.

Big Bear markets quickly opened throughout New Jersey and New York. At the same time, former Kroger executive Michael Cullen opened the King

Kullen Grocery Company in Queens, New York. His chain of supermarkets quickly expanded, and by 1935 there were fifteen King Kullen stores up and down Long Island.[63] These early East Coast supermarkets made a name for themselves by selling at very low prices—occasionally selling below even their own cost on "loss-leaders." Indeed, ads referred to a store as "Price Crusher" or "Price Wrecker."[64]

These cavernous, ungainly stores were remarkably successful. In its first three days, according to historian Richard Tedlow's calculations, the first Big Bear store sold more than $31,000 worth of goods, about what an A&P store sold in six months.[65] By 1936, there were twelve hundred self-proclaimed supermarkets across the country.[66]

Supermarkets opened later in Chicago than on the East Coast; but by 1937, chains and small independents in the city were facing competition from at least twenty-five supermarkets, one of which claimed annual sales of more than $3 million.[67] These early supermarkets not only were large in size but also featured what can only be called remarkable festivities (many of which became public disturbances). When the Family Market Basket opened a ten-thousand-square-foot store on the city's North Side (about 50 percent larger than most large chain store units), it gave away pictures "suitable for framing" and shopping bags to the twenty thousand people who visited on opening day.[68] Another Chicago supermarket faced a line of customers that stretched around the block on opening day, even though it was offering only walk-throughs and was not selling any food that day.[69] The Twenty-sixth Street Food Mart in working-class Garfield Park celebrated its fifth anniversary by giving away free souvenirs to children, hosting demonstrations of sausage-making, and offering free soup greens to anyone presenting the store's ad.[70] One store owner bragged that opening-day crowds were so large that he'd had to call the police.[71]

It was this social disorderliness, as much as their large size, for which early supermarkets came to be known, none more so than Chicago's largest supermarket, Dawson's. Dawson's was the brainchild of one of the founders of the very first supermarket, New Jersey's Big Bear. Located in an abandoned paper bag factory on the city's South Side, the store catered quite openly to a truly mass clientele; on a busy Saturday it could serve as many as ten thousand customers. Luckily, the store's seventy-two-thousand-square-foot sales floor and its five-acre parking lot could accommodate such large crowds. Both analysts and proprietors, however, claimed that the key to the firm's success was neither its size nor its scale, but its massive and unrefined marketing campaigns. Featuring twelve-page advertising circulars, towering and elaborate displays of canned goods, and frequent spectacles and entertainment, Dawson's sought to persuade Chicagoans to see its space as a playground, as well as a store.[72] However unrefined its methods appeared, other supermarket operators admired Dawson's success. "The secret," wrote the new trade journal *Super Market Merchandising*, "is just such ballyhoo—just such mass impressions, even to the display of merchandise."[73]

Although chains had followed the lead of independents in expanding the size of their stores, they remained entirely unwilling to copy the overt price appeals, massive size, and dramatic promotions of the early supermarkets. Many believed that such stores were inherently unstable. "The super-store in its present form may prove to be a 'depression baby,'" noted one observer, implying that the "baby" would not survive the depression.[74] Fierce price competition and the ire that below-cost price wars stirred up seemed to promise a quick end to these unwieldy creatures.[75]

More often, however, chain store operators expressed concern over what they believed was the flouting of social order, especially of gender norms, in such stores. These newcomers to the grocery field were regularly called "wild animal stores"—a reference both to the names (Big Bear, Big Tiger, Big Bull)[76] and to the decidedly unfeminine, lower-class behavior that such stores' promotions seemed to bring out in customers.[77] Referring to what he dubbed a new generation of "can-opener cooks," who would rather purchase canned food than do their own cooking with fresh ingredients, a business research analyst speaking at an annual convention of food chains noted other surprising aspects of women's behavior: "Apparently there are very few people who are ashamed to go into one of these 'wild animal' markets and lug a basket around," he wrote. Moreover, he went on, they shopped at suspicious times of day: "There is the desire or willingness on the part of many customers to do some shopping in the evening. I do not understand this desire fully, but it seems to exist."[78] (The evening hours were, of course, a way to attract wage-earning women who had a difficult time shopping at smaller chain stores, which usually closed around 6:00 P.M.)[79] Supermarkets' sheer lack of regard for middle-class conventions of domesticity presaged a dangerous gender disorder—something that top-down, centrally managed chain stores, ever searching for respectability, could not tolerate. One concerned chain store researcher wrote, "The man and wife don't know each other as they pass through the turnstile, each with the 'limit' bagged for the exit."[80]

Chain stores, struggling to build profits by appealing to middle-class customers and by limiting the price discounts, resisted opening their own supermarkets. Jewel Food Stores explicitly rejected the supermarket model, concentrating instead on smaller "neighborhood stores."[81] By 1935, Kroger operated only fifty self-styled supermarkets among its thousands of stores; years later, company historians noted that the firm's reluctance stemmed from the fact that "the early supermarkets were bare-bones bargain houses that emphasized price, while Kroger felt it owed its growth and strength to its insistence on quality."[82] The question of supermarkets literally pitted brother against brother at A&P, as co-owners George and John Hartford argued fiercely over the merits of opening larger stores.[83] When National Tea finally opened its first supermarket in 1937, it felt compelled to disassociate the firm from the store, calling its new venture "Sterling Food Mart."[84]

In some ways, chain store executives were right to look askance at these first supermarkets and at the chaotic shopping that went on in them. Many did prove unwieldy. Price appeals, selling below cost, and sheer infighting among the many parties involved in running such a store proved to be too much of a strain for several of these early enterprises. Dawson's, for instance, disappeared within a few years of its opening in a cloud of lawsuits and counterlawsuits.[85] The first trade association of supermarkets, the Super Market Institute, had to urge its members to *raise* their prices and avoid price wars.[86] Moreover, supermarkets soon faced their own political nightmare, as municipalities and state legislatures entertained bills meant to slow the growth of very large stores. In Illinois, only a state supreme court decision saved supermarkets from having to close on Sundays.[87]

By the late 1930s, however, supermarkets were coming to have more in common with older chain stores. An increasing number of firms operated more than one supermarket. Although they never owned as many stores as the largest chains, firms like Big Bear in New Jersey, Food Fair in Philadelphia, and Alber's Super Markets in Cincinnati often operated stores in different neighborhoods of the same city. Some of the largest operators of supermarkets, King Kullen, for instance, also operated stores across state lines. As they expanded, they also trended toward the central management style that was such a distinctive feature of chain stores. In their success and expansion, these grocers undermined their identity as independents.[88]

As early supermarkets lost their claim to being independent stores, they also lost their emphasis on mass spectacle and appeal. Gradually coming to embody a more stable, less price-oriented model, they more closely resembled the chains' upscale stores and chains' claims about women's desires. One Chicago grocer explained that he was reopening a store that had been "a promotional scheme" as a "profitable food business."[89] Speakers at the annual convention of the Super Market Institute urged supermarket owners and managers to avoid the "circus-like" atmosphere of the past and to use a "feminine touch" in store decorating and in a new emphasis on services.[90] So noticeable were the upmarket features of new supermarkets that an analyst writing in the *Harvard Business Review* felt compelled to comment on the change. Stores that previously had featured cheaper baskets now offered more expensive wheeled shopping carts. Delivery was increasingly available, and some stores even provided customers with help in carrying groceries to the car.[91] Social order and overt feminization, and not a price-shaving free-for-all, characterized these second-wave supermarkets.

Slowly but surely, chain stores began opening their own upscale supermarkets.[92] Observers described Jewel Food Stores as "a chain of supermarkets" as early as 1939.[93] That same year, A&P signed a ten-year lease (very long by chain store standards) on the largest store that it had ever operated in the Chicago area.[94] Within three months, it had either opened or announced the openings of three more supermarkets in the city.[95] This trend continued, especially before the war limited the supply of building materials. For instance, in July 1940 alone, National Tea Company and A&P each opened three new supermarkets in the city.[96] Even Jewel Foods, still referring to its enlarged stores as "combination" stores, nearly doubled the number of its locations selling meat (from fifty-four to one hundred) in just one year.[97]

There were good economic reasons for chains to begin operating supermarkets. Selling in high volume was, after all, their primary strategy, and supermarkets increased the volume of food any one store could sell; in this way, the move to supermarkets seemed logical. Even here, however, where the emphasis might have been on lower prices and selling to poorer Chicagoans, chain store operators continued to craft appeals to better-off customers. In 1937, National Tea opened one of its first Chicago supermarkets to great fanfare. Observers noted that the new store would surely bring in "the better class of trade."[98] Similarly, Kroger opened its own "double food mart" in the very well-to-do South Shore, "a section where all other chains have modern stores."[99] A&P chose to build its first supermarket in the city in the same neighborhood.[100] Within a few years, supermarkets went from "depression babies" to markers of middle- and upper-class status.

THE SHIFT TOWARD SUPERMARKETS narrowed the differences not only between chains and independents but also between these privately owned firms and the more democratic consumer cooperatives. In a move that would have enormous implications for all facets of their operations, consumer cooperatives also began building supermarket-style stores.

The roots of the co-ops' new efforts at standardized mass retailing lay in the

FIGURE 5.1. *This 1939 upscale A&P supermarket was bigger than earlier stores (see figure 2.2) and sold meat. Note, however, that it does not appear to have extensive parking. (Chicago History Museum, HB 05291, June 22, 1939, photographer, Hedrich-Blessing)*

consolidation of the agencies that advised them. Although each cooperative society was independent, it often relied on voluntary trade associations and wholesalers for advice on such crucial topics as when to expand and how to decorate stores. The associations and advisory agencies so important to small consumer cooperatives were consolidated in the 1930s and 1940s, so that the advice to cooperators tended to come from the same source—in particular, from the Cooperative League of the USA (CLUSA), a national trade association. For instance, Cooperative Wholesale (CW), a local wholesaler controlled by urban midwestern co-ops, formally allied itself with the Central States Cooperative League (CSCL), a CLUSA affiliate, in 1940.[101] Advisory groups followed a similar trajectory toward consolidation. The Chicago Cooperative Federation (later the Chicago Cooperative Union) began as an upstart citywide federation in 1937. Its organizers conceived of it as a challenge to the CLUSA-affiliated Central States Cooperative League, which they believed did not adequately assist the urban co-ops in and around Chicago. In 1943, however, this challenge effectively ended when the Chicago Cooperative Union merged into the CSCL, even as the CSCL tightened its ties to CLUSA.[102]

The Cooperative League of the USA and the groups that it influenced emphasized standardization, expansion, and an appreciation for aesthetics. Leaders believed that standardized design and expansion of the number of stores and of product lines carried, although developed by private chains, were intrinsic to mass retailing regardless of firm type.[103] Thus, training literature from regional and national trade associations constantly admonished cooperators to modernize, using techniques strikingly similar to those engineered by chain stores. Societies were encouraged to enlarge stores, to use the standard "Co-op" logo, to increase the number of product lines carried, and to make stores brighter and generally more attractive.[104] Stores that remodeled, added refrigerators, or added product lines like meat and produce were lauded in newsletters and periodicals.[105]

CLUSA provided everything from financial assistance for expansion to educational brochures that explained the Rochdale principles to classes that taught bookkeeping techniques to staunch praise for cooperatives that opened branch stores or remodeled their existing stores.[106] In 1942, for example, CLUSA's newly created National Architectural Committee established standard co-op colors for use in store signs and décor; cooperative societies quickly adopted the recommended ivory and forest green palette.[107] Like the chain stores that had traded up in the 1930s by building larger stores with embellished decoration and more diverse product lines, co-ops worked toward standardization, expansion, and better-looking stores. Visually, cooperatives were coming to resemble the chain and independent supermarkets against which members so often protested.

The similarities that emerged among these stores in the late 1930s went beyond the visual. Co-ops also sometimes shared the chains' impetus toward hierarchical authority structures. The Council for Cooperative Development (CCD) demonstrated the new lessons being taught to cooperators. Funded by department store magnate and social visionary Edward Filene and staffed by regional trade association leaders, the CCD saw its task as "educating" wayward or struggling cooperative societies and speeding up the growth process of co-ops.[108] Its work consisted of encouraging co-ops to emulate private businesses by keeping stores clean and attractive-looking and by consolidating authority.[109] A CCD-sponsored conference on urban co-ops exemplified this emphasis on top-down decision making. The council's report concluded that cooperatives should "work toward greater centralization wherever [centralization] can provide greater efficiency." Small stores, it added, were best run by well-established, older societies rather than via their own self-contained governance structures.[110] The organization began operations in Chicago in 1944,

FIGURE 5.2. *The newly opened Altgeld Gardens store, 1945.*
(U749956ACME | Standard RM | © Bettmann/CORBIS)

and exerted immediate influence over cooperatives in the city. For instance, the CCD was instrumental in developing plans for the Altgeld Gardens Co-op that required the store to diversify and expand as quickly as possible.[111]

The CCD and the impulse toward expansion in consumer cooperation reflected the successes of the cooperative movement as well as divisions within it. Wholesalers' adherence to co-op standards provided real benefits. Indeed, by the early 1940s, local societies benefited by being able to claim that the goods they sold had already been tested and graded by their wholesaler.[112] Moreover, even the sometimes-demanding advisory agencies like CLUSA and the CSCL provided needed services. Many co-ops did fail; others struggled for years, never quite collecting enough capital to achieve real stability, let alone to expand. These co-ops clearly needed advice on how to run a business and how to attract customers. As late as 1937, Chicago co-ops were, according to a Labor Department observer, badly divided.[113] The fact that only a few years later they were supporting several advisory bodies and a wholesaler suggests not only that cooperation was growing but also that co-ops were finding mass retailing useful.

This emphasis on expansion and remodeling, however, meant that co-ops had joined chains and independents in their new focus on trading up—on attracting richer and steadier customers. Centralization and standardization required significant amounts of capital. Even a small remodeling job—for instance, to use the new official colors of cooperatives—could strain a co-op society's resources. Thus, calls to expand product lines and store size depended on sustaining large monthly sales from the very beginning.

As a result, fundraising became a theme of cooperative life. In Chicago and the Midwest, the Central States Cooperative League organized a capital drive and organized the Chicago Co-operative Finance Association.[114] The logic of mass retailing and mass distribution, as cooperators understood it, required this all-out effort to raise enormous sums.

Similar drives happened nationally. The clearest sign of national associations' commitment to expansion and their recognition of the concomitant need for increased capital was the formation of the National Cooperative Finance Association in 1940. Organizers noted that it would help co-ops expand more quickly and "eventually free the movement from private or political financial control."[115]

However, despite the trade associations' efforts to provide central sources of capital, the majority of co-ops' funds came from their members.[116] The amounts raised for expansion were highly contingent on members' own resources. Simultaneous fund drives by the white, middle-class North Shore Co-op; the white, working-class Garfield Park Co-op; and the African American People's Co-op yielded, respectively, $3,000 (plus an additional $1,000 in pledges), $1,500 (and $1,500 in loans), and $150 in new shares.[117]

Unsurprisingly, co-ops in middle-class or upper-class neighborhoods were able to expand more easily than were those in working-class neighborhoods. For prosperous co-ops, money from shares might be coupled with loans from members, and the combined total could meet the costs of expansion. That was the formula used by Consumers' Cooperative Services (later the Hyde Park Cooperative Society) to open its supermarket in 1942. The society was able to raise all of the $15,000 it needed by conducting a drive among its members and by taking a loan out from a neighborhood bank. The average pledge was $200.[118]

For co-ops that were smaller, or those whose membership was working class, expansion represented more serious risks. The Altgeld Gardens Co-op, sustained by lower-middle- and working-class African American members, had only $1,360 of its $3,775 in initial capital from its own members. The balance represented loans from other Chicago co-ops and donations from "sympathetic cooperators" who were not members of the society.[119] The popular support that these co-ops enjoyed could not make up for the limited resources of their members.

Constant admonishments to open supermarket-style stores could lead even very successful cooperatives to expand beyond their means. The People's Co-op, a popular African American Co-op in the city's Black Belt, expanded both its store size and the lines it carried throughout the 1940s. Enthusiasm could hardly make up for the risks that such expansion engendered: "Undaunted by a $10,982 accumulated deficit and a $2,116 loss for 1942–43, members of People's Consumers Cooperative . . . pledged themselves at their membership meeting . . . to snap their co-op out of the red."[120] Put simply, expansion worked best for middle-class cooperatives, just as it worked best for private retailers in middle-class neighborhoods. The new program preached by cooperative leadership required co-ops to find new, and richer, members.

Even financially prosperous co-ops that could afford to make the changes suggested by leadership still faced the threat that too much top-down direction and standardization would undermine the democracy that had attracted so many to cooperation in the first place. A. W. Warriner, a veteran cooperative organizer, pointed out as early as 1934 that citywide organizations were far less successful at building member loyalty than were locally rooted societies. The "independent neighborhood type of organization," he wrote, "encourages the individual member to assume more direct responsibility for the success of the enterprise and gives him also a great opportunity for experience in controlling and directing its affairs."[121] Similarly, the outgoing president of Consumers' Cooperative Services warned "that in becoming too large the Co-op might lose some of its characteristic and essential advantages: the rather close and personal acquaintanceship among members."[122] His warning proved prescient. By the early 1940s, the pages of the co-op's newsletter carried constant admonishments to members to become more active. One typical article, reporting on a recent drive by the co-op's education committee, was titled "CCS Members Are Found to Be Alive after All."[123]

If large co-ops struggled to motivate neighbors, citywide chains of co-ops— the clearest embodiment of mass retailing—found the going even tougher. When the Chicago Consumers' Cooperative, Inc., began operations in 1945, hopes ran high. Selling shares on a citywide basis rather than in neighborhoods where stores would be located, organizers promised a chain of ten cooperative grocery stores.[124] The projected advantages of the plan did not, however, prove themselves in practice. Although the first store in the CCC chain opened to huge fanfare in November 1946, claiming 350 members, it did not live up to expectations. Its capital was $120,750—a significant amount for a small store, but far less than the $350,000 that the organization had hoped to have on hand when it launched the project. By the time the first store began serving customers, CCC was no longer projecting opening dates for other stores. Organizers said only that they hoped to marshal support across the city "before beginning large-scale operations." The chain of stores seems never to have developed.[125]

Attempts to standardize, centralize, and adhere to the aesthetics of modernization within consumers' cooperation in the late 1930s and 1940s accompanied signs that gender relations within cooperatives were also changing. Women's presence on boards of directors declined in several established co-ops over the course of the mid- and late 1940s.[126] Large co-ops that opened toward the end of the war and in the postwar period had few, if any, women board members.[127] Meanwhile, male-dominated staffs on regional associations and in the CCD were gaining in authority throughout this period. In spite of women's importance to the movement, only men spoke at the CCD's conference.[128] Women consumer cooperators were slowly losing their leadership roles, even as they continued to shop at and support the cooperatives. Although new stores never explicitly limited women's authority, expansion into supermarkets meant larger stores, more conservative gender relations, and dependence on wealthy members.

Profound similarities among stores operated by chains, independents, and consumer cooperatives began to outweigh the differences by the late 1930s and early 1940s. Slowly, these firms converged around a set of strategies. All built stores far larger than anyone had imagined only a decade earlier. Many were able to participate in truly mass retailing—selling high volumes of standardized goods in standardized settings. All were committed to a kind of retailing that depended on top-down organization, elaborately outfitted stores, middle-class shoppers, and a claim that these kinds of stores would best appeal to women performing their roles as wives and mothers.

The convergence of different kinds of firms around the same strategy (and the creation of very similar kinds of stores) marked a transformation in mass retailing. It was the feminized luxury, as much as the scale, of the new stores that was remarkable. How and where grocery stores operated had changed dramatically over the previous twenty years, a result of economies of scale and low prices of new supermarkets but also of grocers' desire to find richer customers and to stabilize and then to reify gender relations in their stores.

Winning the Home Front

Gender and Grocery Stores during World War II

Through much of World War II, mass retailers worried that new government directives would upset efforts to bring order to their stores and to food distribution. Indeed, wartime rationing and price control policy not only imposed new constraints on what and how firms could sell; they also gave consumers new authority to police retail spaces. Over the course of the war, however, federal policymakers moved away from democratic methods of regulation that would have delegated authority to shoppers and instead (and in ways that mirrored the government's growing cooperation with large manufacturers) formed alliances with large, centrally managed supermarkets and especially with chain store supermarkets that could ensure their employees' and customers' adherence to government regulations.

This chapter tracks the political economy of consumption that emerged during World War II through a close examination of the everyday workings and practical difficulties of rationing and price controls. These were unavoidably localized programs and by their very nature forced policymakers to delegate important administrative tasks to individual retailers and to their customers. This had unpredictable results, however. The perspectives of everyday participants reveal a complicated story in which women shoppers embraced and encouraged but also resisted and violated rationing and price control policies set by the Office of Price Administration (OPA).

Policymakers came to see both kinds of responses—enthusiastic support for enforcement of OPA directives, as well as willingness to overlook them—as problems. The first raised the specter of politicized housewives, and the other raised concerns that women, by nature of their work as food procurers, were unlikely to be effective watchdogs over stores. Over the course of the war gender ideology as well as women's own behavior created a context in which

OPA officials grew skeptical of democratic controls on consumption and moved toward tighter alliances with large, centrally controlled stores that could better administer government policy. They did so, this chapter argues, not only for the sake of efficiency but also because of their distrust of politically powerful women they consistently referred to as "housewives."

This chapter also raises a broader point: ideas about how to administer the emerging consumer-centered political economy were embedded in retailers' history (and contemporary experience) with difficult, uncontrollable, women consumers. As Alice Kessler-Harris has argued about economic policies such as Social Security and the income tax, decisions about rationing and price control offered instances in which "gendered worldviews" determined which policies appealed to politicians.[1] The story of the OPA illuminates how laws about stores, food, and prices were embedded in the social relations and ideologies of gender.

It also illustrates the ways in which certain kinds of stores became crucial for the state. Organizational sophistication and the ability to impose policies on customers conferred critical advantages on large, centrally managed firms. By the end of World War II, the federal government had openly recognized the benefits of and made accommodation for top-down chain store supermarkets. For instance, they allowed chain grocery firms to apply a single price throughout all their stores. In the chaotic atmosphere of wartime price control, large, centralized mass retailers and government found common ground in the shared project of controlling consumption and in the shared belief that the most important consumers were women.

LONG BEFORE THE JAPANESE ATTACK on Pearl Harbor, American policymakers worried about the domestic effects of World War II, in particular, about the risk of wartime inflation and postwar depression. In part, this reflected past experience: dramatic inflation and deflation had marked U.S. participation in previous wars. As Meg Jacobs has argued, this commitment to anti-inflation programs also grew out of New Dealers' commitments to widespread consumption and their willingness to devolve political authority on consumers.[2]

Whatever the government's motivations, it became clear that stores would be vital to the success of these new programs. Anti-inflation policy and consumer politics ultimately mattered only to the extent they shaped the actions of grocers. In the everyday interactions in the commercial spaces of stores the line against prices would be held, or it would dissolve. It was there that civilian Americans would most immediately experience the wartime state and there that the New Deal legacy of politicized consumerism might most directly affect the everyday operations of businesses. To understand the meaning of wartime anti-inflation policies, one must also understand what those policies asked of stores and of the consumers who used them.

This is a difficult task. Rationing and price control were huge, unwieldy programs. Their requirements changed constantly, and both grocers and customers were often hard-pressed to know what sorts of responsibilities they had. In theory, consumers had significant power over stores, but in practice their ability to report violations and to enforce punishments was limited. Federal policymakers consistently stated that women stood at the center of their efforts, but they also expressed strong concerns over women's actual ability to assist in wartime food programs.

The federal government began fighting the problems of wartime inflation and scarcity in 1940 (much earlier than it began openly fighting the threat of fascism and Nazism) with establishment of the National Defense Advisory Commission. On the eve of America's entry into the war, Roosevelt expanded his administration's anti-inflation efforts and introduced rationing of goods made with rubber—especially car tires. Food rationing and price controls became the two mainstays of government efforts, and both grew quickly in the early days of World War II. In December 1941, the government announced plans for sugar rationing.[3] Volunteers, already responsible for overseeing the tire program, were quickly organized into local rationing boards. By April 1942, price control had come to the grocery store. The General Maximum Price Regulation (GMPR) required all grocers to freeze their prices at what they had been in March 1942.[4] Seven months later, 93 percent of all retail foodstuffs were covered by price controls.[5] "Dollars-and-cents" ceilings, used with increasing frequency over the course of the war, replaced the cumbersome equations and the expectation that grocers figure their own prices. This policy further expanded the purview of local boards. Board volunteers were charged with the tremendous tasks of distributing and explaining new procedures, as well as ensuring their efficacy by taking complaints from local residents and retailers.[6]

Price control and rationing during World War II constituted the largest effort ever put forth by the federal government to regulate retail transactions. The programs were massive. Sugar rationing alone required registering every individual in the United States, as well as five hundred thousand retailers and five hundred thousand institutional and industrial users (for example, firms that manufactured or processed sweets).[7] Price control officials went to extraordinary lengths to build popular support, organizing outreach campaigns to a broad spectrum of Americans. At the height of these programs, the city of Chicago alone had 167 local price and rationing boards staffed by thousands of volunteers, who in turn worked to mobilize their neighbors.[8] From rural African American sharecroppers to large national firms operating massive chains of stores, few individuals or institutions went unnoticed by the federal government.

Women's Importance to the Office of Price Administration

The Office of Price Administration immediately saw women as especially important to the success of price control and rationing. Although both men and women shopped, price and rationing administrators put particular effort into campaigns directed at women. Promotional literature was often geared toward women's groups, and the office made special efforts to recruit women volunteers. Women, too, were to be drafted into national service.

Policymakers' desire to draw women into their price control efforts drew on the popular identification of consumption—especially food buying—as women's responsibility. Both administrators and scientists subscribed to the widespread belief that women were the people who brought food into homes and prepared it; therefore, women were the people who were most important to the success of domestic food rationing and price control. In doing so, they relied not only on their own predilections but also on polling conducted by the Committee on Food Habits (CFH), an arm of the National Academy of Sciences. The CFH survey found outright antipathy toward the idea of including men in wartime nutrition campaigns. Researchers urged the government to focus its efforts around women.[9]

OPA officials were only too willing to comply with what they, too, perceived to be prevailing gender norms. Officials regularly used the feminine pronoun in official documents. In 1944, when these officials felt pressured to include consumers in the decision-making process, they set up a committee made up of representatives of women's groups.[10] The OPA so conflated the categories of "women" and "consumer" that, according to historian and OPA administrator Caroline Ware, the idea permeated the agency's very structure. When a consumer division was created in the National Defense Advisory Commission, it became a de facto home for women's activities despite the objections of its chief, Harriet Elliott: "Because the Consumer Commissioner was a woman, and no other special provision had been made for considering the role of women in the defense program, the Consumer Division was continually being called upon to advise on something involving women, or to represent women's interests. The Consumer Commissioner made it very clear that she was responsible for the consumer function, not for women, but the calls continued to come, e.g. the question of participation of women in war industry training, and the inclusion of other functions than strictly 'war work' in the training."[11] As Elliott discovered, the very term "consumer" carried heavy gendered connotations.

The substitution of "women" for "consumers" carried over to OPA propaganda and volunteer efforts. Women's groups were expected to furnish the bulk of the volunteers needed to check prices in stores and to enthusiastically support price control and rationing in their own homes—on top of their paid war work. Officials often pressured local boards to recruit more women volunteers and included copies of the "Home Front Pledge," a promise to observe government rationing and price control, in mailings to women's organizations.[12] (Takers of the oath received a badge that pictured a well-coiffed woman solemnly raising her hand.)[13] Virtually every piece of price control and rationing propaganda was directed at women.[14] Most important, as this chapter will demonstrate, the OPA focused its efforts on mobilizing and controlling women's shopping. For the OPA, "consumer" meant "woman."

This conflation of categories might well have led to an expansion of women's political authority.[15] Just as women clearly had become important to federal policy, so too could they demand more power over the system that created and enforced that policy—and certainly they could now more easily disrupt federal plans. Policymakers knew all too well that putting women at the center of wartime food-related policies would mean officially extending women's influence beyond their homes, to government and to businesses, as had happened during previous wars. What this new political influence would mean proved to be among the most difficult issues faced by the OPA.

The Mechanics of Price Control and Rationing: New Questions for Grocers

The federal government wanted to ensure an equitable distribution of goods and to prevent inflationary booms, even as supplies were diverted for the armed forces. That meant that officials had to reshape how grocers ordered, priced, and sold merchandise and that the government would need to have a hand in virtually all aspects of food distribution, from harvest to home. Price control and rationing challenged the resolve of all parties and raised the possibilities for dramatic changes of all kinds.

The complexity and scope of regulations is especially clear in the government's rationing program. Under this program, heads of household were issued ration coupons that entitled them to buy any number of rationed goods (tires, shoes, sugar, canned goods, and meat, to name a few). The number of ration coupons issued (and hence the amount of rationed goods that could be purchased) was determined by the number and age of people in their families. Thus, families with many young children were entitled to buy more meat than families with few or no young children. But the federal government also wanted to be able to change quickly the amount of goods on the market. To do so, program administrators would have to be able to restrict consumer access to rationed goods—to abruptly lower the amount to which a family was entitled. The solution was to assign each ration coupon and each rationed commodity a point value. Thus, ration coupons acted like a kind of parallel currency in which point values were prices. The government simply controlled how many points a basic commodity "cost." To make the matter more complicated, and to give the government more control, each coupon was colored (for example, red for meat, blue for canned goods). The government could very quickly control consumer demand simply by announcing that all coupons of a certain color were invalid and that shoppers would have to use a new set of coupons.

The system of rationing made life complicated for grocers as well as consumers. Grocers were responsible for collecting ration coupons from their customers and turning them over to government officials or wholesalers. The simple act of selling sugar required retailers (1) to have enough ration points on hand to entitle them to order more sugar from a supplier, (2) to know how many ration points a customer needed in order to buy sugar, and (3) to know which color of ration coupons were valid that particular week.[16] The government also set price ceilings on many foods throughout the war, so grocers also had to know the allowable price for that weight and grade of sugar.

As if to makes things worse, the Office of Price Administration often changed its policies and procedures. Because Congress generally authorized the agency for only a year at a time and because both representatives and senators frequently criticized its administrators on a range of issues—from being too hard on business to being too easy and failing to control prices—the OPA had to justify its activities and administer policies in such a way as to win the support of key lawmakers.[17] Decisions to bring new foods under price control or to allow employers of migrant workers in Texas to distribute ration coupons or to revise the procedures that smaller stores had to follow were as much about political expediency as about achieving the agency's ultimate goals.

Subsidies to manufacturers and processors are a prime example of the changing nature and political vulnerability of the OPA. Subsidies were not wholly a result of political pressure. They were part of the government's plan to focus on certain key nodes of production and to hold down prices at those points by subsidizing firms whose efforts were needed for the war but that could not survive on the low prices that they were officially allowed to charge. Subsidies were intended to prevent rising production costs from pushing up retail prices. But they became a much-sought-after reward from politicians and a regular bone of contention with retailers, who were ineligible for subsidies and who could not pass their rising costs on to customers. Producer subsidies contributed to a system that many retailers felt was especially unfair to them. Grocers in Chicago and elsewhere regularly complained that they were bearing the brunt of price control.[18]

Aside from subsidies, there is little question that OPA policies posed challenges to retailers. For instance, rapid changes in OPA policy further complicated what was already a complex set of regulations. Not only did the allowable prices of goods rise and fall; the procedures by which stores figured their allowable prices also changed. At various times during the war, price was determined by the store's status as chain or independent, by its sales for the previous year, by what it had charged for the product before price control went into effect, and by a list of maximum prices formulated by OPA administrators.[19] After numerous experiments with voluntary price schedules (for wholesalers and producers only) and mandatory price ceilings (under which grocers had to determine their own prices and allowable profit margins based on a complicated formula), in April 1943 the federal government finally settled on a combination of community dollars-and-cents lists with prices and profit margins set by regional field offices.[20]

Each new price control procedure brought new sets of forms, new record-keeping requirements, and new restrictions on grocers' activities. For instance, the General Maximum Price Regulation issued in late April 1942 required grocers to calculate their own ceiling prices based on what they had charged for the same items in March 1942, just before price controls went into effect. This procedure worked, however, only if retailers had kept records of their prices from that period and if they still carried exactly the same items they had stocked during the baseline period. When new products were carried for the first time, retailers had to use the prices of "similar" items. If the second method failed and nothing similar had been carried previously, they were to use the prices charged by their competitors for similar items. Finally, if an item was totally new (as was not uncommon under the frequent shortages and substitutions of wartime), retailers were to add the highest percentage markup that they had used in March 1942 for that line of goods to the cost of the new item. Only then would they be able to determine the item's final price.[21] Specific Maximum Price Regulations added to the complications by establishing ceilings and flat prices that were particular to certain products.[22] Once a price was calculated, grocers were still not done. Individual items were frequently taken off the list of regulated commodities only to return to it later, so grocers had to watch for changes in policy or risk penalties.[23] One report on the effects of price control on Chicago- and Detroit-area retailers summarized the situation neatly: the general feeling of both retailers and local officials was that "the whole procedure of price control is too complicated."[24]

"It was an awful hardship on a lot of people": Women and Shopping during World War II

Shoppers might have said the same thing, too. Wartime rationing and price control increased women's household responsibilities at precisely the moment when many of them had less time for such work. While much of the literature on women during World War II emphasizes their participation in the paid workforce, women's unpaid work also changed, often becoming more difficult in light of wartime exigencies. The work of observing and enforcing price control and rationing is an often unappreciated aspect to women's home front service.[25]

For some women, entry into the industrial workforce meant less housework, as some tasks were taken over by other family members and others (long days of baking, for instance) were eliminated in favor of paid work. Nonetheless, most American women seem to have maintained their responsibilities at home during the war. In this time of very limited organized feminism, few Americans called for men to take over women's work at home. Indeed, the bulk of wartime advice literature encouraged women to continue their household labors, even as it acknowledged the ways in which the war had complicated cooking, cleaning, running errands, rearing children, and maintaining a household. Women frequently recall both the excitement and the challenges of working outside their homes. Emily Gotzion, a war worker, mother, and wife who had as many as nine people at a time living in her small home, remembered simply, "It was an awful hardship on a lot of people."[26]

Time constraints and the hurried pace of life were among the most common problems facing women during the war. Paid work certainly provided increased incomes to many families, but because women still were expected to perform or at least supervise the bulk of the housework, it also created enormous problems of time management. The pages of women's magazines were

FIGURE 6.1. *Woman buying groceries during World War II. Note the ration stamps in the center of the image. This is a stark contrast to the image projected by the government (see figure 6.2).* (*BE035192* | *Standard RM* | © *Bettmann/CORBIS*)

filled with advice about how to balance the new double shift of home and work life. One article, certainly less than comforting, encouraged women to accept their husbands' offers to help with the breakfast dishes. "Then you'll have more time for tidying the house," the author explained.[27] Other articles encouraged women to rely on new gadgets like pressure cookers, to speed preparation times;[28] to prepare foods before leaving for work; and to cook them upon their return.[29] Even this advice was not enough. Turnover and absenteeism among employed women was notoriously high—particularly so among women who worked the day shift or who needed time to carry out the shopping, childcare, and meal preparation that households required.[30]

The work of food procurement was, I want to emphasize, done in addition to the other pressures of day-to-day life in a very dangerous time. Women who

FIGURE 6.2.
*The Home Front
Pledge. This image of
dedicated, calm, and
rule-abiding women
shoppers was
distributed widely
during World War II.*

labored on the home front were not unconcerned with happenings on the actual front. Both letters written at the time and women's own memories of the war suggest that women tracked the battles with great assiduousness. Red pins that marked possible locations of husbands, brothers, fathers, or boyfriends; fears of German sabotage or of an invasion along a coast; blackout curtains; and the sound of radio broadcasters anxiously updating Americans on the status of a particular battle—all of these made up the texture of American life during the war. Women on the home front were in no way immune to wartime fears. Ella Meiselwitz, a middle-class young woman from small-town northern Wisconsin, remembered proudly her service at a local draft board during the war. But she also remembered terrible anxiety about the fate of her two brothers and the loss that she felt when her husband was drafted in the first five months of their marriage: "We were married for five months and we're so happy and then all of a sudden he's gone. It's almost like death. I would reach for him like that at night and he wasn't there."[31] Countless women were in Meiselwitz's situation, balancing their new responsibilities with aching concern for the outcome of the war.

New time constraints and demands loomed during the war. Volunteers were more in demand than ever, and USOs, the Red Cross, the Office of Price Administration, and the Office of Civilian Defense joined the usual number of organizations that depended on women's volunteer labor. Simply carrying out traditional household tasks took longer during the war. Procuring food was especially time consuming in an era of shortages, since grocers and customers had to tally ration points as well as cash. For all the emphasis on efficiency and planning ahead, there was no denying that it simply took longer to cook the tougher cuts of beef that were often all that was available or to prepare the beans that had become a major source of protein. Women also were asked to salvage fats and to turn them in to their butchers. Cultivating Victory Gardens and canning and preserving produce were other wartime duties that added to household labors.[32]

At the same time that they were made more challenging, cooking and provisioning achieved new discursive and physical importance. At the beginning of the war, draft officials found that many recruits were simply too weak to perform adequately. This was disturbing enough in the military context, but home front production work was also physically demanding. Thus, national propaganda—and, no doubt, hungry war workers themselves—vociferously reminded the family cook to produce plentiful, protein-rich, filling, and nutritionally balanced meals. The government produced an eight-category (later reduced to seven) food chart that included green and yellow vegetables, citrus fruits, potatoes, milk, protein, carbohydrates, and fats. Officials urged women to keep the chart close at hand and to be sure that family meals did not overemphasize or skimp on foods from any one category.[33] In addition to this instrumentalist emphasis on nutrition for the war effort, women faced new pressures simply to preserve the home as both a haven for the present and a goal for soldiers fighting for the future. One article cheered, "Bank high the greens on the mantel . . . . Hang wreaths in the windows. Trim the tree. Keep alive, this year of all years, the old traditions of Christmas, against the day when 'peace on earth, good will to all mankind' will ring true again."[34] As Maureen Honey has skillfully documented, fiction designed to recruit women war workers emphasized that "war workers were homemakers at heart."[35]

Nowhere did wartime tensions become more visible than in grocery stores, where shopping was both increasingly difficult and increasingly important. A few glimpses of everyday shopping in Chicago make this clear.

In the opening days of the war, shortages brought about dramatic encounters in grocery stores. Limited supplies of coffee, for example, sparked physical aggressiveness. Women shoppers "remembered scuffles they did not mean to get into," and store managers claimed that anxious shoppers mobbed clerks as they tried to stock the shelves.[36] Shortages of paper discouraged the use of shopping bags and the wrapping of store-bought goods. Government conservation directives asked women to bring their own bags with them or to carry packaged goods home unwrapped. (They did not specify how such goods should be kept clean.)[37]

One of the most common themes from this period was the crowded intensity of stores. Not only were clerks in short supply, but checking out also took longer because cashiers had to tally ration point values as well as dollar amounts of purchases. War work made this congestion even worse. Women who held down paid employment had limited control over when they shopped, and so Saturday afternoons, always the busiest times, became even more crowded.[38]

In this context, usual concerns with grocers' stock and service became nearly insurmountable. One woman cheerily recounted rushing out of the house at nine o'clock in the morning and traveling to three different stores in search of butter, soap, and meat. When she was unable to find quality beef for the amount of ration points that she had, she went to a fourth store, seeking a chicken. There, the butcher charged her for a four-pound chicken, even though the bird weighed only three and a half pounds. She acknowledged, "I know I should have refused the chicken. But after two hours of waiting in lines and shopping, I just couldn't go thru another line."[39]

Shortages at stores, limited ration points, and sheer exhaustion pushed many people to violate government guidelines. For some, this involved actions that were clearly illegal. Chicago was purported to have some of the most active black markets in the country, and local retailers were important nodes in the chain of under-the-counter purchases.[40] Observers at the time recounted stories of men being sent to buy meat at taverns and of wives of police officers using their status to get butchers to provide cuts of meat that were in short supply.[41] Sometimes butchers would sell or submit counterfeit ration coupons.[42] Other violations occurred on a smaller scale, embedded in networks of borrowing and lending that had long been part of neighborhood life. Many women's memories of the war include such minor violations as trading ration stamps with neighbors. A columnist in the *Chicago Tribune* offered one of the few open acknowledgments of such practices when she urged women not to participate in "bootlegging rationed things."[43]

That people occasionally "bootlegged" should not, however, suggest that women as a group resisted rationing or price control. In spite of the extra work that they engendered, most people seem to have abided by regulations, most of the time. Respondents to national polls expressed strong support for price controls.[44] Many, especially working-class whites and African Americans, welcomed the move to rationing goods, since this assured them of at least *some* supplies. On the eve of coffee rationing, one woman plaintively wrote, "I wish the government would hurry and ration coffee. At least in this way we can be sure of a certain amount each week instead of having to go from store to store without getting any."[45] In her appreciation for the benefits of rationing and price control, this woman was not alone.

Most women, including those who remembered skirting the law, simply did what they had long done—relied on themselves and their marketing savvy to obtain food to keep themselves and their households going. Standing in long lines, keeping up with changing values of ration points, learning how to cook unfamiliar cuts of beef or chicken, and strategizing how to go without or to save up customary amounts of sugar—all of this added to the work of wartime shopping. Women learned to rely on grocers even if they also doubted their motives. One woman, explaining why she did not bother to check ration point values herself, explained that she simply did not see the point: "I buy what I can get, pay what they tell me, and that's about all anybody can do."[46] Wartime rationing and price control reinforced the work of shopping and the importance of personal ties to retailers.

Grassroots Enforcement and Its Discontents

During the war, however, the government depended on women to do precisely what this woman admitted that she could not—to force grocers to adhere to price controls and ration point values; to resist the demands of budgets, families, culinary traditions, and plain hunger; and then to turn in grocers who violated the regulations.

The Office of Price Administration could not hope to employ enough paid staff to police all the retailers in the country. Therefore, it tried to mobilize volunteers to verify stores' compliance in periodic preplanned price checks and encouraged all citizens to report violations that they noticed in the course of their shopping. Complaints went first to local price panels or rationing boards, which called in the accused retailers for a hearing. The panel or board then determined innocence or guilt and meted out punishments. These local enforcement bodies were made up of private citizens; paid staff (generally female) provided secretarial assistance. The OPA made concerted efforts to involve all important constituencies in a neighborhood—business, organized labor, "housewives" (presumably not working full time), and, especially important in Chicago, African Americans and first- or second-generation European Americans. Although boards were made up of both men and women, price panel assistants—those responsible for doing much of the actual price checking in stores—were overwhelmingly female.[47] Thus, the enforcement procedure relied heavily on women.

This enforcement system was unprecedented in the annals of the federal government—very different from earlier efforts to enlist women in food conservation during World War I via propaganda and semi-organized meatless days.[48] New programs threatened the always unstable dynamic between grocers and their customers. The power of women consumers over the stores in which they shopped was no longer potential, but real and a matter of government policy.

Like price control procedures, however, federal policy toward price panels and volunteer price checkers was constantly changing. Neither grocers nor OPA volunteers were ever confident of the amount of power they had. On the one hand, the panels seemed to be granted far-reaching and important powers. They could take complaints, hear cases, even assess penalties and pass on recalcitrant violators to the district enforcement office. On the other hand, policymakers often assured retailers that angry women customers were not about to take over their stores. Both in rhetoric and in policy, they constrained would-be complainants. The press release accompanying the issuance of the general price controls in the spring of 1942, for example, urged women to refrain from letting themselves become "a Price Policeman."[49]

Even if officials had not been ambivalent about delegating authority, it would have been difficult for customers to report violations. In a context of unsteady supplies, friendly relations with neighborhood grocers were often the only way to assure access to needed goods.

There is much evidence of the importance of personal relations in negotiating price control. Chicago grocers openly acknowledged holding goods in the back for valued customers.[50] Shoppers, meanwhile, found themselves buying more from grocers who might then favor them with sugar, butter, soap, or other difficult-to-come-by goods.[51] One woman's experience stresses the ways in which these relationships were worked out informally: "After trudging from store to store, she finally tried a small place. To make a good impression, she bought several groceries and asked about coffee. The store manager told her he was sorry, but he had no coffee: 'How long since you were in here last?' he asked. 'Two weeks,' the woman bravely admitted. The storekeeper went into the back room, came back and slipped a pound of coffee into her sack of supplies. 'You come in more often after this,' he suggested, 'and everything will be all right.' "[52] In countless situations like these, loyalty to neighborhood grocers loomed large in women's ability to procure needed items.

Reporting grocers, then, carried a high cost. Helen Badal, a Chicago housewife, was so fearful of repercussions that she refused to face the neighborhood grocer whom she had accused. She even requested extra assurances from the board that her name would not be revealed. Apparently her fears were well-founded. When the board was forced to reverse its guilty verdict, the grocer expressed his deep anger at someone with the gall to report him: "I have no objections until you run across some housewife like this. I would like to meet this woman and talk to her."[53]

The grocer whom Badal had offended was not alone in his resentment and anger. An operator of a supermarket in Syracuse, New York, voiced the feelings of many when he wrote, "The specter that haunts the store manager today is the dissatisfied, disgruntled customer. No matter how cooperative the housewives of the nation may be, or how understanding of the war effort, the store manager knows that they resent the merchandise shortages that make their selection of menus more difficult; the red tape of rationing and tokens; the absence of alert and willing sales people and the mistakes that are continually made as the result of inexperience."[54]

Undergirding the resentment and tensions described by these grocers was the long tradition of complex, sometimes rewarding and sometimes frustrating relationships sustained by neighborhood stores. In many ways, the resentment of Badal's grocer and the Syracuse supermarket operator's fear of alienating his customers were not new to food shopping. What *was* new was that the intense and precarious relations between grocers and their customers were suddenly the subject of federal policy.

The Problem of Small Stores

As one might imagine, the challenge posed by personalized commerce was most visible in small stores. The federal government did little to hide the fact that small, independent stores were less helpful in the war on prices than were larger stores. Indeed, the difference between these stores was written into law in June 1943, when the government decreed that stores' price ceilings would be determined by their sales and by their membership (or lack thereof) in a chain. Stores with less than $50,000 in annual sales that were not part of a chain were expected to have the highest margins and so could charge the highest prices. Chains and supermarkets were assumed to have the smallest margins and so had lower ceiling prices.[55] Small independents complained vociferously, but to no avail, that their price disadvantage was now being advertised for all to see. The federal government had officially recognized mass retailers' lower prices.

Higher price ceilings—seen by policymakers as an accommodation to small stores—do not seem to have helped these retailers avoid violations. Small grocers repeatedly proved themselves to be less-than-reliable enforcers of government policy. In virtually every price check that distinguished among types of stores, those with the lowest sales were also the most common violators. Particularly detailed records exist for Chicago's African American neighborhoods. A price check in 1943 found that 31.2 percent of all class 1 stores (independents with under $50,000 in sales) were selling dry groceries above ceiling prices, while only 5.7 percent of all class 2 stores (independents with between $50,000 and $250,000) were doing so.[56] Similar, though less precise, data emerge from price checks done in the winter of 1945 for African American neighborhoods. In February of that year, price checkers found that 48 percent of stores in classes 1 and 2 (smaller independents) were in violation, compared to just 18 percent of stores in classes 3 and 4 (large independents and chains).[57]

The difficulties of small independent grocers arose from a number of causes—some structural and some cultural. Each of these causes made small groceries far less amenable than larger stores to top-down regulation.

Small independent grocers complained constantly that wholesalers abused them by artificially inflating the cost of goods, forcing grocers to charge consumers higher prices. For instance, grocers commonly accused their suppliers of forcing them to buy nonrationed goods that were in high supply in order to buy rationed ones.[58] Such "tying" agreements effectively increased grocers' costs on the rationed goods because they often could not sell the less-desirable products. Grocers wanting carrots from produce vendors, for instance, might be told that they would also have to buy cabbage. Wholesalers were often accused of changing the grade or packaging of a given item, so that grocers had to pay more per item than had been the case before the war.[59] Sometimes wholesalers were accused of actions that were clearly illegal—buying goods back and forth from each other in order to inflate the base cost and establish a high ceiling price,[60] charging above-ceiling prices for goods, and demanding "side payments" for items in especially short supply.[61]

Small grocers' difficulties with wholesalers were common across the Chicago area, regardless of neighborhood. Kosher poultry markets regularly reported that their suppliers charged above-ceiling prices and required additional payments off the books—charges supported by the findings of district investigators.[62] Numerous Chicago-area grocers, called before their local boards to explain over-ceiling prices, said simply that a representative from their wholesaler had come in and told them what the item cost and what to charge for it without ever referring to price ceilings.[63] Even grocers serving the predominately upper-middle-class, native-born population of Evanston expressed these frustrations. An OPA official explained, "They . . . frankly admit they are powerless in the hands of the wholesalers. They state they can only write out the orders for what they need without mentioning prices, and permit the wholesaler to fill in the price and if any questions arise the wholesaler simply tells them that they can look elsewhere."[64]

Proprietors of small stores also seem to have had particular difficulty in coping with the careful accounting demanded by war regulations, problems similar to those first experienced in the 1930s, when state governments had begun demanding more careful record keeping in relief and sales tax programs. During World War II, many grocers furnished the sorts of records demanded by federal officials reluctantly, if at all. One 1945 survey of seventy-seven independent grocers in Chicago was cut short when data proved nearly impossible to come by. Ten grocers refused to answer the questionnaire, and another ten maintained no records and therefore could not furnish the required information. Finally, nine grocers turned in forms that were so incomplete as to be unusable to analysts.[65]

Often, neighborhood grocers could not provide exasperated price panels with even the most basic information about pricing policies in their stores and so could not justify over-ceiling prices or suspicious transactions. Angelo Morreale, for instance, seemed to have taken a smaller profit than he could have, but he could not defend himself from a consumer's accusation of overcharging because he had lost his invoices for the month in question. Helen Fukuda, wife of a partner in the York Grocery Store, also could not locate the invoices used to figure prices. The store was eventually fined. Kay Spada, accused of selling above ceiling prices in a June price check, offered only that she was "no good at figures."[66]

Small grocers' difficulties with record keeping were symptomatic of a profound lack of fit with enforcement procedures in general. Small grocers had difficulty leaving their stores to attend hearings at local price and rationing panels.[67] They did not always list their prices precisely, but often produced a range—an indication that they did actually have fixed prices, but allowed customers to negotiate.[68] Voluntary chains, in which independents paid monthly membership fees that figured heavily into their costs, made it difficult for the OPA to categorize these stores and complicated the job of determining a retailer's cost per item.[69] The sheer number of stores made it difficult for government officials to ensure that each proprietor received the necessary forms and regulations.[70] If these problems were frustrating for officials, they were no less so for grocers. J. Frank Grimes, president of the voluntary chain Independent Grocers Alliance (IGA), spoke for many grocers when he told a congressional committee that "many of the restrictions are unnecessary, that many of the regulations under which he [the grocer] is obliged to live are bungling and unintelligible and impossible to comply with."[71]

"But I have nice people": Social Ties in Small Independent Stores

Social ties to customers and among employees also made independents far more likely to violate wartime regulations. Both grocers and customers could— and often did—undermine price control and rationing in small-scale, everyday interactions. Here, the gender politics of the prewar era came to pose a clear political problem for the state. Women who knew their grocers were more likely to bargain with them and, hence, more likely to wrest exceptions from them. In this way, small neighborhood stores came to be understood, with some reason, as bastions of the black market.

At their least threatening, grocers might simply undermine rationing by saving rationed goods for their best customers. This practice increased general resentment of rationing and price control and prevented an equitable distribution of goods—and was nearly unstoppable.[72] In a letter responding to one such complaint, district OPA officials noted, "Unfortunately . . . rationing regulations do not compel the grocer to sell his sugar to a particular person if he does not wish to sell to that person."[73] Another grocer unintentionally alluded to this practice when defending himself from charges that he had sold a woman butter under the table: "Even my best customers never got a half-pound [of butter] during the shortage, and I certainly would not sell it to a stranger."[74]

At other times, however, grocers provided rationed goods to people who were not legally entitled to them. Sometimes the motivation was sheer sympathy. The owner of one neighborhood Polish grocery remembered that "sometimes the people, they beg for quarter pound of butter or something, they got the kids . . . the babies, they like something . . . so there was hard [sic]. . . . Sometime, you know, I give them, a little something, so I was short on stamps, and I says to the guy [presumably an OPA official] but I have nice people."[75]

More materially motivated employees of the Lincoln-Lawrence Food Mart openly sold rationed goods to customers for higher-than-ceiling prices. In the course of the investigation, the employees claimed that the idea had started with the manager himself, who told one (female) clerk "to get a higher than ceiling price for butter she sells point-free."[76]

Consumers also realized that reporting grocers would hurt their chances of receiving extra portions of rationed goods and might involve confessing their own participation in black market transactions. The problem of consumer compliance was especially acute with regard to meat because it was rationed for so long and was in such high demand.[77] The Consumer Advisory Committee of the Chicago Metropolitan Area OPA concluded that retailers' violations could be explained by consumers' demand for their product: "It was the conclusion of the members of the staff that consumers no less than retailers are responsible for the wholesale breach of retail price ceilings on meat. If consumers are willing to pay a premium to get meat, the retailers can scarcely resist temptation to slap on a markup that will in part compensate him for his reduced sales volume."[78] One report described the difficulty of getting statements from people who had participated in illegal transactions: "Sales are seldom made to people who are not well known to the dealers and of course these people are very hesitant about making statements either incriminating themselves or the dealer."[79]

As these stories demonstrate, personal relationships with grocers stood in the way of equitable distribution of scarce commodities and threatened crucial anti-inflation measures. The problem, as policymakers and most retailers understood it, was not simply wartime hardship but shoppers' natural loyalties to the grocers who helped them. As articulated in OPA documents, female consumers simply could not be trusted to put politics above immediate needs. Mobilizing women as consumers was a problematic issue, one in which gender ideologies and consumers' ties to local grocers combined to undermine the possibilities for a more decentralized administration of policy.

Consumer Cooperatives and Organized Consumers' Political Power

The conventional neighborhood store proved to be an unlikely site for the sort of careful financial and political accounting required by government policy. But it was certainly not the only type of grocery store operating during World War II. Large centrally managed chain stores and smaller democratically operated consumer cooperatives were also important presences on the retailing landscape.

Indeed, many Americans expected that World War II would bring about new political support for the latter. Consumer cooperatives had access to active and politically aware customers who could be convinced to buy or to boycott based on political sympathies (in this case, on their support for the war effort). If consumers were bullied by their grocers or were uncomfortable with the notion of putting political goals above personal ones, then the kind of democratic control and politically minded shopping facilitated by co-ops seemed a likely solution.

In the ongoing competition among chains, smaller independents, and consumer cooperatives, co-ops seemed poised to gain crucial advantages in the period of wartime mobilization. Leon Henderson, the first head of the OPA, was a confirmed New Dealer and strong proponent of a consumer-centered economic policy.[80] The Office of Price Administration had a decentralized structure and an explicit mission to draw consumers into the war effort.[81] It needed politically minded consumers who would turn a critical eye toward the stores in which they shopped. In this context, co-ops provided the federal government with more than access to a pool of volunteers. Consumer cooperatives seemed to exemplify the consumer-regulated economy that the OPA was fostering.

In this remarkably fluid moment in the politics of food retailing, cooperatives and government officials found common ground. Local OPA administrators spoke openly about their respect for consumer cooperatives. Whereas the Washington office was guarded in its support for co-ops, district and regional offices publicly courted influential cooperators. For example, price control administrators used co-ops' mailing lists to send out their own requests for volunteer price checkers.[82] Members of the OPA Chicago district office spoke at meetings of individual societies and of regional associations, reporting enthusiastically about their efforts.[83] Representatives of the national and local offices of the Consumer Division cultivated close relationships with local co-op leaders.[84] Finally, OPA offices often openly asked leading cooperators to join district and regional boards that advised on and designed local price control and rationing programs.[85]

Chicago's cooperators welcomed the opportunities presented to them by federal representatives and celebrated the fact that consumer cooperation had gone from facing accusations of being un-American to being perceived as something positively patriotic.[86] Co-ops were quick to see the possibilities for extending both their own influence and that of consumers. The Cooperative League of the USA urged members of cooperatives to join in all local OPA activities, even if the local community price control and rationing boards were suspicious of cooperators.[87] African American cooperators were especially enthusiastic about the promise of real leverage over the stores in which they shopped and about government efforts to ensure that retailers in their neighborhoods abided by the laws.

Records of the Hyde Park Cooperative Society suggest some of the ways in which cooperators could mobilize around the OPA and its mission. The co-op's weekly newsletter, the *Evergreen*, had a bevy of notices about ways to make do without buying under-the-table goods, and it regularly urged members to write to their congressional representatives to support the OPA and encouraged women members to take the Housewives' Pledge. The HPCS's butcher taught other co-op stores how to cut meat in line with OPA regulations. Finally, in February 1943, the cooperative formed an all-female Public Affairs Committee to investigate "legislation of interest to the consumer and report on it to the membership." This sort of sustained effort was typical; members of all co-ops volunteered for service with the OPA, distributed information on rationing and price controls, and hosted community meetings with government officials, all the while being urged by central headquarters to do even more to promote themselves.[88]

In spite of this activity, co-ops ultimately failed to win new political authority. To understand why, we must look beyond co-ops' adherence to OPA regulations (which was impressive) and toward the growing distrust among policymakers of mobilized female consumers. The stories of cooperatives and the issue of women's control are part of a larger story of policymakers' ambivalence toward political power for women.

Although some OPA staff members saw empowered consumers as critical to enforcement of price control and rationing, others were vocal critics of price panels. For instance, members of the Chicago district office regularly discussed feelings that "[the] Volunteer Price Panel assistant program was 'unworkable' in Chicago."[89] So deep was the distrust that the Chicago district enforcement office—responsible for collecting the fines and penalties from recalcitrant retailers—renegotiated the settlements reached by local price panels.[90] The suspicion voiced by enforcement office staff was returned by local boards, which occasionally accused the district of favoring chain stores and of discounting local boards' findings of violations at chains.[91] Perhaps not surprisingly, the Chicago office had an extraordinarily difficult time recruiting price panel volunteers and performing routine checks of grocery stores.[92]

Although both men and women served on price panels, OPA officials' suspicions and doubts nearly always centered on women. Just before the first national sweep of stores to check for price violations, the economist and OPA administrator John Kenneth Galbraith publicly promised retailers that "no Gestapo of volunteer housewives" would sweep down upon their stores.[93]

When price controls were first introduced, women were urged to refrain from being "price policemen" and "to use methods of persuasion" rather than refer violators to district OPA offices.[94] Even when officials had the opposite concern—that price checkers would not be assertive enough—they still thought of the problem as a peculiarly feminine one. The regional enforcement attorney for the upper Midwest candidly wrote that he doubted that the OPA would ever overcome "the normal timidity of the average volunteer whose only contact with the retail store is as a customer."[95] Whether administrators thought of women as overly assertive or easily intimidated, they saw them as a weak link in their efforts to curb inflation.

OPA administrators were not speaking simply from an irrational dislike of women. Their concerns were shaped by the same understandings that had made them focus on women in the first place: the responsibilities that most women had as procurers and preparers of their families' food. Officials understood these pressures all too well. Many believed that the demands of husbands and children, coupled with women's own preferences, would make black market purchases of coveted goods almost inevitable. OPA administrators' sense of gender practice, as well as their adherence to more inchoate gender ideologies that posited women as essentially weak-willed, shaped their concerns about conferring authority on women.

This profound distrust of women as political actors was reflected in policies that undermined consumers' autonomy and bottom-up organizing. At the national level, the government was unwilling to involve consumers in policy-making decisions, in part because it meant giving women political and economic authority. For instance, plans to establish Consumer Advisory Committees were slowed by administrators' unwillingness to talk with women. The director of field operations for the OPA's Information Division explained in an internal memo, "We are very fortunate in OPA that Chester Bowles [then the head of the OPA] . . . [has] seen the vital importance of having a consumer advisory committee, and [has] pushed this idea, but in general you do have resistance on the part of most men to it. It is tied up with the idea that this is a women's organization, and why should we bother with getting them in here."[96]

Even when the public did gain an opportunity to influence OPA policies (as eventually happened with the Consumers Advisory Committees), its efficacy was often undermined by the very agency that had granted the authority. For instance, the federal government bowed to retailers' pressure and admitted its own distrust of women price checkers when it backed out of a plan to distribute maximum price lists to women shoppers. In this way, shoppers would be dependent on stores to post the maximum prices they should be charged.[97] In spite of the dedication and labor that the OPA expected of women, the agency discouraged their independence.[98]

The OPA's distrust of women extended to a distrust of popular participation more generally. Panels were able to sue violators for punitive damages (by filing "administrator's claims"), but panel members had to follow elaborate procedures, which left them almost no room to decide when and how to pursue those claims.[99] By war's end, the government was discouraging local boards from passing on repeat violators to the OPA's Enforcement Division.[100]

Cooperators remained crucial supporters of price control and rationing, seeing in both a chance for real power. Their hopes, however, went unrealized. Policymakers did not take advantage of cooperative stores or of the nascent support for democratic consumption that co-ops might have tapped into. The conflation of "women" and "consumers," officials' distrust of women as a group, and the importance that officials attached to price control and rationing made any distribution of economic authority politically unworkable.

The Advantages of Supermarkets

Large stores had several important advantages, which together served to defuse the anti-chain sentiments of earlier decades. Centralized stores impressed policymakers with their ability to hold down prices, keep records, and observe the often arcane requirements of federal regulations. But, just as important, large stores proved best able to impose policy on women customers. It was gender relations, as well as low prices and efficiency, that gave large stores such decisive advantages. Larger operations were likely to have lower costs and hence a greater ability to assist in the overall goal of keeping wartime inflation at bay. This was made a matter of policy when the OPA assigned chains and supermarkets the lowest price ceilings.[101] The lower prices of chains and supermarkets were now codified in public policy and price control.

The degree of centralization and vertical integration that most supermarkets and large chains had achieved by World War II helped preserve their advantage. Unlike many independent grocers, they had integrated backward into wholesale, so that for the most part, they controlled their own supplies. Even when chains did not receive a product through an internal division, they bought in such large amounts that private wholesalers were loath to overcharge them. Obtaining supplies was simply less of a problem for large chains than for small independents.

Moreover, like large manufacturers, these stores combined a relatively low cost with a strong, centrally directed bureaucracy that allowed them to keep up with complicated federal regulations and record-keeping requirements. Chain store representatives, unlike small independents, almost never complained that they did not know what price ceilings should be or what their inventory had been. For instance, after meetings with several proprietors who claimed never to have heard of let alone received price ceiling lists, members of one price board were clearly relieved to meet with a representative of The Fair, a large Chicago department store chain that also sold groceries. The representative straightforwardly explained why his store was allowed to charge above-ceiling prices on certain goods and produced records to back up his claim. The board was positively apologetic, noting that they were "sorry to have inconvenienced" the store representative. District-level officials also appreciated the accessibility of chain store records. When Kroger's internal wholesaling division was investigated for the prices that it charged Kroger stores, investigators not only found no violation but also praised the division's general manager for maintaining "very complete books and records of all transactions."[102] These experiences stood in stark contrast to the difficulties that smaller stores had in keeping even the most basic accounts.

The advantages of chain store firms went far beyond their ability to keep adequate records. Large firms, especially chain store firms, often had enough specialization in their bureaucracies that a single person could devote his or her time to communications with federal officials and the implementation of new regulations. Unlike the proprietors and managers of smaller stores, this person could develop expertise in the vagaries of government policy.[103] Thus, chains had the advantage of expert knowledge in interpreting the complicated and constantly changing price control and rationing guidelines.

Finally, large chains and supermarkets built on their prewar strategy of trading up. During the 1930s, many firms had retooled and relocated stores to attract higher-income consumers. Wartime trading up was more often expressed by grocers' substitution of higher-priced goods for lower-quality ones. The practice helped stores achieve stability and even prosperity amid wartime exigencies. OPA officials frowned on trading up, but stores widely pursued the strategy during and after the war.[104] Sometimes the availability of higher-end goods depended on new technology. A&P, working with United Airlines and Wayne State University, was one of the first firms to test the possibilities of shipping produce by air.[105] Not to be outdone, Kroger and the U.S. Department of Agriculture celebrated the overnight delivery of California lettuce to Kroger's Detroit stores—and the five-cent-per-head price increase that it ensured.[106] At other times, however, trading up simply depended on new marketing angles. In Chicago, both Jewel Food Stores and National Tea Company stores urged women customers to get full value for their precious ration points by purchasing higher-quality, and presumably more expensive, goods.[107] Stores throughout the city used similar reasoning in pushing ready-made meals and deli foods; these purchases might not have saved on cost, but they did save on ration points (and time).[108] This emphasis on higher-priced lines of goods only increased as the war wound down. Jewel Food Stores, for instance, sent a representative to California to talk with packers and suppliers about how best to supply "the homemakers of Chicago" with wider varieties of produce.[109] A&P featured precut and prewrapped chickens in its 1946 advertisements, and Kroger began selling its own top grade of canned goods under a distinctive label in this same period.[110] Jewel noted in its 1945 annual report that its profits under price control depended on "changing buying patterns"—to higher-end goods.[111]

Even the largest chain stores did not always fulfill policymakers' hopes for full compliance with wartime regulations and anti-inflation initiatives. Sometimes, chains violated the spirit of the law by pushing higher-priced merchandise. At other times, the violations were more direct. High-Low Stores—a local Chicago chain—had so many over-ceiling prices after one price check that the regional OPA legal office considered court action.[112] Kroger's Chicago operations—which consisted of nearly two hundred stores—had enough price violations to merit a federal injunction against further violations.[113] Numerous chains seem to have been slow in posting changes in price ceilings and in lowering their prices accordingly.[114]

But problems with large chains also were easier to address than similar problems with independents. For instance, when the National Tea Company was accused of selling butter below its rationed point value, the district's enforcement division simply met with a single company representative. Similar meetings with representatives of chain stores in nearby Gary, Indiana, and throughout the metro area won promises of full cooperation with government regulations.[115] Officials had only to bring the problem to the attention of the stores' higher-level administrators rather than meet with individual store managers.

Selling higher-end goods and responding promptly to government directives were not the only strategies that helped chain store firms during the war. Because the marketing efforts of large firms reached more people than those of smaller stores, these larger operations were especially valuable partners in propaganda campaigns. Sometimes the ad campaigns of chain stores had special importance to federal officials. Just before the 1944 elections, Chester Bowles noted that his office had induced several chains to advertise that prices were lower than they had been in 1943. Not only did this build support for the war effort in general, but Bowles also noted that advertising the success of the OPA would help Democratic candidates in the upcoming elections.[116]

Chains' efforts, like the OPA's, centered on women. During one war bond campaign, just five chain store firms were able to distribute more than 8 million copies of the booklet *Mrs. Brown Goes to War*.[117] Kroger and A&P both bought radio time and produced shows designed to build support for price control and rationing among women.[118] A&P happily offered its magazine, *Woman's Day*, to the government for use in the war effort.[119]

Chains' ability to keep women behind the war effort went beyond distribution of propaganda. Noting that chains could "more easily be kept in line" than could other sorts of stores, a Chicago-area price control official contended that women were more willing to report violations in these stores. They generally had no personal ties to the store, and customers could not pressure managers and employees into selling goods under the table.[120] Put simply, the resources of chains, their lack of community ties, and their ability to integrate women into the war effort made them especially well suited to the job of imposing federal regulations.

Federal officials, in turn, were willing to accommodate the special requirements of large, top-down chains. By 1944, chain stores were allowed to bypass district OPA offices and their price lists and apply to regional OPA offices for "uniform pricing"—the right to assign the same prices to the same items throughout a chain, as long as those prices did not break community price ceilings. Regional or national OPA offices then helped chains develop their uniform prices.[121] Chains also gained help with an entirely different problem—their lack of standardization. In mid-1943, chains won the right to use higher margins on prices at their full-service stores than at their self-service stores. Noting that "all stores in a chain do not necessarily operate on the same basis," federal officials informed local boards that they could grant the higher margins to chain stores that operated on margins of more than 25 percent.[122] Similarly, chains and large supermarkets were eventually granted the right to higher margins when they (however infrequently) bought goods from outside wholesalers.[123]

In the chaotic mobilization of World War II, chain store supermarkets and the federal government found common ground. Both strove to stabilize consumer purchasing and, by extension, to cut short customers' ability to disrupt store operations. Both also participated in a broader project of stabilizing gender relations. Both saw central control and economies of scale as the tools to achieve those ends. Each came to rely on the other for continued stability. Chains became important administrators of government directives, and the federal government became friendlier toward large chains and mass retailers.

PROMISES OF OVERSIGHT OF RETAILERS and protection of consumer autonomy disappeared entirely from government rhetoric with the end of the OPA. In early 1946, the Truman administration began undermining the OPA's authority by lifting price controls without regard to the agency's recommendations. Within six months of the end of the war, the compliance program was, in the words of one scholar, "crippled." The resistance of retailers and manufacturers (particularly grocers and food processors) to federal regulation overcame support from organized consumer groups and from vocal women's organizations for such regulation.[124] Federal-level oversight of prices ended for all practical purposes in October 1946, and with it ended the country's largest experiment in democratic consumption.

The speed and finality with which Congress withdrew price controls obscured the original ambitions of program administrators. World War II had been a time of enormous experimentation in food distribution. It had seemed possible to many Americans that the federal government would monitor prices with an eye toward equalizing the treatment of individual shoppers in stores—for instance, by setting maximum prices and making overcharges illegal. Many Americans also had thought that the government would endow individual consumers with significant political authority over stores—for instance, by making it easy to report violations. That sort of increased state oversight—and increased influence for consumers—might have radically altered the dominance of chain stores, encouraged the growth of more democratic alternatives (like consumer cooperatives), and presented Americans who did not engage in paid or unionized labor with new avenues to political and economic authority. It certainly would have led to more economic and political authority for women.

Although the federal government succeeded in keeping price inflation at bay, it did not significantly increase consumers' authority in stores. Chains effectively became agents of the state in ways that consumer cooperatives and independent stores never could. One story is particularly poignant: In 1947, the Hyde Park Cooperative Society, an early and vocal proponent of price controls, advised its supporters that their membership in a co-op might now be taken by the federal government as a sign of communist sympathies.[125]

The political economy that developed during World War II favored the top-down structures of many of these stores and rewarded women shoppers' adherence to store policy. This trend continued after the war. Women's shopping before World War I had required assertiveness and agency; after World War II, their shopping and their citizenship were characterized by a new passivity. Over time, a discourse that emphasized the apolitical and narrowly self-interested nature of women's shopping became crucial not only to images of consumer culture but to the very workings of the state and business. A particular gender system—one that assigned to women the work of everyday shopping, but not any consequent public authority—was critical to exchange in mass retailing and to a growing body of federal and state-level initiatives, regulations, and policies.

Babes in Consumerland

Supermarkets, Hardware Stores, and the
Politics of Postwar Mass Retail

In the 1950s and 1960s, accounts of women's grocery shopping differed remarkably from the gritty descriptions of earlier decades. Trips to the supermarket were described as exciting adventures. A 1962 piece reminded women that "one of the biggest revolutions going is in the neighborhood grocery. Its shelves are bursting with excitement. You'll discover delicacies once reserved for kings' feasts."[1] Another unabashedly asserted, "Nowhere else in the world is such an abundance of food so lavishly displayed and so reasonably priced."[2] Women, it seemed, had finally found the perfect store.

This chapter concludes the story of the emergence of supermarkets by providing examples of the success that large-scale, standardized, hierarchical food retailing found in the immediate postwar years. To document fully a widely resonant discourse of women and supermarkets requires a national perspective. Although Chicago stores figure prominently in this story, so too do the voices of actors from across the country.

Celebrations of women's food shopping were ubiquitous in the 1950s and 1960s. In the years after World War II, policymakers, business owners, journalists, and domestic advisers writing in the popular and business press repeated the refrain that women were thrilled with the new, streamlined, and aesthetically pleasing supermarkets. In these accounts, supermarkets were the key not only to low-priced food but also to much that was considered "good" in post–World War II consumer society—the abundance of products, the convenience that they offered housewives, the pleasure of shopping, the affordability of such items, and the ways in which they facilitated family togetherness. Writers of magazine articles, textbooks, cookbooks, and political speeches created a rich discourse of conservative femininity in which women's desires revolved around low prices, abundant goods, and elaborate decor.

The editors and authors who established this discourse ascribed the stores' success to women's long-standing concern with the work of meeting family budgets and tastes, as well as to women's supposed natural appreciation for the benefits of large systems. As the case of hardware stores makes clear, these rhetorical flourishes took on material meaning. In hardware—a sector in many ways similar to food retailing but dominated by men's purchases—mass retailing had proved a more awkward fit. Acquiescence in the systems devised by mass retail (whether that acquiescence was critiqued as problematic or celebrated as a mark of American superiority) characterized women's shopping, but not men's.

These celebrations of women's satisfaction with stores continued, even though the reality of women's shopping was far different. In acts that ranged from public critiques of marketing practices to organized boycotts or simply looking on as two friends blocked an aisle to chat, women subverted the claims that supermarkets pleased them all. Sometimes their displeasure was especially problematic; the limits of mass retailing were unmistakable in the urban insurrections of the mid- and late 1960s and in retailers' pallid responses to them. Nonetheless, writers, academics, and business analysts of all sorts forwarded the supermarket as an emblem of smooth-running consumption and domesticity—and economic prosperity.

But their writings did something else, too. These accounts obscured the politics surrounding supermarkets, the contingencies that led to their growth, and the long history and present state of women's difficult, complicated, and sometimes unsuccessful shopping in food stores. They conflated women's decisions about where to shop and what to buy with an expression of their "demand"—and posited that demand as itself lying at the center of retailers concerns.

I argue here that the political significance of supermarkets remained an undercurrent in narratives that instead highlighted the importance of women's desires in stores' operations. The disavowal of the political qualities of supermarkets can be understood as itself political; these were spaces in which the discourses that marked postwar liberalism and gender relations were reified, enforced, and linked. To ask for individualized treatment or to complain loudly to a clerk was to put at risk one's femininity *and* access to the benefits of postwar shopping. Asserting independence came, literally, at a very high cost. In the constructions and celebrations of women's demand as the driver of retail practices lie the roots of policies and movements that would transform policy and political discourse in later years.

Supermarkets' Growth in the Postwar Years

In 1954, in response to a decline in the number of grocery stores that did not sell meat, the U.S. Bureau of the Census ceased categorizing grocery stores that did not sell meat separately from grocery stores that did.[3] While that pronouncement has understandably not received the strong reaction that has greeted some other conclusions of the bureau (for example, that the frontier was closed or that the nation had become predominantly urban or, more recently, that non-Hispanic whites are a minority in one in ten U.S. counties), it nonetheless heralded an important change that, at least for grocers, was even more striking. Designers of the census tacitly acknowledged that the nature of grocery stores had changed. After decades of diversity and unsettledness in food retailing, there was a general convergence of grocers, regardless of size, around the model of the modern supermarket selling multiple lines of goods.[4]

The bureau's pronouncement would have made little sense only twenty-five years earlier. When the census first enumerated grocery stores, census takers had felt compelled to differentiate a store on the basis of an astonishing number of variables, including whether it was a grocery store that sold meat or a meat store that sold groceries, or a grocery store that did not sell meat or a meat store that did not sell groceries.[5]

The story of the National Tea Company and its changing fortunes illustrates this transformation via the success that many large chains—and, more precisely, many upscale supermarkets that targeted women shoppers—achieved in the postwar period. National Tea was the largest chain in Chicago and one of the largest in the Midwest. In 1940, it operated more than 1,000 stores, 220 of them in Chicago. The firm was still haunted by the losses it suffered during the 1930s, however—profits were steady but not spectacular, and the firm continued its policies of closing stores and negotiating short-term leases for the remaining ones. Wartime conditions were yet another impediment—price ceilings did not reflect the firm's increased costs, procuring fresh meat proved a challenge, and remodeling and expansion were nearly impossible under the constraints of the war.[6] By 1943, sales were the highest in the firm's history, but profits, limited by price ceilings, had fallen. Employee turnover was astronomical: fewer than half of National Tea's managers had held their positions for more than a year. The firm was forced to close stores because it simply did not have the personnel to run them.[7]

By 1944, however, the firm's fortunes were improving. The Office of Price Administration had become slightly more accommodating, and many of its officials had clearly articulated their preference for chain stores. At the same time, sales and profits reached new heights, and company directors announced that the year had been "the most successful . . . in many years."[8] Glowing reports continued in 1945 and 1946, as the OPA removed price ceilings and the store could once again focus on "larger self-service stores with meat departments."[9]

In 1947, the firm announced that it had purchased a small chain of stores in Indianapolis and now was selling in such high volume that it could safely reduce its average profit margin per item from 1.86 percent to 1.65 percent.[10] 1950 was another record-setting year for National Tea. More than 90 percent of its stores had their own meat departments, and the firm had bought a new warehouse from the War Assets Administration. National Tea also had purchased a 25 percent interest in Everywoman's Magazine, Inc., which included exclusive rights to distribute *Everywoman's Magazine* in any territory where National Tea stores were located.[11] By 1957, the firm had achieved previously unimaginable sales: $750 million in a single year. In 1964, sales topped $1 billion.[12]

The sort of stores that National Tea operated and the sort of shopping that it facilitated would dominate Americans' experience of consumption in the decades following the Second World War. Its success was typical of large grocery firms in the 1950s and 1960s. The Super Market Institute, founded with thirty-five members in 1935, had seven thousand by 1950.[13] One 1951 article claimed that supermarkets had been opened at a rate of three a day during the previous year.[14] Moreover, these stores did big business. Although supermarkets made up only 4 percent of all grocery stores, they accounted for 44 percent of all retail food sales in 1952, according to *Business Week*. The journal saw no end in sight: "The trend is still away from small stores, and toward the big self-service marts with giant stocks, elaborate assortments of groceries, meats and sundries, and jumbo parking lots."[15] Between 1948 and 1958, supermarket sales grew far faster than either the population or per capita income.[16] Supermarkets had achieved what one researcher called "overwhelming dominance" in food retailing.[17]

The popularity of a particular set of strategies among all grocers, regardless of the size or structure of firm that they operated, exemplifies that dominance. As might be expected, national firms operating chains of stores were able to invest in big stores.[18] But operators of large independent stores often also had significant capital. They also maintained supersized stores and followed the chain store strategy of opening several stores at a time, so that by 1958, only 20.7 percent of all supermarkets were single units.[19] Even owners who continued to operate relatively few stores worked to coordinate purchasing, to standardize selling, and to mimic multiunit operations. Affiliated independents had already made nearly half of all sales by independent grocers in 1946, but they increased that market share to 73 percent by 1958.[20] In Chicago alone, more than three thousand individually operated grocery stores were members of such voluntary chains in 1951.[21]

Observers readily remarked that even independently owned stores were coming to resemble chain-operated stores, both in terms of their relations with customers and in terms of their ability to achieve economies of scale.[22] Smaller stores were labeled "superettes." Classified by most trade associations as stores posting moderate sales, but less than the amount needed to be classed as a supermarket, these stores "operated in the main much like their larger counterparts, the supermarkets, with departmentalized organization, and self-service operation."[23] Proprietors worked to install new equipment that would enable them to sell refrigerated and frozen products and keep up with the supermarkets. For example, members of the IGA, one of the largest associations of independent grocers, opened "Foodliner" stores.[24] Consumer cooperatives were part of this convergence, as well. In the early 1950s, as cooperative societies and the journals that had publicized their growth shut down across the city, the few consumer cooperatives that remained increasingly resembled privately owned supermarkets in their aesthetics, size, and business model.[25]

The strategies of grocers had converged to such a degree that one manual for supermarket operators, published in 1963, made no distinction between chains and independent supermarkets, even in a chapter on store organization. Instead, the author assumed that all stores would rely on self-service, offer elaborate displays and a vast range of goods, and strive to bedazzle their female customers with new and modern sales techniques.[26]

Supermarkets of the 1950s and 1960s embodied the strategies engineered in the 1930s and 1940s. Stores were quite large—averaging nine thousand square feet by the late 1940s and twenty-two thousand square feet by 1957. With the increased size came increased stock. In 1946, the average supermarket carried three thousand items; by 1956, that number had increased to five thousand; and by 1966, the average store had more than seven thousand items.[27] These included meat, produce, and dry groceries, as well as nonfood items, such as cleaning supplies, paper goods, and health and beauty supplies.

FIGURE 7.1.
Exterior of the new
Hyde Park Consumers'
Co-op supermarket.
(Chicago History
Museum, HB-17554-C,
August 30, 1954,
photographer,
Hedrich-Blessing)

Post–World War II supermarkets also exemplified the possibilities of self-service.[28] Although grocery stores had long had some degree of self-service, this trend did not extend to meat departments until the 1950s. The advent of self-serve meat was hastened by several forces: for instance, Freon, which made it easier to cool open-topped refrigerated cases, was developed by Du-Pont only in the late 1940s. Another factor in the spread of self-serve meats was retailers' insistence on it, even, as Roger Horowitz has shown, when increased labor costs for wrappers canceled out the savings from having fewer skilled butchers on the payroll. By the 1960s, selecting prepackaged meat at open cases in large supermarkets was the "typical way to shop for meat."[29]

New supermarkets were often elaborately decorated. A 1951 article declared the final realization of chain stores' long-standing efforts to move away from straightforward price appeal: "Low prices are no longer the supermarket's only attraction. Recent surveys indicate that shoppers are even more impressed by the appearance of both the food displays and the stores themselves, plus the way customers are treated."[30] Publix supermarkets of Florida, which promi-

FIGURE 7.2. *Interior of the new Hyde Park Consumers' Co-op supermarket. (Chicago History Museum, HB-17554A, August 30, 1954, photographer, Hedrich-Blessing)*

nently displayed the motto "Where shopping is a pleasure," epitomized this aestheticization. One Publix store featured, among other things, eight-foot-wide aisles, a "candy-stripe terrazzo floor, pastel walls, and air conditioning."[31] Chicago supermarkets echoed this trend. Kroger hired Howard Ketchum, a well-known interior designer (most famous for designing the interior of the new Boeing jets and for creating the Lustron color scheme for homes), to put together the lighting and color scheme of its new stores. One such shop, opened in September 1952, featured "all the colors of an artist's palette," as well as frozen foods, refrigerated and self-serve fruits and vegetables, an automatic juicer for customers' use, and "nationally advertised beauty and health aids."[32] Other firms followed suit. Although Chicago did not have Florida's warm climate, new markets were often air-conditioned.[33] When National Tea opened a new store in 1958, it featured many "ultra-modern conveniences," including "magic carpet doors" (that is, automated doors).[34]

By the mid-twentieth century, then, supermarkets had achieved both a new coherence and success in food retailing. Edward Brand, the author of a textbook for would-be supermarket operators, described these stores in especially

FIGURE 7.3. *Interior of a new National Tea "superstore." This upscale store was located in the suburb of Addison. (Chicago History Museum, HB-32244-B, February 26, 1969, photographer, Hedrich-Blessing)*

vivid language, making it clear that the term "supermarket" meant much more than simply high-volume sales:

> Today's supermarket represents the last word in modernization of . . . the food industry. It is housed in a modern building . . . complete with parking lot. Customers entering the store pass through an automatic door that opens "magically" without manual effort. . . . The interior of the store, including fixtures, has a pastel decor. Low gondolas and wide, spacious aisles make all parts of the store visible. . . . Meat cases, dairy cases, and in most stores, produce cases are fully refrigerated. . . . The increasing volume, made possible by self-service, is bringing about operating efficiencies which have lowered the cost of food to the consumers.[35]

For retail analysts like Brand, modernity, convenience, value, and feminine decor explained supermarkets' tremendous success: "The story of supermarkets is, in a very real sense, the story of America. The food industry is not great because of any unified power or monopolistic control, nor has it attained its greatness through government aid. It is great because of the pioneering spirit and the leadership of the owners and operators, and because it answers a need—low cost merchandising of food."[36] In this telling, supermarkets showcased modern American solutions to universal needs.

Supermarkets in Cold War Politics

The "needs" supermarkets answered were not, however, just for low-cost food or aesthetically pleasing interiors. The image of the supermarket as a kind of pleasure palace took on special political significance in cold war rhetoric, domestic politics, and foreign policy at this time. Whatever they offered the public, supermarkets had much to offer politicians.

Supermarkets achieved new importance as the government haltingly adopted Keynesian economic policies and also as the belief that sustained consumption was crucial to economic growth became a kind of truism among policymakers.[37] When the press celebrated the bounty of American life, it increasingly celebrated the ways in which Americans' shopping kept the economy strong enough to produce such bounty. Consumer spending at supermarkets and other mass retailers was crucial to a Keynesian vision of American political economy.

When price controls were reintroduced during the Korean War, the government continued its move away from mobilizing individual women consumers. The only whisper of consumer involvement—which once had been the federal government's main strategy for controlling inflation—was a weak Consumer Advisory Committee located inside the Office of Price Stabilization.[38] Instead of price limits, federal officials merely set limits on firms' profits (the "cost-plus system"), relying on retailers and other firms to report their costs honestly. Controls were much weaker than they had been during World War II, and many firms exceeded the already generous government guidelines on profits.[39]

In addition to this reliance on firms to offset inflation, long-standing government programs—for example, sales taxes and food relief (now called welfare)—became even more extensive in the postwar period. Supermarket employees continued to perform such vital functions as collecting sales taxes and food stamps, administering (or undermining) state and federal guidelines as they did so. Finally, municipal regulations involving zoning and hours and days of operation made their impact on urban and suburban landscapes through the actions of these increasingly large firms.

In addition to these elaborations of older functions, supermarkets also assumed new importance in foreign policy. In the cold war context, there was particular political utility in supermarkets' claims of being apolitical. In the 1950s and 1960s, the U.S. government and trade associations relied on supermarkets to epitomize the freedom, choice, and bounty of American society. It was precisely supermarkets' perceived distance from law, power, and constraint that made them so important and so valuable to the federal government.

As many historians have demonstrated, the cold war was fought in cultural realms just as much as diplomatic ones.[40] Supermarkets, as positioned by policymakers and trade associations, were especially effective vehicles for establishing the superiority of America and, more broadly, of capitalism itself. Proponents argued that because supermarkets lowered food prices, celebrated freedom of choice, and made customers feel that they were being treated equally, they reduced the appeal of communism and showcased the real value of American capitalism and free enterprise.[41] They were, in the words of *Super Market Merchandising*, "as powerful a weapon in the arsenal of western democracy as any to be found."[42]

As a result, elaborately fitted, large supermarkets figured prominently in cold war propaganda efforts. Visiting dignitaries often were taken on visits to grocery stores. Media were especially gleeful over Nikita Khrushchev's open admiration for a Safeway store that he visited in 1959. In addition, supermarkets often traveled to Europe, with frequent exhibitions in countries that were, to greater or lesser degrees, within the communist orbit. Yugoslavia and Italy (where there was a vigorous communist movement), for instance, were both treated to exhibits of American supermarket technology, including checkout lanes, refrigerated cases for produce and frozen foods, and, of course, gravity-defying towers of canned goods.[43] The most elaborate of these efforts was the model American Way Supermarket that was erected in Rome in 1956 and then in Zagreb, Yugoslavia, in 1957 by the American-dominated International Congress of Food Distribution. According to historian Victoria de Grazia, the U.S. Department of Agriculture and the U.S. State Department "prevailed upon" the National Association of Food Chains to build the original model store, and policymakers continued to work alongside private firms and trade associations to expand it the following year.[44] The business press claimed that "nearly half a million Italians paraded through the aisles, literally gasping at the display of 2,500 different household items."[45]

Supermarkets' role in anticommunist propaganda remained long after the model store had closed. When a supermarket opened in Milan, American journalists gleefully noted that local communists could not claim that it was an "imperialist plot" because "workers were swamping the store at a rate of 23,000 customers a week."[46] Similarly, Victoria de Grazia has argued that Nelson Rockefeller's International Basic Economy Corporation decided to open supermarkets in Milan not because it expected immediate profits but in order to stave off the appeal of communism by lowering food prices.[47] The perceived power of supermarkets to sway people from communism informed both the media's descriptions of these exhibits and the construction of actual supermarkets by U.S. firms in Europe.

It was, in particular *women's* appreciation for supermarkets that, to U.S. observers, was their biggest guarantee of success. One newspaper article, which featured photos of excited Italian women mobbing the entrances to stores, noted succinctly, "Italian housewives . . . took their first enthralled look at a U.S. supermarket this week and last—and bought it." The article went on to describe what it saw as the drudgery of Italian shopping practices—including shopping "as much as two hours daily" at small stores.[48] Women's needs were thwarted, however, by the state. One news reporter deplored the ways in which local licensing laws and opposition from small grocers impeded the development of Italian supermarkets, "even though thousands of Italian housewives feel the same as one old woman, who gazed at the mountains of food in the American-model supermarket and sighed, 'Heaven must be like this.' "[49] In the cold war context, regulation had emerged as a roadblock to women's bliss.

Women's Work and Domesticity: Food and Supermarkets in Cold War Domestic Politics

For all the media discussion of Europeans' love of supermarkets, many countries adopted supermarket strategies only slowly, if at all.[50] Supermarkets unquestionably dominated American food distribution, however, and became central economic and cultural spaces in this time period. In the widespread celebration of particular supermarket strategies, especially their ability to make mundane food shopping both pleasurable and calming, we can detect a grocery store version of Elaine Tyler May's notion of cold war domestic containment.[51] Just as the home contained sexuality, the supermarket contained women's demand for public authority.

Supermarket owners, managers, and analysts made it clear that stores' strategies focused on women. George Jenkins, owner of the Publix chain, explained the success of his supermarkets by saying that his firm had "made it [i.e., a supermarket] into the kind of place we thought a woman would design if she were in the grocery business."[52] A celebratory piece in *Parents'* magazine defined supermarkets as "a system of merchandising that would cut the price of food to fit the homemakers' budget."[53] A journalist explained the early success of A&P in very similar terms: "It has always operated on the theory that all the housewife really wants is top quality at the lowest price, and by holding to that belief, A&P became the Goliath of the industry."[54] Using even more direct language, Kroger presented its new store as "a shopper's dream, planned, designed and created for women like you."[55] Despite a new discourse of "family" shopping, women remained at the center of retailers' concerns.

Behind these claims was the belief—sometimes implicit and sometimes explicit—that women exerted enormous power over the policies, strategies, and practices of these stores. Journalists and proprietors shared a tongue-in-cheek tone that both mocked grocers and gave them credit for elevating women. One article described the supermarket magnate George Jenkins as serving "Her Highness, the never-satisfied housewife" and referred to the "woman-haunted food business."[56] The owner of Colonial stores, based in Atlanta, bragged that a survey of his shoppers enabled him to make changes they had asked for—including chandeliers over the checkout stands.[57]

Chicago shoppers, too, were enmeshed in a discourse of housewives' empowerment. A *Chicago Tribune* article on decisions to locate supermarkets in "open" areas (that is, newer business districts, especially in suburbs) claimed that although these moves reflected the need for parking lots and the availability of large home freezers in nearby homes, the impetus came from "housewives" (to use the article's term) who had suggested these changes to grocers.[58] Similarly, to celebrate the twentieth anniversary of its first venture into food stores, Jewel re-ran the ad that had announced its 1934 remodeling campaign, "18,389 Women Planned This Store."[59] The elaborate surveys devised by trade associations and retailers, as well as the increasingly subtle methods for tracking customers' reactions in stores—hidden cameras, machines that measured the rapidity with which customers blinked, "traffic pattern" studies in which a researcher shadowed a particular customer—testify to the lengths to which retailers went to obtain the elusive answer to the question of what women wanted.[60] Over and over, grocers claimed that women's desires drove business strategy.

An image that appeared on the front cover of *Life* magazine in 1955 epitomized this discourse. The editors chose to open the magazine's special issue on the "mass luxury" of postwar society with a cover that featured a shopping cart with a seated, smiling toddler and filled to overflowing with Technicolor packaged goods. A woman's fashionably gloved hand pushed the ensemble. Articles inside documented the stunning array of choices awaiting Americans in the

FIGURE 7.4.
Cover of Life magazine,
January 3, 1955. (Life
logo and cover
treatment © Time Inc.,
used with permission;
photograph courtesy of
The Getty Collection,
Arnold Newman
Collection)

new supermarkets and used the story of food distribution to celebrate the vir-
tues and advantages of centrally managed, large-scale, standardized capitalist
enterprises.[61] Everywhere, editors assured their readers, consumers' demands
were being answered by the incredible innovation of American enterprise.

In a world in which consumption was overdetermined—assigned vast political, social, and economic meaning—the importance of food stood out. It was
with food, countless experts assured Americans, that both consumer goods
and familial ties were made most meaningful. The particular importance of
supermarkets in the postwar period is difficult to understand without examining emerging prescriptions for and discourses around food, women's cooking,
and domesticity.

Cookbooks of the postwar period illustrate the scale of economic and cultural investment in home-cooked food. Beginning most famously with the
first edition in 1950 of *Betty Crocker's Picture Cookbook*, cookbooks became

best sellers.[62] Both the number and the production value of cookbooks were impressive. Whereas older cookbooks had been relatively straightforward, new ones featured high-end illustrations. For instance, Andy Warhol, already a very successful commercial artist and already a well-known exhibitor in New York galleries, did the illustrations for Amy Vanderbilt's 1961 cookbook.[63] Perhaps the most memorable examples of the new visual appeal of cookbooks were the vivid color photos that Betty Crocker made famous. In this and other cookbooks, women were encouraged to make meals into festive events—and to dress not only for dinner but also for breakfast, lunch, and kitchen dishwashing. Authors presented food and the labor behind cooking, as they long had, as undergirding social success. James Beard, who otherwise shared little with Betty Crocker, reinforced the importance of food to social success. Encouraging cooks to study basic techniques carefully, Beard noted only somewhat facetiously, "Good food has a magic appeal. You may grow old, even ugly, but if you are a good cook, people will always find the path to your door."[64] Others were even more direct, blaming everything from political threats to juvenile delinquency, from nervous stomachs to disagreeable family life, on poorly prepared meals.[65]

Indeed, food remained such a crucial touchstone of the post–World War II gender system that cooking figured prominently in sex manuals of the period. Good home cooking would "catch" a man, "keep" a husband, and as Jessamyn Neuhaus has argued, serve as a convenient metaphor for sexual behavior. One 1951 manual encouraged women to think of sexual intercourse (and their failure to achieve orgasm) with the same spirit of generosity that they brought to their cooking. The authors reminded women that they often cooked for their husbands out of love, although doing so did not provide "a climactic thrill," and that they might tap into the same feeling to provide "sexual comfort"—even if that, too, failed to bring on an orgasm.[66] In this context, food served to link modern sexuality to older discourses of women's cooking. Food was the glue that kept families intact and women in their place.

A very specific kind of food figured prominently in the postwar discourse of domesticity. Observers, authors, and many others touted the processed and preserved foods that shortened preparation times as clear benefits of, and requirements for, modern American life. One home economics textbook reminded its audience of high school girls that canned and frozen fruits and vegetables offered low prices, convenience, and the promise of healthier meals, because they had been "packed at the peak of freshness."[67] Similarly, one cookbook author titled her preface "Atom and Eve" and noted that "young brides . . . love all the new quickie casseroles, the packaged mixes, the heat-and-eat foods" because these goods allowed them to keep up with the many children that they were having and kept them from being "a slave to the kitchen stove."[68]

Indeed, processed foods occupied places of particular prominence in these cookbooks. The 1963 edition of *McCall's* cookbook featured an entire chapter on "convenience foods" (including recipes like "Orange-Glazed Luncheon Meat," p. 613) and another that relied heavily on processed foods ("Casseroles and Other Main Dishes," pp. 206–27).[69] The *New Good Housekeeping Cookbook* similarly praised prepared foods as time-savers, even as its recipes incorporated them as fodder for more creative dishes. The editors encouraged the purchase of breakfast cereals, for instance, as "a wonderful time-saver" while also encouraging women to "discover the many recipes using the special qualities of breakfast cereals—appetizers, breads, cakes, confections, cookies, entrées, frozen desserts, fruit crisps, muffins, piecrusts, puddings, salads, soups, sundaes, and vegetables." Much cooking advice of the 1950s celebrated creative combinations of canned, frozen, or otherwise ready-made foods.[70]

As these descriptions suggest, the emphasis on processed foods reflected a concomitant interest on the part of cookbook authors, as well as cooks, in efficiency and speed. The Pillsbury Bake-Off contest (established in 1949), for instance, used "speed or ease of preparation" as one of the primary criteria for determining winning recipes.[71] Cookbook after cookbook, both those that were aimed at working women and those that were not, featured recipes, and often whole menus, that could be prepared quickly. The anonymous authors at Betty Crocker kitchens echoed this concern when they acknowledged that planning a week's meals for the newly married could be daunting but promised that "with shortcut methods, streamlined schedules and lots of wonderful convenience foods, the battle's almost won!"[72] Amy Vanderbilt, better known for her etiquette guides, assured readers of her 1961 cookbook that "although I find the actual preparation of food—from scratch—interesting, creative, and challenging, I by no means, as you will see in the pages of this cookbook, spurn the use of quick methods." Vanderbilt made good on her promise, including in her lengthy cookbook, which focused mainly on tony and fashionable cuisine, sections on "casserole meals" and "go-together soups" (made by mixing together various canned soups), as well as recipes that used prepared or processed ingredients (for instance, frozen, deveined shrimp in a paella).[73]

Supermarkets were indispensable to this lifestyle. "Grandma," lamented one cookbook editor, "had no supermarket around the corner where every conceivable food was available in several forms at any time of year."[74] The same home economics textbook that praised the possibilities of new supermarkets also advised its readers that chain supermarkets offered these goods at low prices and in huge variety, in contrast to smaller, independent stores that often had relatively high prices and were "in trouble."[75] This celebration of supermarkets as important purveyors of processed food was widespread. A 1962 *Ladies' Home Journal* piece approvingly described the offerings of supermarkets this way: "It's difficult to find food that has not been washed, trimmed, measured, cooked, canned, frozen, or dried. Feasts once requiring days and dollars to prepare come quickly, economically to the table. Creativity doesn't end with the package—but most of the chore of cooking does! You can serve dinner almost as quick as a cash register can click."[76] As these authors implied, supermarkets and the goods that they offered provided access to foods so crucial to household relations and gave women a chance, at least in theory, to ease their labors.

Like the grocers and business journalists who celebrated supermarkets, these food writers frequently put forth the notion that women did, and should, enjoy this new way of food shopping. The 1959 edition of the General Foods cookbook made this case in especially vivid language. The authors (identified as "the women of General Foods Kitchens") observed that although "marketing may sometimes be a chore," they believed "that in their heart of hearts, most women love it. After all, we're born shoppers, and there's nothing more exhilarating than nosing out a wonderful buy or pouncing on a new product that promises much." The authors went on to compare a modern-day "food market" to "a sort of Arabian Nights bazaar." "No wonder everybody has such a good time," they concluded.[77] Similarly, a lengthy essay on supermarket operators' efforts to redo their stores concluded reassuringly, "They have learned this much. To women, buying food for their families is not a chore. It is a joyful ritual that gives them an inner glow of satisfaction and deep sense of fulfillment."[78] Supermarkets, like sex, achieved new prominence in postwar celebrations of abundance and pleasure.

Women and the Hard Work of Shopping

These descriptions bear little resemblance to women's accounts of shopping. In spite of retailers' claims, shopping continued to be hard work, and it was described in those terms. Checking store ads in newspapers, compiling shopping lists long enough to encompass a week's worth of meals, "shopping around" rather than concentrating purchases at a single store, locating a particular item among shelves and shelves of possibilities, comparing nonstandardized sizes of canned goods, watching the register to avoid overcharges and to ensure that specials were noted, saving the coupons and trading stamps offered by stores and manufacturers—all these activities took time and energy that worked against the promises of supermarkets. (One researcher found that packaging was so confusing that often not even "college-educated women" could accurately determine which canned goods provided the most food for the money.)[79] Yet, shoppers did and were encouraged to do all these things.[80] One woman in 1968 summed up the work of shopping: "It is difficult enough to watch the children, check how the bags are being packed ('please don't squeeze the bananas . . . watch that leaky roast') and count the change. But to add stamps, games and coupons to all this is only insulting the shopper."[81] These anecdotal accounts of the work of food shopping are reinforced in studies by social scientists. The sociologist Joanne Vanek concluded in 1974 that although time spent preparing meals had dropped between 1920 and the late 1960s, the work of shopping and driving to stores had increased so dramatically that virtually no time was saved.[82]

Even without this increase in labor, the smooth efficiency of supermarket shopping turned out to be easily disruptable. One of the easiest ways to do this was simply by talking. Socialization—so crucial to the operation of food stores in earlier decades—now presented a special problem. In 1955, a columnist explained that the challenges of shopping with "the sisters in the housewives' sorority" was more stressful than caring for her two young children. Shopping carts askew, they stopped to "gossip, completely inconsiderate of the rights of other shoppers."[83] Thirteen years later, the "problem" of women talking in stores had not abated. "Women," charged a member of a 1968 shoppers' panel, "shouldn't go to the store to visit with neighbors and talk about their Mah-Jongg game."[84]

Shopping with family members presented other challenges to the carefully ordered spaces of stores. Keeping children entertained, calm, and contained during the relatively lengthy time required to navigate a large supermarket was no easy task—as numerous admonitions about the dangers of unsupervised children bore witness.[85] Sandra Thomas, caring for several young children in the 1950s, remembered that bringing the children along to the store regularly led to impromptu exits, the shopping still uncompleted.[86] Husbands were notoriously susceptible to impulse purchases and posed their own problems.[87] Many women worked hard to shop alone, finding the work of shopping for the family easier when the family was excluded from shopping.

Finally, many women made it clear that they understood full well the lie of retailers' claims that consumers were the ones in power. When representatives from trade groups and food manufacturers asked a 1968 panel of female supermarket shoppers why they had talked so freely about their shopping habits, their response went right to the heart of their limited authority in these stores. Participating in the panel, they answered, allowed them to influence store policy in a direct way. As one woman explained, "It has given all of us a feeling of importance that we don't usually get." Others made similar claims: "It beats going to an individual store manager with a problem."[88] Supermarkets' claims of being influenced by women shoppers were not reflected in women's accounts of the shopping experience.

This gap between the advice of experts and women's lived reality spoke to larger contradictions in the gender prescriptions of the postwar period. For instance, women's paid work and outside interests were celebrated in the popular press, as Joanne Meyerowitz has pointed out.[89] At the same time, however, experts also called on women to prepare, plan, and serve regular meals to their families.[90] Indeed, food preparation was a particular site of contradictions: cooking was an outlet for creativity, but it also—especially given the new techniques and ingredients—required strict adherence to recipes.[91] Moreover, for all the promises of processed foods, cooking continued to invite displays of individual skill and to involve real labor. As Laura Shapiro has importantly documented, women's reuse of prepared foods as ingredients in recipes of their own devising speaks to the pervasiveness of processed foods but also to their limits: the prescriptive instructions for three-can meals were rarely followed.[92] Stores, I contend, worked similarly. As with processed and manufactured food, women worked to turn new supermarket resources to their own ends.

The hard work around food, the contradictions of prescriptive literature, and a reality of shopping that resisted retailers' celebrations, make it easy to dismiss overblown claims of female-controlled pleasure palaces as mere rhetoric, with little resonance for consumers.[93] It would be a mistake, however, to dismiss the appeal of these stores. In the post–World War II years, the ideology of domesticity was particularly compelling. Even women who saw themselves as challenging conventional cold war norms—civil defense protesters, for instance, or those who maintained their identity as leftists—used the language and the priorities of domesticity and motherhood to wage their battles.[94] The pervasiveness of a language of domesticity speaks not only to the strictures of cold war life but also to the ways in which the work of raising children and provisioning families continued to occupy an enormous amount of women's time and effort. Cookbooks, popular articles, and advertising that validated women's domestic work resonated with the women who performed the daily labor of caring for homes, husbands, and children—as well as with the many unmarried women who saw the identity of "housewife" as a likely end point for themselves. Whether or not their experiences of supermarket shopping or motherhood or cooking were pleasurable, such activities were undeniably important aspects of their lives.

The promises of prepared foods and mass retail were, in the context of the hard work of daily life, very meaningful. Grocers and business writers were not wrong when they said that supermarkets could alleviate women's work, even if they understated the difficulties of shopping. There were many reasons to appreciate supermarkets without swallowing whole their promises. Supermarkets and their processed foods allowed women to hold down a job *and* prepare meals at home. The towering displays, the array of goods, the cleanliness, brightness, and possibilities were both impressive *and* assurances that women could find what they needed in the store.

Lower prices made a new range of goods available to people who might previously have felt themselves restricted by class or ethnicity. Finally, going food shopping remained what it always had been, a social experience. One woman recalled that going to the local Safeway was her "one outing of the week. . . . [W]e'd go in a group, a bunch of women, in a car pool."[95] These stores really did represent, as one article put it, "efficiency, service, progress"—and lower prices.[96] A great part of supermarkets' appeal lay in helping women negotiate and resolve the contradictions of 1950s and 1960s gender ideology.

As previous chapters have shown, grocery stores had long functioned as sites in which competing pressures around food and meals came to a head and, ideally, in which they were defused. What made post–World War II supermarkets different was that tensions could no longer be resolved simply by demanding or bargaining for changes in or exceptions to store policy. Whereas in earlier decades women might have entreated their local grocer to stay open late or to allow a child sent on an errand to take a product without paying immediately, such strategies were now clearly discouraged. To be unable to shop during scheduled hours or to shop in person was seen as an individual failing—perhaps regrettable, but certainly not one that ought to impinge on grocers' policies. Surveys, comment cards, and increasingly elaborate tools of surveillance replaced the one-on-one communication that had characterized food shopping in previous decades. In smaller and less systematized stores, grocers could not help but know what their customers wanted—nor could they help but know that the category of women was itself diverse and unstable, made up of individuals. By the 1950s, however, personal frustrations—even when grocers acknowledged them—were difficult to address because they seemed to disrupt the very strategies that "pleased women." To resist store policy, then, was also to resist gender norms. Femininity and passive shopping, once opposed, were now nearly conflated.

Do-It-Yourself: Sex, Masculinity, and Full-Service Hardware Stores

Men's consumption, on the other hand, flourished under very different retail policies. Between 1920 and the 1970s, hardware proprietors tried over and over again to "modernize": to adopt the strategies so dominant in grocery stores and supermarkets—self-service, low-priced goods sold in high volume, and clean and bright stores. Some proprietors made this transition. But many more were deeply ambivalent about the change, asserting that personal service was required for increasingly popular "DIY projects" and the men who did them. The contrasting stories of grocery stores and hardware stores suggest how norms of gender and sex came to be reified, embedded, and reasserted in the structures of consumer culture.

Like supermarkets, hardware stores became icons of middle-class domesticity and were central to its material realization. Hardware stores, however, were associated with tools, not food, and thus with what the historian Steven Gelber has termed "domestic masculinity."[97] Tools allowed men to make important and useful economic contributions to their families while also fulfilling broader cultural prescriptions around gender—in this case, that men be a presence in their homes and take an active role with their children, particularly their sons. Buoyed by the do-it-yourself movement of the 1950s and 1960s, tools and tool purchases became associated with precisely the sort of investment in domestic space (single-family homes, state-of-the-art kitchens and kitchen appliances, home workshops and garages) that fostered the rise of supermarkets. Finally, while they never approached the level of grocery stores in terms of sales, hardware stores were themselves an important retail sector, consisting of more than twenty-seven thousand stores that sold a little less than $3 billion worth of goods in 1967.[98]

Yet, hardware stores followed a path very different, both structurally and discursively, from that of grocery stores. As late as 1967, more than 95 percent of all hardware stores were operated independently. Moreover, relatively small stores made the majority of sales; stores selling more than $500,000 worth of goods, the cutoff used to define a food supermarket, made only 18 percent of all sales.[99] Moreover, hardware stores were famous both for the wide array of tools they offered and for the personal service that accompanied the sales. Hardware stores, for all their embeddedness in postwar consumer culture, were institutionally quite distinctive.

That the trajectory of hardware stores into mass retailing differed from that of grocery stores would have surprised pre–World War II hardware store operators. In the 1920s and 1930s, hardware and groceries were sold in similar ways. Hardware store margins were similar to those of grocery stores (averaging around 26 percent between 1923 and 1925, according to one national study),[100] and the average range of profits was also similar (rarely more than 4 percent in hardware stores).[101] Although hardware stores were often of greater physical size, this reflected the large space needed for stocking goods rather than the functions of a large-scale enterprise; the vast majority of hardware stores in 1928 consisted of five or fewer "selling employees."[102]

Finally, hardware store proprietors shared with small grocers a fear of incursion by chain store firms—and drew from their strategies to stay afloat. Hardware retailers, for instance, shared grocers' interest in voluntary chains. As a result, a move toward central buying and, in some cases, central management typified hardware retailing between the end of World War I and the end of World War II. In the early 1920s, wholesalers occasionally had tried to integrate manufacturing operations and then to continue vertical expansion by signing on store owners who agreed to make a large proportion of their purchases from the new firm. This, for instance, was the plan of the Winchester Agency stores—a result of the merger of Simmons Hardware Co. (a wholesaler) with the Winchester Co.[103] Most viable organizations, however, consisted of dealer-owned voluntary chains or buying associations operated by wholesalers. While the plans varied, they generally included some assurance that dealers would purchase most of their goods from the same source and, often, that they would engage in collective advertising campaigns or use similar logos in advertising their stores.[104]

Some of the most striking and most compelling examples occurred in Chicago. Ace Stores originated in 1925, when four hardware dealers on the North Side decided to begin buying collectively.[105] Ace was among the strictest in terms of requirements on members—proprietors agreed to make all their purchases through the Ace buying organization, the firm would sell only to its members, and similar signage and aesthetics demonstrated strong central control.[106]

Ace remained an important name in the hardware business after the war, but the trend that it had seemed to represent—that of increasing standardization—did not come to pass. Instead, postwar hardware stores remained small, often family-run enterprises that emphasized personal attention. This is not to say that hardware stores did not adopt and adapt to mass retailing. Many did. Proprietors installed open shelving and began keeping goods on the store floor rather than on inaccessible shelves or in back storage rooms. Some stores expanded in size and began carrying more varieties and larger stocks of goods. Conventional hardware stores continued to face competition, both from building and lumber supply firms that were now reaching out to amateur handymen and, in the 1950s and 1960s, from "discount houses" (like Topps, in Chicago). These firms mimicked the strategies of early supermarkets, opening bare-bones facilities in old warehouses or factory lofts and selling housewares, including hardware, at prices far lower than most retailers could afford to match.[107]

None of this, however, immediately transformed hardware retailing in the way that it had food retailing. Although by the late 1970s chains of large home repair supercenters had opened (among them, Home Depot), in the 1950s and 1960s—at the height of postwar consumption, the moment when mass retail seemed everywhere—price competition and chains did not invade hardware, nor did hardware retailers drop their emphasis on personalized service. Instead, individual proprietors affiliated themselves with larger wholesaler-organized chains or, more commonly, with retailer-owned cooperatives (in which individual proprietors owned a central buying system, often operating much like a wholesaler). True Value (originally called Cotter and Co.) grew from 25 members at its founding in 1948 to 460 in 1958.[108] When Hibbard, Spencer, and Bartlett, one of the nation's largest hardware wholesalers, initiated an "associates" program for retail customers, eight hundred stores enlisted within a year.[109]

In these chains, and in hardware stores generally, dealers were encouraged to modernize, as independent grocers had, by instituting self-service, by cleaning and decorating store interiors, and by standardizing offerings. This proceeded slowly, however. Independent proprietors continued to make the vast majority of sales, and stores, while they might carry a brand name on the outside, could vary remarkably on the inside. As late as 1968, the president of Ace found himself repeating calls that had been made since the early 1920s—that hardware stores ought to expand their size, invest in advertising, and feature the brands, items, and names carried by their central supplier (in this case, Ace).[110]

Moreover, stores continued to feature personalized attention. Ace celebrated its "Helpful Hardware Man" through ads and publicity. The firm was careful to describe the change to open shelving and self-service as one that enhanced the advisory function of store staff. Rather than run to back rooms to obtain the right merchandise, self-service meant that a clerk's only job would be to act as a helpful guide available to make suggestions and answer questions.[111]

True Value, likewise, "cautiously endorsed self-service wherever appropriate in hardware stores, so long as knowledgeable personnel remained available to assist customers." Similarly, when Central Hardware Co. in Kirkwood, Missouri (outside Saint Louis), adopted the "supermarket way" in a new store that featured self-service and shopping carts, it maintained "experts" to staff each department: "This way, a customer having a plumbing or electrical problem can get suggestions as to what to buy and even how to fix it."[112] As hardware stores began using self-serve display racks, the writers of *Business Week* noted that "supermarket techniques are capturing the staid old hardware store." Even here, however, "hardware merchants find definite limits on how far they can go in self-service and mass display. . . . [T]he hardware dealer has always had a major function as guide and counselor to his customers. You can't hang advice on the wall or package it neatly in a bottle."[113] Self-service, like expansion into regional or national chains, met only limited success.

Along with the emphasis on service, the other distinguishing feature of hardware stores in this period was the focus of so much of merchandising on men. For instance, campaigns often centered on temptations particular to heterosexual men. One display at a national trade show made this connection vividly: perched on the edge of the display, directly under the sign and gesturing vaguely toward the products being shown was a bare-legged woman wearing a very tight blouse and very short shorts. She sat under a large sign that identified this as the "Squeeze-It-Yourself Department"—a reference to collapsible metal tubes (the kind used to dispense caulk or glue) being touted by the manufacturer as well as to the model's sexual availability.[114] This connection between hardware and primal masculine impulses was made by many observers: describing the electrical and plumbing supply department of a new hardware store on Chicago's Far South Side, a reporter wrote, "It takes a very strong-willed man indeed to stroll through this department without being tempted to make purchases."[115] When stores adopted self-service, the explanation was made in terms of men's most basic instincts: "The customer, egged on by the man-child's ancient desire to grab cutting tools will serve himself."[116]

It is not surprising that the distinctive selling strategies of hardware stores were focused on male customers. Tools, the mainstay of the hardware trade, had long been understood as being used by men more than by women.[117] However, in the 1950s and 1960s, hardware stores became lynchpins of the burgeoning "do-it-yourself" movement, which brought tool purchases and hardware stores into cold war domesticity and consumer society.

The DIY movement encouraged men to undertake home repair and larger-scale remodeling projects themselves. Rather than hiring professionals, the growing corps of individual homeowners now took on everything from the installation of new curtain rods to the remodeling of entire rooms.[118] (Perhaps the most extreme example of DIY was blueprints for bomb shelters that fathers might construct with their sons.)[119] A new industry in home repair advice—from books to columns to entire magazines—encouraged and facilitated DIY projects. The *Chicago Tribune*, for instance, employed a full-time "home shop editor" who authored weekly columns between 1949 and 1968 under the moniker "Mr. Fix-It."[120] These advisory products seem to have found a willing audience. By the mid-1950s, home repair was listed as the third-most-popular hobby among married men (behind only television watching and reading).[121] Although women often participated in remodeling projects, it was men's work that stood at the center of the movement, both discursively and materially.

Like the meals that women prepared in their homes, men's repair and remodeling were understood to facilitate child-rearing, providing a vehicle through which men might bond with their sons. Fathers who built birdhouses (or bomb shelters) with their sons were promised that they were setting a "fine example."[122] Moreover, this work had clear economic incentives—at least in theory, men could add to the value of their homes by making them larger or more useful.[123] As more and more families came to own their homes—stretching themselves financially to do so—do-it-yourself projects grew in popularity. Finally, men who spent time in garages and workshops—like women who cooked and shopped carefully—became part of a broader emphasis on heteronormativity in the advice literature and popular culture of the day.[124] In Steven Gelber's phrase, "By the 1950s being handy had, like sobriety and fidelity, become an expected quality in a good husband."[125]

Hardware stores were the places from which DIYers obtained the literal "tools of the trade," a fact that did not go unrecognized by hardware dealers. The keynote speaker of the 1955 annual convention of the Illinois Retail Hardware Association announced, "The growing interest in all sorts of projects by millions of Mr. and Mrs. Do-Its has a pronounced influence on the retail hardware industry. . . . We recognize it as opening new vistas of possibilities and add our enthusiastic approval to that of the nations' home workshop fraternity."[126] As this speaker's use of "fraternity" suggests, while women engaged in DIY projects, their participation was understood to be limited. Men's purchases provided the foundation of hardware store sales.

Hardware stores relied more and more on sales of tools to amateurs. Although manufacturers initially had feared alienating the professional builders and handymen who made up the bulk of their market, they began expanding into retail sales to the ultimate consumer in the postwar period. Pre-World

War II annual sales of power tools averaged $25 million, reflecting the purchases of professional skilled home repairers, carpenters, and industrial machinists who used these tools in their work. By 1954, sales of power tools topped $200 million—a number powered by the purchases of individuals.[127] In 1953, self-proclaimed DIYers "sawed through 500 million square feet of plywood, brushed on 100 million gallons of paint, applied 150 million rolls of wall paper and laid enough asphalt roof tiles to cover the entire state of Oregon."[128] Black and Decker sold fifteen million drills between 1946 and 1954, a dramatic increase from prewar years.[129] As projects became more elaborate, so too did the tools required, and the hardware stores were more than happy to expand their offerings accordingly. (The *Chicago Tribune*'s Mr. Fix-It columns, for instance, referred to coping saws and "an assortment of drill and auger bits" as "standard equipment"—a dramatic expansion in the tool chests of urban and suburban homeowners.)[130] One journalist at the 1955 national hardware trade show described the new "gimmicks" and "glamour" on display—not the elaborately stacked cans, color palettes, or murals of supermarkets—but instead items like "a portable jig saw, router, and shaper" billed by the manufacturer as the "first tool of its kind performing all three jobs."[131]

In these stores, men purchased advice as much as tools. As homeownership spread, and as more and more homeowners took on the work of remodeling, repair, and maintenance, hardware dealers became the only "professionals" with whom homeowners were likely to have contact before tackling home repairs.[132] Home projects were rife with potential for disaster. Indeed, even proponents of DIY projects often celebrated the spectacular failures—implicitly and explicitly pointing to the need for advice from professional hardware dealers.[133] It was not what stores sold so much as the way in which they sold it that gave new homeowners entrée into postwar world of home repair.

Masculinity meant more than cheesecake displays and puttering in garages. In the hardware stores of the 1950s and 1960s, it was big business. However, it was big business conducted in relatively small spaces. In the personalized spaces of these stores—in the conversations between clerks and customers, in the hesitance of owners to fully adopt mass marketing and self-service, in the expectation that customers would want and need guidance as they undertook domestic labors, in the very systems of exchange and distribution—the meanings of masculinity took on structural importance. Even the designs of hardware stores reflected the belief that distinctively male projects involved difficult and challenging work and hence required personal attention and service.

The story of hardware suggests how gender and sex inhered in the very structures of consumer culture—not only in the products people bought but also in the ways they bought them. Put briefly, retailers worked to please women by standardizing the ways in which they were treated; they worked to please men by focusing on their individualism. As subsequent sections will show, these divergent strategies both reflected and contributed to the gendering of citizenship and of political positions. Women's demands for more rights or for more responsibility were complicated because it was easier for society to see them as an easily led mass than as individuals; men's individualism remained a precious and vital aspect of their public and economic lives—a fact that explained their authority over stores (both as operators and as consumers) and over the workings of exchange more generally.

The Problem of Women and the Problem of Mass Consumption

The cultural and material importance of hardware stores might suggest that they, too, figured in another vital postwar discourse—the critique of mass consumption and mass retailing. Although hardware purchases increased during the war and although these purchases made possible crucial features of postwar consumption—domesticity, single-family homeownership, and dramatic increases in consumer spending—critics of mass retailing and mass consumption rarely suggested that men's tool shopping was problematic.[134] Instead, when authors criticized consumer excess, women were their subjects.

One of the most popular exposés of advertising, Vance Packard's *The Hidden Persuaders*, famously documented the subtle and sometimes subliminal marketing methods of package designers, psychologists, producers of advertising copy, and retailers. Packard never discussed hardware stores. Packard did, however, repeatedly reinforce the idea that food shopping was a mindless pursuit and that women grocery store shoppers were especially vulnerable to marketers' techniques. In his chapter on supermarkets, "Babes in Consumerland," Packard painted an image of women mesmerized by the "fairyland" of colorful and well-stocked shelves, in a "trance-like" state, so distracted by the store that "they passed by neighbors and old friends without noticing or greeting them."[135]

Packard's image of the passive, disconnected female shopper echoed other social scientific and popular literature of this era. The 1959 issue of the *Science Digest* described the results of the new tests with the "Van Rosen Videometric Comparator," which found that "65 percent of women shoppers do not get beyond one word identifying a package on display" and that manufacturers therefore, needed to focus on large letters and package design; women shoppers could not be expected to actually read.[136] Relying on more qualitative "data," a woman writing for *Harper's* in 1960 used sarcasm to unmask deep concerns with the politics of supermarkets. In one of many passages decrying the difficulties of supermarket shopping, she asserted that "it has been proved that shoppers respond to these assaults on the senses [that is, the huge array of gaudy goods, elaborate packaging, use of music in stores] by wandering around in a semi-hypnotic state, unable to remember where they parked their cars or why they came to the market at all."[137] Writing more seriously in his essay "Sad Heart at the Supermarket," Randall Jarrell imagined a dialogue between an interviewer and "a vague gracious figure, a kind of Mrs. America." When asked, " 'But while you waited for the intercontinental ballistic missiles what did you do?' She answers, 'I bought things.' "[138]

Indeed, the notion of women as inherently passive shoppers was so pervasive that it informed responses to events that would seem to have suggested just the opposite—women's organized protests of high prices in grocery stores. In the mid-1960s, a new wave of consumer activism hit retailers across the country, spurred, as Lizabeth Cohen has argued, by renewed government support of consumers' fair treatment.[139] While policymakers and journalists publicized particularly stark examples of misleading packaging and other attempts to manipulate consumers, unions and grassroots organizations sustained, energized, and politicized the exposés.

In the fall of 1966, retailers faced an onslaught of grassroots protests against rising food prices. These protests were waged by self-identified "housewives" and, worst of all in the eyes of grocers, focused on retailers rather than producers or wholesalers. Urging vocal picketing of chain supermarkets and boycotts of their products, the protesters garnered enormous publicity for their cause.[140] Supermarket firms reacted with alarm to the public protests of women. They hosted an emergency meeting in the Chicago headquarters of the Super Market Institute, created talking points for retailers hit by boycotts, launched an enormous public relations campaign explaining why grocers were not to blame for high prices, and reminded all grocers that they were at risk in these turbulent times.[141]

In the short term, the protests clearly worked. Prices fell, the promotional games and trading stamps that had been a particular target of the protesters assumed a smaller place in store marketing efforts, and grocers expressed genuine alarm at the prospect of disaffected and organized women shoppers. In one well-publicized and dramatic response, the directors of trade associations and chains sat down with "typical" cross-sections of shoppers in a series of panels that stretched across the country and over several years.[142]

Yet, the protests had little impact on the top-down structures of food distribution or the belief that women were ill-suited for authority over stores. Although stores continued to try to win over male customers, the panels were made up entirely of women.[143] Even at the height of the movement, the activists' femaleness was taken by many as an impediment. Protesters were regularly criticized in heavily gendered terms. Boycotts, for example, were referred to as "ladycotts."[144] Policymakers, even those who were nominally consumer advocates, expressed doubt that "housewives" could mount an effective protest. A representative of the Federal Trade Commission said, "The housewives' activities may or may not serve a purpose. . . . It depends on how careful they are. It isn't enough just to scream, 'Cut prices by 15 per cent.'"[145] This skepticism toward the movement was reinforced when the newly appointed special assistant to the president for consumer affairs, Esther Peterson, was asked to resign after she openly supported the boycotters. Efforts to create a permanent federal-level consumer agency failed—as they had in the 1930s.[146]

The broader discourse of the politically inept and ill-prepared female consumer seems to have been left relatively untouched by these events. In 1970, two books that focused on the dissatisfactions of women shoppers were published. Each was written from a different side of the consumption debate. Robert Chisholm, writing for the largest trade association of chain grocery stores, saw the gender relations of supermarkets as the basis for their success. In *The Darlings*, Chisholm explained, "The Darlings are those enchanting people, the housewives, the purchasing agents of the world to whom we beam our advertising and promotional appeal, and whom we must woo and win in our affairs and our affaires."[147] Authors more sympathetic to the consumer movement shared a similar understanding of women as blank slates—women were important but ultimately dependent. In *The Supermarket Trap*, Jennifer Cross addressed women consumers' growing anger over high prices. She explained that rising costs of food "not only pinched the ladies' pockets, they hit at their instincts as homemakers, aggravating them in a way that the rising costs of other things, such as medical care, did not."[148] However, although this anger had led to a spurt of boycotts and direct confrontations in the late 1960s, Cross neither encouraged nor expected her audience to follow up on those dramatic expressions of frustration. Noting that "housewives' groups" had dissolved quickly because "many of the ladies found protesting a searing experience . . . and grew discouraged at the impossibility of changing the system," Cross urged her audience simply to adopt conventional money-saving techniques, such as buying in bulk, resisting the temptations of packaging and processed foods, and pushing for labeling laws that would help them choose goods more intelligently.[149] Broad reforms—and certainly those led by women—were unrealistic. Indeed, in her analysis, women could barely be critical of marketing techniques, let alone engineer systemic changes in distribution. In the postwar period, the notion of women's vulnerability to spectacle, low prices, and elaborately decorated stores seemed natural, reified in the structures of distribution and in the discourses used to understand those structures. The older view of women's shopping as inherently and necessarily antagonistic, a result of two parties with divergent interests meeting over a store counter, had been lost.

Why did the larger discourse remain untouched in light of the long history of women's claims to authority in stores and their contemporary resistance to store policies? Here the response of the supermarket industry is instructive. In addition to lowering prices, grocers initiated a campaign that emphasized the idea that supermarkets were already giving people what they wanted, so structural change would be difficult, if not impossible. Part of what supermarket operators did was to reveal statistics about themselves (for instance, that their actual net profits were a little over 1 percent, not the 10 to 70 percent that some customers imagined). They also pointed to the ways in which, they claimed, consumer demand hampered any easy remedy to high prices. When confronted with the widespread belief that eliminating games and trading stamps from stores would reduce prices, the president of the National Association of Food Chains "patiently explained" that prices were a function of volume, not only costs, and that games and trading stamps increased volume—removing them ultimately would raise prices since it would reduce the volume of sales. Pleasing women, he reiterated, remained grocers' primary goal. Indeed, the panel discussions that supermarket operators sponsored were evidence of their efforts to reinforce the idea that women's demand remained at the center of their strategy. They were, in the words of *Business Week* journalists, "aimed at finding out just what consumer complaints are and determining what can be done to resolve them."[150] To fix the problems of stores, these responses implied, would be to go against women's natures. Implicitly and by extension, the women who wanted those changes were either ill-informed or missing crucial feminine qualities—or both.

The Limits of the Mass Market

The biggest challenges to supermarkets' claims that they pleased people were the moments when they did not even reach them. For Chicago's poor African Americans and for many retailers of all races, the claims that food stores were apolitical and that women's power determined store strategy and practices simply made no sense. Food stores and the firms that ran them remained vehicles for imposing—or resisting—inequality.[151]

One example of such inequality and resistance was the civil rights project Operation Breadbasket. A program of the Southern Christian Leadership Conference, Operation Breadbasket sought to bring the civil rights movement into northern cities by opening access to jobs and capital to urban African Americans. Because organizers focused on businesses that drew profits from African American customers, many of their campaigns focused on grocery stores and food manufacturers. The group proved extraordinarily successful, winning concessions from larger chain store operations as well as from the associations that coordinated the efforts of smaller groceries and that did so much business in African American neighborhoods. These were sizable gains—protesters won more than twenty-five hundred jobs in Chicago and, according to local sources, added $1.5 million to the assets of black-owned banks.[152]

Operation Breadbasket highlighted the long-standing efforts of African Americans to win employment in white-owned firms that benefited from spending by African Americans. Its strategies differed from earlier efforts in one telling way. Whereas in the 1930s boycotts had been effective weapons against local retailers who were heavily invested in particular neighborhoods, the limited presence of national chains in black Chicago made boycotts more difficult now. Only one of Operation Breadbasket's campaigns involved a consumer boycott—the campaign against independently owned Certified stores.

The decline of boycotts against local stores in the urban North, a mainstay of African American efforts to obtain jobs in white-owned retail in the 1930s, points to another difficulty commonly experienced by the city's blacks—not that they didn't work in grocery stores, but that they had such limited access to them and such limited choices when they got inside.[153]

By the mid-1960s, it was a truism that food shopping was difficult in poor African American neighborhoods. A writer for the *New Republic* described the units of an unnamed chain store firm that were located in poor neighborhoods of Washington, D.C., as having only limited choices of the least expensive brands of staples and low-quality produce. The meat, brown around the edges, was "not comparable to that displayed in fashionable Georgetown" and yet was more expensive. Many staples—dried beans, sugar, and lard—were unpriced. When the shopper asked the price, the checker quoted a figure higher than that charged by the same firm in its stores in other parts of Washington. Produce was also a problem. "In a store in a poor neighborhood the lettuce would be wilted, the apples bruised, the green peppers shriveled." Yet customers remained dependent on this store. The author reported that "customers aren't willing to stand up to store managers," perhaps in part because "small branches of supermarkets" that operated in poor neighborhoods were, for all of their faults, still "more pleasant places to shop than small groceries" that were the alternative.[154]

Similar problems were documented in cities across the country. In Chicago, a social worker who moved to a West Side "slum" in the summer of 1966 left after three weeks, in large part because food was so expensive and such household necessities as a ball of string were nearly impossible to obtain.[155] Investigations of chain supermarkets in many northern cities revealed that those in poor neighborhoods were dirtier and stocked goods of lower quality and in fewer sizes than did their counterparts in middle-class and suburban locations.[156]

In language similar to that used by retailers, reformers treated the facts (that food of lower quality was being sold in poor neighborhoods in lesser quantities and at higher prices) as intransigent and inevitable. The *New Republic*'s investigator in Washington, D.C., found alarming inequities in the quality and price of goods but did not see government interventions as effective or realistic. Instead, in an otherwise sharp critique of distribution, he encouraged the stationing of home economists in local stores so that they might provide advice to customers. He also, quite tellingly, suggested busing poor people to neighborhoods of better-off people and better stores.[157]

These limited responses come to seem positively radical in comparison with the solutions that supermarket operators came up with. The president of the National Association of Food Chains asked for patience and sympathy when confronted by a Philadelphia housewife who said she had heard that chain supermarkets sold goods of lower quality in black neighborhoods. A *Business Week* journalist paraphrased his reply: "Adamy and his colleagues deny everything—and then explain why it happens. Suburban stores, they say, are bigger than ghetto stores, with more parking space, roomier aisles, better display, and greater store traffic. The implication to experienced merchandisers is plain: fresher product, greater variety. . . . By contrast, land in ghetto areas is often costly, and parking space in short supply. The result: fewer stores, cramped, crowded, and offering few products."[158] Finally, in the wake of increased criticism of supermarkets, the head of the NAFC began working with the U.S. Department of Agriculture and President Nixon's consumer affairs adviser to create a series of skits to "be performed by local [African American] residents in churches and schools." The skits were to be "written in simple, down-to-earth language" so that they might best "communicate the industry's complex problems."[159] Suggesting that the African American families who paid for those "problems" would be interested in such skits, let alone allow their children to participate in them, is nothing short of astonishing.

In these analyses, both progressive and conservative, poor Americans suffered not because of discrimination or racism, but because their neighborhoods or buying styles were unsuited to large supermarkets. The rhetoric reflected the one circulating in response to the contemporaneous protests over high prices and needless marketing techniques. In each case, both the industry and self-proclaimed consumer advocates refused to imagine that structural change was possible. Complaining individuals simply had to "pay the price"— both economically and socially—for not fitting the system of food distribution that had developed. What went unsaid was that the actions that this system required from customers—the ability to buy in large quantities, to travel to the store and back home with groceries in tow, to navigate a large store, to pay the price that the store charged with little resistance or negotiation and generally in cash—were recent changes that had transformed food distribution. That a retail format famous for pleasing women did not actually do so, that it might be structurally incapable of pleasing whole groups of women, and that it might even exclude large numbers of people from the "mass" market, remained a bald contradiction.

No event better demonstrates the power relations still being played out in grocery stores or the limits of the "mass" market, than the urban insurrection that took place in Chicago in April 1968. In the three days following Martin Luther King Jr.'s assassination on April 4, Chicago's police and firefighters joined National Guard troops in confronting residents of black neighborhoods who had seized control of streets and attacked neighborhood businesses. The results of that confrontation were profound: curfews were imposed, the mayor issued an infamous "shoot-to-kill" order, and at least a hundred buildings were burned to the ground. Whole stretches of Madison and Roosevelt avenues lay in ruins. Marked first by gutted buildings and later by empty lots, these neighborhoods made visible the problems that seemed to symbolize cities more generally.

In Chicago's 1968 insurrection and the many similar disorders in other cities in the mid- and late 1960s, much of the activity centered on retail—either its protection or its procurement.[160] The fires, the looting, and the police presence occurred in the spaces of stores (or the spaces where stores had been). Food and grocery stores were a particular catalyst for fury—and their destruction became a kind of symbol of the social disorder of the insurrection.

Newspaper reports made prominent mention of attacks on Chicago grocery stores. Articles described people running off with cases of liquor or stores' stock lying in disarray (indeed this became a kind of motif in journalistic coverage). Photographers snapped images of shopping carts full of food—or even more powerful ones of shopping carts full of incongruent, nonfood items like televisions or clothing.

Attacks on stores were a special feature of coverage of the riots in predominantly black areas of the city's Near North Side. One journalist described a neighborhood in which "food rotted on sidewalks outside food stores which were looted and virtually torn apart." The *Chicago Tribune* featured the story of Jack Levin, whose store near the Cabrini Green housing project had been set on fire the previous day. Stunned by the smoking ruins of his store, the owner (a resident of the North Side suburb of Niles) mourned what he perceived as the injustice of the situation: "When I moved [and opened a new store, several years earlier] those people owed me $5,000, I wiped it off the books for them. . . . Why me? What did I do to them? My prices weren't only fair, they were the lowest around. This is the thanks I get. I've lent my customers money when they were short. They all knew me. I tried to be good to them."[161] This grocer, like many others, saw extensions of credit and personalized relations as exceptions to the rule of mass retail. They also understood these exceptions as privileges for which residents should be grateful.

Such destruction and such personalized analyses tragically illustrate the social resentments that continued to permeate grocery stores. Not only had social ties to local residents not saved stores, but such ties were also marked by more resentment than many white people had imagined.

As might be expected, given the industry and government responses to other expressions of dissatisfaction with stores, "solutions" to the violence and destruction of property centered on education and integration into preexisting systems. Federal authorities sponsored new "consumer education programs."[162] In Chicago, the Hyde Park Bank took advantage of a new loan program from the state of Illinois to provide emergency loans to black small business owners in looted neighborhoods.[163] The Small Business Administration, in Chicago and elsewhere, created several new initiatives to jump-start and sustain black entrepreneurship.[164] When these failed, the urban insurrections were taken as reasons to cease doing business along what had been busy commercial streets—the violence was seen as a cause, rather than a symptom, of the isolation of black neighborhoods and the difficulties of living there.[165]

Discussions of women's work were almost entirely absent from discussions of the riot, its causes, or its solutions. Despite images and anecdotes of women openly taking and cooking food, the burning and looting of stores were understood as being either about racial injustice or about rioters' materialistic

FIGURE 7.5. *Interior of a Chicago supermarket, 1968. This store, like many others in Chicago, was attacked in the violent aftermath of the assassination of Martin Luther King Jr.* (*BE051483 | Standard RM | © Bettmann/CORBIS*)

desire for consumer goods. In this analysis, the long-standing and complicated relationship between black women and food—indeed, the frustrations and necessity of food shopping generally—were lost.[166] Rather than discuss the difficulties of reproductive labor (which would have pointed to the shortcomings of capitalism and commercial exchange), analysts and policymakers oriented later discourses around productive labor and the ways in which higher wages and more business ownership (in other words, *more* commerce and capital) would address root causes of the unrest. In this way, the 1968 riots marked the disappearance of women's labor, their authority, and the shortcomings and frustrations of *all* markets from discussions of food shopping.

The looting of stores and the efforts of supermarket operators to celebrate their hard work on behalf of women, like the arresting images put forward by Vance Packard and supermarket designers, and like the cartoons that lampooned men's DIY fiascos and the newspaper columns that celebrated handymen's projects, point to the many concerns Americans expressed through consumption (and fears of consumption) in the postwar period. Many contradictory concerns—the enjoyment of bounty and prosperity, a dislike for the suburbs, an appreciation for single-family homes, excitement at discovering new products, and the danger of losing individuality and succumbing to peer pressure and social forces—swirled around consumer goods.

What is striking, however, is that the possibilities and pitfalls of consumer society were so commonly denoted by the image of women shopping in a supermarket. Even in the face of women's accounts of the disorder and labor required for food shopping, their organized resistance to elaborate and costly marketing practices, and open physical attacks on stores themselves, authors, artists, and policymakers continued to use supermarkets and women's food shopping as showcases of smooth-running consensus. Not only was this connotation misleading, but it was also an abrupt change from earlier in the century, when many Americans had perceived grocery stores as arenas of disorder and women's assertiveness.

At the heart of this change was the erasure of politics from descriptions of food shopping and from dominant explanations of grocers' motives. Instead, women's pleasure and demand were highlighted. Women's difficult balancing of neighborhood and familial politics, grocers' efforts to win authority in the everyday work of buying and selling food, the government's laws and regulations, and distribution systems that made retailers' authority so important to broader political economy—all of these were obscured by the growing consensus that the current structure of distribution rested on women's most basic desires.

Put simply, retailing did not work that way. Supermarkets and grocery stores did *not* always put demand at their center. Demand has never been the only, indeed not even always the most important, variable in the decisions made by grocers. That we think that it is, and that creating more equitable or more just or more politically informed mass consumption seems so difficult, owes much to the obscured history of grocery stores and the discourse of apolitical, passive, female consumers articulated and embedded in 1950s and 1960s supermarkets.

Conclusion

The Point of Purchase

The 1976 sleeper hit *The Stepford Wives* vividly evokes the cultural and social importance of supermarkets in the last decades of the twentieth century. In the film's haunting final scene, smiling women in long, flowing summer dresses calmly roll shopping carts through an immaculate, well-stocked supermarket. The scene is a fitting finale for the film's disturbing plot, which slowly reveals that the Stepford Men's Club has been systematically kidnapping the wives of its members and replacing them with robots who act as self-sacrificing and devoted homemakers, robots identical to the original women in all respects but for their vacant eyes. The heroine uncovers the plot, but not in time to save her own life—she, too, is turned into an animatronic look-alike. As elevator music plays softly in the background, previously vivacious and thoughtful women nod to one another with blank expressions on their faces as they stroll the aisles of the nearly silent grocery store.[1]

The filmmakers' use of the supermarket as a setting for soul-deadening passivity suggests the hidden violence against women in seemingly peaceful domestic arrangements. When this film and the novel on which it was based were created, supermarkets seemed ideal settings for such juxtapositions. By 1975, supermarkets figured prominently both in celebrations of consumers' choices and in critiques of their consumption. They had become crucial to Americans' access to food and to much of the nation's modern political economy. Supermarkets were, as all grocery stores had long been, distinctively identified with women's domesticity and the commercial and public spaces that had become central to domestic life. For the filmmakers, a supermarket must have been an obvious site in which to explore the tensions of modern life.

Even in its efforts to critique contemporary suburban patriarchy, how-

FIGURE C.1. The Stepford Wives, *publicity still, 1975. (Image courtesy of PhotoFest Photo Archive)*

ever, the film did something else, too. It implied that everyday food shopping required only routinized, mindless labor, that consummate food shoppers—women—could not both perform domestic labor and maintain autonomous thoughts or a desire for authority. They could not both oversee families' grocery shopping and remain independent individuals. *The Stepford Wives* leaves the viewer with the notion that modern food procurement is best accomplished by robots.

Much of this book has been dedicated to proving that this was not the case. Food shopping had long required work—physical labor as well as social and cultural strategizing, as well as assertions of individual needs against larger marketplace structures. While the operations of supermarkets and mass retail often concealed individual expressions of authority over stores, they did not create a world in which individual effort of that sort was unnecessary.

Food shopping has changed since *The Stepford Wives* was filmed, but the implications of the final scene, and its version of supermarket shopping, remain. Below I analyze two examples of recent changes in food shopping that suggest both the new retail landscape and the ongoing challenges and pressures faced by women who undertake the task of food procurement. Expectations of pacified food shopping continue to haunt discussions of food distribution, women's domestic labor, and possibilities for change. To understand fully the significance of supermarkets and mass retail, we must appreciate the broad resonance of the image of dead women peacefully pushing shopping carts.

In recent years, food procurement has, for a variety of reasons, become more heterogeneous.[2] Two new terms that portray opposing images of food shopping evoke the new landscape of food provisioning. "Food desert" came into use in the last decades of the twentieth century to describe urban areas bereft of grocery stores. These areas are "deserts" in the sense that food, especially fresh or unprocessed food, is very difficult to obtain. Many of the neighborhoods I've described earlier in this book are now characterized in this way.[3] In contrast, the term "locavore" evokes precisely the opposite image of eating locally. Here, local surroundings are recast as sources of bounty and health, producing foods and businesses that can support environmental well-being. Originally coined by a group of women in 2005, and declared "word of the year" for 2007 by the editors of The Oxford American Dictionary, it has very quickly become a touchstone of new efforts to combine a taste for high-quality foods with ecological concerns.[4] The language of the new food landscape—"locavore" and "food desert"—offers contradictory analyses of the conditions under which people shop. Their juxtaposition highlights bitter class divisions but also demands further exploration. How is it possible that practices of food shopping—or at least discussions of food shopping—could have diverged so sharply?

ALTHOUGH THE ROOTS OF CONTEMPORARY FOOD deserts are long, the most dramatic change occurred in the wake of the 1968 riots. Very quickly, Chicago's poor neighborhoods emptied of grocery stores. In the immediate aftermath of the insurrections, food had to be brought into some areas from outside the community and distributed from makeshift sidewalk stalls and out of the trunks of cars.[5] A year later, "dozens of square blocks [remained] totally vacant."[6] Food distribution remained sporadic and uneven, decades after the rioting was over. Writing about Chicago women and their food work in the early 1980s, Marjorie DeVault described a "poor single mother who lived in a neighborhood with few stores or services." When asked about her concerns with food shopping, the woman began talking neither about price nor about quality—but about the problem of getting to stores. Another woman proudly described how she managed to "make it so good," even on welfare, by being willing to spend extraordinary amounts of time traveling: "'I go to No-Frills, I go to Diamond's, I go to the fruit market. I mean, I don't care, if I have to walk all over the city to get it.'"[7]

This story could have been repeated twenty years later: it was not until 1999, for instance, that Lawndale, a neighborhood on the city's Near West Side, saw the construction of a new grocery store.[8] As recently as 2003, Austin, located farther west, had only one chain supermarket. The locally owned stores in which residents shopped featured produce that was of far lower quality than what was available in neighboring middle-class Oak Park.[9]

Even when stores are present, problems obtaining food are ongoing. At the turn of the twenty-first century, One Stop Food & Liquor, located on the city's South Side, began opening at midnight on the first of each month so that neighborhood residents could spend their electronic benefit transfer credits (EBT, a digital version of food stamps) as soon as they were valid. In a news story designed to illustrate the plight of the poor amid rising food prices, a reporter from MSNBC interviewed several shoppers. Lynda Wheeler described her monthly routine—an endless round of visits to stores, then food pantry shelves and friends' homes, and finally just waiting for new money to be deposited into her EBT account. All the while, she tried to make the food that she had last as long as possible—for example, by watering down the milk. Finally, she had the privilege of staying up until midnight, taking her children with her or finding someone to watch them, so that she could buy the cereal, milk, and eggs with which to cook them breakfast the next day—their first full meal in weeks. This story is typical; for many poor families, food stores, while still important, are at best a limited presence in their lives.

The contrast with the beginning of the twentieth century, when this book began, could not be starker. These same neighborhoods that are now "food deserts" were once sites of intensely competitive food distribution. The presence of peddlers, the close concentration of small stores, and in many cases the proximity to public markets made working-class neighborhoods places where fresh food was often available for purchase in small amounts by people whose financial resources changed from day to day. In those older systems of dense networks and multiple kinds of food vendors expecting to serve the particular needs of female customers, the complete absence of grocery retail of any kind would have been inconceivable. In this context, simple *access* to fresh food was hardly the marker of class status that it has become.

Food retailers have changed not only in number but also in terms of their policies. Groceries at the turn of the century regularly stayed open extremely late for customers and offered them credit to get through until the first of the month. That a store like One Stop Food & Liquor would allow customers to shop late, that poor people had uneven spending patterns, and that the hardships and work of poverty affected stores' practices would have surprised no one, least of all grocers.

The dominance of a single model for food retailing—and the consensus that it is what women want—has contributed to the dramatic decline in poor peoples' shopping options. As grocers converged around the policies that defined the modern supermarket, emphasizing top-down organization, economies of scale, and streamlined service, they quite simply moved away from poor neighborhoods and the unsteady, difficult customers who lived there. Rather than a natural part of doing business, complaints and demands by customers (for instance, that stores open at midnight on the first of the month) can become a reason *not* to do business in a particular community.

A full account of these women's stories of food procurement shows the rifts, fissures, and gaps in a project that is supposed to be seamless. Their stories stand in stark contrast to those told by people who are a better fit with contemporary stores. Supermarkets encourage the production of subjects who shop steadily, in large quantities, and without challenging store policy or demanding too much in the way of help or personal attention. Everyday struggles to stretch food and food budgets, struggles that used to be apparent in stores, are now obscured because the sort of negotiating, informal credit relations, and bargaining that formerly characterized these spaces now rarely takes place in public. Demands for changes in store policy or offerings increasingly occur away from the shop floor, and often far away from neighborhoods where poor people live. Policies of stores and the state make it difficult to see labor, anger, and acts of assertiveness—even when they do occur. Perhaps the most startling aspect of these stories of food procurement and the shortcomings of stores, in historical perspective, is not the limited presence of stores but the absence of politically charged encounters in them, and the absence of any indication that Lynda Wheeler and people like her should be outraged and that they might bring that outrage to bear on grocers or the state.

Although the stakes and costs are quite different, food shopping can be tension-filled for anyone, even for more affluent people. Middle-class and upper-class women also negotiate the uncertain terrain of food prices, family preferences, and shortages. They, like poor women, are expected to oversee food shopping. They are also disciplined by stores that make it difficult to change policy, offerings, and treatment. Their stories, too, would reveal the ongoing challenges, frustrations, and rewards of satisfying all the stakeholders in family meals.[10]

Local foods movements—famously middle- and upper-class in their make-up—exemplify the ways in which even calls for dramatic change in food shopping rely upon women's commitments (sometimes contradictory) to family, politics, efficiency, and fiscal health—and the labor that they expend in fulfilling them.

To avoid the environmental costs of food produced far away, many Americans are attempting to source more of their food from their immediate surroundings. Eating local often accompanies efforts to garden urban lots more intensively, to eat seasonally, and to learn about the sources of food. Such a change often (although, of course, not necessarily) involves class-based "taste" (for instance, looking for especially fresh and high-quality "gourmet" ingredients) and heavy investments of time and money. Shopping at farmers' markets, buying shares of farms' produce (via community supported agriculture, or CSAs), and growing or processing large amounts of one's own food are all examples of local eating. Michael Pollan has been at the forefront of this movement away from conventional food systems and stores, famously arguing in an open letter to the president of the upscale Whole Foods grocery chain that "17 percent of US fossil fuel consumption goes to feeding ourselves."[11] As the writer Barbara Kingsolver vividly puts it, "The average food item on a U.S. grocery shelf has traveled farther than most families go on their annual vacations."[12] This sort of dedication to local food procurement must be an important part of more just and more sustainable living.

However, these strategies that otherwise demand radical changes in food shopping continue to obscure the inevitable work of navigating food markets and to deny the workings of power at the point of purchase. They celebrate and predict seamless commercial interactions. Advocates of local buying rarely acknowledge that since one cannot obtain all of one's groceries at farmers' markets, buying from local producers greatly expands the amount of time required for food procurement—and that this work has disturbing implications for the pressures placed on women. When such gendered divisions of labor are discussed, they are generally celebrated. Kingsolver moves on from her concerns about fuel usage to speak glowingly of the "nurturing routines" that emerge from daily cooking and eating. She praises Spanish and French women who go to market every day after work, "feeding their loved ones with aplomb," and celebrates the women writers she met who successfully moved conversations "from postcolonial literature to fish markets . . . [and] had no apparent concern with sounding unliberated."[13] Issues of equity within families' division of labor and concerns about the goodness and pleasures of domesticity (let alone its separate existence), are dealt with in passing, if at all, in this and in many other celebrations of local eating.

In these progressive arguments, commercial exchange works when shoppers (usually, but not always female) can come to depend on producers without needing to assert themselves. Advocates describe local markets in which people know each other and, as a result, have fair, beneficial, and open exchanges. Too often, issues of racial equality and power relations are overlooked in celebrations of all that is good about local foods. The possibilities for disempowerment at the hands of a limited group of providers; the resentments of farmers (often of a lower class or different ethnic group than the relatively well-off shoppers); the fact that, for many poor people restricted to their neighborhoods, eating locally means being exploited by high prices for inferior goods; the bitter irony of the much larger "local" space that serves wealthier people; and the unthinking romanticization of the work of shopping for, cooking, processing, and serving food procured in this way, all too often remain obscured.[14]

Such visions miss important truths about commerce—namely, that products must always be made, however awkwardly, to fit actual people's needs and perceptions of needs. Even the relatively resource-rich shoppers targeted in "local foods" writing are asked to work. However, just as poor women's laborious shopping is a marker of their poverty in other accounts, in these celebrations of the possibilities of more sustainable food provisioning, middle-class women's *lack* of labor acts as a kind of class marker. In these tellings, one sign of being affluent is that markets work for women, vendors provide what is needed, and food shopping rarely involves exhausting decisions. Perhaps it is, according to these authors, even fun and rewarding. Juxtaposing the phenomenon of local foods with that of food deserts reveals a reactionary implication of contemporary understandings of food shopping: if food procurement requires extra authoritativeness or is unsatisfying, it is because of individual shortcomings and individual lack of resources, not because of problems inherent in markets and capitalism. This faith in the market and in intimate exchange limits even ostensibly progressive visions of change.

In both food deserts and food cornucopias, consumers' assertiveness, antagonism, and demands for authority would be disruptive. In analyses of all sorts, the success of a market—whether an inner city liquor store or a high-end farmers' market—is epitomized in the image of a woman walking away satisfied by what others have given her.

The long history of gender relations in grocery stores is crucial to seeing why this model of consumer-as-dependent has taken hold so fiercely, why it resonates so deeply. It was not everyone's demands, but *women's* demands that figured prominently in the discourse of supermarkets. Claims to understanding their needs and concerns legitimized store growth and fed a broader faith in an invisible market that would satisfy all participants.

Older debates about women's authority over stores thus have high stakes for contemporary discussions about how all consumers, not just women, should act and about what they should want. People in the first decades of the twentieth century understood food shopping as necessarily disruptive, profoundly worklike, and obviously political. That understanding changed between the end of World War I and the end World War II. It was in these unsettled times that policymakers, retailers, and Americans came to rely on the gender ideologies and relations that undergirded postwar supermarkets, structured postwar consumer society, and that reified the notion that consumption was not and ought not be a politically dangerous act. By the 1950s and 1960s, the work of procuring goods for families had come to be understood as rendering its practitioners unfit to exercise direct power over stores or governments and uninterested in doing so.

The older notion that food shopping invited, or even required, assertiveness and personal attention from retailers, that it could be a route to broader economic and political authority, and that it was as difficult as other forms of work all but disappeared from public policy, business strategy, and social movements in the wake of the 1968 insurrections. Even when feminism revived in the 1960s and 1970s, feminists rarely looked to consumption as a site from which women might gain economic authority. Indeed, many second-wave feminists articulated compelling criticisms of the effects of advertising and consumer goods on women's self-images and urged women to resist "buying into" male-dominated institutions whenever possible.[15] Consumption, once a point of activism and seemingly the gateway to new freedoms, now seemed to many Americans simply an indication of materialism and alienation.

In subsequent years, the possibilities for structural changes in the system of food retailing also disappeared. Indeed, the possibility of providing some authority over food distribution to the people responsible for food procurement seems only rarely to have been articulated as a solution to the problem of poor food availability, then or now. Even to raise the idea was to be critiqued as naïve because people's use of supermarkets and their purchase of processed foods were so often taken as evidence that few Americans wanted anything else.

In the last decades of the twentieth century, celebration of the power of "the market" to satisfy—unimpeded by analysis of the power relations that sustain exchange—was extended to many realms of American life. Policymakers, activists, and many scholars explicitly and implicitly asserted that consumption was the best way to distribute *anything* and that all institutions and all interactions could be understood in the language of markets and choice.[16]

Many scholars have labeled the emergence of this language and the strategies associated with it "neoliberalism," and they have pointed to neoliberalism's triumph in the 1970s and 1980s, especially in development policies abroad.[17] We can also see its roots, however, in politics that are older and closer to home—policies that are domestic in every sense of the word. The argument presented here places its roots in the widely held cold war notion that consumer demand drives firms and that carefully managed consumer spaces (malls, supermarkets, amusement parks, and so on) can buffer political, economic, and social threats. Hence, any shortcomings of these marketplaces are the problem of idiosyncratic or otherwise nonnormative consumers and businesses rather than of capitalism itself.

In other words, neoliberal ideas about choice and the benefits of markets resonate precisely because a certain gendered ideology of consumption also does. It is no accident that, as scholars of queer history have documented, neoliberalism entered 1980s debates around sexual freedom and familial responsibilities. Neoliberalism emerged alongside postwar celebration of commercially enabled domesticity.[18] Decades earlier, a discourse of women's blissful satisfaction in the hands of systematized, carefully managed markets anchored the earliest examples of neoliberalism.

Gender matters to grocery stores and to the problems of mass retail—not because women do all the shopping but because the structures of supermarkets have been justified in their name and built around their supposed desires. Undoing current systems of distribution requires undoing ideas about what women want. Indeed, it requires undoing the very idea that "women" exist as a coherent entity, are particularly amenable to mass retailing, and want any one thing. Women, as a discursive category and a lived identity, ground mass retailing's politics and its historical development.[19]

FOR SUPERMARKETS, AS FOR OTHER THINGS, analyses of the past shape prescriptions for the future. In this case, apolitical histories of supermarkets suggest that only apolitical solutions to food provisioning are possible. If demand drove the creation of supermarkets and mass retail, then it is difficult to imagine public policy initiatives (for instance, to make locally produced foods more accessible) as being appropriate to the realm of consumption—that seems somehow undemocratic. Moreover, seeing the desires of self-interested individuals as the most important variable in retailing makes calls for any sort of political change seem naïve at best. After all, it would be hard to change grocery stores (or anything else) to a more sustainable or more just model if doing so required changes to individuals' sincere preferences. Current politics—both progressive and conservative—would seem to reinforce the intransigence and the fixed nature of stores and the sort of shopping that sustains them.

This book uses a feminist perspective to point to a more hopeful and more politicized analysis of mass retail. Current systems of food distribution emerged from historically contingent power relations and can, therefore, be changed by politics—both everyday and institutional. At different times, different political economies have accommodated grocery vending through a variety of retail formats; laws and policy shaped the emergence of the top-down supermarkets that we now have, and, in other moments, have revealed women's desires for authority over stores.

Moreover, while one might think of participation in consumption as itself undoing the possibilities (and the need) for resistance and change, the history of women's food shopping bears witness to a different result: women often embraced the benefits of mass retail while navigating it for their own purposes. Shoppers were neither only impulsive nor narrowly self-interested. Sometimes, shopping has allowed for claims of power and has encouraged desires for radically different ways of organizing distribution (or family life).[20] Without unthinking romanticization, historically minded observers can point out that no one set of power relations and no one system of distribution is inevitable. What people buy and how they buy it does not reveal, and never has revealed, the boundaries of what they want.

In a climate in which consumption is so often portrayed as resistant to politics, it is important to remember that shopping has been political for a very long time. Even when consumers could not imagine radical alterations to stores, they and the stores they shopped in were embedded in broader systems of governance and political economy. All those grocery store sales, and all the policies and political economies that they sustained, depended on behavior that was as much social as economic. If, for instance, shoppers had continued to successfully demand personalized attention, it is difficult to imagine Keynesian policies predicated on consumption seeming realistic, sales taxes being so easily and predictably collected, or consumer sales coming to be such a powerful symbol of American prosperity and abundance. In the spaces of supermarkets, the social underpinnings of American political economy and retail—that is, the ways in which institutional structures depend on socially embedded exchange—become clear. These are spaces that reveal the power relations that run through, but are so often hidden, in modern liberal society.

RECAPTURING THE HARD WORK of food shopping encourages two other kinds of hard work—integrating sex and gender systems into analyses of distribution and integrating complicated visions of the instability of distribution and consumption into analyses of capitalism and the market. Ultimately, a book about gender and modern consumption is necessarily also about capitalism. Capitalism is embedded, undermined, reinforced, and indeed constituted and made meaningful through social relations at the point of purchase. In any moment of exchange, much is at stake. Seeing shopping in this way suggests both the importance of mass retail to everyday life as well as its contingencies and the ways in which interventions might occur.

Indeed, it has been the point of much of this book to suggest that a reconfiguring of economic systems and social power relations happens, whether planned or not, in the everyday work of food shopping. In the work of keeping things going, of making do, of deciding what to buy for dinner, larger structures are resisted, upheld, and, sometimes, undone. What changes is not whether that work happens, but whether we see it and, in so doing, whether we see the connection between economics and gender.

Notes

Introduction

1. R. V. Rasmussen, "We've Profited by the Times to Build or Remodel 250 Stores," *Chain Store Age, Administration Edition* (hereafter *CSA-A*) 8 (November 1932): 644, 698.

2. See, for instance, Tedlow, *New and Improved*. Other work on grocery stores and supermarkets has focused on their aesthetics and architectural importance. See Longstreth, *Drive-In, the Supermarket, and the Transformation of Commercial Space*; and Mayo, *American Grocery Store*.

3. For a statement to this effect and an overview of grocery stores' importance, see Bureau of the Census, *Census of Business, 1954*, vol. 1, *Retail Trade, Summary Statistics*, 7–8. Census officials noted that grocery stores "have been the most important single kind of business in every Census of Business." Later censuses bear this out. By 1967, grocery stores were second only to restaurants in numbers of establishments and far outpaced every other kind of business in sales. Bureau of the Census, *1967 Census of Business*, vol. 2, *Retail Trade Subject Reports*, table 1, 1–4.

4. There were 7,266 in the city proper in 1929, and 10,893 in the metropolitan area in 1948. Bureau of the Census, *Fifteenth Census of the United States: 1930, Distribution*, vol. 1, *Retail Distribution*, pt. 1, table 14, 350; Bureau of the Census, *U.S. Census of Business 1948*, vol. 2, *Retail Trade—Area Statistics*, O26. There were only 4,802 in the metro area in 1967. However, the lower number in 1967 does not reflect lower food sales, but the fact that grocery firms were building fewer, but larger, stores. Thus, Chicagoans had fewer stores from which to choose and had to travel further to get to a store. *1967 Census of Business*, vol. 2, *Retail Trade Area Statistics*, table 9, 1–64.

5. See, for example, Lizabeth Cohen, *Consumers' Republic*; Jacobs, *Pocketbook Politics*; Koehn, *Brand New*; Marchand, *Advertising the American Dream*; McGovern, *Sold American*; and Parkin, *Food Is Love*.

6. An enormous and important literature critiques the construction of globalization as fully hegemonic, and it has influenced my own perspective on domestic firms. Among the most prominent authors are Tsing, *Friction*, and Gibson-Graham, *End of Capitalism*.

7. Lizabeth Cohen, *Consumers' Republic*; Jacobs, *Pocketbook Politics*; McGovern, *Sold American*.

8. DeVault, abstract of "Women and Food," iii. On the long history of women's responsibility for food work, see Boydston, *Home and Work*; DeVault, *Feeding the Family*, 13–14, 98–99; Forson, *Building Houses out of Chicken Legs*; and Ulrich, *Good Wives*. Academic and popular literature documents women's ongoing responsibility for shopping and the ways in which retailers continue to see women as responsible for this work. See, for instance, Miller, *Theory of Shopping*. A recent *New York Times* article reports that grocers tailor new "money-saving" classes to women because they continue to control the food-buying budget. In the piece, a Wal-Mart executive explains, "'We have to be interested in what moms are interested in.'" Stephanie Rosenbloom and Andrew Martin, "Thriftiness on Special in Aisle Five," *New York Times*, October 14, 2008, B1.

9. Studies produced in the 1970s and early 1980s suggest the structural significance of these tasks to the organization of families and the economy. See Hartmann, "Family as the Locus of Gender, Class, and Political Struggle"; and Mainardi, "Politics of Housework." The work cited here is among the best known and most accessible, it but represents only a fraction of the work generated in informal and formal group meetings.

Since this surge of interest in domesticity among second-wave feminists, subsequent scholarship on women and capitalism has, without focusing on housework, restated the more general point that systems of production require particular arrangements of family life and systems of sexuality. In this regard, the work of Miranda Joseph, Sylvia Yanagisako, and Viviana Zelizer has been especially helpful. See Joseph, *Against the Romance of Community*; Yanagisako, *Producing Culture and Capital*; and Zelizer, *Purchase of Intimacy*. An important early work that does discuss the labor of housekeeping is Strasser, *Never Done*.

10. Orleck, "'We Are That Mythical Thing Called the Public'"; Frank, *Purchasing Power* and "Housewives, Socialists, and the Politics of Food." Discussions of politicized food shopping and women are especially developed among European women's historians, who have already documented the ubiquity of food protests for this period. Among the most relevant texts is Davis, *Home Fires Burning*. More recently, Lawrence Glickman's study of the centrality of consumption to American political culture, *Buying Power*, has documented participation in consumer protests by white women and African Americans.

11. As I have focused on the institutional implications of the difficult work of shopping, I have also been grateful for the theoretically rich (and, I would say, underutilized) work of Susan Porter Benson, whose accounts of the working conditions of department store clerks and, more recently, of negotiations over spending in working-class households suggest the charged nature of the moment of purchase. Benson, *Counter Cultures* and *Household Accounts*.

12. See, for example, Laird, *Pull*; and Blaszczyk, *Imagining Consumers*.

13. The emphasis on politics is indicative of a general move among business historians to problematize the inevitability of large firms. Relevant examples include Dunlavy, *Politics and Industrialization*; and McCurdy, "American Law and the Marketing Structure of the Large Corporation." Richard John offers an important example of this thinking, as well as an overview of this "turn" among business historians, in "Governmental Institutions as Agents of Change."

I have been especially influenced by the work of those who study "flexible specialization": for instance, Sabel and Zeitlin, *World of Possibilities* and "Historical Alternatives to Mass Production"; Scranton, *Endless Novelty*; and Tolliday and Yonemitsu, "Microfirms and Industrial Districts in Japan." An excellent book that also attends to the social politics that undergirded "flexible" production is Walton, *France at the Crystal Palace*. Walton's work is the exception, however. As this list suggests, scholars focusing on the question of the viability of small firms, and on flexible specialization, have tended to focus on producers rather than retailers and on the structures of firms themselves. Their work identifies but does not often interrogate the social politics responsible for the kinds of "taste" expressed by buyers of that firms' products or the dynamics that come into play in retail spaces.

14. Beckert, *Monied Metropolis*; Mihm, *Nation of Counterfeiters*; Guterl, *American Medi-*

terranean; Johnson, "Pedestal and the Veil" and *Soul by Soul*. These examples are meant only to be suggestive. The number of historical projects that analytically engage with capitalism is growing, even as I write (although many continue to focus on nineteenth-century history and emerge from studies of slavery).

Few works that self-identify as the history of capitalism also attend to gender, and those that do so tend to be generated by interdisciplinary studies of imperialism and labor. See, for instance, Stoler, *Haunted by Empire*; Ferguson, *Aberrations in Black*; and Hong, *Ruptures of American Capital*. While these projects are understood as being about queerness, gender, or sex, I contend that they also raise questions crucial to theorizing about economics, commerce, and capitalism. For instance, authors regularly demonstrate that gender, sexual performance, and socially formed identities in general are simultaneously integral to and vulnerabilities of capitalism.

15. Lévi-Strauss, *Totemism*, 89. Lévi-Strauss's original text was about animals used as totems, not as food: "Natural species are chosen not because they are 'good to eat' but because they are 'good to think.'" However, Lévi-Strauss's own work, as well as that of many anthropologists, certainly supports the idea that he did find food "good to think."

Chapter 1

1. DeVault, *Feeding the Family*.

2. Both retailers and many analysts celebrate neighborhood stores and public markets as unproblematic builders of community and social good. See, for just a few examples, the lament of the chairman of Starbucks that the chain had lost its connection to buyers as it grew, "A Double Shot of Nostalgia," *New York Times*, March 3, 2007, C1; a tribute to local hardware stores in Woodsworth, "Service a la Your Neighborhood Store"; and the letters section of the September 11, 2006, issue of the *Nation*, in which readers were asked to name their "most beloved food institutions." Our limited knowledge of the complicated work of food shopping allows this romanticization to continue. This is not to say that local stores and their proprietors do not occupy vital roles in the health of neighborhoods and the identity-making efforts of their residents; but such important work, particularly in a capitalist context, is never distant from the work of profit-making and economic exploitation.

3. "Girls to Learn Shopping," *Chicago Tribune*, September 18, 1911, 3. For an earlier article making a very similar point (though about butchers, not peddlers), see "About Marketing," *Chicago Tribune*, June 24, 1875, 11.

4. The letter was published in Mary Eleanor O'Donnell, "Fighting Cost of Living," *Chicago Tribune*, March 3, 1913, 14.

5. Marion Harland, "How to Buy Cheap Cuts," *Chicago Tribune*, November 3, 1912, F3.

6. "Expert in Marketing," *Chicago Tribune*, August 29, 1896, 23.

7. "Markets and Marketers," *Chicago Tribune*, June 22, 1919, D6.

8. Duddy, "Distribution of Perishable Commodities," 162–63.

9. Alice Stoll, "Some Difficulties of the Housewife," *Chicago Tribune*, February 5, 1911, F2.

10. For an example of the growing number of business historians who investigate social relations in firms, see Laird, *Pull*.

11. Ulrich, *Good Wives*; Boydston, *Home and Work*, 77.

12. See, for instance, Strasser, *Never Done*. Many scholars have reached similar conclusions about women in other parts of the Euro-American world. The normativity of this division of labor was remarkably stable across time and place. See Ellen Ross, *Love and Toil*; and Spruill, *Women's Life and Work in the Southern Colonies*. See also Kreskas, "Division of Domestic Work," for a more recent example.

13. Boydston, *Home and Work*, 81; "Aunt Hannah Scores Bachelor Husband," *Chicago Tribune*, September 5, 1897, 45.

14. Boydston, *Home and Work*, 90–91.

15. The literature on separate spheres and the associated ideology of domesticity is enormous. For a classic work, see Cott, *Bonds of Womanhood*. More recently, authors have complicated the notion of separate spheres, exploring the ways in which women deployed the ideology to gain political authority and arguing both for its limited effects and for its significance to politics. For two examples, see Norling, *Captain Ahab Had a Wife*; and Michel and Koven, *Mothers of a New World*.

16. The extensive anthropological and sociological literatures on the rituals of serving and eating make this point very effectively. Some of this work—the present included—embeds meals in exchange systems. For examples, see Mintz, *Sweetness and Power*; and Wilk, *Home Cooking in the Global Village*.

17. Goldstein, "Mediating Consumption." See also Laura Shapiro, *Perfection Salad*; Cowan, *More Work for Mother*; Fitzpatrick, Edmunds, and Dennison, "Positive Effects of Family Dinner Are Undone by Television Viewing"; and Fulkerson et al., "Family Dinner Meal Frequency and Adolescent Development." For a popularized version of this discourse, see Weinstein, *Surprising Power of Family Meals*.

18. Dreiser, *Sister Carrie*, 250–302. Hurstwood justifies his unwillingness to look for waged work by offering to run to the butcher and grocer (246–47) and urges Carrie to travel to the Gansevoort Market, where prices are cheaper than at neighborhood grocery stores (249). Over time, as the relationship deteriorates, Carrie begins to use him for such errands, although "accompanying his plan came skimpiness" (250).

19. Strasser, *Never Done*, 41.

20. There is very limited scholarly work on relations between servants (especially cooks) and female employers in the late nineteenth and early twentieth century. Phyllis Palmer has argued that between 1920 and 1945, white women were willing to stay at home and provide unwaged work even after winning suffrage because the existence of poorly paid female domestics significantly eased their labors and provided them with managerial authority. It is not clear, however, how much authority employers exercised over meal preparation and food procurement or what credit they took for it. See Palmer, *Domesticity and Dirt*. For a social history of African American household servants and the difficult work around food, see Clark-Lewis, *Living In, Living Out*; and Bentley, "Islands of Serenity," chap. 3 in *Eating for Victory*.

21. Women had, of course, purchased some foodstuffs throughout much of U.S. history. On the early importance of food procurement, see Strasser, *Never Done*, 23; Ulrich, *Good Wives*, 26–27.

22. Strasser, *Never Done*, 22–27, 16–18.

23. Duddy, "Distribution of Perishable Commodities," 157. See also Duis, *Challenging Chicago*, 116.

24. Mechanical refrigerators were not common until well into the 1930s and 1940s. Strasser, *Never Done*, 265–72.

25. Boydston, *Home and Work*, 71–72.

26. It is true that many poorer urban Americans and those from rural areas continued to get much of their food from gardens. See Strasser, *Never Done*, 11–14; Boydston, *Home and Work*, 132 (on gardens). Many families kept cows and chickens in backyards through the first decades of the twentieth century. Nonetheless, over the course of the nineteenth century, this practice slowly diminished. Americans increasingly looked to markets to provide the supplies of everyday life. On the production of canned goods, see Levenstein, *Revolution at the Table*, 37. On the use of industrialized and processed foods in general, see Matthews, *Just a Housewife*, 103–4.

27. Matthews, *Just a Housewife*, 105.

28. Ann Smart Martin, *Buying into the World of Goods*, 158–59, 164–67.

29. Catherine Beaumont, "What an Exasperated Englishwoman Thinks of her American Sisters," *Chicago Tribune*, June 21, 1874, 2; "Family Marketing," *Chicago Tribune*, July 24, 1881, 16; "Training for Servants," *Chicago Tribune*, July 26, 1896, 42. See also Boydston, *Home and Work*, 102–3.

30. Strasser, *Never Done*, 243.

31. Mary Eleanor O'Donnell, "How to Fight the Cost of Living," *Chicago Tribune*, January 14, 1913, 14, and January 15, 1913, 10; "Readers of 'The Tribune' Tell Their Plans for Reducing the Cost of Living," *Chicago Tribune*, February 16, 1913, F6; "Mrs. Kate Watson on Marketing," *Chicago Tribune*, December 11, 1894, 3; "Market Fable for Housewives," *Chicago Tribune*, October 25, 1908, E3.

32. Jane LeBaron Goodwin, "Domestic Science," *Chicago Tribune*, November 10, 1906, 9.

33. "Doris Blake's Advice: Marketing by Telephone," *Chicago Tribune*, November 27, 1913, 15.

34. *Six Hundred Dollars a Year*, 83, 100. Coffin is quoted in Boydston, *Home and Work*, 134 and 193 n. 28. See Boydston, *Home and Work*, 132, for a rich discussion of how much money could be saved by careful food shopping.

35. Untitled, *Chicago Tribune*, October 2, 1858, 1. See also "Food Plenty and Cheap," *Chicago Tribune*, August 14, 1896, 7; "Now's the Time to Can or Dry Carrots, Beets," *Chicago Tribune*, July 3, 1918, 4; "Market Guide," *Chicago Tribune*, April 23, 1919, 17.

36. Wandersee, *Women's Work and Family Values*, 8.

37. By comparison, the estimated annual cost to "professional families" in San Francisco in 1926 was 16 percent of income, or $1,043.28 for a family of four. Heller Committee for Research in Social Economics, *Cost of Living Studies*, table 1, 133 and 135–36.

38. Mary Eleanor O'Donnell, "How to Fight the Increased Cost of Living," *Chicago Tribune*, October 27, 1912, F1; Mary Eleanor O'Donnell, "How to Fight the Cost of Living," *Chicago Tribune*, June 30, 1913, 16. A similar series ran at the end of World War I (e.g., "How to Fight the Cost of Living: Letters Keep Coming," *Chicago Tribune*, August 24, 1919, C2).

39. Mary Eleanor O'Donnell, "High Cost of Living," *Chicago Tribune*, July 2, 1913, 10. By this time, the term "marketing" had come to connote buying food, although it was still

sometimes used to indicate participation in a market, either as a buyer or a seller. It did not come to refer to the techniques used to sell a good (as in a "marketing campaign") until much later in the twentieth century. *Oxford English Dictionary Online*, s.v. "Marketing," [http://dictionary.oed.com.floyd.lib.umn.edu/cgi/entry/00302203?query_type=word &queryword=marketing&first=1&max_to_show=10&sort_type=alpha&result_place= 1&search_id=cnmz-ypVJUW-11254&hilite=00302203] (accessed July 2, 2008).

40. See, for instance, Mary Eleanor O'Donnell, "How to Fight the Cost of Living: 'Two Heads Better Than One,'" *Chicago Tribune*, January 14, 1913, 14.

41. "Readers of 'The Tribune' Tell Their Plans for Reducing the Cost of Living," *Chicago Tribune*, February 16, 1913, F6.

42. Ibid.

43. Mary Eleanor O'Donnell, "High Cost of Living," *Chicago Tribune*, July 2, 1913, 10.

44. For a classic account of Chicago and the emergence of large-sized businesses, see Cronon, *Nature's Metropolis*.

45. On the early history of Maxwell Street, see Eastwood, *Chicago's Jewish Street Peddlers*, 21. See also Balkin, Morales, and Persky, "Utilizing the Informal Economy."

46. "Motley Crowds at City Market," *Chicago Tribune*, September 25, 1914, 13; "H.C. of L. Cut in Two by 12,000 at Public Mart," *Chicago Tribune*, July 14, 1918, 14; Duis, *Challenging Chicago*, 177.

47. "H.C. of L. Cut in Two."

48. More than forty-eight thousand railroad cars of produce were unloaded in its environs every year. Duddy, "Distribution of Perishable Commodities," 175.

49. Ibid., 153–54.

50. Duis, *Challenging Chicago*, 116; Duddy, "Distribution of Perishable Commodities," 151.

51. Ferber, *So Big*, 175.

52. "The Marketing Problem," *Chicago Tribune*, December 28, 1884, 9.

53. "Everyday Life in the Philippines," *Chicago Tribune*, September 17, 1899, 45.

54. Wirth, *Ghetto*, 232. Also quoted in Eastwood, *Chicago's Jewish Street Peddlers*, 21. This image of markets as distastefully multiethnic followed a much older European discourse of anti-Semitism and a concept of marketplaces and merchants as exciting but potentially dangerous. On medieval suspicions of transactions and markets generally, see Farber, *Anatomy of Trade in Medieval Writing*.

55. Polacheck, *I Came a Stranger*, 78–80. I am grateful to the anonymous reader of the manuscript of this book who brought this source to my attention.

56. Untitled, *Chicago Tribune*, April 30, 1858, 1; Duis, *Challenging Chicago*, 115.

57. "Opening Day at Chicago's New Municipal Market," *Chicago Tribune*, September 25, 1914, 13; "H.C. of L. Cut in Two"; "Real Estate News: Motor and Walk to 'Fresh from Farm Market,'" *Chicago Tribune*, February 29, 1920, A10. As late as 1994, as many as twenty thousand potential customers walked through Maxwell Street Market on peak days. Balkin, Morales, and Persky, "Utilizing the Informal Economy," 3. On being advised to shop there, see "The Marketing Problem," *Chicago Tribune*, December 28, 1884, 1.

58. Strasser, *Never Done*, 15–16. They also had closely governed days of operation and

opening and closing hours. On efforts to prevent "forestalling" and to govern markets generally, see Tangires, *Public Markets and Civic Culture*, 3–68; and Novak, *People's Welfare*, 94–102.

59. Duis, *Challenging Chicago*, 117–18.

60. On market masters' oversight of foul language at markets, see "Public Market Rules Changed," *Chicago Tribune*, September 20, 1914, 4. The Chicago Municipal Code of 1911 assigned to the superintendent of the Randolph Street Market the authority to arrest anyone who "conducted himself in a disorderly manner" or who violated any of the ordinances over fruit, meat, poultry, and vegetables. *Chicago Municipal Code of 1911*, § 1591.

61. Duis, *Challenging Chicago*, 114–15.

62. "A New Market House," *Chicago Tribune*, April 20, 1857, 2.

63. Untitled, *Chicago Tribune*, April 30, 1858, 1.

64. Jane Eddington, "Tribune Cookbooks: Need of Public Markets," *Chicago Tribune*, March 28, 1919, 18. See also Duis, *Challenging Chicago*, 117.

65. "They Go to Market," *Chicago Tribune*, December 25, 1897, 16.

66. Jane Eddington, "Economical Housekeeping," *Chicago Tribune*, September 16, 1913, 13.

67. "Girls to Learn Shopping," *Chicago Tribune*, September 18, 1911, 3. Less affluent women were present in the market as sellers, but often as itinerant peddlers who sold at markets rather than as stall owners. These spots were often reserved for widows or other women who were understood as having been forced outside the sphere of domestic labor by economic duress. Tangires, *Public Markets and Civic Culture*, 57. For a fictional, but plausible, account of one such woman's efforts to find a place among mostly male sellers, see Ferber, *So Big*.

68. Duddy, "Distribution of Perishable Commodities," 152.

69. Ibid., 174–75, 165.

70. Ibid., 176.

71. Eastwood, *Chicago's Jewish Street Peddlers*, 19; Duis, *Challenging Chicago*, 121.

72. Eastwood, *Chicago's Jewish Street Peddlers*, 17–18.

73. Quote from Duis, *Challenging Chicago*, 121. My sense of the range of foods is based on Duis and on Pollak, "Jewish Peddlers of Omaha," 481.

74. Eastwood, "Study of the Regulation of Chicago's Street Vendors," 43–44.

75. Quote is from Strasser, *Never Done*, 16. Other info is from Strasser, *Never Done*, 19; and Eastwood, "Study of the Regulation of Chicago's Street Vendors," 46. The role of prepared foods in working-class neighborhoods is underrated by scholars. On restaurants, taverns, and other commercial sources of already-cooked foods, see Turner, "Buying, Not Cooking."

76. Bertha Michaels Shapiro, *Memories of Lawndale*, 43.

77. Eastwood, *Chicago's Jewish Street Peddlers*, 29. 19.

78. Ibid., 23.

79. Pollak, "Jewish Peddlers of Omaha," 491–92, 494; Boyd, "Ethnicity, Niches, and Retail Enterprise," 90; Eastwood, "Study of the Regulation of Chicago's Street Vendors," 29, 48–49, 51–52; Eastwood, *Chicago's Jewish Street Peddlers*, 11.

80. Abbott, "Study of the Greeks in Chicago," 389–90.

81. Quoted in Eastwood, "Study of the Regulation of Chicago's Street Vendors," 30. On wages, see ibid., 47–48.

82. Abbott, "Study of the Greeks in Chicago," 379–93; Eastwood, "Study of the Regulation of Chicago's Street Vendors," 29–58. On peddling's importance to Jews in particular, see Eastwood, *Chicago's Jewish Street Peddlers*, 15–17. As late as 1923, peddling was the second-most-popular occupation among recent Russian Jewish immigrants, behind only needle trades.

83. Eastwood, *Chicago's Jewish Street Peddlers*, 24.

84. Ibid., 31.

85. Quoted in ibid., 32.

86. Ferber, *So Big*, 186.

87. Eastwood, *Chicago's Jewish Street Peddlers*, 36.

88. Eastwood, "Study of the Regulation of Chicago's Street Vendors," 52.

89. "The Retail Grocers," *Chicago Tribune*, September 21, 1881, 8; "Retail Grocers," *Chicago Tribune*, October 19, 1881, 8.

90. Quoted in Eastwood, "Study of the Regulation of Chicago's Street Vendors," 53.

91. Vaillant, "Peddling Noise."

92. Eastwood, "Study of the Regulation of Chicago's Street Vendors," 56–57.

93. Duis, *Challenging Chicago*, 117; Vaillant, "Peddling Noise," 266.

94. Balkin, Morales, and Persky, "Utilizing the Informal Economy," 1; Pollak, "Jewish Peddlers of Omaha," 484.

95. Duddy, "Distribution of Perishable Commodities," 156. See also Duis, *Challenging Chicago*, 121.

96. Eastwood, "Study of the Regulation of Chicago's Street Vendors," 55–56.

97. *Journal of the Proceedings of the City Council of the City of Chicago for the Council Year 1926–27*, November 3, 1926, 4554–55 (hereafter, *Journal of Proceedings of Chicago City Council*).

98. *Journal of Proceedings of Chicago City Council*, 1922–23, December 6, 1922, 1462.

99. Strasser, *Never Done*, 15. For more recent examples, see Eastwood, "Study of the Regulation of Chicago's Street Vendors," 265–66.

100. Eastwood, "Study of the Regulation of Chicago's Street Vendors," 56.

101. "Fruit Plenty and Cheap," *Chicago Tribune*, August 14, 1896, 7; "Public Market Rules Changed," *Chicago Tribune*, September 20, 1914, 4; Al Chase, "Real Estate News: Motor and Walk to 'Fresh from Farm Market,'" *Chicago Tribune*, February 9, 1920, A10; Leo J. Tausio, "In Defense of the Farmer's Market," *Chicago Tribune*, July 1, 1922, 6. On peddlers' uses of markets, see also Eastwood, *Chicago's Jewish Street Peddlers*.

102. *Journal of Proceedings of Chicago City Council*, 1932–33, February 1, 1933, 3363.

103. Peddlers continued to be an important, if more sporadic, presence. When it became difficult to operate their joint-buying service in 1939, Chicago's consumer cooperatives experimented with purchasing produce from neighborhood peddlers. Untitled, *Co-op News* 4 (July 1939): 5. Peddlers' continued presence in lower middle-class neighborhoods can be gleaned from the city council's attempts to keep them out. See, for instance, Ald. Feigenbutz's order that the city council "remove the peddler from the corner of Melrose

street and Lincoln Avenue," in *Journal of Proceedings of Chicago City Council*, 1932–33, February 1, 1933, 3363. See also Ald. Jackson's request that the city install "No Peddlers Allowed" signs at the corners of Forty-fifth and Vincennes and Forty-sixth and Vincennes, ibid., March 31, 1933, 3529.

104. Tedlow, *New and Improved*, 230; Mayo, *American Grocery Store*, 86, 140. Safeway wanted only 2,100 square feet for its prime locations. H. S. Wright, "Locating Grocery Stores," *Chain Store Age* (hereafter, *CSA*) 1 (August 1925): 10. As late as 1930, the Kroger company's "standard store" was only 3,000 square feet. Laycock, *Kroger Story*, 37.

105. This average is computed from total net sales for Chicago stores. Net sales are approximately, but not quite, the same as gross sales. They include all final sales (i.e., sales on goods that were not returned). Definition of "net sales" from Bureau of the Census, *Fifteenth Census of the United States: 1930, Distribution*, vol. 1, *Retail Distribution*, pt. 1, 41. Food stores ranked near the bottom of all retailers in terms of sales per store. By this measure, only cigar stores and filling stations sold less than a typical grocery store in Chicago. Data assembled from ibid., pt. 2, table 19, 633.

106. Quoted in Lizabeth Cohen, *Making a New Deal*, 109–10.

107. See, for instance, Strasser, *Satisfaction Guaranteed*, 67.

108. Jean Brichke, "Report on Term Paper under Miss Nesbitt's Direction (Standard Budget for Dependent Families) Sociology 264," 13–14, March 11, 1931, folder 2, box 156, Ernest Watson Burgess Papers, Special Collections Research Center, University of Chicago Library, University of Chicago, Chicago (hereafter, Burgess Papers). The Burgess Papers are a rich collection of research conducted under the direction of one of the University of Chicago's most distinguished sociologists, Ernest Watson Burgess. Burgess had a special interest in qualitative descriptions of Chicago's neighborhoods, and so many of his students provided invaluable descriptions of the everyday happenings in and around local grocery stores. I make use of several such papers in the course of this book.

109. Shideler, "Chain Store," chap. 2, 8–9.

110. "Housewife Finds Lack of System Keeps Prices Up," *Chicago Tribune*, June 11, 1919, 21.

111. "Doris Blake's Advice: Marketing by Telephone," *Chicago Tribune*, November 27, 1913, 15; Mary Eleanor O'Donnell, "How to Fight the Costs of Living," *Chicago Tribune*, January 15, 1913, 10.

112. "Readers of 'The Tribune' Tell Their Plans for Reducing the Cost of Living," *Chicago Tribune*, February 16, 1913, F6.

113. In this time period, phone orders were most likely to be placed by middle-class families, and so this critique was aimed primarily at middle-class shoppers. However, even working-class families often had access to common phones in the hallways of apartment buildings and increasingly relied on phones. (On working-class families' use of telephones, see Claude Fischer, *America Calling*, 107–18.) In this context, it is useful to see ordering via the telephone as a variant of the longstanding and common practice of making purchases without traveling to stores (for instance, by sending servants or, for working-class families, by sending children).

114. Strasser, *Satisfaction Guaranteed*, 84–88, 187–95.

115. Christine Frederick, "My Idea of a Good Storekeeper," *CSA* 1 (August 1925): 16.

116. Brichke, "Report on Term Paper under Miss Nesbitt's Direction," 14.

117. "Millions Lost Annually by Thoughtless Buying," *Chicago Defender*, January 16, 1934, 4.

118. Bureau of Foreign and Domestic Commerce, *Louisville Grocery Survey*, pt. 1, *Census of Food Distribution*, 14. This finding was very similar to that of a national study conducted in 1924 by the Harvard Bureau of Business Research: the average retail grocer made 61 percent of its sales on credit. See Harvard Bureau of Business Research, *Operating Expenses in Retail Grocery Stores in 1924*, 11.

119. Anna Blazewich, interview, transcript, 95, November 11, 1977, Oral History Archives of Chicago Polonia, Chicago History Museum, Chicago. For more accounts of grocers who felt pressured into granting credit, see Strasser, *Satisfaction Guaranteed*, 69.

120. "Tendency of Grocers is toward More Credit," *Progressive Grocer* 9 (December 1930): 34.

121. See, for instance, "Are Outstanding Bills Eating Up Your Profits?" *Progressive Grocer* 1 (December 1922): 32–34; "Collect Your Bills—and Keep the Friendship of Your Customers," *Progressive Grocer* 3 (April 1924): 27–29; Pop Keener, "Educate Credit Customers to Pay Promptly," *Progressive Grocer* 8 (January 1929): 16–18; Bureau of Foreign and Domestic Commerce, *Credit Extension and Business Failures*, 1.

122. On customers' resentment of the terms of credit arrangements and their reliance on credit, see Strasser, *Satisfaction Guaranteed*, 69; and Lizabeth Cohen, *Making a New Deal*, 112, 234–35.

123. Independent grocers were notorious for keeping records poorly, if at all. Researchers at the Harvard Bureau of Business Research noted somewhat disdainfully that "a surprisingly large proportion of the retail grocers of the country . . . do not keep records that are even approximately accurate. . . . Records are [either] inadequate for their needs or none at all." Harvard Bureau of Business Research, *Management Problems in Retail Grocery Stores*, 16. See also Strasser, *Satisfaction Guaranteed*, 231–35.

124. African Americans owned only 1.4 percent of all retail stores nationally, according to the 1935 Census of Business. Grocery stores and restaurants accounted for nearly half of all sales by African American–owned businesses in 1935. Bureau of the Census, *Census of Business: 1935, Retail Distribution*, vol. 1, *United States Summary*, I-42.

125. In Chicago, there was one black-owned store for every 287 African Americans; the ratio was 1:37 for Polish-owned stores and Poles, and 1:40 for Italian-owned stores and Italians. Lizabeth Cohen, *Making a New Deal*, 152.

126. On African American businesses in Chicago during this time, see Lizabeth Cohen, *Making a New Deal*; and Grossman, *Land of Hope*.

127. On Chicago's racial violence during the first decades of the twentieth century, see Grossman, *Land of Hope*. On the "race riots" of 1919, see Chicago Commission on Race Relations, *Negro in Chicago*; and Tuttle, *Race Riot*.

128. *Journal of Proceedings of Chicago City Council*, 1919–20, special meeting, August 5, 1919, 1112; "Important Meeting of Jewish Storekeepers on the South Side," *Daily Jewish Courier*, August 13, 1919, ID1b, box 23, Jewish, Chicago Foreign Language Press Survey, Special Collections Research Center, University of Chicago Library, University of Chicago,

Chicago (hereafter, CFLPS); untitled, *Forward*, August 9, 1919, ID1b, box 23, Jewish, CFLPS. CFLPS documents were translated by the Works Progress Administration workers who compiled them from Chicago's foreign-language newspapers.

129. Tingley, *Structuring of a State*, 310; Hunter, "'Don't Buy from Where You Can't Work,'" 81.

130. Hunter, "'Don't Buy from Where You Can't Work.'" See also Lizabeth Cohen, *Making a New Deal*, 153–54.

131. Hunter, "Don't Buy from Where You Can't Work," 53–55.

132. "Patronize the Stores of Your Countrymen," *Osadne Hlasy*, December 9, 1932, ID1b, box 40, Slovak, CFLPS.

133. "An Unexploited Branch of Commerce," *Lietuva*, September 6, 1918, ID2b, box 28, Lithuanian, CFLPS.

134. Ibid.

135. Kushar, untitled, c. 1934, file 3, box 130, Burgess Papers.

136. Christine Frederick, "Listen to This Sophisticated Shopper!" *CSA* 1 (June 1925): 36.

137. On working-class immigrants, see Gabaccia, *From Sicily to Elizabeth Street*; Glenn, *Daughters of the Shtetl*; and Weinberg, *World of Our Mothers*. African American women's household labor had a history very different from that of white women, since work for their families was often understood by them as a way of resisting inequality and oppression. Nonetheless, African American families generally worked to retain a gendered division of labor in which women were responsible for cooking and food shopping. See Jones, *Labor of Love, Labor of Sorrow*, 187–88, 223, 227–29.

138. R. L. Hobart, "Rubbing a Sophisticated Male Shopper the Wrong Way," *CSA* 1 (December 1925): 20–21; "It Was a Great Saturday Night at the Empire Grocery," *Progressive Grocer* 3 (July 1924): 29–30; N. Mitchell, "The Kind of Showcard That Brings Results," *Progressive Grocer* 1 (September 1922): 10–12; F. S. Clark, "Does Tobacco Belong in the Grocery Store?" *Progressive Grocer* 1 (June 1922): 7–10. There is significant anecdotal evidence from working-class neighborhoods that stores could sometimes be male spaces. Working-class Chinese and Sicilian grocery stores were both described as sites of men's clubs and social gatherings. One member of a Sicilian men's club in Bridgeport, which met in the back of a store, explained it this way: "Home is for the women to cook and take care of the kids. This is our home." Henry B. Steele, "Bridgeport, #60, Organizations, Bridgeport area west side of Halsted to east limit," file 60, box 87, Federal Writers' Project Records, Illinois State Historical Library, Manuscripts Division, Springfield. On stores in Chinatown, see "Chinese Families in Chicago," c. 1930, and Paul R. Sui, "Family Matters," c. 1930, both in file 7, box 136, Burgess Papers.

139. Bureau of Foreign and Domestic Commerce, *Louisville Grocery Survey*, pt. 2, *Costs, Markets, and Methods in Grocery Retailing*, 4.

140. Emmett F. Harte, "Honk and Horace Hit a Boycott but Horace Saves the Day," *Progressive Grocer* 1 (December 1922): 43.

141. "The Eved-Ivri [Hebrew Slave]—The Grocer," *Daily Jewish Courier*, June 12, 1918, ID1b, box 23, Jewish, CFLPS.

142. Untitled, *Forward*, February 6, 1921, ID1b, box 23, Jewish, CFLPS.

143. "Charm . . . A Quality of Growing Importance in Grocery Stores," *Progressive Grocer* 9 (March 1930): 26.

144. Advertisement, "Grocers Want to Help Lower Food Costs," *Chicago Sunday Tribune*, October 23, 1921, pt. 7, 2. See also a similar ad from the same trade organization in *Chicago Tribune*, October 5, 1921, 15.

145. Kushar, untitled.

146. Cayton and Drake, *Black Metropolis*, 441.

147. Ibid., 444.

Chapter 2

1. Few historians have attended to questions of chain stores' origins. Those who have, have relied on relatively straightforward explanations based on efficiency and low prices. For examples of this, see Chandler, *Visible Hand*, 233–35; and Tedlow, *New and Improved*, 182–258. Although discussion of chain store firms is sparse, it has been quite influential. Authors working on other historical questions frequently proceed from the assumption that chain store firms and mass retailers were able to charge lower prices as a result of their organizational efficiencies and that these lower prices were key to their success. See, for instance, Cronon, *Nature's Metropolis*, 333–38.

2. This figure is based on data collected by the Bureau of Labor Statistics between 1914 and 1923 and included in Douglas, Hitchcock, and Atkins, *Worker in Modern Economic Society*, table 34, 288. See also Hawley, *Great War and the Search for Modern Order*, 27.

3. National Industrial Conference Board, *Changes in the Cost of Living*, 7. For an extended discussion of the effects in New York City, see Frank, "Housewives, Socialists, and the Politics of Food," 256–57.

4. "Changes in the Cost of Living in the United States," *Monthly Labor Review* 11 (February 1921): 93. See also National Industrial Conference Board, *Changes in the Cost of Living*, table 2, 6.

5. Hawley, *Great War and the Search for Modern Order*, 47.

6. Chicago City Council, *Journal of the Proceedings of the City Council of Chicago for the Council Year 1919–20* (hereafter, *Journal of Proceedings of Chicago City Council*), April 26, 1919, 788.

7. For instance, for information on the Bureau of Food and Markets, see ibid., July 7, 1919, 698–700. On the difficulties of the bureau and the rocky transition to the Committee on High Costs, see *Journal of Proceedings of Chicago City Council*, 1920–21, May 3, 1920, 110; May 26, 1920, 210; June 23, 1920, 525, 531; December 22, 1920, 1414; and December 29, 1920, 1472.

8. On mail order, see "See Prices Curb in Shipping Food," *Chicago Tribune*, September 1, 1914, 5.

9. "Want Farmers Given Increase in Milk Prices," *Chicago Tribune*, September 3, 1914, 5; Duis, *Challenging Chicago*, 123.

10. "Opening Day at Chicago's New Municipal Market," *Chicago Tribune*, September 25, 1914, 13; "Bargain Prices Rule Today at New Fish Sale," *Chicago Tribune*, December 4, 1919, 19; "Buy Fish Today," *Chicago Tribune*, December 11, 1919, 1.

11. "Evanston to Establish Public Market Monday," *Chicago Tribune*, August 12, 1920, 3.

12. On Toledo, see "Women of Toledo Fight to Reduce High Living Cost," *Chicago Tribune*, December 26, 1913, 1. See also Hitchcock, "Relation of the Housewife to the Food Problem," 130–40.

13. "Hop Along to Market with Your Basket on Your Arm," *Chicago Tribune*, July 10, 1918, 3; "H.C. of L Cut in Two by 12,000 at Public Market," *Chicago Tribune*, July 14, 1918, 14; "Real Estate News: Motor and Walk to 'Fresh from Farm Market,'" *Chicago Tribune*, February 9, 1920, A10.

14. Leo J. Tausio, "In Defense of the Farmer's Market," *Chicago Tribune*, July 1, 1922, 6.

15. "Evanston Eggs and Tomato Riot: Judge Hit," *Chicago Tribune*, August 24, 1920, 1.

16. "South Chicago Public Market Dies at Birth," *Chicago Tribune*, September 12, 1916, 1.

17. Duis, *Challenging Chicago*, 123.

18. Jane Eddington, "Tribune Cookbook: Need of Public Markets," *Chicago Tribune*, March 28, 1919, 18.

19. "Hunger and Poverty in Chicago," *Dziennik Zwiazkowy*, February 23, 1917, ID1a, box 32, Polish, CFLPS; Meditation of the Day (in English), *Sunday Jewish Courier*, May 13, 1923, ID1a, box 23, Jewish, CFLPS.

20. Frank, "Housewives, Socialists, and the Politics of Food," 255–86; Levenstein, *Revolution at the Table*, 109–10. On European riots, see, for instance, Stovall, "Du vieux et du neuf," 85–113; Davis, *Home Fires Burning*; and Hessler, *Social History of Soviet Trade*.

21. "War Profiteers" (editorial), *Denni Hlasatel*, November 10, 1917, ID1a, box 1, Bohemian, CFLPS.

22. "The Harvest Moon," *Chicago Tribune*, August 12, 1919, 1.

23. Sol Posner, "Why Was the Price of Bread Raised?" *Daily Jewish Courier*, March 9, 1922, ID1b, box 23, Jewish, CFLPS.

24. Morris Ziskind, "The Problems and Aims of the Mother's League," *Forward*, March 12, 1922, ID2b, box 23, Jewish, CFLPS.

25. Women's Club Page, *Chicago Sunday Tribune*, October 9, 1921, pt. 8, 5; Women's Club Page, *Chicago Sunday Tribune*, November 13, 1921, pt. 8, 5; Women's Club Page, *Chicago Sunday Tribune*, January 8, 1922, pt. 8, 5–8.

26. "Don't Eat Turk [*sic*] Till Christmas, Poole's Advice," *Chicago Tribune*, November 22, 1921, 3.

27. "Keep Eyes Open, High Price Foes Advise Women," *Chicago Tribune*, September 7, 1914, 5.

28. "Hold Housewife for Living Cost," *Chicago Tribune*, September 25, 1912, 15.

29. Julian Heath, "Are Wives Wasting Their Husbands [*sic*] Money?" *Ladies' Home Journal* 31 (January 1914): 4. Over time, Heath's sympathy for manufacturers was rewarded and reinforced by their frequent payments to her and her organizations. After conflict of interest investigations by New York State's attorney general, the Housewives' League was dissolved. See Strasser, *Satisfaction Guaranteed*, 266–68.

30. "Butchers Put H.C.L. Blame up to Housekeepers," *Chicago Tribune*, August 5, 1924, 3.

31. Hitchcock, "Relation of the Housewife to the Food Problem," 130–31.

32. Ibid., 140.

33. Warne, *Consumers' Co-operative Movement in Illinois*, 176 and table 14, 188.

34. For a fuller discussion of the Cooperative Society of America, see Warne, "The Growth of Spurious Cooperative," ibid., chap. 14. Only a few scholars have attended to 1920s U.S. co-ops since Warne's efforts. For one of the most thoughtful discussions of this movement, see Frank, *Purchasing Power*, 40–65.

35. "300 Women Storm U.S. Court in 'Co-op' Case," *Chicago Daily News*, March 8, 1922, 1.

36. Vaclas Karuza, "An Unexploited Branch of Commerce," *Lietuva*, September 6, 1918, ID2b, box 28, Lithuanian, CFLPS.

37. Hunter, " 'Don't Buy from Where You Can't Work,' " 52–53.

38. For examples of this critique of chain stores, see Shideler, "Chain Store"; and Lizabeth Cohen, *Making a New Deal*.

39. Foreword to Bjorklund and Palmer, *Study of the Prices of Chain and Independent Grocers in Chicago*, vii; Alexander, "Study of Retail Grocery Prices," 9; Converse, "Prices and Services of Chain and Independent Stores in Champaign-Urbana, Illinois," 1–37. For a complete list of these studies, see Tedlow, *New and Improved*, table 4-5, 200–201.

40. Bjorklund and Palmer, *Study of the Prices of Chain and Independent Grocers in Chicago*, 2, 14.

41. The extension of the one-price system beyond department stores was one of chains' most important innovations. See Strasser, *Satisfaction Guaranteed*, 204–5.

42. A. C. Jones, "An Analysis of Piggly Wiggly Progress," *Chain Store Age* (hereafter, *CSA*) 2 (January 1926): 44.

43. Lizabeth Cohen, *Making a New Deal*, 152–53.

44. On the hiring of African Americans, see Lizabeth Cohen, *Making a New Deal*, 154; Greenberg, "Or Does It Explode?," 122–23, 134; "History of District '40,' " 30, file 40, box 86, Federal Writers' Project Records, Illinois State Historical Library.

45. See for instance, the 1942 claim by the retail clerks' union that clerks at Kroger's "colored" stores (who were themselves "colored") did not earn as much as clerks at Kroger's other Chicago-area stores. Complaint in equity for injunction, October 20, 1942, and answer to complaint in equity for injunction, October 21, 1942, *Kroger Grocery and Baking Company, a corporation v. The Retail Clerks International Protective Association, etc., et al.*, case no. 42 C 13019, Clerk of the Circuit Court of Cook County, Archives Department, Chicago (hereafter, Circ. Ct. Archives). Chain store managers were participants in local cultures of racial segregation and consequently enforced racial orders. Tolbert, " 'Aristocracy of the Market Basket.' "

46. For overviews of the introduction of self-service and concern about it, see Strasser, *Satisfaction Guaranteed*, 248–49; and Tenhoor, "Eating by Machinery."

47. A. C. Jones, "An Analysis of Piggly Wiggly Progress," *CSA* 2 (January 1926): 39. In Piggly Wiggly, as at most chain stores, clerks were generally, although not exclusively, male.

48. On women's experience of commercial culture and of stores, see Peiss, *Cheap Amusements* and *Hope in a Jar*; Meyerowitz, *Women Adrift*; and Benson, *Counter Cultures*.

49. For a survey of this literature, see Ryan, *Mysteries of Sex*, 163–214.

50. Hall, "Disorderly Women."

51. On women's shared culture as facilitating their activism, see especially Enstad, *Ladies of Labor, Girls of Adventure*; and Finnegan, *Selling Suffrage.*

52. Allen, *Only Yesterday*, 89.

53. On this point, see Ryan, *Mysteries of Sex*, 226.

54. See, for instance, Cott, *Grounding of Modern Feminism.*

55. For a theoretical discussion of the possibilities of gender sameness, see Riley, *Am I That Name?* In a different way, Gayle Rubin has also made a very similar point. Rubin, "Traffic in Women."

56. Marchand, *Advertising the American Dream*, 167–88; Cott, *Grounding of Modern Feminism*, 135–36; Cowan, *More Work for Mother*; Peiss, *Hope in a Jar*, 134–66.

57. Marchand, *Advertising the American Dream*, 168.

58. Parkin, *Food Is Love*, 67–68.

59. Ibid., 68.

60. "The A&P Takes the Woman's Side in a New Advertising Campaign," *CSA* 4 (April 1928): 62–64.

61. Lionel Ralph Martin, "Grocery Chain Competition in Chicago," 10. For examples of chains' focus on women customers, see Fred B. Barton, "Some More Advertising Ideas for Chain Store Grocers," *CSA* 4 (January 1928): 41–42; "How a 250-Store Chain Handles Its Produce Department," *CSA* 4 (March 1928): 43–44; "A Store Manager," "Is the Personality Idea Overdone?" *CSA* 4 (April 1928): 87–88. On evening newspapers' targeting of women readers, see Emery and Emery, *Press and America*, 206.

62. Advertisement, *Chicago Tribune*, September 30, 1921, 26.

63. Lizabeth Cohen, *Making a New Deal*, 108.

64. Laycock, *Kroger Story*, 37; Tedlow, *New and Improved*, table 4-2, 195; "Investors' Aid: Information Service to Subscribers," *Chicago Journal of Commerce and LaSalle Street Journal*, March 24, 1929, 8.

65. National Tea Company, *Annual Report*, 1919; National Tea Company, *Annual Report*, 1929. Chain store firms owned stores in the sense that they were responsible for the goods and fixtures in these stores, bore the risk of financial losses, and claimed the profits earned there. The physical buildings were generally rented, rather than owned.

66. Godfrey M. Lebhar, Editorially Speaking, *CSA* 7 (September 1931): 36; Tedlow, *New and Improved*, table 4-2, 195.

67. Edwin Hoyt, *That Wonderful A&P!* 130; Tedlow, *New and Improved*, table 4-1, 194.

68. Tedlow, *New and Improved*, 193.

69. Ernest F. Witte, "How to Operate a Chain of One-Man Meat Shops," *CSA* 4 (January 1928): 49–50.

70. *Chicago Telephone Directory* (alphabetical), July 1925.

71. For more on business progressivism, see Wiebe, *Search for Order*, 292–96; and Hawley, *Great War and the Search for Modern Order*, 100–107.

72. There is significant literature on Ford, Fordism, and the associated "science" of employee productivity, "Taylorism." Much of it suggests that even Henry Ford had a difficult time fully implementing mass production. For a classic statement of this argument, see Hounshell, *From the American System to Mass Production.*

73. Hawley, *Great War and the Search for a Modern Order.*

74. Moskowitz, *Standard of Living*. On the rise of brands and brand names in consumer goods, see Strasser, *Satisfaction Guaranteed*.

75. This information has been compiled from the firm's annual reports for 1920 to 1929 and from an internally produced company history, National Tea Company, *Historical High-Lights of National Tea Co., Home Offices—Chicago, Ill., 1899–1955*.

76. Business Highlights, *Progressive Grocer* 8 (January 1929): 46; "Kroger-Consumer Stores," *Chain Store Age, Administration Edition* (hereafter, *CSA-A*) 7 (August 1931): 57.

77. Tedlow, *New and Improved*, table 4-2, 195.

78. Advertisement, *Chicago Sunday Tribune*, February 19, 1922, 10.

79. Advertisement, *Chicago Daily News*, March 9, 1922, 10.

80. "Canadian Grocery Chain to Enter Chicago," *CSA* 4 (February 1928): 219.

81. Edwin Hoyt, *That Wonderful A&P!* 130.

82. For more on bankers' and policymakers' efforts to encourage individuals to buy stock, see Ott, "When Wall Street Met Main Street."

83. Clement Cartwright, "Chain Store Stock Issues in 1927," *CSA* 4 (January 1928): 206.

84. Criscuolo, "Financing the Chain."

85. "National Tea 1925 Net is $1,569,636," *Chicago Journal of Commerce and LaSalle Street Journal*, March 8, 1926, 7.

86. Perkins, *From Wall Street to Main Street*, 113.

For examples of other investors' faith in chains, see Franz Neilson, "The Outlook for Chain Store Securities in 1928," *CSA* 4 (January 1928): 177; and John Hancock, "The Outlook for Chain Store Stocks," *CSA* 6 (January 1930): 77.

87. Consumer Butter Company Chicago, "Increase of Stock $12,000 to $100,000, Increase of Directors 3 to 5 and Change of Name," October 12, 1917; "Increase of Capital Stock from $1,250,000 to $2,750,000," May 27, 1927, both in Corporate Records, Secretary of State's Office, State of Illinois Archives, Springfield.

88. Shideler, "Chain Store," chap. 7, 17.

89. By the late 1920s, virtually every large chain store firm doing business in Chicago operated one or more stores along this street, sometimes in very close proximity to each other. The National Tea Company, for instance, operated fourteen stores between the 1600 and 5600 blocks of West Madison Street in 1929. See listing for the National Tea Company in the *Polk City Directory of 1929* and for Loblaw Groceterias, Royal Blue stores, and A&P in the *Chicago Telephone Directory* for 1929 (listed in the classified directory under "Grocers, Retail").

90. "Says Independent Is Indispensable," *Progressive Grocer* 7 (November 1928): 96.

91. See, for instance, "A Live Grocer Can Beat Any Chain," *Progressive Grocer* 7 (November 1929): 34–36; Carl Dipman, "Chain Store Problems as Seen by the Owners Themselves," *Progressive Grocer* 3 (November 1924): 25–27; Paul Findlay, "Sell 'Em by the Box—a Chain Store 'Secret,'" *Progressive Grocer* 2 (December 1923): 28–30; "Charm . . . A Quality of Growing Importance in Grocery Stores," *Progressive Grocer* 9 (March 1930): 26–29. See also Strasser, *Satisfaction Guaranteed*, 229–42.

92. Carl Dipman, "What Happens to Sales When You Modernize," *Progressive Grocer* 8 (August 1929): 39.

93. "Uncle Sam Builds a Model Grocery Store," *Progressive Grocer* 8 (April 1929): 18–25.

94. Godfrey M. Lebhar, Editorially Speaking, *CSA* 6 (March 1930): 44; "New Book out on Voluntary Chains," *Progressive Grocer* 9 (November 1930): 44; Lizabeth Cohen, *Making a New Deal*, 118–19.

95. See, for example, Lizabeth Cohen's discussion of the A-G chain, *Making a New Deal*, 119.

96. The 1929 telephone directory listed ninety-two stores under the Royal Blue entry, and one hundred in 1930. *Chicago Telephone Directory*, 1929 (classified edition) and *Chicago Telephone Directory*, 1930 (classified edition).

97. W. L. Pohn, "How We Run a Chain of Independent Stores," *CSA* 4 (February 1928): 21–22.

98. Copy of indenture, attached to "Narr. and Cognovit," December 7, 1926, *Howard S. Evans v. Royal Blue Stores, a corporation*, case no. 449473, Circ. Ct. Archives.

99. Criscuolo, "Financing the Chain," 16.

100. Godfrey M. Lebhar, *CSA* 4 (March 1928): 28.

101. For good explanations of this term and the system behind it, see "Chain Store Expansion in 1930," *CSA-A* 7 (January 1931): 76; and Frank S. Slosson, "Chain Store Locations," *Chicago Realtor* 40 (November 1927): 9–12.

102. Shideler, "Chain Store," chap. 7, 6, 11–12; Charles D. Nicholls, "Some of the New Factors in Chain Store Leasing," *CSA* 1 (June 1925): 6–7; Criscuolo, "Financing the Chain," 16.

103. Frank G. Phillips, "How Our Printing Press Boosts Our Sales," *CSA* 4 (April 1928): 35–37.

104. "Second settlement" is a term used to describe areas to which first- and second-generation immigrants moved when they left the area where most recently arrived immigrants lived (the area of primary settlement). Areas of second settlement tended to be populated by slightly more prosperous, less traditional immigrants. On Humboldt Park as an area of second settlement, see Holli and Jones, *Ethnic Chicago*.

105. Shideler, "Chain Store," chap. 8, 17, 23.

106. On the growth of Uptown's business district, see "Thriving Era Dawns for Wilson Avenue," *Chicago Daily News*, February 18, 1922, 13; Shideler, "Chain Store," chap. 8, 6–8. For a general description of this phenomenon, see Nicholls, "Some of the New Factors in Chain Store Leasing," 6–7.

107. Robert D. Bulkley, "South Berwyn, for Sociology 264," 5–7, March 24, 1933, file 2, box 159, Ernest Watson Burgess Papers, Special Collections Research Center, University of Chicago Library, University of Chicago, Chicago (hereafter, Burgess Papers).

108. Jean Brichke, "Report on Term Paper under Miss Nesbitt's Direction (Standard Budget for Dependent Families) Sociology 264," 17–18, March 11, 1931, folder 2, box 156, Burgess Papers.

109. H. S. Wright, "Locating Grocery Stores," *CSA* 1 (August 1925): 11.

110. Shideler, "Chain Store," chap. 7, 7.

111. Godfrey M. Lebhar, Editorially Speaking, *CSA* 1 (September 1925): n.p.

112. Homer Hoyt, *One Hundred Years of Land Values in Chicago*, 249–65.

113. Shideler, "Chain Store," chap. 7, 13–14; Nicholls, "Some of the New Factors in Chain Store Leasing," 6. This was especially true for stores that targeted women, since "women's locations" (districts in which stores selling to women were concentrated) were generally the most expensive. See Slosson, "Chain Store Locations," 11.

114. See, for instance, Wright, "Locating Grocery Stores," 10; Shideler, "Chain Store," chap. 9, 22 n. 2; Mark Levy, "Address on How to Determine Rental Values for Business Properties," *Chicago Realtor* 28 (July 1923): 5–6; Ray N. Brinkman, "Chain Store Leasing from the Chain Stores [sic] Viewpoint," *Chicago Realtor* 37 (September 1924): 13–14; George A. Young, "Chain Store Rental Values," *Chicago Realtor* 41 (February 1928): 15; Criscuolo, "Financing the Chain," 16. For an example of the lengthy leases signed by Chicago chains, see bill for specific performance," October 9, 1933, *Loblaw Groceterias v. Harry Alter*, case no. 33S587465, Circ. Ct. Archives, which contains a fifteen-year lease signed by Loblaw Groceterias.

115. George A. Young, "Chain Store Rental Values," *Chicago Realtor* 41 (February 1928): 15–16.

116. McNair, "Expenses and Profits in the Chain Grocery Business in 1929," 13. Rents were a key ingredient in stores' rising costs. The same study found that 2.3 percent of an average chain's sales went for rent, but that that number *increased* as the number of stores owned by the firm increased (table 4, 28). Even that proportion was twice as high as that reported by grocery stores in 1918, when only 1.1 percent of sales, on average, went to cover rental costs. Harvard Bureau of Business Research, *Management Problems in Retail Grocery Stores*, table 1, 9.

117. W. Lowe, "The Story of Woodlawn: The Social History of a Community, Paper for Sociology 264," 9, March 1931, folder 4, box 156, Burgess Papers.

118. Christine Frederick, "Why Chain Stores Must Offer More Than Price Advantage," *CSA* 1 (September 1925): 38.

119. M. H. Karker, "Our Operating Plan Nets Better Than 8%," *CSA* 4 (April 1928): 39. Jewel Tea was, however, able to overcome its concerns about women's housekeeping long enough to open a chain of grocery stores only five years later, as discussed in Chapter 5.

120. Christine Frederick, "My Idea of a Good Storekeeper," *CSA* 1 (August 1925): 16.

121. Julian Heath, "Another 'Sophisticated Shopper' Has Her Say," *CSA* 1 (July 1925): 19.

122. Carl Reimers, "The Trend in Chain Store Advertising," *CSA* 2 (March 1926): 55.

123. "The Chain Stores Hold a Convention," *Progressive Grocer* 7 (November 1928): 36.

124. Fred B. Barton, "Some More Advertising Ideas for Chain Store Grocers," *CSA* 4 (January 1928): 42.

125. A Practical Housekeeper, "Feeding the Average Family on a Limited Income," *Chicago Tribune*, October 19, 1913, D5.

126. Business Highlights, *Progressive Grocer* 8 (June 1929): 60.

127. Fred W. Albrecht, "It Pays to Sell the Best to the Best," *CSA* 4 (April 1928): 68.

128. Hatfield, "Analysis of Some Grocery Store Practices," 20.

129. Shideler, "Chain Store," chap. 4, 8; R. V. Rasmussen, "We've Profited by the Times to Build or Remodel 250 Stores," *CSA* 8 (November 1932): 698.

130. Fred B. Barton, "Do Chains Offer Men Careers?" *CSA* 6 (May 1930): 34–35. Edward Kearns, interview, August 28, 1977, tape 1, side 1, Oral History Archives of Chicago Polonia, Chicago History Museum, Chicago.

131. Hatfield, "Analysis of Some Grocery Store Practices," 1.

132. Parkin, *Food Is Love*, 3.

133. Strasser, *Satisfaction Guaranteed*, 86–87, 248–51.

134. For a longer discussion of the politics of this relationship, see Strasser, *Satisfaction Guaranteed*, 227–29, 265–83.

135. Ibid., 256–63.

136. Hatfield, "Analysis of Some Grocery Store Practices," 44, 50. In spite of this, chain store operators regularly noted that it was difficult to get "foreign" populations to try chains. Wright, "Locating Grocery Stores," 56; Milward Pick, "Where Shall We Open Next?" *CSA* 4 (February 1928): 17–18; Fred B. Barton, "Do Chains Offer Men Careers?" *CSA* 6 (May 1930): 34–35; Barton, "Do Chains Offer Men Careers?"; Kearns interview, tape 1, side, 1. For a more recent analysis of food shopping by less affluent women, in which they express particular concern with the quality of goods from which they had to choose, see DeVault, *Feeding the Family*.

137. Hatfield, "Analysis of Some Grocery Store Practices," 50, 54.

Chapter 3

1. See, for instance, Jacobs, *Pocketbook Politics*. Lizabeth Cohen's sweeping history of American consumption suggests that policies shaped retailing—for example, in her discussions of racial discrimination in Veterans Administration mortgages, residential segregation, and the policing of free speech in malls. Here I argue for a more direct effect, in which the state shaped the very terrain of consumption, even in unintended ways. Cohen, *Consumers' Republic*, esp. chaps. 5 and 6.

2. On the significance of local laws to retail in the nineteenth century, see Novak, *People's Welfare*.

3. For an overview of Chicago politics, see Bukowski, *Big Bill Thompson, Chicago, and the Politics of Image*. Andrew Cohen also details the significance of informal (and, in his examples, often violent) negotiations of law and power in Chicago's political economy in this period. Cohen, *Racketeer's Progress*.

4. The tradition of local oversight of weights and measures is a long one in Anglo-American law. For an overview, see Novak, *People's Welfare*.

5. *Chicago Municipal Code of 1922*, §§ 2044, sec. 4173, 4182–84.

6. On licensing fees by the health department, see Ibid., §§ 2012–13. In addition to paying the fee, applicants had to satisfy the mayor that they were "of good character and reputation." Ibid., § 4174.

7. Ibid., § 315.

8. Chicago City Council, *Journal of the Proceedings of the City Council of the City of Chicago for the Council Year 1924–1925* (hereafter, *Journal of Proceedings of Chicago City Council*), January 2, 1925, 4412.

9. *Journal of Proceedings of Chicago City Council*, 1925–26, July 15, 1925, 995. Retailers who

observed their Sabbath on another day of the week could sell on Sundays, but the ordinance required them "to make suitable arrangements as to inspection."

10. "Open Second Co-op Mart at 91st St. Today," *Chicago Tribune*, November 5, 1924, 21. "Direct Marketing Starts," *Chicago Daily News*, November 7, 1924, 9.

11. For an overview of the legislative history of the zoning bill, see King, *Law and Land Use in Chicago*, 365–78. For popular support for the zoning ordinance, see "Mayor's Annual Message," in *Journal of Proceedings of Chicago City Council*, 1919–20, April 28, 1919, 7.

12. Both the membership and the authority of the appeals board were highly controversial topics. Fully aware of the tremendous power an appeals board would have, the state government tried, unsuccessfully, to make the board independent of the city council. *Journal of Proceedings of Chicago City Council*, 1923–24, June 13, 1923, 467; June 20, 1923, 541–42. The Appeals Board remained firmly under the city's control, however, with all appointments made by the mayor, and funding coming from the city council. Board members and employees were remarkably well paid, even by 1920s city council standards. In the ordinance creating the board, the chair received a $7,000 annual salary and each of the four other members received a $5,000 salary. The secretary was paid $6,000. Ibid., June 20, 1923, 763–64. By the late 1920s, board members were also receiving city funds for the purchase of autos (including Cadillac sedans), and maintenance of their cars. See, for instance, "The Annual Appropriation Bill for the City of Chicago for the Year 1928," in *Journal of Proceedings of Chicago City Council*, 1927–28, January 9, 1928, 1727–28; "Supplementary Appropriations for Various Departments," June 29, 1927, 663; July 13, 1927, 826; December 28, 1927, 1579; and "Annual Appropriations Bill for 1929," in *Journal of Proceedings of Chicago City Council*, 1928–29, January 5, 1929, 4258–59.

13. For a fuller and fascinating history of zoning as a mechanism to enforce middle-class aesthetic standards and a mechanism for creating middle-class districts, see Moskowitz, *Standard of Living*. Of course, zoning also proved a way of enforcing race and isolating environmental problems in working-class and African American neighborhoods. On the role of planning in general, and zoning in particular, in creating segregated neighborhoods, see, for instance, Cruikshank and Bouchier, "Blighted Areas and Obnoxious Industry"; and Wiese, *Places of Their Own*. Much of this work is complicated, although not contradicted, by other work which points to the ineffectiveness of zoning and municipal regulations generally at effectively creating orderly and homogenous urban spaces. See, for example, Hartog, "Pigs and Positivism." Focusing on the 1920s, Christopher Wells has effectively demonstrated that urban zoning rarely effectively eased traffic congestion in pre-existing business districts. See Wells, "Car Country." My own analysis suggests that the personalized, uneven enforcement common in urban governance meant that although zoning might achieve racial and class segregation, it rarely achieved the sort of orderly and homogeneous districts that urban planners had envisioned.

14. *Journal of Proceedings of Chicago City Council*, 1923–24, May 23, 1923, 295.

15. For the mayor's powers, see *Journal of Proceedings of Chicago City Council*, 1920–21, November 10, 1929, 973; and *Journal of Proceedings of Chicago City Council*, 1928–29, July 11, 1928, 3419–20. For the scale of license fees, see *Journal of Proceedings of Chicago City Council*, 1920–21, August 26, 1920, 817; January 19, 1921, 1647; and *Journal of Proceedings of Chicago City Council*, 1921–22, December 28, 1921, 1516.

16. *Journal of Proceedings of Chicago City Council*, 1923–24, July 2, 1923, 769.

17. *Journal of Proceedings of Chicago City Council*, 1925–26, October 28, 1925, 1358; *Journal of Proceedings of Chicago City Council*, 1926–27, November 3, 1926, 4559.

18. See, for instance, *Journal of Proceedings of Chicago City Council*, 1920–21, May 26, 1920, 238; November 19, 1920, 958–59; *Journal of Proceedings of Chicago City Council*, 1921–22, May 6, 1921, 100; November 23, 1921, 1311; *Journal of Proceedings of Chicago City Council*, 1922–23, April 19, 1922, 39; November 1, 1922, 1220; *Journal of Proceedings of Chicago City Council*, 1923–24, June 20, 1923, 542, 558; *Journal of Proceedings of Chicago City Council*, 1924–25, December 3, 1924, 4171; December 23, 1924, 4350; *Journal of Proceedings of Chicago City Council*, 1925–26, June 17, 1925, 669; *Journal of Proceedings of Chicago City Council*, 1926–27, February 16, 1927, 5575; *Journal of Proceedings of Chicago City Council*, 1927–28, July 25, 1927, 937; *Journal of Proceedings of Chicago City Council*, 1928–29, September 12, 1928, 3514; and *Journal of Proceedings of Chicago City Council*, 1929–30, May 15, 1929, 304.

19. Stores were classified by number of employees, by number of stores owned by the proprietor, and by whether they were self-service. They paid fees that based on their classification and on the number of delivery wagons that they owned. The inclusion of self-service as a criterion may have hurt chains, but other features seem to have been geared toward large stores rather than toward chain stores per se. For the creation of this system, see *Journal of Proceedings of Chicago City Council*, 1920–21, June 23, 1920, 538–39; August 26, 1920, 817; and November 24, 1920, 1073. For the elimination of certain protections for small stores, see *Journal of Proceedings of Chicago City Council*, 1928–29, July 11, 1928, 3419–20; and May 14, 1928, 2918. There is some indication that the city was unsure of its power to regulate chains explicitly. A 1923 state law constrained the city's taxation powers. See *Journal of Proceedings of Chicago City Council*, 1923–24, October 17, 1923, 844, for a discussion of the failure of a bill that would have allowed the city to tax retail stores (and would have greatly enlarged its licensing provisions).

20. For examples of ordinances and regulations directed against department stores and traveling peddlers, see *Welton v. Missouri*, 91 U.S. 275 (1875); and *Robbins v. Shelby County Taxing District*, 120 U.S. 489 (1887). David Jaffee's thoughtful analysis of itinerant peddlers and the creation of a consumer market includes an excellent discussion of local ordinances aimed at keeping peddlers out of small towns. Jaffee, "Peddlers of Progress," 511–35.

21. Most of the Commerce Department's efforts focused around two projects, a close study of grocery stores in Louisville, Ky., and a simultaneous educational campaign. See, for instance, Bureau of Foreign and Domestic Commerce, *Louisville Grocery Survey*, pt. 2, *Costs, Markets, and Methods in Grocery Retailing*; Bureau of Foreign and Domestic Commerce, *Louisville Grocery Survey*, pt. 3A, *Merchandising Characteristics of Grocery Store Commodities: General Findings and Specific Results*, 48–52; Bureau of Foreign and Domestic Commerce, *Retail Grocer's Problems*; Marketing Services Division to District Offices, *A Manual for Retail Grocery Group Discussion and Application Work*, May 31, 1932, Commerce—Foreign and Domestic Commerce, Bureau of Elimination of Waste in Marketing 1932 January–June 2, box 11, Herbert Hoover Presidential Papers, Herbert Hoover Library, West Branch, Iowa.

22. Tedlow, *New and Improved*, 218. For a general discussion of the anti-chain movement, see ibid., 214–26; and Bean, *Beyond the Broker State*. See also Ryant, "Kentucky and

the Movement to Regulate Chain Stores," 270–85; Harper, "'New Battle on Evolution'";
and Sparks, "Locally Owned and Operated."

23. "The Indiana Chain Store Tax Decision," *Chain Store Age, Administration Edition*
(hereafter, *CSA-A*) 7 (July 1931): 37.

24. Robert W. Lyons, "Annual Report for 1930–1931," *CSA-A* 7 (October 1931): 25.

25. Albert H. Morrill, "What's Ahead for the Chains?" *CSA-A* 7 (October 1931): 22.

26. Godfrey M. Lebhar, As We See It, *CSA-A* 6 (April 1930): 25–26; C. O. Sherrill, "How
We're Decentralizing," *CSA-A* 6 (August 1930): 21–23; C. O. Sherrill, "How Our Managers
Help Spread Facts about Chain Stores," *CSA-A* 10 (May 1934): 13–15. See also Lyons, "Annual
Report for 1930–1931," 25; Godfrey M. Lebhar, As We See It, *CSA-A* 8 (November 1932): 634;
"New Chain Store Association Launched in Washington," *CSA-A* 9 (November 1933): 14.

27. Edwin Hoyt, *That Wonderful A&P!* 170; "How A&P Talks to the Public," *CSA-A* 8 (June
1932): 359–61; Godfrey M. Lebhar, As We See It, *CSA-A* 10 (September 1934): 11–12; "A&P
Scores Anti-Chain Tax as Raising Living Costs," *CSA-A* 8 (March 1932): 198.

28. See, for instance, Harper, "'New Battle on Evolution,'" 407–26; David Horowitz,
"Crusade against Chain Stores," 340–68; and Ryant, "Kentucky and the Movement to Regulate Chain Stores," 270–85. Moreover, the small business owners who organized against
chain stores were not seeking to preserve their own businesses unchanged. Indeed, they
were among the most vocal proponents of modernization campaigns for independent
stores. Sparks, "Locally Owned and Operated," 4–5.

29. See, for instance, "How Detroit Grocers Are Fighting Chain Stores," *Progressive Grocer* 9 (June 1930): 36; and Sparks, "Locally Owned and Operated," 4, 57, 59–62.

30. Real estate agents used Chicago's reputation as a city friendly to chains to induce
businesses to locate there. "Chain Store Leasing Outlook," *CSA-A* 10 (January 1934): 48.

31. Lizabeth Cohen, *Making a New Deal*, 358; Joseph Wagner, "Berwyn: A Short Study
of a Residential Suburb of Chicago," 54, term paper, winter quarter 1933, folder 3, box 159,
Ernest Watson Burgess Papers, Special Collections Research Center, University of Chicago
Library, University of Chicago, Chicago (hereafter, Burgess Papers); "Caslow to Talk at L.
View High," *Uptown News*, February 31, 1930 [*sic*], attached to R. Fischer, "The Local Com-
munity Studied through the Community Paper," 1931, folder 5, box 156, Burgess Papers;
Shideler, "Chain Store," chap. 10, 6; "Howard District Group to Hear Winfield Caslow,"
Chicago Tribune, March 8, 1931, G5; "What's Doing This Week," *Chicago Tribune*, January 25,
1931, H1; Sparks, "Locally Owned and Operated," 57; Parke Brown, "Bundesen out of
Mayor's Race to Aid Cermak," *Chicago Tribune*, March 4, 1931, 3.

32. Illinois General Assembly, House, *Report of Committee on License and Miscellany*, HB
979, 59th General Assembly, May 28, 1935, General Assembly Papers, Legislative Records,
Illinois State Archives, Springfield (hereafter, Legislative Records).

33. Illinois General Assembly, Senate, *A Bill Requiring Every Person, Firm, Association or
Corporation Operating Stores in This State to Obtain a License*, SB264, 55th General Assembly,
1927, *Journal of the Senate of the General Assembly of the State of Illinois*, 1200.

34. Robert W. Lyons, "Annual Report for 1930–31," *CSA-A* 7 (October 1931): 46.

35. Godfrey M. Lebhar, As We See It, *CSA-A* 8 (March 1932): 155.

36. SB 24, SB 124, and SB 283 would have forced firms owning several stores to pay high
fees for licenses. SB 124 passed the Senate, and it was considered, along with the similar

bills HB 119 and HB 121, in the Illinois House of Representatives. No bill made it out of the legislature in this session, however. Illinois General Assembly, Senate, *Journal of the Senate of the General Assembly of Illinois*, 58th General Assembly, 1933; Illinois General Assembly, House, *Journal of the House of Representatives of the General Assembly of the State of Illinois*, 58th General Assembly, 1933.

37. See, for instance, HB 521, 57th General Assembly, 1931; HB 119, 58th General Assembly, 1933; HB 126, 58th General Assembly, 1934; and HB 979, 59th General Assembly, 1935, all in General Assembly Papers, Legislative Records.

38. "Address delivered by Winfield H. Caslow, station WJJD, Chicago, Friday, July 14, 1933," Chain Stores, 1933–34, Official Files (hereafter, FDR Official Files), Franklin D. Roosevelt Papers, Franklin D. Roosevelt Presidential Library, Hyde Park, N.Y. (hereafter FDR Library).

39. Advertisement, *Chicago Tribune*, July 13, 1933, 10–11.

40. Albert H. Morrill, "What's Ahead for Chains?" *Chain Store Age* (hereafter, *CSA*) 7 (October 1931): 22.

41. On the preference of the federal government for working with large firms during World War II, see Brinkley, *End of Reform*, 120–23; and McQuaid, *Uneasy Partners*, 14–16.

42. Lizabeth Cohen, *Making a New Deal*, 218–29.

43. In a famous speech, Mayor Cermak warned the U.S. House Banking and Currency Committee that they could send money then or troops later. Biles, *Big City Boss*, 23.

44. On private fund-raising efforts, see Lizabeth Cohen, *Making a New Deal*, 223; and Biles, *Big City Boss*, 23.

45. On the low levels of county- and state-level relief before the 1930s, see Lizabeth Cohen, *Making a New Deal*, 63. On the creation of the IERC and FERA, see ibid., 269. Of course, other states also worked to alleviate poverty. See New York State's efforts to regulate the price of milk in *Nebbia v. New York*, 291 U.S. 502 (1934). Barry Cushman has traced the doctrine in this case to the Supreme Court's eventual acceptance of the rights of New Dealers to extensively regulate private enterprise. See Cushman, *Rethinking the New Deal Court*.

46. "Urge $8,000,000 Saving in Relief Food Purchases," *Chicago Tribune*, February 17, 1933, 8.

47. In one case, IERC officials discovered that some of their own employees had been aiding a National Tea Company store manager in collecting benefits for nonexistent clients. Officials estimated that he had defrauded the state of a total of $2,577.85. IERC, "Refund—National Tea Co.," September 28, 1936, attached to agenda, September 29, 1936, box 16, Illinois Emergency Relief Commission Records, Illinois State Historical Library, Springfield (hereafter IERC Records). By October 1936, the Cook County office of the IERC employed twenty-one people whose sole job was to pursue investigations and claims. IERC, "Exhibit G: Disposition of Cases Involving the Obtainment of Relief by Fraud: Restitution of Money Obtained Thereby from the Illinois Emergency Relief Commission," October 15, 1936, attached to agenda, October 15, 1936, box 16, IERC Records.

48. IERC, agenda, Illinois Emergency Relief Commission, December 1, 1932, box 1, IERC Records; "County Board Raps Relief Commission Food Contract," *Chicago Tribune*, December 6, 1932, 9.

49. "20 Witnesses Subpoenaed in Relief Inquiry," *Chicago Tribune*, July 23, 1934, 4.

50. IERC, "Exhibit J: Illinois Emergency Relief Commission, Statement of Status of Claims as Reflected in the Records of the Refund and Restitution Department as of November 30, 1936," attached to agenda, December 18, 1936, box 16, IERC Records. For the focus on Chicago, see IERC, "Exhibit G: Disposition of Cases Involving the Obtainment of Relief by Fraud . . . ," October 15, 1936.

51. For evidence of the IERC's ongoing campaign to reshape clients' spending and cooking habits, see Lizabeth Cohen, *Making the New Deal*, 235; and IERC, "Standards of Relief in Cook County," 7, March 30, 1933, attached to agenda, April 3, 1933, box 2, IERC Records; IERC, "Exhibit G: Report and Recommendation to the Commission by the Executive Staff Relative to the Proposal to Substitute for Grocery Orders an Allowance of Cash to Those Relief Clients Capable of Spending Such Cash Wisely," September 29, 1933, attached to agenda, September 29, 1933, box 2, IERC Records.

52. The IERC used precisely this argument in explaining its resistance to moving to cash relief. IERC, "Standards of Relief in Cook County," March 30, 1933; IERC, "Exhibit G: Report and Recommendation . . . ," September 29, 1933; IERC, "Exhibit A-1: Minutes of a Meeting of the Illinois Emergency Relief Commission," October 13, 1933, attached to agenda, October 20, 1933, box 3, IERC Records.

53. On the difficulty of changing vouchers, see IERC, "Standards of Relief in Cook County," March 30, 1933; and IERC, "Exhibit H: Minutes of Meeting of Joint Committee on Relief Administration in Cook County," January 27, 1933, attached to agenda, February 6, 1933, box 2, IERC Records. On the limited nature of the list, see Joseph L. Moss to Special Committee on Unemployment, in *Journal of Proceedings of Chicago City Council*, 1932–33, March 15, 1933, 3410–11.

54. "Stores to Start Refund of Sales Tax Cash at Once," *Chicago Tribune*, May 13, 1933, 22.

55. IERC, "Exhibit H: Minutes of Meeting of Joint Committee on Relief Administration in Cook County"; IERC, "Exhibit A: Minutes of IERC Meeting," May 19, 1933, attached to agenda, May 26, 1933, box 3, IERC Records.

56. "Proposed Investigation of the Alleged Inequitable Distribution of Relief Funds in the Purchase of Supplies, Etc.," in *Journal of Proceedings of Chicago City Council*, 1932–33, February 1, 1933, 3353; "Proposed Investigation of the Alleged Inequitable Distribution of Money Expended to Reimburse Chain Stores, Etc., for Furnishing the Unemployed with Food and Supplies," in *Journal of Proceedings of Chicago City Council*, 1933–34, April 26, 1933, 98. See also "Address Delivered by Winfield H. Caslow"; and Walter J. Nichols, "Sales Tax," *Caslow's Weekly*, Saturday, July 29, 1933, 2, found in Chain Stores, 1933–34, FDR Official Files.

57. "Agenda, Illinois Emergency Relief Commission (Federal) Meeting," 4, September 16, 1932, attached to agenda, September 16, 1932, box 1, IERC Records; Illinois Commission on Taxation and Expenditures, *Report and Recommendations of the Illinois Commission on Taxation and Expenditures*, 11, January 24, 1933, Legislative Reference Collection, Illinois State Archives, Springfield.

58. IERC, "Exhibit A: Minutes of a Meeting of the IERC," 1, February 9, 1934, attached to agenda, February 23, 1934, box 4, IERC Records.

59. "Proposed Investigation of the Alleged Inequitable Distribution of Relief Funds in the Purchase of Supplies, Etc.," 3353; "Proposed Investigation of the Alleged Inequitable Distribution of Money Expended to Reimburse Chain Stores, Etc.," 98.

60. Joseph L. Moss to Special Committee on Unemployment, in *Journal of Proceedings of Chicago City Council*, 1932–33, March 15, 1933, 3410–11.

61. IERC, "Minutes of a Meeting of the Illinois Emergency Relief Commission," March 9, 1934, attached to agenda, March 23, 1934, box 4, IERC Records.

62. Moss to Special Committee on Unemployment, 3410–11. The proportion of relief orders written for chain stores exceeded the chains' citywide proportion of sales and represented far more money than working-class families had spent at chains in the 1920s. In 1929, chain groceries made 50 percent of all sales, and in 1939 they made 56 percent. Although mass culture had made inroads into working-class neighborhoods in the 1930s, most chain groceries were still in middle-class communities (Lizabeth Cohen, *Making a New Deal*, 107, 109, 235–36). Indeed, my findings about chain store expansion, discussed in Chapter 5, suggest that the number of stores increased, while chains' presence in working-class neighborhoods decreased. It therefore seems especially unlikely that relief recipients would have chosen chains in the early 1930s without outside encouragement.

63. IERC, "Instructions Relating to Accounting Procedure, as Required by 'An Act in Relation to State Finance' and in Conformity with the Requirements of the Illinois Emergency Relief Commission," March 8, 1932, attached to agenda, March 17, 1932, box 1, IERC Records.

64. Anna Blazewich, interview, transcript at 91, November 11, 1977, Oral History Archives of Chicago Polonia, Chicago History Museum, Chicago.

65. National Tea was not the only firm to benefit from "the relief business" in this way. By May 1933, A&P was owed nearly $5 million by public welfare agencies and charitable organizations across the country. "A&P Tonnage Drops Only 4% as Dollar Sales Fall 14.3%, Annual Report Shows," *Chain Store Age, Administrative Edition* (hereafter, *CSA-A*) 9 (May 1933): 48.

The National Tea Company was awarded the contract on at least two occasions. Together, these contracts were worth nearly $3 million to the firm. See IERC, "Exhibit B: Food Rations for Cook County," June 22, 1934, attached to agenda, June 29, 1934; and "Exhibit B-7: Food Rations for Cook County," January 18, 1935, attached to agenda, January 18, 1935, both in box 7, IERC Records. See also "County Board Raps Relief Commission Food Contract." Some indication of the extent to which NTC dealt with relief officials can be gauged from a civil case filed by the firm to collect on money owed it by the suburbs of Leyden, Elmwood Park, and River Grove. See complaint at law, January 30, 1940, *National Tea Co. v. Leyden Township*, case no. 40 C 913, Clerk of the Circuit Court of Cook County, Archives Department, Chicago.

66. "Grocers Object to Restrictions on Relief Sales," *Chicago Tribune*, May 15, 1933, 10.

67. Lizabeth Cohen, *Making a New Deal*, 235–36.

68. Quoted in IERC, "Exhibit I: To: The Illinois Emergency Relief Commission, Subject: Cash Relief," December 27, 1935, attached to agenda, December 27, 1935, box 12, IERC Records.

69. The ethnic categories were "Italian," "Jewish," and "Southern." See IERC, "Exhibit H: Food Rations," March 9, 1934, attached to agenda, March 9, 1934, box 4, IERC Records.

70. Thomas Steep to Harry Hopkins, November 17, 1934, Steep, Thomas, IL and IND, box 66, Harry Hopkins Papers (hereafter, Hopkins Papers), FDR Library.

71. A. Aaron, comp., "From: *The New York Daily Worker* (National Ed) Month of January 1933 (1-1-33–1-24-33)," Social Service Study, Relief, Admin, etc., box 79, Federal Writers' Project Records, Manuscripts Division, Illinois State Historical Library, Springfield; "Charge Federal Relief Purchase of Spoiled Eggs," *Chicago Tribune*, July 25, 1934, 4.

72. For a fuller discussion of organized protests, see Lizabeth Cohen, *Making a New Deal*, 262–67; and Piven and Cloward, "Unemployed Workers' Movement," in *Poor People's Movements*, 41–95.

73. Piven and Cloward, *Poor People's Movements*, 59; Lizabeth Cohen, *Making a New Deal*, 265; "Aldermen Consider Request to Permit Parade of Jobless," *Chicago Tribune*, October 27, 1932, 2; "Reds Storm City in Food Plea," *Chicago Tribune*, November 5, 1932, 1; Edsforth, *New Deal*, 107. The November march was part of a national day of protest organized by Unemployed Councils. Edsforth, *New Deal*, 108.

74. "Unemployed Ask for All Relief in Form of Cash," *Chicago Tribune*, November 5, 1932, 15.

75. Aaron, "From: *The New York Daily Worker* (National Ed) Month of January 1933."

76. IERC, "Exhibit A-1: Minutes of a Meeting of the Illinois Emergency Relief Commission," 6–7, September 29, 1933, attached to agenda, October 13, 1933, box 3, IERC Records; IERC, "Exhibit A: Minutes of a Meeting of the Illinois Emergency Relief Commission," 15, November 30, 1934, attached to agenda, December 4, 1934, box 7, IERC Records; IERC, "Exhibit A-2: Minutes of a Meeting of the Illinois Emergency Relief Commission," 7, August 2, 1935, attached to agenda, August 30, 1935, box 11, IERC Records.

77. Steep to Hopkins, November 17, 1934.

78. Ibid.

79. On chains' support, see "22,798 Relief Workers Aid in City Projects," *Chicago Tribune*, April 12, 1935, 2. On support from critics of relief spending, see Betty Browning, "100,000 Protest Relief Tax Raise," *Chicago Tribune*, March 10, 1935, S1.

80. IERC, "Exhibit H: Minutes of Meeting of Joint Committee on Relief Administration in Cook County," January 27, 1933, 4.

81. IERC, "Exhibit A-2: Minutes of a Meeting of the Illinois Emergency Relief Commission (Federal)," April 21, 1933, attached to agenda, May 1, 1933, box 2, IERC Records.

82. IERC, "Exhibit G: Report and Recommendation . . . ," September 29, 1933.

83. IERC, "Exhibit A: Minutes of a Meeting of the Illinois Emergency Relief Commission," September 13, 1935, attached to agenda, September 29, 1935, box 11, IERC Records, 8.

84. IERC, "Exhibit A: Minutes of a Meeting of the Illinois Emergency Relief Commission," 4, December 20, 1935, attached to agenda, December 27, 1935, box 12, IERC Records.

85. IERC, "Exhibit I: To: IERC Subject: Cash Relief," December 27, 1935, 4–7.

86. IERC, "Exhibit D: Recommendation for Payment of Relief in Cash from State Funds in Cook County Effective January 1, 1936," December 20, 1935, attached to agenda, Decem-

ber 20, 1935, box 12, IERC Records; IERC, "Exhibit D: IERC Analysis of Present Administrative Staff of the IERC with Special Reference to the Effects of Cash Relief," March 13, 1936, attached to agenda, March 13, 1936, box 13, IERC Records.

87. "Plan to Restore Cash Relief to Chicago's Needy," *Chicago Tribune*, July 18, 1936, 3.

88. The problem of payment was covered extensively at the time. See, for instance, Jacoby, *Retail Sales Taxation*, 73; Illinois Tax Commission, *Fifteenth Annual Report*; and Haig et al., *Sales Tax in the American States*, 227–28. A brief history of the legislation is helpful here. The sales tax was first passed in March 1933. On May 10 of that year, however, the Illinois Supreme Court declared it unconstitutional on several counts (*Winter v. Barrett*, 352 Ill. 441 [1933]). The court's original decision was based on the fact that the tax exempted some retail sales (in particular sales of motor fuels, which were subject to a separate tax, and sales of goods produced by the seller) and that it allowed Cook County to use the receipts either for relief or for the common schools fund and so, according to the court, appropriated funds for more than one purpose. The state legislature almost immediately passed a second tax, which went into effect July 1, 1933. That tax was declared constitutional in *Reif v. Barrett*, 355 Ill. 104 (1933). Illinois Tax Commission, *Fifteenth Annual Report*, 76, 93.

89. Jacoby, *Retail Sales Taxation*, 75; Illinois Legislative Council, *Exemption of Food under Sales Tax Statutes*, 1.

90. Jacoby, *Retail Sales Taxation*, 76.

91. Both the Reconstruction Finance Corporation (under Hoover) and the Federal Emergency Recovery Administration and the Works Progress Administration (under Roosevelt) were ostensibly meant to boost, but not supersede, state funding of relief. While FERA and the WPA allocated more money to the state, they also demanded matching funds from the Illinois legislature (Biles, *Big City Boss*, 27). Indeed, federal officials seem to have pressured the Illinois legislature to pass a sales tax and take over some the responsibility for funding relief. Jacoby, *Retail Sales Taxation*, 78; Haig et al., *Sales Tax in the American States*, 230; Howard Hunter to Harry Hopkins, December 11, 1934, and April 27, 1935, Illinois Field Reports, 1933–1935, box 57, Hopkins Papers.

92. Jacoby, *Retail Sales Taxation*, 28. There is little secondary literature on the sales taxes and the controversies surrounding them, although a growing number of historians have come to see taxation itself as crucial to the building of the American state. See, for instance, Julian Zelizer, *Taxing America*; Einhorn, *American Taxation, American Slavery*; Mehrotra, "Envisioning the Modern American Fiscal State," 1793–1826.

93. Jacoby, *Retail Sales Taxation*, 84, 229. Even after the measure was passed, amid continued deflation and depression, the state described the sales tax as offering "an assured and certain payment of tax receipts into those funds for which they are intended." Illinois Tax Commission, *Fifteenth Annual Report*, 100.

94. Jacoby, preface to *Retail Sales Taxation*, iii, and table 14, 72.

95. Ibid., 71.

96. Illinois Legislative Council, *Major Potential Sources of State Revenue*, table 1, 2; Jacoby, *Retail Sales Taxation*, 219–20.

97. Jacoby, *Retail Sales Taxation*, 21. Jacoby quickly became vice president of the business school at the university, and then dean of the Graduate School of Management at the University of California at Los Angeles from 1948 to 1973. Jacoby had significant reservations

about the sales tax and, in particular, that it was regressive (meaning that consumers at the lower end of the income scale pay a much higher percentage of their income than do consumers at the higher end of the scale). He combined his faith in the free market with concern for social welfare in his work as a consultant to the Rand Corporation, as a member of Eisenhower's Council of Economic Advisors, and in many international development agencies and local economic policy think tanks from the 1950s to the 1970s. J. Fred Weston, Harold D. Koontz, George W. Robbins, and George A. Steiner, "University of California: In Memoriam, 1980," *Online Archive of California*, [http://content.cdlib.org/xtf/view?docId=hb1j49n6pv&brand=oac&doc.view=entire_text] (accessed February 18, 2009); Eisenhower Presidential Library and Museum, Finding Aids to Neil Jacoby Papers, [http://www.eisenhower.archives.gov/Research/Finding_Aids/J.html] (accessed July 27, 2009).

98. Biles, *Big City Boss*, 23–24; Cermak, *Address of Hon. A. J. Cermak.*

99. Haig et al., *Sales Tax in the American States*, 225.

100. *Journal of Proceedings of Chicago City Council*, 1932–33, August 4, 1932, 2909; December 14, 1932, 3154–55.

101. *Journal of Proceedings of Chicago City Council*, 1933–34, May 10, 1933, 174.

102. Haig et al., *Sales Tax in the American States*, 228; Biles, *Big City Boss*, 22. One indication of the inequity of these property assessments is that the standard deviation from the average assessment was 36.5 percent. Chicago newspapers published numerous accounts of glaring favoritism shown to city and county officials, including an infamous picture of two neighboring homes, one assessed $2,450 and the other, owned by Chicago's chief of police, assessed $500. Beito, *Taxpayers in Revolt*, 39.

103. In order to support city and county agencies, the city issued "tax anticipation warrants"—securities redeemable when taxes were finally collected. Even this measure proved to be fiscally unsound. When the reassessment was completed in 1929, tax rates were almost uniformly lowered, so that revenues failed to match the amounts borrowed. Biles, *Big City Boss*, 22.

104. Beito, *Taxpayers in Revolt*, chaps. 2–4.

105. Jacoby, *Retail Sales Taxation*, 78–79; Haig et al., *Sales Tax in the American States*, 230–32 and table 83, 498.

106. Haig et al., *Sales Tax in the American States*, 228–29.

107. Ibid., 8.

108. Ibid., 229. For social workers' support, see IERC, "Exhibit A: Minutes of a Meeting of the Illinois Emergency Relief Commission," 7–8, May 31, 1935, attached to agenda, June 7, 1935, box 10, IERC Records. The Chicago press was also determinedly against any income tax. See Haig et al., *Sales Tax in the American States*, 228.

109. Although declared unconstitutional by the state supreme court because it exempted motor oil and farm produce, the first tax was quickly followed by a revised one, which remained in place; tax collection was only minimally disrupted. Haig et al., *Sales Tax in the American States*, 228–29; Jacoby, *Retail Sales Taxation*, 86 n. 16. The Sixteenth Amendment, ratified in 1913, made possible a federal income tax but did not apply to the states.

110. Illinois Tax Commission, *Fifteenth Annual Report*, 61, 99.

111. Ibid., table 6, 44. The sales tax made up a larger proportion of the state's budget

than the property tax levy that it was designed to replace. The property tax had been only 14 percent of the state's total revenues. Ibid., 100.

112. Illinois Legislative Council, *Major Potential Sources of State Revenue*, table 2, 2.

113. Illinois Tax Commission, *Fifteenth Annual Report*, 46–47.

114. Haig et al., *Sales Tax in the American States*, 225, 28. The tax rate increased from 2 to 3 percent for an initial period of eighteen months beginning July 1, 1935; the 3 percent rate was retained through the 1930s. Illinois Tax Commission, *Sixteenth Annual Report*, 65.

115. Illinois Tax Commission, *Sixteenth Annual Report*, 66; Haig et al., *Sales Tax in the American States*, 228.

116. On railroads and recordkeeping, see Welke, *Recasting American Liberty*.

117. *Preliminary Rules and Regulations Relating to Tax upon Persons Engaged in the Business of Selling Tangible Personal Property at Retail in This State Pursuant to Act Effective April 1 1933*, March 28, 1933, attached to agenda, April 21, 1933, box 2, IERC Records; Haig et al., *Sales Tax in the American States*, 488; SB 665, §§ 3 and 7, 58th General Assembly, 1933, General Assembly Papers, Legislative Records.

118. SB 665, § 7, 58th General Assembly; Haig et al., *Sales Tax in the American States*, 488.

119. SB 348, 61st General Assembly, 1939, General Assembly Papers, Legislative Records.

120. Jacoby, *Retail Sales Taxation*, 124, 277; SB 665, § 5, 58th General Assembly.

121. Haig et al., *Sales Tax in the American States*, 235; SB 665, §§ 4 and 5, 58th General Assembly. By the end of the decade, the penalties were even more severe—the state could place liens on retailers' real and personal property (excepting "tools of the trade") to recoup taxes and penalties. SB 348, 61st General Assembly.

122. Haig et al., *Sales Tax in the American States*, 235.

123. Quoted in ibid., 432. The first tax, declared unconstitutional for unrelated reasons, had taken a very different tack, stating explicitly that retailers could not pretend to consumers that the tax was not an element of the price they were being charged. Ibid., 431–32.

124. "New Sales Tax Goes in Effect; Adds 2 Per Cent," *Chicago Tribune*, July 1, 1933, 3.

125. Quoted in Haig et al., *Sales Tax in the American States*, 432.

126. For merchants' requests that this be written into legislation in Illinois, see ibid., 232.

127. Ibid., 433.

128. Ibid., 438.

129. Some retailers issued fractional-cent devices for use in sales tax collection. Both retailers and consumers found the devices clumsy and cumbersome, and they were quickly discontinued. Ibid., 433, 436.

130. Their stores were large, but not necessarily located on State Street.

131. Haig et al., *Sales Tax in the American States*, 434.

132. Ibid. The schedule adopted for the 2 percent tax, accordingly, grouped sales differently. On sales of 1 to 25 cents, no tax was added; from 26 to 75 cents, one cent was added, and from 76 cents to $1.25, two cents were added. Only half the sales in each bracket were charged more than 2 percent. Overcharging still occurred but was at least minimized. Advertisement, *Chicago Tribune*, July 1, 1933, 6.

133. Haig et al., *Sales Tax in the American States*, 232, 433.

134. "Voice of the Traffic," *Chicago Tribune*, July 16, 1933, A6.

135. "Wage Arbiters Get Picture of Milkman's Day," *Chicago Tribune*, August 13, 1940, 8.

136. "Low Food Prices Almost Offset Sales Tax Today," *Chicago Tribune*, April 1, 1933, 7.

137. "Friend of the People," *Chicago Tribune*, October 6, 1935, 16.

138. Haig et al., *Sales Tax in the American States*, 433 and table 48, 449.

139. Ibid., table 65, 475. This was cited by 1,507 of 2,366 firms that did not shift the tax. The low dollar value of merchandise and severe competition were also common reasons for not passing along the tax. These were cited, respectively, by 1,157 and 1,429 of the firms.

140. See, for instance, Walter J. Nichols, "Sales Tax," *Caslow's Weekly*, July 29, 1933, 2, found in Chain Stores, 1933–34, FDR Official Files.

141. Haig et al., *Sales Tax in the American States*, table 75, 489; Jacoby, *Retail Sales Taxation*, 124–27.

142. "36 Merchants Named in Sales Tax Warrant," *Chicago Tribune*, September 15, 1938, 16.

143. Jacoby, *Retail Sales Taxation*, 124, 252.

144. On skepticism of retailers' collection methods, see "A Line o'Type or Two," *Chicago Tribune*, April 1, 1937, 14. Here a writer charges the local grocer with regularly rounding up to the next whole cent when collecting the tax, so that he regularly collected more than he would have to pay to the state. On opposition to the tax, see Voice of the People, *Chicago Tribune*, April 15, 1935, 14; for a letter from the Chicago and Cook County Retail Grocers and Butchers' Association protesting the extension and increased rates of the sales tax, see Voice of the People, *Chicago Tribune*, April 15, 1935; for protests based on the regressive nature of the tax, see Thyra Edwards, "Thyra Edwards Speaks . . . ," *Chicago Defender*, December 18, 1937, 17, and January 1, 1938, 17.

145. "Housewives Gird to Kill with Shopping Bags," *Chicago Tribune*, March 21, 1940, 6; "G.O.P. Campaign Hums in High Note of Victory," *Chicago Tribune*, March 24, 1940, 3.

146. See, for instance, Cott, *Grounding of Modern Feminism*. Laura L. Behling makes the important point that, both in spite of and because of the suffrage movement's deployment of gender sameness, "masculine women" and "sexual inversion" were recurring criticism of women activists. See Behling, *Masculine Woman in America*. Sometimes, however, this discourse could be strategically very effective. For an insightful study of women's deployment of gender sameness and commercial culture, see Finnegan, *Selling Suffrage*. For a useful theoretical discussion of the limits and possibilities of gender sameness, see Riley, *Am I That Name*.

147. Quoted in Jacobs, *Pocketbook Politics*, 109. As many historians have documented, other legislation passed at this time followed similar reasoning. See, for instance, Jacobs, *Pocketbook Politics*, 137; and Lizabeth Cohen, *Consumers' Republic*, 54–56. For a fuller discussion of this line of thinking in the Roosevelt administration, see Brinkley, "New Deal and the Idea of the State."

148. The NRA's concern with consumption marked the culmination of a new school of economic thought, one that emphasized the importance of steady purchasing. Very often, advocates sought to secure consumers' faith in the economy by pushing for formal repre-

sentation of "consumers'" interests in government agencies. Prominent New Dealers who worked toward such representation included Paul Douglas, Gardiner Means, and Rexford Tugwell. Their hopes were realized in the NRA, the Agricultural Adjustment Administration, and the Tennessee Valley Authority. On the frustrations and successes of those advocating for consumer representation, see Persia Campbell, *Consumer Representation in the New Deal.*

149. Jacobs, *Pocketbook Politics*, 114–16, 121–25, 167; Lizabeth Cohen, *Consumers' Republic*, 28–31; Storrs, *Civilizing Capitalism*, 96–99.

150. See, for instance, Pattie Jacobs to chairmen of NRA Women's Committee, undated, file 4, box 43, CAB, General Files, Women's Section, RG 9, National Archives II, College Park, Md.

151. Godfrey M. Lebhar, "The Chains and the New Deal," As We See It, *CSA-A* 9 (July 1933): 22.

152. "Compliance Status of the Retail Food and Grocery Industry in the Chicago Area with Particular Emphasis on the Large Chain Organizations," attached to W. L. Kilcoin to Captain W. Robert, August 12, 1935, Illinois State NRA Office, box 79, Administration Records, series 552, Records of Region VI, National Recovery Administration, RG 9, National Archives and Records Administration—Great Lakes Region (Chicago) (hereafter, Records of Region VI, NRA, NARA-Chicago).

153. Hawley, *New Deal and the Problem of Monopoly*, 248–49.

154. As We See It, *CSA-A* 10 (May 1934): 11.

155. William Kilcoin to J. A. Nelson, September 11, 1935, Illinois State NRA Office, box 79, series 552, Records of Region VI, NRA, NARA-Chicago.

156. "Policing a Million Retailers," *Chicago Daily News*, October 25, 1933, 16. Quotes from "Retail Code Is Signed by Roosevelt," *Chicago Journal of Commerce and La Salle Street Journal*, October 24, 1933, 1–2.

157. Godfrey M. Lebhar, As We See It, "The Chains and the New Deal," *CSA-A* 9 (July 1933): 12; Godfrey M. Lebhar, As We See It, *CSA-A* 9 (September 1933): 11.

158. Godfrey M. Lebhar, As We See It, *CSA-A* 9 (September 1933): 20 (emphasis in the original).

159. Godfrey M. Lebhar, "Chains and the New Deal," As We See It, *CSA-A* 9 (July 1933): 11–12, 22; Godfrey M. Lebhar, As We See It, *CSA-A* 9 (September 1933): 11–12.

160. Edwin Hoyt, *That Wonderful A&P!* 144–45; R. V. Rassmussen, "We've Profited by the Times to Build or Remodel 250 Stores," *CSA-A* 8 (November 1932): 644.

161. Untitled, c. 1935, box 16, series 554, Records of Region VI, NRA, NARA-Chicago.

162. Kilcoin, "Compliance Status of the Retail Food and Grocery Industry in the Chicago Area."

163. Ibid. Black workers' willingness to file complaints about their employers under the NRA fits with Risa Goluboff's argument that in the years before the Brown decision, African American workers and civil rights lawyers used new labor laws as key tools in a broad civil rights strategy that included redress for economic as well as political wrongs. See Goluboff, *Lost Promise of Civil Rights.*

164. "Hearings before Regional Compliance Council," Compliance Council Hearings, box 74, Records of Region VI, NRA, NARA-Chicago.

165. Frederic Massmann, a vice president of Chicago's National Tea Company, was also the head of the Chain Store Code Authority, a trade association that helped create the blanket Retail Code and the Food and Grocery Retail Code. In one report of violations, analysts noted that large businesses were so much more successful at observing requirements than were small businesses because the codes had been designed to reflect the wages and hours common at large firms. Untitled, c. 1935, box 16, series 554, Records of Region VI, NRA, NARA-Chicago. On Massmann's work, see Godfrey M. Lebhar, As We See It, *CSA-A* 9 (September 1933): 11.

166. R. E. Wenzel to Regional Director, Region #6, Legal Reports, box 84, series 552, Records of Region VI, NRA, NARA-Chicago; A. W. DeBirny, regional litigation attorney, to C. R. Rumley, regional director, NRA, Miscellaneous Cases (Closed), box 15, series 552, Records of Region VI, NRA, NARA-Chicago.

167. *A.L.A. Schechter Poultry Corp., et. al. v. United States*, 295 U.S. 495 (1935).

168. "The N.R.A.," *Chicago Defender*, March 23, 1935, 14. On widespread criticism of the NRA, particularly its price-fixing provisions, see Jacobs, *Pocketbook Politics*, 119–36.

169. For a fuller description of the fate of consumer advisory boards and the hopes of organized consumers, see Jacobs, *Pocketbook Politics*, 122–24, 133; and Lizabeth Cohen, *Consumers' Republic*, 28–30.

170. See Jacobs, *Pocketbook Politics*, 131–34.

171. For a longer discussion of Chase and Schlink, see McGovern, *Sold American*.

172. Chase and Schlink, *Your Money's Worth*. See also McGovern, *Sold American*, 217–44. As McGovern points out, Chase and Schlink shared with many other business firms a profound faith in science, rationality, and the benefits of standardization.

173. McGovern, *Sold American*, 246. On the split that resulted in the creation of Consumers Union, see Glickman, "Strike in the Temple of Consumption."

174. For instance, Kallet and Schlink, *One Hundred Thousand Guinea Pigs*.

175. Alicia B. Gibson to Consumers' Project, Department of Labor, July 31, 1936, file 2, box 11, Consumers' Division, National Emergency Council's Consumer Division County Council Files, 1933–1935, RG 9, National Archives, Washington, D.C.

176. Mary Zuk to the president, August 16, 1935, OF 2246 Cooperatives, FDR Official Files; Werner K. Gabler, *Labeling the Consumer Movement: An Analysis from the Retailers' Point of View of Organization and Agencies Engaged in Consumer Activities*, found in Consumer Materials, Consumer Movement, box 21, Caroline Ware Papers (hereafter, Ware Papers), FDR Library. The best account of Zuk's housewife protests, and their success, remains Orleck, "'We Are That Mythical Thing Called the Public.'"

177. "The Consumer Movement," *Business Week*, April 29, 1939, 47.

Chapter 4

1. Ann Tweedle, "Kitchen with a View," *Co-op News* 2 [*sic*: should be vol. 8] (January 1944): 2 (emphasis in the original).

2. On women as idealized consumers, see Marchand, *Advertising the American Dream*; Wendt and Kogan, *Give the Lady What She Wants!*; Benson, *Counter Cultures*; and McGovern, *Sold American*, 214–15.

3. See Lizabeth Cohen, *Consumers' Republic*; Glickman, "Strike in the Temple of Con-

sumption"; and McGovern, *Sold American*. Annelise Orleck's discussion of the United Conference against the High Cost of Living is an important exception to this; her work points to the extensive network of the UCHCL and the possibilities for working-class (although not cross-class) alliances in 1930s protests. Orleck, "'We Are That Mythical Thing Called the Public.'"

4. See Smith, "Food Rioters and the American Revolution"; and Hyman, "Immigrant Women and Consumer Protest." For numerous instances of women's public protests over food during the French Revolution, see Levy, Applewhite, and Johnson, *Women in Revolutionary Paris*. For examples of such protests in the antebellum United States, see Glickman, "'Buy for the Sake of the Slave.'"

5. For a useful overview, see Sklar, "Two Political Cultures in the Progressive Era." On the history of the NCL during the 1930s, see Storrs, *Civilizing Capitalism*.

6. On European protests during this era, see Davis, *Home Fires Burning*; Engel, "Not by Bread Alone"; and Fridenson, "Impact of the War on French Workers."

7. For a description of these new tactics in the Seattle labor movement, see Frank, *Purchasing Power*.

8. Bayor, *Neighbors in Conflict*, 68–69.

9. *Good Housekeeping* had provided its "seal of approval" to products based on payments from manufacturers—not, as had been implied, on the quality of the product. McGovern, *Sold American*, 214; McGovern, "Sold American," 310.

10. Orleck, "'We Are That Mythical Thing Called the Public,'" 377.

11. Orleck, *Common Sense and a Little Fire*, 224, 226, 241.

12. McGovern, *Sold American*, 215.

13. McGovern, "Sold American," 210.

14. Orleck, *Common Sense and a Little Fire*, 239.

15. On the anti-Japanese boycotts, see Frank, *Buy American*, 95–100. See also Glickman, "'Make Lisle the Style.'" It should be noted that this boycott was especially effective. Imports from Japan were 47 percent lower in the first six months of 1938 than in the first six months of 1937.

16. Cayton and Drake, *Black Metropolis*, 430–32.

17. On women's importance, see Greenberg, "Or Does It Explode?" 114–31; and McDowell, "Keeping Them 'In the Same Boat Together'?" 222–24, 227.

18. For a fuller description of these campaigns, in Chicago and elsewhere, see Hunter, "Don't Buy from Where You Can't Work"; and Lizabeth Cohen, *Consumers' Republic*, 44–47.

19. Lucius B. Harper, "Dustin' Off the News," *Chicago Defender*, April 16, 1938, 16.

20. Ibid.

21. Baldwin, *Chicago's New Negroes*.

22. "Chicago Northern District Reviews Quarter's Work," *Chicago Defender*, December 18, 1937, 1.

23. "Six More Merchants Were Convicted as Chiselers," *Chicago Defender*, July 13, 1940, 8; "Housewives Install Officers at Reception," *Chicago Defender*, January 2, 1937, 8; "Condemn 934 Pounds of Meat in 4-Week Drive," *Chicago Defender*, September 7, 1940, 7. Although the name resembles that used by various European "housewives'" organizations, there is no

evidence that American housewives' groups modeled themselves on European groups. The influence of American housewives' organizations was much smaller and their politics less visible and less conservative than that of its European counterparts. For a discussion of the European housewives' movement, see Reagin, *Sweeping the German Nation*.

24. "I Go to Market," *Chicago Defender*, June 15, 1940, 13–15.

25. "Meat Protest Spreads, Livestock Is Quiet," *Chicago Tribune*, June 11, 1935, 32. On the UCHCL, see also Jacobs, *Pocketbook Politics*, 169–70.

26. Orleck, "'We Are That Mythical Thing Called the Public'"; "Women Protest Meat Prices at Packing Plants," *Chicago Tribune*, August 22, 1935 [illegible].

27. UCHCL program, December 1, 1940, file 21, box 130, Jessie Lloyd O'Connor Papers, Sophia Smith Collection, Smith College, Northampton, Mass. (hereafter, O'Connor Papers).

28. Minutes of the conference on profiteering, Hull-House, November 5, 1939; "An Open Letter to the US Dept of Justice Calling for Protection of the American Consumer against Profiteering," October 28, 1940; press release, February 24, 1943, all in file 21, box 130, O'Connor Papers.

29. Alice Belester to "Consumer," September 2, 1937, file 21, box 130, O'Connor Papers.

30. U.S. Congress, House, Temporary National Economic Committee, *Hearings before the Temporary National Economic Committee*, pt. 8, *The Problems of the Consumer*, 3303. For a full description of working-class "housewife" activism in the 1930s, see Orleck, "'We Are That Mythical Thing Called the Public,'" and "Spark Plugs in Every Neighborhood," chap. 6 in *Common Sense and a Little Fire*.

31. Jessie Lloyd O'Connor to Sidney James, November 7, 1939, folder 5, box 116, O'Connor Papers; Jessie Lloyd O'Connor to Mr. Lahey, May 1, 1942, League of Women Shoppers Papers, Sophia Smith Collection, Smith College, Northampton, Mass. (hereafter, LWS Papers); "Winnetkans Numbered among Shoppers' League," clipping dated February 10, 1938, file 2, box 119, O'Connor Papers.

32. Calling card, file 10, box 1, LWS Papers.

33. "A Woman Gentle and Wise: Fond Memories of My Mother, Alice Elsie Lesser Shephard," box 1, file 1, LWS Papers; "Mrs. Arthur G. Hays, Lawyer's Wife, Dead, Founded Shoppers' League to Aid Workers in Stores," *New York Times*, June 4, 1944, 42.

34. Agenda, c. 1939, file 11, box 1, LWS Papers.

35. Agenda, February 1941, file 11, box 1, LWS Papers.

36. Katharine Armatage to "Member," October 24, 1941, file 4, box 1, LWS Papers.

37. For more on the CR's transformation into a red-baiting organization, see Glickman, "Strike in the Temple of Consumption." On increasing anticommunist activism around consumer groups generally, see McGovern, *Sold American*, 305–6 and 319–21; and Schrecker, *Many Were the Crimes*.

38. For a deft untangling of these networks in the life of one LWS member, see Storrs, "Red Scare Politics and the Suppression of Popular Front Feminism." The Dies Committee investigation of the LWS received significant press coverage and earned group members intense study by the FBI. See, for instance, "Dies Group Holds Seized Red Papers," *New York*

Times, April 5, 1940, 10; and telegram [author and addressee illegible], December 16, 1940, released through FOIA request for materials on the League of Women Shoppers from the FBI's files, in possession of the author.

39. Board meeting, League of Women Shoppers, September 27, 1938, file 8, box 1, LWS Papers.

40. "Hull House: Some Facts about Chicago's Most Famous Settlement," c. 1939–40, file 6, box 116; minutes of the conference on profiteering," November 5, 1939; Alice Belester to "Consumer," September 2, 1937; statement of UCHCL to Illinois Commerce Commission, January 14 and February 2 [1942], file 21, box 130; "Government Grading Exhibit," January 29, 1940, file 21, box 130; "Open Letter to the US Dept of Justice"; press release, February 24, 1943; minutes of UCHCL meeting, July 23, 1940, file 21, box 130; UCHCL untitled brochure, file 21, box 130, all in O'Connor Papers.

41. Flyer, c. 1938, file 21, box 130, O'Connor Papers.

42. Statement of the UCHCL about the Dies Committee, c. 1939, file 21, box 130, O'Connor Papers; *Organization, Education, Action*, undated brochure, O'Connor Papers.

43. "Meat Boycott Is Planned for July 26-7-8," *Chicago Defender*, July 20, 1935, 3.

44. Agenda of UCHCL meeting, July 23, 1940, file 21, box 130, O'Connor Papers. On the Illinois Housewives Association as an African American organization, see "Facts Concerning the Organization," *Original Illinois Housewives Association Bulletin*, 2 (November–December 1936): 3, found in Thelma Wheaton Papers, Chicago History Museum, Chicago. So many organizations had adopted the name "Illinois Housewives Association" that the group began calling itself "The Original Illinois Housewives Association."

45. "Judge Blocks Move to Oust Girl from Office," *Chicago Defender*, October 25, 1941, 6.

46. Minutes of the conference on profiteering, November 5, 1939, O'Connor Papers.

47. Untitled flyer, c. 1938, file 21, box 130, O'Connor Papers.

48. League of Women Shoppers, program of board meeting, September 27, 1938, file 8, box 1, LWS Papers.

49. "Consumers Co-Op Theme of Congress," *Chicago Defender*, June 27, 1936, 18.

50. On the importance of Scandinavian immigrants to Rochdale-style co-ops and to cooperation generally, see Furlough and Stirkwerda, "Economics, Consumer Culture, and Gender," 10; and Keillor, *Cooperative Commonwealth*. On the importance of cooperatives to ethnic communities, especially in the upper Midwest, see Gabaccia, *We Are What We Eat*, 87–91.

51. For an astute discussion of this wave of labor activism and cooperatives, see Frank, *Purchasing Power*; and Warne, *Consumers' Co-operative Movement in Illinois*.

52. In Chicago, see "Action on Co-op Receiver to be Urged to Judge," *Chicago Tribune*, September 30, 1921, 15; "Parker Admits Evasion to Avoid Co-op Shortage," *Chicago Tribune*, October 16, 1921, 3; "Court Annuls Bankruptcy of Co-op Society," *Chicago Tribune*, December 29, 1921, 7; "Parker Refuses to Quit as Head of Co-op Society," *Chicago Tribune*, February 26, 1922, 5.

53. Florence Parker, "Consumers' Cooperation in the United States, 1920–1936," *Monthly Labor Review* 38 (August 1938): 231.

54. Ibid., 234.

55. "Operations of Consumer Cooperatives in 1944," *Monthly Labor Review* 61 (September 1945): 471–72.

56. Sidney Gubin, "Consumers' Cooperatives in Chicago," *Monthly Labor Review* 45 (October 1937): 833; "Cooperatives on the March," *Cooperation* 25 (February 1939): 29.

57. On cooperatives' alliance with the consumer movement, see, for instance, "The Consumer Movement (Report to Executives)," *Business Week*, April 29, 1939, 38–52; Burley, *Consumers' Cooperative as a Distributive Agency*, 17; Gubin, "Consumers' Cooperatives in Chicago," 828–29; "Consumers Awakening!" *Cooperation* 19 (November 1933): 184. Business advisor and University of Chicago marketing professor James Palmer warned business executives that co-ops would only continue to grow so long as retailers engaged in price-fixing and opposed consumer protection measures. See, for instance, "Palmer Gives Suggestion on Co-op Threat," *Chicago Journal of Commerce and La Salle Street Journal*, October 10, 1936, 5. Palmer received attention for his remarks from all the major Chicago newspapers. See also "Price-Boosting Laws Are Aid to Co-Ops, Advertisers Told," *Chicago Daily News*, October 9, 1936, 49; the inexplicably titled "Finds Consumer 'Co-ops' Having Small Effects," *Chicago Tribune*, October 10, 1936, 31; and "Resolutions Adopted by the Ninth Biennial Congress of the Cooperative League," *Cooperation* 20 (November–December 1934): 180.

58. See, for instance, Education Committee Annual Report, April 30, 1936; and the many recipes and quality comparisons made in the Hyde Park Co-op's weekly newsletter, the *Evergreen*, both in Hyde Park Cooperative Society Papers (hereafter, HPCS). Documents identified as being in the Hyde Park Cooperative Society Papers were held by the Hyde Park Co-op when I examined them. The co-op has since closed and its papers have been donated to the Hyde Park Historical Society and in turn to the Special Collections Research Center at the University of Chicago. As I write this, it is impossible to know whether all the materials I examined were transferred. On the wholesaler's reliance on testing and grading, as well as the early adoption of government grades, see "Cooperatives on the March," *Consumers' Cooperation* 25 (February 1939): 29; and "Consumer Co-op Progress in 1941," *Consumers' Cooperation* 28 (January 1942): 12. Both National Cooperatives, Inc., a processor, and Cooperative Wholesale, the wholesaler serving Chicago-area co-ops, prided themselves on their development of and adherence to grading standards. All products sold under the "Co-op" label were categorized as one of three different grades and had color-coded labels corresponding to each grade. See H. E. Bogardus, "Grading of All Products Begins," *Co-op News* 6 (October 1941): 1.

59. "Selling to or through Cooperative Organization Ruled No Violation of Code," *Monthly Labor Review* 38 (April 1934): n.p.; "Cooperative Societies Permitted . . ." *Monthly Labor Review* 39 (December 1934): 1358.

60. Although co-ops never sold the majority of commodities, they often sold large percentages of them. Peter Gurney finds that co-ops were responsible for 7 to 9 percent of all retail sales in Britain in 1920—about the same proportion represented by nascent "multiple shops" (chain stores). Gurney, *Co-operative Culture*, 247. See also Gurney, "Battle of the Consumer in Postwar Britain." Martin Purvis finds that in some localities, they accounted

for as much as 30 percent of sales. Purvis, "Societies of Consumers and Consumer Socie-ties," 164. Co-ops accounted for as much as 20 percent of all sales of grocery and household goods. Furlough and Stirkwerda, *Consumers against Capitalism?* 18–19.

61. See, for instance, "Board Named by Roosevelt for Study for Co-ops," *Chicago Tribune*, June 24, 1936, 26; "3 Members of Roosevelt's Comm Sail for Europe," *New York Times*, July 2, 1936, 24; "Ed from Louisville Courier Journal," *New York Times*, July 12, 1936, section 4, 8; "Commission in Sweden," *New York Times*, July 13, 1936, 7; "Comm Arrives in London," *New York Times*, August 18, 1936, 21. The commission was originally composed of Jacob Baker, an assistant WPA administrator; Leland Olds, secretary of the New York State Power As-sociation; and Charles Stuart, a New York City engineer. "U.S. Commission off for Europe to Study Co-Ops," *Chicago Tribune*, July 2, 1936, 12.

62. Godfrey M. Lebhar, As We See It, *Chain Store Age, Administration Edition* (hereafter, *CSA-A*) 12 (September 1936): 12; Lincoln et al., *Consumers' Co-operatives and Private Busi-ness*, 17; "Grocers' Head Terms Co-Ops Worse Peril Than Chain Stores," *Chicago Tribune*, October 11, 1936, 6. The U.S. Chamber of Commerce publicly called for the government to cease all activities that promoted or gave unfair advantages to consumers' cooperatives. "Demands End of Favoritism for 'Coops,'" *Chicago Journal of Commerce and La Salle Street Journal*, October 5, 1936, 1.

63. "Fight Tugwell's Co-ops or Crash, Merchants Told," *Chicago Tribune*, October 8, 1936, 12.

64. "Co-op Report Available," *Consumers' Cooperation* 23 (April 1937): 52. Jacob Baker, a member of the commission, wrote to Roosevelt's secretary, "I hope the President will find the printed copy more convenient for reading than was the typewritten form in which the advance copy was submitted. . . . We [the members of the commission] are somewhat in the situation of the members of an exploring expedition, which upon returning finds that the home folks do not quite recognize them." Jacob Baker to Marvin McIntyre, May 12, 1937, Commission of Inquiry on Cooperative Enterprises in Europe, 1937, Official Files, Franklin D. Roosevelt Papers, Franklin D. Roosevelt Presidential Library, Hyde Park, N.Y.

65. Richard Giles, "Co-Ops [sic] and Politics," *Printers' Ink* 176 (August 13, 1936): 15–17.

66. "Government Backs Cooperatives," *Business Week*, September 11, 1937, 30–32; "Co-op Transfer," *Business Week*, July 29, 1939, 16; "Co-op Stores Grow in Greenbelt," *Busi-ness Week*, May 14, 1938, 17–18.

67. "Notes on Cooperative Development," *Monthly Labor Review* 30 (June 1930): 120–23.

68. "News and Comment," *Cooperation* 19 (January 1933): 12.

69. "Central States Cooperative League Congress Draws Record Attendance," *Coopera-tion* 20 (June 1934): 89–90.

70. "Consumers' Cooperatives in Action," *Consumers' Cooperation* 23 (March 1937): 46.

71. Gubin, "Consumers' Cooperatives in Chicago," 816.

72. Ibid., 819–20, 824. The 61 percent growth rate represented fourteen new societies. Other figures back up Gubin's claim of sudden growth. Membership had increased in the thirty-five societies reporting from 2,500 to 3,886—or 55.4 percent. Twenty-nine societies had records of their 1936 sales—they reported sales of $476,439, an increase of 52 percent

over those of the previous year. Newly formed stores reported an even more astonishing increase in sales—116 percent. Nearly all the growth was the result of increased membership in food and grocery co-ops. Ibid., 820, 825.

73. Ibid., 820.

74. "Co-op National Brand," *Business Week*, February 11, 1939, 41; Gubin, "Consumers' Cooperatives in Chicago," 833; Wallace J. Campbell, "Cooperative Highlights of 1938," *Consumers' Cooperation* 25 (January 1939): 12.

75. "1943—Another Cooperative Year," *Consumers' Cooperation* 29 (January 1943): 1.

76. Pipeline, *Co-op News* 9 (January 1944): 4. Consumers' Cooperative Services claimed that it was actually losing customers because of its small quarters. On CCS's expansion, see "CCS on Lookout for a Bigger Home," *Co-op News* 6 (November 1941): 4; "Manager's Report," presented at CCS membership meeting, April 29, 1943; and *Evergreen*, January 22, 1943 (which announced that the new store would be 4,000 square feet), all in HPCS. Worker's Home Co-op, one of the oldest cooperative societies in the city, enlarged and remodeled an old storefront, renaming it the "Rochdale Trading Association" in 1941. "Rochdale Trading Association Modernizes," *Co-op News* 6 (September 1941): 1.

77. "Central States Co-ops in 1943–44," *Co-op News* 2 [*sic: should be vol. 8*] (October 1944): 8.

78. "Co-op Stock Registered with SEC," *Chicago Daily News*, August 6, 1945, 18; "Corporate: Co-op Files Common," *Chicago Journal of Commerce and LaSalle Street Journal*, August 7, 1945, 8; Ruth Schumm, "First Link Forged in Chicago Co-op Chain," *Co-op Magazine* 3 (January 1947): 8.

79. "Report of the General Manager," May 1947, Hyde Park Cooperative Society, HPCS; "Two More Co-op Stores Ready to Go," *Co-op News* 2 [*sic*] (September 1944): 1.

80. For accounts of Rochdale principles, see "Resolutions Adopted by the Ninth Biennial Congress of the Cooperative League," 183; Furlough and Stirkwerda, "Economics, Consumer Culture, and Gender"; and Frank, *Purchasing Power*, 44.

81. The Hyde Park Co-op, one of the city's most successful, estimated that most members bought less than half of their groceries at the store. "Report on Member Buying," May 16, 1938, HPCS. The Evanston Consumers' Cooperative had similar problems—twenty of its members were officially listed as "non-purchasers." Wade Crawford Barclay, "Cooperation Advances in a Mid-West Community," *Consumers' Cooperation* 23 (April 1937): 57.

82. Gubin, "Consumers' Cooperatives in Chicago," 828–29; Hyde Park Cooperative Society Records, Chicago History Museum, Chicago (hereafter HPCS-CHM); minutes of board of directors meeting, May 15, 1939, HPCS. Apparently, the tests had a direct effect on what products the co-op purchased. Participants reported, "In many cases highly advertised brands failed to meet stringent tests of consumer needs and the cooperative was able to stock higher quality goods at lower prices than competing private profit stores." "Cooperatives in Action," *Consumers' Cooperation* 22 (January 1936): 13. See also the report of a Mrs. Bogart to the board of directors, minutes of board of directors meeting, c. 1937, HPCS.

83. Articles of incorporation, Ida B. Wells Consumers' Co-operative, Corporate Records, Secretary of State Records, Illinois State Archives, Springfield.

84. Gubin, "Consumers' Cooperatives in Chicago," 815.

85. "Resolutions Adopted by the Ninth Biennial Congress of the Cooperative League," 183.

86. In 1936 CSCL spun off its wholesale business into a separate organization, Cooperative Wholesale, Inc. After first opening in Bloomington, Indiana, Cooperative Wholesale moved to Chicago in 1937. Gubin, "Consumers' Cooperatives in Chicago," 833–35; "Consumers Cooperatives in Action," *Consumers' Cooperation* 23 (March 1937): 46; "League Admits National Cooperatives, Inc.," *Cooperation* 19 (December 1933): 205; "Co-op National Brand," *Business Week*, February 11, 1939, 41.

87. In practice, the central buying agencies had an ambiguous relationship to cooperative principles and were not always welcomed by local societies. These wholesalers were nominally cooperative in that they were financed through shares owned by member co-op societies. These member societies then determined the buying and selling policies of the wholesalers. Unlike most Rochdale coop societies, however, national cooperatives offered members increased voting power in proportion to the number of shares bought. Gubin, "Consumers' Cooperatives in Chicago," 833. Gubin noted that in practice, most co-ops had only one vote. Similarly, Cooperative Wholesale established a system whereby voting rights increased with the amount of goods purchased. Ibid., 834. Under CWI's system, member societies were asked to buy stock equaling 10 percent of their purchases from the wholesaler.

88. The Central States Cooperative League had had only thirteen member societies in the region in 1926, but thirty-two member societies in Chicago alone by December 31, 1935, and fifty-five total member societies by December 31, 1936. Ibid., 834–36. The 1937 CSCL meeting drew three hundred delegates and members, and the association represented sixty co-op societies. A. W. Warriner, "Central States League to Move Headquarters to Chicago—Plans New Cooperative Wholesale," *Consumers' Cooperation* 21 (June 1935): 116. By June 1938, CSCL was credited by the national cooperative trade journal with serving sixty-six urban co-ops. "Cooperatives on the March," *Consumers' Cooperation* 24 (June 1938): 94.

89. C. B. Larrabee, "That Cooperative Gap," *Printers' Ink* 168 (September 20, 1934): 96–98. Proponents of cooperation also applauded its increasing centralization. See, for instance, "The Coops Grow Up," *New Republic* 90 (April 7, 1937): 253–54. The concern with co-ops' growth resulted in very close coverage of them in the business press in the late 1930s. See, for instance, "Coops Gained 20% Last Year," *Business Week*, February, 26, 1938, 23–24; "Co-op Stores Grow in Greenbelt," *Business Week*, May 14, 1938, 17–18; "Consumer Cooperatives," *Fortune* 15 (March 1937): 133–40.

90. "Consumer Cooperative Growth Challenges Profit Business," *Printers' Ink* 209 (December 29, 1944): 17–19.

91. "Co-ops Plan United Front," *Business Week*, October 22, 1938, 33–35.

92. Richard Giles, "Co-Ops [sic] and Politics," *Printers' Ink* (August 13, 1936): 15–17; J. J. Baskin, "How Co-ops Work in the Middle West," *Retailing*, August 24, 1936, 2. As late as 1946, the editor of the major chain store trade journal warned his readers to guard against any future "unfair advantages" that coops might gain. Godfrey M. Lebhar, As We See It, *CSA-A* 22 (February 1946): 7.

93. U.S. Congress, House, Committee on the District of Columbia, *Hearings before the*

Subcommittee of the Committee on the District of Columbia, A Bill to Amend the Code of the District of Columbia to Provide for the Organization and Regulation of Cooperative Associations and for Other Purposes.

94. "Girding for Co-ops," *Business Week*, September 25, 1943, 98–99; "Co-ops Cheer," *Business Week*, November 11, 1944, 24.

95. Wallace J. Campbell, "Radio Controversy Establishes Fundamental Points," *Consumers' Cooperation* 29 (January 1943): 6–7; "Radio Fight Ends in Victory for Co-ops," *Co-op News* 8 (January 1943): 1.

96. "A Record of the Past Year," *Evergreen*, April 4, 1938, HPCS.

97. Folk dancing and celebration of folk culture more generally were popular pastimes of many liberal and leftist organizations in the 1930s. See Pells, *Radical Visions and American Dreams*, 100–102; Graff, *Stepping Left*, 35, 133–38.

98. "7 High Spots in Chicago Coops' Drive," *Co-op News* 2 [*sic*] (September 1944): 5. The ABC coop was located in the Jane Addams and Robert Brooks housing projects and was the result of a merger between two older buying clubs. "The Pipeline," *Co-op News* 9 (May 1944): 4.

99. "Shelving May Be Weak but Co-op Spirit is Strong," *Co-op News* 7 (August 1942): 4.

100. Circle Pines developed quite a following among Chicago cooperators. See "The New Circle Pines Center," *Evergreen* (November 1940); "Circle Pines Reunion to Be March 7," *Co-op News* 7 (March 1942): 3.

101. For mention of the lease on the camp, see "Cooperatives on the March," *Consumers' Cooperation* 4 (April 1938): 61. Beginning in 1937, the national trade journal *Consumers' Cooperation* carried a regular feature on recreational activities in cooperatives. See "National Cooperative Recreation School," *Consumers' Cooperation* 23 (October 1937): 156–58. Circle Pines is still in existence, is still run as a cooperative, and still provides facilities to other co-ops. It also offers its own elaborate programming for adults and youth designed "to demonstrate cooperative alternatives for social justice, recreation, environmental stewardship, peace, and to teach cooperation as a way of life." Circle Pines Center Cooperative, "History," *Circle Pines Center*, [http://www.circlepinescenter.org/history.php] (accessed July 23, 2007).

102. "Recreation News," *Consumers' Cooperation* 28 (April 1942): 59. See also Co-ops at Play, *Consumers' Cooperation* 26 (August 1940): 125; Co-ops at Play, *Consumers' Cooperation* 26 (September 1940): 141–42; and Viola Jo Kreiner, "Circle Pines Center," *Cooperation* 27 (January 1941): 9. In 1943, a Circle Pines Club formed in the city to "promote the co-op camp throughout the year." Members had already subscribed $1,000 by the time of this notice. Pipeline, *Co-op News* 8 (March 1943): 1.

103. See, for example, "Folk Dancing Every Tuesday in Beliajus' Class," *Co-op News* 5 (October 1941): 2; the announcement of a citywide party and a reminder about weekly "Play Co-op" meetings in Pipeline, *Co-op News* 9 (April 1944): 4; and the "fair" at the Thrift Co-op, as well as four socials that had been held as a joint project of Thrift and the newer Frederick Douglass Co-op, described in Pipeline, *Co-op News* 7 (July 1942). See also the notice of banquets sponsored by the Morgan Park Co-op's Men's Club, More Pipeline, *Co-op News* 8 (May 1943): 5; More Pipeline, *Co-op News* 8 (May 1943): 4; and "What They Are Doing," *Co-op News* 7 (May 1942): 4.

104. "Rochdale Trading Association Modernizes," *Co-op News* 6 (September 1941): 1; Pipeline, *Co-op News* 2 [*sic*] (December 1944): 8.

105. When the HPCS opened a supermarket in 1942, it included a permanent home for its Education Department. See *Evergreen*, May 14, 1942.

106. Pipeline, *Co-op News* 2 [*sic*] (December 1944): 8.

107. "First Glimpse of That Smart New Co-op," *Co-op News* 6 (October 1941): 3; "Modernizing Hikes Co-op Sales," *Co-op News* 7 (February 1942): 8.

108. CLUSA, *Brief Report of the Proceedings of the Fifth Congress of the Co-operative League, Nov. 4, 5, 6, 1926*, 8, Papers of the Cooperative League of the USA, Wisconsin Historical Society, Madison (hereafter, CLUSA Papers).

109. CLUSA, *First Yearbook: The Cooperative League of the U.S.A.* (New York: Cooperative League of New York, 1930), 108; CLUSA, *Third Yearbook: The Cooperative League of the U.S.A.* (Minneapolis, Minn.: Northern States Cooperative League, 1936), 47.

110. "Yes, Women Are Active!" *Consumers' Cooperation* 29 (October 1943): 110.

111. After a survey of regional wholesales, CLUSA announced that women were indeed active, but mostly with educational programs. "Yes, Women Are Active!" 110. See also "Education Pushes Ahead," *Co-op News* 2 [*sic*] (June 1944): 7. For Altgeld Gardens, see "It's the First Smile of Victory at Altgeld Gardens," *Co-op News* 2 [*sic*] (October 1944): 4. The Brotherhood Co-op, originally begun by the Ladies' Auxiliary of the Brotherhood of Sleeping Car Porters, included men in its membership and its recruitment staff by 1948. In a letter explaining the decision, the president of the auxiliary wrote, "Since there are both men and women on the Membership Committee, it was decided to place a man and a woman together for the purpose of making a house to house contact." Halena Wilson to the Membership Committee, January 26, 1948, Brotherhood of Sleeping Car Porters Papers, Chicago History Museum, Chicago (hereafter, BSCP Papers). All papers on the co-op and buying club are contained in box 118.

112. The Hyde Park Co-op was home to a Youth League and the "Cracker Barrel," a couples group that met for suppers and dancing. See *Evergreen*, July 1941 and December 1941, HPCS.

113. CLUSA, *Report of the Proceedings of the Third Congress of the Cooperative League*, 63–64, October 26–28, 1922, CLUSA Papers.

114. "Women's Conference," August 1942, CLUSA Papers. Women's guilds continued to operate, particularly at older cooperatives, through the 1950s.

115. Cora C. Alderton to Benjamin Hayenga, April 7, 1936, HPCS-CHM.

116. Untitled report of 1936 CLUSA Convention, 33–52, held in Columbus, Ohio, October 8–10, 1936, CLUSA Papers.

117. Leo LeLievre, "American People Are Sold on Brands—Give Them What They Want," *Cooperation* 15 (April 1929): 67.

118. Oscar Cooley, "What Does Cooperation Mean to Women?" *Cooperation* 19 (February 1933): 54–55.

119. "'What Does Cooperation Mean to Women?' A Letter from the National Committee to Women's Guilds," *Cooperation* 19 (May 1933): 98.

120. Josephine Johnson, "The Consumer Consumed or Pure Applesauce?" *Cooperation* 25 (April 1939): 60–64.

121. See, for instance, "Lulu Says She's Sorry Milkmen Have to Come So Early in the Morning," *Co-operator of the North Shore Co-operative Society*, May 1939, 1–2; and "Lulu Gives Credit Union a Lot of Credit but She Can't Find Anything Romantic," *Co-operator of the North Shore Co-operative Society*, July 1939, 3, both in file 8, box 137, O'Connor Papers.

122. On attempts to recruit women, see the untitled report on education and the problem of recruiting women, October 1936, box 16, CLUSA Papers; Wade Crawford Barclay, "Cooperation Advances in a Midwest Community," *Consumers' Cooperation* 23 (April 1937): 57–58; Henry Davis, "Consumers' Cooperation in Chicago," *Consumers' Cooperation* 23 (August 1937): 117–19; Cooley, "What Does Cooperation Mean to Women?" Cooperation 19 (May 1933): 54–55; " 'What Does Cooperation Mean to Women?' " Cooperation 19 (May 1933): 98.

123. More Pipeline, *Co-op News* 8 (March, 1943): 4.

124. "Cooperative Youth," *Cooperation* 19 (February 1933): 56; Barclay, "Cooperation Advances in a Mid-West Community," 57.

125. Management Committee minutes, January 9, 1939, HPCS; minutes of board of directors meeting, March 22, 1937, HPCS.

126. When the Ida B. Wells Co-op was incorporated in 1941, it had five women on its nine-person board of directors. Ida B. Wells Cooperative, certificate of incorporation, Corporate Records, Secretary of State Records, Illinois State Archives, Springfield. The most extreme example of women's control was the Brotherhood Co-op, founded and run by the Ladies' Auxiliary of the Brotherhood of Sleeping Car Porters.

127. For one example of such support, see the correspondence between the Brotherhood Cooperative and two co-op advisory associations—the Central States Cooperatives and the Council for Cooperative Development. Margedant Peters, Congress Publicity Committee, Central States Cooperatives, to Halena Wilson, May 6, 1943, BSCP Papers; Jim Blackburn, Council for Cooperative Development, to Halena Wilson, May 19, 1944, BSCP Papers; William Torma, Central States Co-operatives, Inc., to Halena Wilson, August 11, 1944, BSCP Papers.

128. "Central States Cooperative League Congress Draws Record Attendance," *Consumers' Cooperation* 20 (June 1934): 89.

129. S. I. Hayakawa, Second Thoughts, *Chicago Defender*, October 21, 1944, 13.

130. J. L. Reddix, "The Negro Finds a Way to Economic Equality," *Consumers' Cooperation* 21 (October 1935): 175; "It's the First Smile of Victory at Altgeld Gardens," *Co-op News* 2 [sic] (October 1944): 4.

131. S. I. Hayakawa, Second Thoughts, *Chicago Defender*, November 3, 1945, 15; S. I. Hayakawa, Second Thoughts, *Chicago Defender*, September 14, 1946, 15.

132. Pipeline, *Co-op News* 8 (May 1943): 1; minutes of the board of directors meeting, July 5, 1943, HPCS.

133. Minutes of board of directors meetings, May 17, 1937; August 7, 1944; October 23, 1944, HPCS.

134. "Democracy," *Evergreen*, December 23, 1943; "Report from the Urban League," *Evergreen*, January 27, 1944, both in HPCS. Another example of the ways in which racial equality appealed to co-op members occurred at the end of World War II. When one member of the HPCS questioned the co-op's annual contribution to the Red Cross on the grounds that the

Red Cross practiced segregation, the HPCS passed a resolution that it would donate only "to organizations rendering a distinct service to the community, and whose purposes and practices were not contrary to cooperative principles." Minutes of Hyde Park membership meeting, May 1945, HPCS.

135. Minutes of board of directors meeting, July 29, 1942, HPCS; minutes of board of directors meeting, January 9, 1944, HPCS.

136. People's Co-operative Union, certificate of incorporation, Corporate Records, Secretary of State Records, Illinois State Archives, Springfield.

137. S. I. Hayakawa, Second Thoughts, *Chicago Defender*, October 20, 1945, 15; S. I. Hayakawa, Second Thoughts, *Chicago Defender*, November 16, 1946, 15.

138. S. I. Hayakawa, Second Thoughts, *Chicago Defender*, September 14, 1946, 15.

139. Reddix, "Negro Finds a Way to Economic Equality," 175.

140. George Schuyler, "Consumers' Cooperation, the American Negro's Salvation," *Cooperation* 17 (August 1931): 145.

141. H. W. to the president, October 17, 1941, BSCP Papers. In a particularly suggestive passage of a later letter, Wilson made clear the hope she held out for the potential of cooperatives. Recounting a request for assistance from Mary McLeod Bethune, Wilson wrote to the D.C. chapter president, "While I have the greatest admiration for Mrs. Bethune and the work she is doing, I am about convinced that our own organization is still too young and too much in need of all out attention to have its energies divided at this time. We are developing an organization that is of greater importance than the National Council of Negro Women's Clubs and it is important that we do not lose sight of that fact." H. W. to Elizabeth Craig, May 3, 1945, BSCP Papers.

142. Payne, *I've Got the Light of Freedom*, 82–83; Ransby, *Ella Baker and the Black Freedom Movement*, 82–91.

143. "Du Bois Traces Rise of World Co-op System," *Chicago Defender*, March 4, 1939, 10.

144. "Brotherhood Consumers Cooperative Buying Rally," January 1944, BSCP Papers. Randolph's sensibility was echoed in starker terms by J. L. Reddix, a founder of an African American coop in nearby Gary, Indiana. The Consumers' Cooperative Trading Company was then the largest African American–owned retail operation in the country. Reddix noted, "The capitalist system has been benevolent to the Negro. It has given him Y.M.C.A.s, schools, and education. It has given him his dole during business depressions and has left him poor for the next one." Reddix, "Negro Finds a Way to Economic Equality," 175.

145. See Ownby, *American Dreams in Mississippi*; Kornbluh, "To Fulfill Their 'Rightly Needs'"; and Lizabeth Cohen, *Consumers' Republic*, chap. 4.

146. Landon Storrs has importantly narrated the antifeminism of anticommunist activists. Storrs, "Left-Feminism," 40–67. Charles McGovern documents sexist attitudes toward women in the Consumers' Research group in *Sold American*, 214–15.

147. Storrs, *Civilizing Capitalism*.

Chapter 5

1. Seaton Fairfield, "The War on Co-ops," *Reporter* (October 10, 1950), offprint in Papers of the Cooperative League of the USA, Wisconsin Historical Society, Madison (hereafter, CLUSA papers).

2. Many historians ascribe the architecture and appeal of supermarkets to retailers' need to accommodate and appeal to automobile-owning Americans. See, for example, Longstreth, *City Center to Regional Mall*; and Tedlow, *New and Improved*. Although grocers, like all retailers, tried to increase the availability and convenience of parking around their stores, the notion that car ownership explains the emergence and evolution of supermarkets does not hold up under a close examination of the timing of these stores' growth. Stores began opening in nonresidential areas (with parking lots, or at least the potential for them) in the early 1930s, long before most Americans owned cars. Moreover, many Americans had owned bicycles, horses, or other conveyances before the 1930s but hadn't chosen stores based on ease of parking. What changed were the requirements and culture of shopping. In short, technology did not determine supermarkets—although people's use of technology did come to seem essential to these stores. I am grateful to Christopher Wells for his discussions with me on this point.

3. I talk about the influence of the supermarket on hardware stores in Chapter 7. For an analysis that privileges California supermarkets but shares my sense of the form's importance more generally, see Longstreth, *Drive-In, the Supermarket, and the Transformation of Commercial Space*.

4. "Supermarket" was written as two words ("super market" for much of the 1930s. Here I use the compound word, except when quoting from documents of that era.

5. Godfrey M. Lebhar, Editorially Speaking, *Chain Store Age, Administration Edition* (hereafter, *CSA-A*) 6 (January 1930): 50.

6. Godfrey M. Lebhar, "Chain Store Progress in 1930," *CSA* 7 (January 1931): 33.

7. Leuchtenburg, *Perils of Prosperity*, 191.

8. Laycock, *Kroger Story*, 37; "Kroger Checks Expansion and Consolidates Stores," *CSA* 6 (May 1930).

9. National Tea Company, *Historical High-Lights of National Tea Co.*, 6–9; National Tea Company, *Annual Report*, 1919; National Tea Company, *Annual Report*, 1929, 1.

10. "Chains Issue Annual Reports," *CSA* 7 (April 1931): 62–63; Edwin Hoyt, *That Wonderful A&P!* 156; "A&P Tonnage Drops Only 4% as Dollar Sales Fall 14.3%, Annual Report Shows," *CSA* 9 (May 1933): 48.

11. "Kroger Dollar Sales Decrease; Tonnage Sales Rise," *CSA* 6 (October 1930): 79.

12. A&P is an important exception to this dependence on the stock market; the Hartford family maintained tight control over the firm through the 1950s.

13. Business Highlights, *Progressive Grocer* 9 (May 1930): 15; "Jewel Reports Drop in Sales," *CSA* 8 (June 1932): 389.

14. Business Highlights, *Progressive Grocer* 8 (December 1929): 15.

15. Clyde William Phelps, "Some Limitations and Disadvantages of the Chain Store System," *Progressive Grocer* 10 (March 1931): 78.

16. "Canadian Grocery Chain to Enter Chicago," *CSA* 4 (February 1928): 219.

17. Display advertisement, *Chicago Tribune*, November 16, 1928, 7.

18. On Jewel's acquisition of Loblaw stores, see "Jewel Tea Said to Be Seeking Chicago Loblaw Stores," *CSA* 8 (March 1932): 193; "Jewel Acquires Loblaw Stores in Chicago Area," *CSA* 8 (April 1932): 257; Frank Bostwick, "Why Jewel Sparkles," *CSA* 33 (December 1949): 23. Jewel's motives for opening stores were as much political as financial. In 1931, the town

of Green River, Wyoming, passed the first of what became known as "Green River Ordinances," which prevented door-to-door sales. Given the possibility of a loss in courts and the seeming popularity of chain stores, Jewel diversified into retail stores in 1932. On the Green River Ordinance, see "Door Slammed," *Time*, March 22, 1937, [http://www.time.com/time/magazine/article/0,9171,757444,00.html] (accessed February 11, 2009). On the losses incurred in these stores, see "Chains Issue Reports," *CSA* 8 (October 1932): 611; and Wright, "Marketing History of the Jewel Tea Company," 374–75.

19. Palamountain, *Politics of Distribution*, 194–95. See also Chapter 3 for a fuller discussion of state-level anti-chain activism.

20. The act was meant to prevent chains' suppliers from lowering their prices simply as incentives for their customers and to prevent chains from demanding payoffs from firms that wanted their sizable business.

21. Tedlow, *New and Improved*, 223. Thomas W. Ross makes the important point that suits brought under the Robinson-Patman Act did tend to lower stock values, if not profits, of chains. Ross, "Winners and Losers under the Robinson-Patman Act."

22. Palamountain, *Politics of Distribution*, 176–77; Tedlow, *New and Improved*, 219.

23. HB 45, 57th General Assembly, October 4, 1932, General Assembly Papers, Legislative Records, Illinois State Archives, Springfield.

24. Jacoby, *Retail Sales Taxation*, 19.

25. Godfrey M. Lebhar, As We See It, *CSA* 10 (June 1934): 24.

26. Elizabeth Woody, "The Consumer and the Super Market," *Super Market Merchandising* 4 (October 1939): 53.

27. R. V. Rasmussen, "We've Profited by the Times to Build or Remodel 250 Stores," *CSA* 8 (November 1932): 644. Grocers were not the only ones who looked to women's spending to end the depression. Eleanor Roosevelt also asked women to help, not necessarily by spending more money but by spending it more evenly, so as to enable businesses to stabilize production. See "Mrs. Roosevelt Urges Women to Aid by Wider Spending," *Chicago Tribune*, October 10, 1933, 16.

28. Edwin Hoyt, *That Wonderful A&P!* 130.

29. Laycock, *Kroger Story*, 37.

30. Business Highlights, *Progressive Grocer* 10 (December 1931): 67.

31. National Tea Company, *Annual Report*, 1930; National Tea Company, *Annual Report*, 1931; National Tea Company, *Annual Report*, 1932.

32. "A&P Tonnage Drops Only 4% as Dollar Sales Fall 14.3%, Annual Report Shows," *CSA* 9 (May 1933): 48.

33. Ibid.

34. "Chain Store Companies Issue Annual Reports," *CSA* 9 (April 1933): 52.

35. "Chain Store Expansion in 1930," *CSA* 7 (January 1931): 87–88; "Chain Store Leasing Outlook," *CSA* 10 (January 1934): 48. The property tax assessment was the result of a long-running investigation of county tax assessments. For more on the controversy surrounding property taxes in the city, see Chapter 3.

36. Renegotiated leases and discussions of landlords' having to re-sign much less favorable leases with Jewel appear in several civil suits filed against the firm. See, for instance, bill for specific performance, October 10, 1933, *Loblaw Groceterias v. William A. Kaufman, et*

al., case no. 33S58740; and bill for specific performance, October 9, 1933, *Loblaw Grocete-rias v. Harry Alter*, case no. 33S587465, both in Clerk of the Circuit Court of Cook County, Archives Department, Chicago (hereafter, Circ. Ct. Archives).

37. Mayo, *American Grocery Store*, 134–36.

38. Bureau of the Census, *Census of Business: 1935, Retail Distribution*, vol. 4, *Types of Operation*, 13.

39. "Chain Store Progress in 1930," *CSA* 7 (January 1931): 33.

40. "Chain Store Modernization Active, Survey Reveals," *CSA* 8 (November 1932): 635.

41. "Chains Spend $33,000,000 to Modernize Stores," *CSA* 9 (November 1933): 12.

42. "Kroger Plans 250 Large Stores for Chicago District," *CSA* 8 (January 1932): 60.

43. Bureau of the Census, *Fifteenth Census of the United States: 1930, Distribution*, vol. 1, *Retail Distribution*, pt. 2, table 18, 633; Bureau of the Census, *Census of Business: 1935, Retail Distribution*, vol. 4, *Types of Operation*, table 3, 71.

44. National Tea Company, *Annual Report*, 1929; National Tea Company, *Annual Report*, 1932, table 5.1.

45. "Kroger Plans 250 Large Stores for Chicago District," 60.

46. Ibid.

47. "Kroger Voices Confidence with Big Downtown Unit," *CSA* 7 (February 1931): 57–58; Carl Dipman, "What the Chains Are Doing These Days," *Progressive Grocer* 9 (October 1930): 85.

48. D. I. Mirrielees, "National Tea Sets Modern Standard in Remodeled Unit," *CSA* 9 (November 1933): 48.

49. For data sources and explanation, see table 5.2, this chapter. Lizabeth Cohen's argument that working-class consumers encountered chain groceries more often in the 1930s than in the 1920s is different from, but not incompatible with, my own. While my data suggest that chains did not seek out working-class customers during the depression, it is entirely possible that working-class customers, prompted by lower prices and the pressure from relief officials, did seek out chains. Moreover, as immigration dwindled in the later 1920s, 1930s, and during World War II, white ethnic communities became both less ethnically differentiated and better-off economically. In this context, it seems likely that acceptance and presence of chains would have increased among previously isolated working-class white ethnic communities. This was not because chains were intentionally enlarging their customer base among the working-class or among immigrants but because of demographic and cultural shifts within immigrant communities. Cohen, *Making a New Deal*, 108–10.

50. Edward Kearns, interview, tape 1, side 1, Oral History Archives of Chicago Polonia, Chicago History Museum, Chicago.

51. A. Aaron, "Excerpts from the Files of the Illinois Workers' Alliance, Found in the Library of the S.S.A. School of the University of Chicago," 13–15, Social Service Study, Relief, Admin, etc., box 79, Federal Writers' Project Records, Illinois State Historical Society, Springfield; Kearns, interview, tape 1, side 1, and tape 2, side 2.

52. Virginia Pattison, "Report of Minimum Budget Study: A Term Paper for Soc. 264," 1, March 1931, file 2, box 156, Ernest Watson Burgess Papers, Special Collections Research Center, University of Chicago Library, University of Chicago, Chicago (hereafter, Burgess Papers); Florence Andrews, "The Minimum Budgeting of Poor Families," 7–8, March 16,

1931, file 2, box 156, Burgess Papers; Betty Wright, "Report on Securing Data for the Minimum Budgetting [sic] of Poor Families," 9–10, c. 1931, file 2, box 156, Burgess Papers.

53. Laycock *Kroger Story*, 73.

54. Ibid., 38.

55. News Highlights, *CSA* 13 (August 1937): 56; News Highlights, *CSA* 13 (October 1937): 56. The magazine was published for decades thereafter, although not distributed exclusively via A&P.

56. Mirrielees, "National Tea Sets Modern Standard in Remodeled Unit," 48. They also began distributing recipes and meal-planning tips to women customers, though women themselves do not seem to have been helped by these "aids." Hatfield, "Analysis of Some Grocery Store Practices," 35.

57. Rasmussen, "We've Profited by the Times," 644.

58. F. M. Kasch, "Increasing Volume by Overcoming Customer Resistance," *CSA* 10 (December 1934): 13–15.

59. Hatfield, "Analysis of Some Grocery Store Practices," 8–9.

60. For an overview of supermarket development, see Zimmerman, *Super Market*; and Phillips, "Supermarket." The most influential supermarkets, the ones on which I will focus here, were those opened on the East Coast, although several high-end supermarkets also opened in California at about this time. These were often touted as "luxury" stores, however, and did not inspire imitators in the way that East Coast supermarkets did. For examples of these markets, see McAusland, *Supermarkets*, 24. For a fuller discussion, see Zimmerman, *Super Market*, 24–26.

61. Department stores had used this model in the late nineteenth century but had developed more unified command structures by the 1930s.

62. Tedlow, *New and Improved*, 233.

63. *Ibid.*; Zimmerman, *Super Market*, 39.

64. Zimmerman, *Super Market*, 40.

65. Tedlow, *New and Improved*, 233.

66. Zimmerman, *Super Market*, 54.

67. M. M. Zimmerman, "Super Markets, Article No. 4—Growth and Progress in Industrial Centers," *Super Market Merchandising* 2 (March 1937): 7; "The Voluntary and the Super," *Super Market Merchandising* 2 (April 1937): 13.

68. "Family Market Basket Reopens in Chicago," *Super Market Merchandising* 2 (July 1937): 5.

69. "Remodeled Super Opens in Suburb of Chicago," *Super Market Merchandising* 4 (March 1939): 47.

70. "Celebration in Chicago Mart," *Super Market Merchandising* 5 (May 1939): 27.

71. "The Romance of the Super Market," *Super Market Merchandising* 1 (November 1936): 24.

72. McAusland, *Supermarkets*, 20. According to the 1935 Census of Business, the average grocery store in Chicago sold $16,447.50 worth of goods in that year. Even chains, the highest-grossing stores, averaged only $54,392.62. Bureau of the Census, *Census of Business: 1935, Retail Distribution*, vol. 4, *Types of Operation*, table 3, 71.

73. "Dawson's Trading Post in Chicago Does a Volume of $3,000,000 Annually," *Super*

Market Merchandising 1 (November 1936): 18; "Dawson's Trading Post, A Pioneer's Vision Fulfilled," *Super Market Merchandising* 1 (December 1936): 6–7.

74. Frank Landau, "Is the Price-Wrecking Market Here to Stay?" *CSA* 13 (March 1937): 24.

75. Ibid.; A. E. Holden, "Is Price-Wrecking Wrecking the Super-Markets?" *CSA* 9 (June 1933): 18–19.

76. For uses of these names, see Tedlow, *New and Improved*, 239; and Phillips, "Supermarket," 193.

77. Landau, "Is the Price-Wrecking Market Here to Stay?" 36; M. M. Zimmerman, "Facing 1939: The Present Status of the Super Market," *Super Market Merchandising* 4 (January 1939): 4.

78. Carl Schmalz, "Why the Food Chains Need Research," *CSA* 13 (February 1937): 38.

79. See, for example, complaint in equity for injunction, October 7, 1939, *The Kroger Grocery and Baking Company v. Retail Clerks International Protective Association, Local 1248, Illinois Federation of Labor, Chicago Federation of Labor, Max Caldwell, Pres and Ben Pollock, Secy. and Treasurer of Retail Clerk's Protective Association, Local No. 1248*, case no. 39C10206, Circ. Ct. Archives.

80. Holden, "Is Price-Wrecking Wrecking the Super-Markets?" 31.

81. *Crusader* 8, special 20 year edition (1953): 23.

82. Laycock, *Kroger Story*, 109. In 1936, the firm operated 4,250 stores. Tedlow, *New and Improved*, 211.

83. Edwin Hoyt, *That Wonderful A&P!* 154–55, 159.

84. "National Tea Company Opens Chicago Food Super," *Super Market Merchandising* 2 (November 1937): 10.

85. "Dawson Files Suit," *Super Market Merchandising* 2 (April 1937): 21; "A Super Market with 135 Bosses," *Super Market Merchandising* 2 (April 1937): 8–9.

86. Zimmerman, "Facing 1939," 4.

87. On the Illinois law, see M. M. Zimmerman, "The Present Status of the Super Market," *Super Market Merchandising* 4 (May 1939): 42. On antisupermarket laws in general, see "Vigilance Needed," *Super Market Merchandising* 4 (May 1939): 30; and "New Jersey Supreme Court Voids Super License Tax," *Super Market Merchandising* 4 (March 1939): 16.

88. On supermarket operators' attempts to come to terms with their status as chain or independent, see Zimmerman, "Facing 1939," 4; Hawley, *New Deal and the Problem of Monopoly*, 247; and "Independent or Chain," *Super Market Merchandising* 5 (November 1940): 44.

89. "Family Market Basket Reopens in Chicago," *Super Market Merchandising* 2 (July 1937): 5.

90. Luis Gibson, "Operating a Super Market to Please Ten Million Women," *Super Market Merchandising* 2 (January 1937): 21.

91. Phillips, "Supermarket," 199–200. The history of the shopping cart has received attention from many historians. For a helpful overview, see Grandclément, "Wheeling One's Groceries around the Store."

92. Edwin Hoyt, *That Wonderful A&P!* 159; Zimmerman, "Facing 1939," 4; "Facing 1939: The Present Status of the Super Market," *Super Market Merchandising* 4 (March 1939):

30–31; "Ten Major Trends Seen Affecting Chains in 1941," *Chain Store Age, Grocery Managers Edition* (hereafter, *CSA-GM*) (January 1941): 22–23.

93. "Jewel Tea Plans Fund for Retiring Employees," *Super Market Merchandising* 4 (February 1939): 14.

94. Only 3.5 percent of National Tea's leases were for terms longer than five years. National Tea Company, *Annual Report*, 1939. Movements in the Super Market World, *Super Market Merchandising* 4 (September 1939): 100.

95. Movements in the Super Market World, *Super Market Merchandising* 4 (November 1939): 53.

96. Movements in the Super Market World, *Super Market Merchandising* 5 (July 1940): 55.

97. *Crusader 8*, special 20 year edition (1953): 36.

98. "National Tea Company Owns Chicago Food Super," *Super Market Merchandising* 2 (November 1937): 10.

99. Movements in the Super Market World, *Super Market Merchandising* 4 (March 1939): 63.

100. "A&P Plans Its First Chicago Super Market," *Super Market Merchandising* 2 (August 1937): 23.

101. "Cooperative Highlights of 1939," *Consumers' Cooperation* 26 (January 1940): 14; "Consumer Cooperatives on the March," *Consumers' Cooperation* 25 (May 1939): 79.

102. Sidney Gubin, "Consumers' Cooperatives in Chicago," *Monthly Labor Review* 45 (October 1937): 837. See discussion of CSCL's growth in Pipeline, *Co-op News* 8 (September 1943): 1; "Spearheads Co-op Expansion Drive," *Co-op News* 2 [sic] (June 1944): 5.

103. See Chapter 2 for a fuller explanation of the characteristics of chain groceries.

104. See, for instance, "Going into Groceries," *Consumers' Cooperation* 28 (February 1942): 32; and "More Midwest Co-op Management Institutes Planned," *Consumers' Cooperation* 28 (August 1942): 125.

105. See, for instance, "Consumers' Cooperatives in Action," *Consumers' Cooperation* 23 (December 1937): 188–91.

106. "Cooperatives in Action," *Consumers' Cooperation* 21 (August 1935): 150. For mention of an accounting bureau run by CLUSA, which was established in Chicago at the request of the Central States Cooperative League, see "Cooperatives on the March," *Consumers' Cooperation* 24 (April 1938): 65. For announcement of a training course for coop employees and prospective employees sponsored by CSCL and Cooperative Wholesale, see "Consumers' Cooperation in Action," *Consumers' Cooperation* 23 (December 1937): 189–91. For notice of advanced training provided to cooperators, see "What's New with Coops," *Consumers' Cooperation* 28 (February 1942): 30–32; and "More Midwest Co-op Management Institutes Planned," *Consumers' Cooperation* 28 (August 1942): 125.

107. "Consumer Co-op Progress in 1941," *Consumers' Cooperation* 28 (January 1942): 9–16; More Pipeline, *Co-op News* 8 (May 1943): 4; "First Glimpse of that Smart New Co-op," *Co-op News* 6 (October 1944): 3.

108. "Council to Extend Work in Chicago," *Co-op News* 2 [sic] (July 1944): 3; "Chicago Gets Larger Staff, Volunteer Corps to Speed Centennial Co-op Stores," *Co-op News* 7 (August 1944): 1. On the CCD generally, see Parker, *First 125 Years*, 198.

109. "CCD: What It Is, What It Does," *Co-op News* 2 [sic] (June 1944): 5.

110. "Study City Co-op Tasks," *Co-op News* 2 [sic] (October 1944): 6.

111. "It's the First Smile of Victory at Altgeld Gardens," *Co-op News* 2 [sic] (October 1944): 4.

112. Gubin, "Consumers' Cooperatives in Chicago," *Monthly Labor Review* 45 (October 1937): 834–36. On National Cooperatives, Inc.'s, adoption of standard labels that correlated to the grade of the item manufactured, see "Cooperatives on the March," *Consumers' Cooperation* 25 (February 1939): 29. On the adoption of grades for all of its products by National Cooperatives, Inc., see Hugh E. Bogardus, "Grading of All Products Begins," *Co-op News* 6 (October 1941): 1; and "Consumer Co-op Progress in 1941," *Consumers' Cooperation* 28 (January 1942): 12. Cooperative Wholesale's sales as a whole increased from $264,000 to $494,307 between 1942 and 1943. "CSC Sales Up 87% in Year," *Co-op News* 2 [sic] (May 1944): 1.

113. Their growth was hampered, the author noted, because of "conflict of ideas and personalities of the leaders of the new cooperatives and those who have been in the movement for many years." Gubin, "Consumers' Cooperatives in Chicago," 816.

114. "Capital Drive Gets Underway," *Co-op News* 8 (September 1943): 1; Harland Allen, "Describes Chicago Co-op Finance Body," *Co-op News* 2 [sic] (November 1944): 3–4. Originally capitalized at $100,000, the association would lend money to active buying clubs or small stores that wanted to expand, as well as to societies looking to diversify into new lines. It hoped to "speed the pace of development by advancing capital."

115. "Co-ops Organize Financing Unit," *Business Week*, October 12, 1940, 36–38; "1942 and 1943," *Consumers' Cooperation* 29 (January 1943): 2–3.

116. Although nothing in the Rochdale principles required consumer cooperatives to be self-financing, most cooperative publications emphasized the importance of member financing for any expansion. See Hugh Bogardus, "Wholesale Asks Reserve Loans," *Co-op News* 7 (March 1942): n.p.; and "Commentary," *Co-op News* 2 [sic] (March 1944): 4. Even the most prosperous co-op had to hold frequent capital drives to convince members to pay for shares they had already pledged to buy or to purchase extra shares. See "Serve Themselves in North Chicago," *Co-op News* 6 (October 1941): 6; " '$25 plus $5' Campaign Routs '$5 Disease,' " *Co-op News* 9 (January 1944): 1; "Winnetkans Get New Store through Community Action, Careful Planning," *Co-op News* 2 [sic] (March 1944): 1.

117. " '$25 Plus $5' Campaign Routs '$5 Disease,' " 1; Pipeline, *Co-op News* 2 [sic] (March 1944): 1, 2.

118. "CCS' Shining New Supermart Is New Co-op Showplace in the Midwest," *Co-op News* 7 (June 1942): 7. See "Hyde Park Leases 1460–66 E. 57th St.," *Co-op News* 7 (February 1942): 1. Other coops serving upper-middle-class and upper-class clienteles were also able to finance expansions relatively easily. When the North Shore Co-op decided to open a branch store in Winnetka, it was able to raise all of the $4,000 it needed over the course of a four-week drive. "Winnetkans Get New Store through Community Action, Careful Planning," 1.

119. "It's the First Smile of Victory at Altgeld Gardens," 4.

120. "What They're Doing," *Co-op News* 7 (April 1942): 3; "People's Co-op Takes Deficit as Challenge," *Co-op News* 8 (November 1943): 1.

121. A. W. Warinner, "City Cooperatives," *Consumers' Cooperation* 22 (December 1936): 178–79.

122. Board of directors minutes, April 18, 1939, Hyde Park Cooperative Society Papers (hereafter, HPCS). See note 58 of Chapter 4 regarding this collection.

123. *Evergreen* (July 1941). For other examples of similar problems, see the *Evergreen* for November and December, 1940. Copies are in HPCS.

124. "Citywide Co-ops," *Business Week*, August 11, 1945, 94; "Co-op Stock Registered with SEC," *Chicago Daily News*, August 6, 1945, 18; "Corporates: Co-op Files Common," *Chicago Journal of Commerce and LaSalle Street Journal*, August 7, 1945, 8. CLUSA had been actively promoting the idea of chains of cooperatives since the late 1930s. "Cooperative Highlights of 1939," *Consumers' Cooperation* 26 (January 1940): 10–14; Ruth Schumm, "First Link Forged in Chicago Co-op Chain," *Co-op Magazine* 3 (January 1947): 8–9. Chains had already opened in Minnesota and Wisconsin. See E. R. Bowen, "Consumer Cooperatives on the March," *Consumers' Cooperation* 25 (May 1939): 79.

125. Schumm, "First Link Forged in Chicago Co-op Chain," 8.

126. Five of the nine directors of the Ida B. Wells Co-op were women when the society incorporated in May 1942. When it amended its articles of incorporation in October 1945, only two of the seven directors were women. Articles of incorporation, May 9, 1942, Ida B. Wells Consumers' Co-operative, and application for license of foreign corporation, October 25, 1945, Corporation Records, Secretary of State, State of Illinois Archives, Springfield. The Brotherhood Cooperative, started by the Ladies' Auxiliary of the Brotherhood of Sleeping Car Porters, was appealing to men to take leadership positions by 1948. Halena Wilson to "'Sir or Brother,'" June 25, 1948, box 118, Brotherhood of Sleeping Car Porters Papers, Chicago History Museum, Chicago.

127. Altgeld Gardens had two women directors (of a total of seven), and the proposed chain (Chicago Consumers' Cooperative) did not list any female directors. See "Two More Co-op Stores Ready to Go," *Co-op News* 2 [*sic*] (September 1944): 1; Chicago Consumers' Cooperative, August 24, 1945, application for license of foreign corporation, Corporate Records, Secretary of State, State of Illinois Archives, Springfield.

128. Extant records on CSCL's board of directors list only male members. "Tenth Annual Congress Central States Cooperative League," *Consumers' Cooperation* 22 (June 1936): 93. By the mid-1940s, it often referred to staff members as "CSC men." See "Co-op Boom in Detroit Area Seen as Societies Form in War Homes, First CSC Field Man Hired," *Co-op News* 8 (November 1943): 1; and "CSC to Add Five Organizers in Drive to Quadruple Volume," *Co-op News* 9 (January 1944): 1–2. For articles that list the staff of CCD, see "Council to Advise Co-op Development," *Co-op News* 9 (January 1944): 1; "Local Problems Are Starting Point for Council Program," *Co-op News* 2 [*sic*] (March 1944); and "Council Grants Renewed," *Co-op News* 2 [*sic*)] (December 1944): 8. On the CCD conference, see "Urban Cooperative Development," *Urban Cooperative Development Conference* (pamphlet), Papers of the Cooperative League of the U.S.A., Wisconsin Historical Society, Madison.

Chapter 6

1. Kessler-Harris, *In Pursuit of Equity*, 6.

2. Jacobs, *Pocketbook Politics*, 179–80; Jacobs, "'How about Some Meat?'"

3. Tilley, *Chronology of the Office of Price Administration*, December 1941. For an overview of rationing and price control policies, see Lizabeth Cohen, *Consumers' Republic*, 65–70.

4. Tilley, *Chronology of the Office of Price Administration*, April 1942.

5. Ibid., February 1943.

6. Mansfield, *Short History of the Office of Price Administration*, 13; Jacobs, *Pocketbook Politics*, 202–4, 210; Lizabeth Cohen, *Consumers' Republic*, 66–67.

7. Mansfield, *Short History of the Office of Price Administration*, 154; Lizabeth Cohen, *Consumers' Republic*, 65–70; Jacobs, *Pocketbook Politics*, 179.

8. "History of Board Division," 1, March 7, 1946, Price Board Management Records, Field Offices, box 10, series 1243, Records of Region VI, Records of the Office of Price Administration, RG 188, National Archives and Records Administration—Great Lakes Region (Chicago) (hereafter Records of Region VI, OPA, NARA-Chicago); Paul A. H. Shults to Alex Elson and Michael Mulcahy, 2, June 12, 1943, Rationing, General Reports, Narrative and Progress, box 1627, series 279, Records of Region VI, OPA, NARA-Chicago, 2.

9. Bentley, *Eating for Victory*, 26.

10. On the use of the feminine pronoun, see, for instance, Mansfield, *Short History of the Office of Price Administration*, 59. On the creation of the advisory councils, see Putnam, *Volunteers in OPA*, 87.

11. Caroline Ware, notes on the history of the Consumer Division of the National Defense Advisory Commission, folder, Article on History of Consumer Division, Consumer Materials, box 27, Caroline Ware Papers (hereafter, Ware Papers), Franklin D. Roosevelt Presidential Library, Hyde Park, N.Y. (hereafter, FDR Library)

12. For Chicago, see, for instance, Bert Atkins to Mrs. Arthur Cavender, June 7, 1945, Field Offices, box 11, series 1243, Records of Region VI, OPA, NARA-Chicago; and A. H. Noelke to district director, February 7, 1944, series 1243, Records of Region VI, OPA, NARA-Chicago.

13. Lizabeth Cohen, *Consumers' Republic*, 76; Bentley, *Eating for Victory*.

14. For more elaborate discussions of this, see Bentley, *Eating for Victory*. On the targeting of women in rationing and price control campaigns generally, see Zweiniger-Bargielowska, *Austerity in Britain*.

15. On women's new political visibility as consumers during the war, see also Lizabeth Cohen, *Consumers' Republic*, 75–83.

16. For discussions of the difficult mechanics of rationing, see Mansfield, *Short History of the Office of Price Administration*, 169–70; and Bentley, *Eating for Victory*, 15–16.

17. For an extensive discussion of the political machinations surrounding the OPA, see Jacobs, "Consumer Goes to War," in *Pocketbook Politics*, 179–220.

18. There are numerous examples of grocers' complaints. See, for instance, "OPA Bungling under Attack from 3 Sides," *Chicago Tribune*, May 19, 1943, 25; "Calls Subsidy Plan Peril to Food Industry," *Chicago Tribune*, June 9, 1943, 4; "Grocers Brand Subsidies 'Tax on Fighting Men,'" *Chicago Tribune*, October 11, 1943, 31; and Bartel, "Politics of Food Control," 235.

19. Mansfield, *Short History of the Office of Price Administration*, 154.

20. Tilley, *OPA Chronology*, April 1943; Bartel, "Politics of Food Control," 255–56, 258–62, 293.

21. Mansfield, *Short History of the Office of Price Administration*, 42–43.

22. Ibid., 53. Even large chains had difficulty knowing what prices to charge. Kroger's Chicago stores figured the prices on eight-ounce packages of peanuts incorrectly because staff did not know that peanuts were covered under a "specific maximum price regulation." See Elmo Hohman to Kroger Grocery and Baking Company, March 30, 1942, Regional Records Sample File, GMPR Filings (Chicago Metropolitan District), Retailers, box 12686, series 1236, Records of Region VI, OPA, NARA-Chicago.

23. See, for instance, R. A. Marmaduke to Food Section, June 9, 1942, Price, GMPR (All Commodities), 2/2, box 12686, series 1236, Records of Region VI, OPA, NARA-Chicago.

24. C. L. Christenson to John C. Weigel, September 28, 1942, Price, GMPR (All Commodities), 2/2, box 12686, series 1236, Records of Region VI, OPA, NARA-Chicago.

25. Much of the literature on women during World War II, and especially that on women's work, emphasizes their participation in the paid workforce—and particularly the changing levels of participation by married white women. See, for instance, Yellin, *Our Mothers' War*; Milkman, *Gender at Work*; and Murphy and Venet, *Midwestern Women*. Perry Duis's essay "No Time for Privacy: World War II and Chicago's Families" suggests but does not explore the possibility of food preparation as an aspect of wartime labor. For one of the only studies that does investigate women's food work during World War II, see Bentley, *Eating for Victory*. Numerous primary sources produced during the war, ranging from the wartime pamphlets discussed in this chapter to cookbooks (e.g., M. F. K. Fischer's *How to Cook a Wolf*), provide evidence of the new challenges faced by household cooks. Lizabeth Cohen also suggests the importance of food work in *Consumers' Republic*, 75–83.

26. Emily Gotzion, interview, June 18, 1992, folder 3, box 3, Wisconsin Women during World War II Oral History Interviews, Wisconsin Historical Society, Madison.

27. Dorothy Marsh, "I've Got My First Job—and I Still Get the Meals," *Good Housekeeping*, February 1943, 84–85.

28. Helen W. Kendall "Quick and Easy Meals out of One Pot," *Good Housekeeping*, September 1942, 128–29.

29. Katharine Fisher, "Good Méals Even with Rationing," *Good Housekeeping*, January 1943, 102–4.

30. Weatherford, *American Women and World War II*, 165; D'Ann Campbell, *Women at War with America*, 133.

31. Ella Meiselwitz, interview, October 9, 1992, folder 14, box 4, Wisconsin Women during World War II Oral History Project, Wisconsin Historical Society, Madison.

32. For more on the ways that the war infiltrated families' time, see Duis, "No Time for Privacy."

33. "Rationing Has Brought a New Cookery," *Good Housekeeping*, July 1943, 92; Hayes, *Grandma's Wartime Kitchen*, 26; Bentley, *Eating for Victory*, 67–69.

34. "Christmas Cooking This Year," *Good Housekeeping*, December 1943, 88. See also Dorothy Kirk, "Let Us Give Thanks . . . ," *Women's Home Companion*, November 1944, 26–27.

35. Honey, *Creating Rosie the Riveter*, quote at 99.

36. "Women, Grocers, Welcome News of Coffee Dole," *Chicago Tribune*, November 1, 1942, S5.

37. Mary Meade, "A New Muffin Mix Available to Homemakers," *Chicago Tribune*, May 29, 1944, 11.

38. "Complaint of a Working Shopper," *Chicago Tribune*, May 7, 1944, 18.

39. "The Tireless Shopper," "Life under the OPA," *Chicago Tribune*, July 20, 1945, 8.

40. "Chicago's Black Market Termed Worst in Region," *Chicago Tribune*, November 9, 1943, 13.

41. Voice of the People, "Policemen Go Shopping," *Chicago Tribune*, June 29, 1946, 10; "Tell How Meat Black Market Boosts Prices," *Chicago Tribune*, April 17, 1946, 2.

42. "Meat Dealer Fined $1,000 for Fake Ration Coupons," *Chicago Tribune*, June 14, 1946, 6.

43. For examples of women's memories of black market activities, see Emma Blair, interview, November 7, 1992, folder 6, box 1, and Jennie Firmano, interview, July 28, 1993, folder 1, box 3, both in Wisconsin Women during World War II Oral History Project, Wisconsin Historical Society, Madison; Doris Blake, "Face Rations Honestly, Is Doris' Advice," *Chicago Tribune*, June 15, 1942, 19.

44. Lizabeth Cohen, *Consumers' Republic*, 102–5.

45. "Women, Grocers, Welcome News of Coffee Dole," *Chicago Tribune*, November 1, 1942, S5; Mrs. F. Schneider "To Ration or Not to Ration," *Chicago Tribune*, October 15, 1942, 14.

46. Quoted in Rita Fitzpatrick, "Tribune Adopts a Simplified Plan for Presenting Ration News," *Chicago Tribune*, July 3, 1943, 9.

47. On this point, see also Lizabeth Cohen, *Consumers' Republic*, 75–77.

48. Food rationing during World War I has been the subject of several quite suggestive articles. See, for instance, Veit, " 'We Were a Soft People' "; Cullather, "Foreign Policy of the Calorie"; and Rich, " 'She Would Raise Hens to Aid the War.' "

49. Putnam, *Volunteers in OPA*, 29.

50. "Women, Grocers, Welcome News of Coffee Dole," November 1, 1942, *Chicago Tribune*, S5.

51. Voice of the People, *Chicago Tribune*, January 21, 1942, 12; "The Tireless Shopper," "Life under the OPA," *Chicago Tribune*, July 20, 1945, 8.

52. "Women, Grocers, Welcome News of Coffee Dole," November 1, 1942, *Chicago Tribune*, S5.

53. Minutes of Price Control Panel Conference Board 61-1.107 2745 N. Clark, April 18, 1946, Sample Panel Minutes, box 13756, series 1349, Price Records of War Price and Rationing Boards, Records of Region VI, OPA, NARA-Chicago.

54. "Easing the Path for Disgruntled Customers," *Super Market Merchandising* 9 (May 1944): 45–46.

55. Mansfield, *Short History of the Office of Price Administration*, 61.

56. Michael Mulcahy to Raymond S. McKeough, October 29, 1943, 12937–45, box 11, series 1243, Records of Region VI, OPA, NARA-Chicago.

57. W. B. Taylor to Rae E. Walters, June 21, 1945, 12937–12945, box 11, series 1243, Records of Region VI, OPA, NARA-Chicago.

58. See, for instance, Jack Oppenheim to Paul A. H. Shults, 2, 4–5, April 27, 1943, Rationing, General Reports, Narrative and Progress, box 1627, series 279, Records of Region VI,

OPA, NARA-Chicago; and Evanston Rationing Board to Mr. Mueller, August 10, 1943, Price Panel Minutes, box 13756, series 1349, Price Records of War Price and Rationing Boards, Records of Region VI, OPA, NARA-Chicago.

59. See, for instance, Mary E. Townsend to Elmo Hohman, June 5, 1943, Board Operations Report, Price Panels, box 11, 12937–12945, series 1243, Records of Region VI, OPA, NARA-Chicago; and C. L. Christenson to John C. Weigel, September 28, 1942, Board Operations Report, Price Panels, 12937–12945, box 11, series 1243, Records of Region VI, OPA, NARA-Chicago.

60. See, for example, James M. Carrithers to Jack H. Oppenheim, "Wilensky and Company," box 56, series 465, Records of Company Investigations, Records of Region VI, OPA, NARA-Chicago; and Neal Billiatt to E. F. Phelps, Jr., MPR 421 Certain Foods, Wholesale, box 12786, series 1236, Records of Region VI, OPA, NARA-Chicago.

61. Paul A. H. Shults to Alex Elson and Michael Mulcahy, Rationing, General, Reports Narrative and Progress, box 1627, series 279, Records of Region VI, OPA, NARA-Chicago; Jack Oppenheim to Paul Shults, April 27, 1943, Rationing, General Reports, Narrative and Progress, box 1627, series 279, Records of Region VI, OPA, NARA-Chicago.

62. On kosher poultry markets, see weekly price panel letter, March 16, 1944, Chicago, box 1507, series 270, Records of Region VI, OPA, NARA-Chicago; and Walter G. Archer to Paul A. H. Shults, Rationing, General Reports Narrative and Progress, box 1627, series 279, Records of Region VI, OPA, NARA-Chicago.

63. See, for instance, the cases of Panayotis Gozio, May 11, 1946; August Townsend, August 8, 1946; Edward Hipps, August 8, 1946; and Carmelo Rizzo, October 21, 1946. All hearing records are contained in Minutes of Price Control Panel Conferences, Food Stores, box 13754, series 1349, Price Records of War Price and Rationing Boards, Records of Region VI, OPA, NARA-Chicago. The only local board dockets that have survived in the Chicago region are from 1946, when the war was already over and the OPA was removing price ceilings. Many goods, especially foods, were still being controlled, however. Price boards continued to hear cases and to enforce ceilings through October 1946, when ceilings on all foods, except for sugar and rice, were lifted.

64. Evanston Rationing Board to Mr. Mueller, August 10, 1943, Price Records, Field Offices, 1942–1946, series 1349, Price Records of War Price and Rationing Boards, General Records, Records of Region VI, OPA, NARA-Chicago.

65. John Pellettiere and Charles F. Herold to Harold B. Eversole, "Survey of Independent Food Retailers," January 23, 1945, Independent Food Retailers, Chicago Metropolitan Area Survey, box 56, series 465, Records of Company Investigations, Records of Region VI, OPA, NARA-Chicago.

66. All cases from Minutes of Price Control Panel Conferences, Food Panel, box 13754, series 1349, Records of War Price and Rationing Boards, Records of Region VI, OPA, NARA-Chicago. The hearings took place, respectively, on July 18, October 7, and August 5, 1946.

67. Weekly price panel letter, 2–3, July 28, 1944, Chicago, box 1507, series 270, Records of Region VI, OPA, NARA-Chicago.

68. Weekly price panel letter, 3–4, March 16, 1944, Chicago, box 1507, series 270, Records of Region VI, OPA, NARA-Chicago.

69. IGA-affiliated stores, for instance, caused no end of consternation and questions within the OPA hierarchy. Some sense of officials' bewilderment can be gleaned from the name of the plan eventually adopted to accommodate these stores—the "X-plan." See Morris Levinson to all cities on teletype circuit, September 1, 1943, MPR 422, Certain Foods, Retail, 2/2, box 12786, series 1236, Records of Region VI, OPA, NARA-Chicago; Henry Heineman to Milton Quint, December 12, 1944, MPR 422, Certain Foods, Retail, 2/2, box 12786, series 1236, Records of Region VI, OPA, NARA-Chicago; Thomas B. Rollins to Kenneth Erickson, September 16, 1946, Board Operations, Chicago Metropolitan District Cooperation with Other Divisions, 12937–12945, box 10, series 1243, Records of Region VI, OPA, NARA-Chicago; and Thomas B. Rollins to all price control boards in the Chicago metropolitan area, September 25, 1946, Board Operations, Board Members, folder 3, 12937–12945, box 9, series 1243, Records of Region VI, OPA, NARA-Chicago.

70. There were frequent problems with shortages of forms. See, for instance, James F. Riley to Michael F. Mulcahy, June 3, 1943, Rationing, General Reports, Narrative and Progress, box 1627, series 279, Records of Region VI, OPA, NARA-Chicago; Frank J. Sloup to Michael F. Mulcahy, April 20, 1943, Rationing, Food Reports, Narrative and Progress, 1943, box 1628, series 280, Records of Region VI, OPA, NARA-Chicago; and Elmo Hohman to G. M. Landon, April 22, 1944, Board Operations Report, Price Panels, Board Operations, 12937–12945, box 11, series 1243, Records of Region VI, OPA, NARA-Chicago.

71. Quoted in Bartel, "Politics of Food Control," 267 n. 68.

72. Weekly price panel letter, 5–6, November 26, 1943, Chicago, box 1507, series 270, Records of Region VI, OPA, NARA-Chicago. See also Bentley, *Eating for Victory*, 38–39.

73. Marion Isbell to Jacob Meier, December 4, 1944, Rationing, Food Interpretations, box 1628, series 280, Records of Region VI, OPA, NARA-Chicago.

74. Minutes of price control panel conference board 61-1.107 2745 N. Clark, April 18, 1946, Sample Panel Minutes, box 13756, series 1349, Price Records of War Price and Rationing Boards, Records of Region VI, OPA, NARA-Chicago.

75. Zofia Kowalczyk, interview, transcript at 4, Oral History Archives of Chicago Polonia, Chicago History Museum, Chicago.

76. Charles W. Quinlan to Daniel D. Lynch and Edward C. Jordan, June 7, 1944, Rationing, Food District Problems and Conditions, box 1628, series 280, Records on Commodity Rationing, Chicago District Office, Records of Region VI, OPA, NARA-Chicago.

77. On the unrest surrounding meat in the immediate post–World War II period, see Jacobs, "'How about Some Meat?'" 934–40.

78. Rachel Goetz to members of the Consumer Advisory Committee, May 21, 1945, Board Operations, Reports—Volunteers, 12937–12945, box 11, series 1243, Records of Region VI, OPA, NARA-Chicago.

79. Paul A. H. Shults to Alex Elson and Michael F. Mulcahy, June 28, 1943, Rationing, General Reports, Narrative and Progress, box 1627, series 279, Records of Region VI, OPA, NARA-Chicago. The Midtown Manhattan War Price Board in New York City reported that "nearly 50 per cent" of the complaints it received were anonymous or otherwise hid information that would identify the writer or grocer. A journalist explained that the OPA board tried to work with these inadequate reports but nonetheless "is aware that many are sent by housewives who are afraid of upsetting their friendly relations with the butcher or grocer"

or from people afraid of "official" documents. "It's a Woman's War Too," *New York Times*, October 31, 1943, X13. On this problem in Chicago, see, for instance, "Face Rations Honestly Is Doris' Advice," *Chicago Tribune*, June 15, 1942, 19.

80. Brinkley, *End of Reform*, 146–48. The Cooperative League of the USA (CLUSA) apparently expected Henderson and his associates to support consumer cooperatives. John Carson, "Capitol Letters," *Consumers' Cooperation* 28 (April 1942): 60–61.

81. For a fuller discussion of the organizational structure of the Office of Price Administration, see Mansfield, *Short History of the Office of Price Administration*; and Bartel, "Politics of Food Control."

82. Untitled memo, June 7, 1945, Board Operations, 12937–12945, box 11, series 1243, Records of Region VI, OPA, NARA-Chicago.

83. James E. Degnant to Thomas F. Kelly, July 12, 1945, Board Operations, 12937–12945, box 11, series 1243, Records of Region VI, OPA, NARA-Chicago.

84. See, for example, the tight relationship between the Brotherhood Cooperative and the OPA. Halena Wilson to Frances Williams, June 9, 1942, Brotherhood of Sleeping Car Porter Papers, Chicago History Museum, Chicago (hereafter BSCP Papers); Frances Williams to Halena Wilson, June 17, 1942, BSCP Papers; Frances Williams to Halena Wilson, May 22, 1943, BSCP Papers. So close was Wilson to the OPA administration that when the agency was disbanded after the war, Wilson received several personal thank-you notes from local- and national-level OPA officials. Typical of these was the note from the district director, James Riley, in December 1946: "It is not easy to terminate the friendly association we have had in such a worthwhile program and I want you to know how greatly we have valued the helpfulness of the Consumer Advisory Committee." James Riley to HW, December 6, 1946, BSCP Papers. All BSCP papers are in box 118.

85. Hazel Kyrk, a professor at the University of Chicago and an active member of the Hyde Park Cooperative Society, served on the national Consumer Advisory Council. Her job was to "suggest improvements in the OPA program, sit in on some of the planning of new programs, and advise the OPA on how better to explain price and rationing regulations to the public." "Chicago Co-operator Heads OPA Advisory Committee," *Co-op News* 9 (January 1944): 1. The OPA contacted Halena Wilson directly, seeking her help in spreading information about the need for OPA regulations. See Ruth W. Ayres to Halena Wilson, October 29, 1943, BSCP Papers. Wilson was also asked to serve on the local Consumer Advisory Committee. Paul Shults to Halena Wilson, July 14, 1944, BSCP Papers.

86. "Consumers' Cooperatives in Relation to the Government," *Consumers' Cooperation* 28 (September 1942): 141–42; "War Effort Gives Co-ops a New 'In,'" *Co-op News* 7 (March 1942): 5.

87. John Carson, "Capitol Letters," *Consumers' Cooperation* 28 (April 1942): 60.

88. See *Evergreen* issues of February 12, 1942; August 27, 1942; December 10, 1942; July 22, 1943; September 16, 1943; and April 13, 1944; as well as "Del Birk to Tell Defense Center Facts on Meats," *Co-op News* 7 (March 1942): 5; and minutes of education committee meeting, February 24, 1943, HPCS. For the activities of other cooperatives and of the regional association (Central States Cooperatives), see "Information Center Aids the Consumer," *Co-op News* 7 (February 1942): 6; and Ruth Neufeld, "Let Honey Sweeten That Sugar Ration," *Co-op News* 2 [*sic*] (June 1944): 1.

89. Rae E. Walters and W. B. Taylor to Marion Isbell and A. E. Bradley, September 28, 1944, Board Operations, Organization and Operation of Boards, 12937–12945, box 11, series 1243, Records of Region VI, OPA, NARA-Chicago.

90. Thomas B. Rollins to Homer Clay, October 31, 1946, Board Operations, Chicago Met, Cooperation with Other Divisions, 12937–12945, box 10, series 1243, Records of Region VI, OPA, NARA-Chicago.

91. John McGuane to James W. Riley, April 27, 1944, Rationing, Food, Board Problems and Conditions (selected documents), box 1628, series 280, Chicago District Office, Records on Commodity Rationing, Records of Region VI, OPA, NARA-Chicago.

92. Rae E. Walters and W. B. Taylor to Marion Isbell and A. E. Bradley, September 28, 1944, Board Operations, Organization and Operation of Boards, 12937–12945, box 11, series 1243, Records of Region VI, OPA, NARA-Chicago.

93. Putnam, *Volunteers in OPA*, 32–33.

94. Ibid., 27, 29; Alex Elson to Thomas Emerson, April 8, 1944, Preliminary Draft of Price Panel Manual, box 1508, series 270, Enforcement, OPA, NARA-Chicago.

95. Alex Elson to Thomas I. Emerson, April 8, 1944, Enforcement, Price Panel Relations Reports of Regional Board Enforcement Coordinator, Springfield Price Panel Manual, box 1508, series 270, Records of Region VI, OPA, NARA-Chicago.

96. "The Setting up of Consumer Committees and Related Subjects," c. 1944, National Defense Advisory Commission, Consumer Advisory Committee, 1944, box 31, Ware Papers.

97. Putnam, *Volunteers in OPA*, 70–75; Mansfield, *Short History of the Office of Price Administration*, 61, 250.

98. Mansfield, *Short History of the Office of Price Administration*, 61, 250.

99. Ibid., 353–54; Bartel, "Politics of Food Control," 362.

100. Putnam, *Volunteers in OPA*, 70–75.

101. Mansfield, *Short History of the Office of Price Administration*, 63.

102. For the Fair, see, minutes of price control panel conference, October 21, 1946, Minutes of Price Panel Conference, Food Panel, box 13754, series 1349, Records of War Price and Rationing Boards, Records of Region VI, OPA, NARA-Chicago. On Kroger, see A. J. Leonard to Homer C. Clay, "Wesco Foods Company," September 19, 1945, Wesco Foods, box 56, series 465, Records of Company Investigations, Record of Poultry, Eggs, and Dairy Products Price Branch, Records of Region VI, OPA, NARA-Chicago.

103. Kroger went so far as to appoint a "rationing executive." Frank J. Sloup to the Kroger Grocery and Baking Co., June 23, 1944, Rationing, Food, District Problems and Conditions, box 1628, series 280, Records on Commodity Rationing, Records of the Cotton Section, Records of Region VI, OPA, NARA-Chicago. Similarly, a Mr. A. J. Fugit, of the department store "The Fair," explained to one Chicago price panel that his job was to "interpret all government regulations." Minutes of price control panel conference, October 21, 1946, Minutes of Price Panel Conference, Food Panel, box 13754, series 1349, Records of War Price and Rationing Boards, Records of Region VI, OPA, NARA-Chicago.

104. On trading up in clothing, see Jacobs, *Pocketbook Politics*, 214.

105. "Air Transport of Produce to Be Tested Soon," *CSA-GM* 20 (July 1944): 222.

106. "Kroger Experiments with Produce Shipped by Air," *CSA-GM* 20 (August 1944): 62.

107. "Quotes . . . from the Food Chain Field," *CSA-GM* 19 (September 1943): 119.

108. "Stress Ready-to-Serve Foods," *CSA-GM* 19 (November 1943): 107.

109. "Names in the News," *CSA-GM* 21 (May 1945): 105.

110. "Ready-Cut Poultry Pushed in Advertisement," *CSA-GM* 22 (March 1946): 169; "New Policy Announced for Kroger Private Labels," *CSA-GM* 22 (December 1946): 71.

111. Jewel Tea Company, *Annual Report for 1945*.

112. Walter C. Archer to Paul A. H. Shults, January 12, 1943, Rationing, General, Reports Narrative and Progress, box 1627, series 279, Rationing Records, Field Office, Records of Region VI, OPA, NARA-Chicago.

113. *Edgewater News*, September 25, 1945, in Board Operations, Volunteers, 12937–12945, box 11, series 1243, Records of Region VI, OPA, NARA-Chicago.

114. Jack H. Oppenheim to Paul A. H. Shults, 4–5, June 10, 1943, Rationing, General Reports, Narrative and Progress, box 1627, series 279, Rationing Records, Records of Region VI, OPA, NARA-Chicago.

115. C. L. Christensen to Kenneth T. Rowe, August 13, 1943, Gary Experiment, box 1508, series 270, Records of Region VI, OPA, NARA-Chicago. For the National Tea Company case, see Frank J. Sloup to Michael F. Mulcahy, c. April 10, 1943, box 1628, series 280, Chicago District Office, Records on Commodity Rationing, Records of Region VI, OPA, NARA-Chicago.

116. Chester Bowles to Stephen Early, July 3, 1944, Chain Stores, 1937–1944, box 1, Official Files, Franklin D. Roosevelt Papers, FDR Library.

117. "Food Chains Are to Distribute Treasury War Bond Booklet," *CSA-GM* 19 (March 1943): 62.

118. "A&P and Kroger Present News in Radio Program," *CSA-GM* 19 (March 1943): 84; "Kroger Renews Radio Programs," *CSA-GM* 20 (October 1944): 43.

119. Bentley, *Eating for Victory*, 33.

120. Rachel M. Goetz to members of the Consumer Advisory Committee, 2–3, May 21, 1945, Board Operations Reports—Volunteers, box 11, series 1243, Records of Region VI, OPA, NARA-Chicago.

121. Tilley, *Chronology of the Office of Price Administration*, February 1944. Numerous chains in Chicago and elsewhere had uniform pricing agreements with the federal government, even before it was made the official practice of the OPA. On the National Tea Company, see Alex Elson to Callman Gottesman, August 24, 1943, MPR 422, Certain Foods, Retail, 2/2, box 12786, series 1236, Records of Region VI, OPA, NARA-Chicago. On Kroger, see Merle Fainsod to L. S. Bruckner, January 7, 1943, Price Department Field Offices, Region VI, Regional Office, GMPR Sample Files, Records of Chicago Office, series 1236, Records of Region VI, OPA, NARA-Chicago. On chain stores generally, see C. L. Christenson and Cale L. Smith to H. K. Allen and Patrick V. Houlihan, January 18, 1943, Price, GMPR (All Commodities), 1/2, box 12686, series 1236, Records of Region VI, OPA, NARA-Chicago.

122. To all cities on teletype circuit, "Adjustment Provisions under RMPR 238, 268, 336, 355, 390, MPR 422, 423," July 17, 1943, MPR 422, Certain Foods, Retail, 2/2, box 12786, series 1236, General Maximum Price Regulation, Records of Region VI, OPA, NARA-Chicago.

123. Berthold J. Harris by Henry H. Shabain to all district price executives and all district

price attorneys, July 10, 1944, MPR 422, Certain Foods, Retail, 1/2, box 12786, series 1236, General Maximum Price Regulation, Records of Region VI, OPA, NARA-Chicago.

124. Bartel, "Politics of Food Control," 368; Jacobs, "'How about Some Meat?'" 934–40. I place greater emphasis than does Jacobs on the centrality of gender ideology (and discomfort with women's authority) in the progression and demise of the OPA.

125. "An Editorial," *Evergreen Weekly*, May 29, 1947, HPCS.

Chapter 7

1. Nancy Crawford Wood and Jean Anderson, "Check Out Feast from the Supermarket," *Ladies' Home Journal* 79 (September 1962): 81.

2. Martin Sontheimer, "Do You Know Your Groceries?" *Women's Home Companion* 76 (March 1951): 42.

3. Bureau of the Census, *Census of Business, 1954*, vol. 1, *Retail Trade, Summary Statistics*, 8. It should be noted that the convergence did not mean that all stores had high annual sales, but simply that they had diversified the number of lines they carried.

4. The convergence in retail strategy is striking in light of the fact that many grocery stores remained quite small. In the 1954 census, stores selling more than $300,000 worth of goods annually comprised only 7.8 percent of all grocery stores. (Data from ibid., table 2A, 2–2.)

5. Bureau of the Census, *Fifteenth Census of the United States: 1930, Distribution*, vol. 1, *Retail Distribution*, pt. 1 (Washington, D.C.: Government Printing Office, 1934), 1–29.

6. National Tea Company, *Annual Report*, 1942.

7. National Tea Company, *Annual Report*, 1943.

8. National Tea Company, *Annual Report*, 1944.

9. National Tea Company, *Annual Reports*, 1945 and 1946.

10. National Tea Company, *Annual Report*, 1947.

11. National Tea Company, *Annual Report*, 1950.

12. "National Tea Has Peak Year in Sales, Net," *Chicago Tribune*, March 3, 1958, C5; "National Tea Sales, Profit, at New High," *Chicago Tribune*, March 3, 1965, E1.

13. De Grazia, *Irresistible Empire*, 381.

14. John Conner, "Supermarkets: There'll Be Another Along Any Minute," *Collier's* 127 (May 1951): 18.

15. The same article explained that the stores' new lease-back arrangements (in which private firms or builders created spaces to chains' specifications and then the chains leased the spaces back from them) insulated them from the volatility of the stock market, interest rates, and rents. These arrangements were available to only the largest firms, which could afford to build their own stores and promise enough sales to interest investors in taking ownership of the building. "Food Chains, Building Supermarkets, See No Trouble Raising Funds," *Business Week*, July 18, 1953, 130–31.

16. Markin, *Supermarket*, 1.

17. Ibid. By 1954, 55 percent of all grocery store sales were made by large stores with annual sales of more than $300,000. Bureau of the Census, *Census of Business, 1954*, vol. 1, *Retail Trade, Summary Statistics*, table 2A, 2–2. By the mid-1960s, supermarkets (now de-

fined as stores with annual sales of more than $500,000) made more than 71 percent of all sales. Markin, *Supermarket*, 20. The criteria for a supermarket used by *Progressive Grocer* and in Markin's study had changed in these years, from $375,000 in annual sales to $500,000.

18. "Supermarket: A Revolution in Retailing," *Business Week*, June 28, 1952, 38–40; "Food Chains, Building Supermarkets, See No Trouble Raising Funds," *Business Week*, July 18, 1953, 130–31.

19. Charvat, *Supermarketing*, 169.

20. Markin, *Supermarket*, 31–34; Mueller and Garoian, *Changes in the Market Structure of Grocery Retailing*, 39.

21. The number is based on stores listed in Joseph Egelhot, "New Grocery Ideas Spice an Old Business," *Chicago Tribune*, March 16, 1952, 7.

22. Charvat, *Supermarketing*, 197.

23. The quote is from Markin, *Supermarket*, 19. For further discussion of these, see Markin, 18–24; Charvat, *Supermarketing*, 192–93; and "Chains Stage a Comeback," *Business Week*, January 25, 1947, 55–56.

24. Numerous issues of the in-house magazine *Grocergram* bear testimony to campaigns by the organization to help members "modernize." On "Foodliners" specifically, see "Super 'Foodliner'; Orchid Brand Revealed by IGA," *Independent Grocergram* 19 (June 1945): 16–31; and "First 'Foodliner' Is Opened in Wisconsin," *Independent Grocergram* 19 (July 1945): 7–15.

25. The local journal *Co-op News* ceased operations in 1951. The Altgeld Gardens co-ops had shut down in the summer of 1951, and the citywide chain also seems to have ceased operations at about this time. "Denies CHA Had Role in Co-op Closing," *Chicago Defender*, June 9, 1951, 1.

26. Brand, *Modern Supermarket Operation*.

27. Mack, "Good Things to Eat in Suburbia," 37.

28. Roger Horowitz, *Putting Meat on the American Table*.

29. Ibid., 139–44; quotes at 141–42.

30. "Supermarkets, There'll Be Another One Along Any Minute," *Collier's* 127 (May 1951): 64.

31. Harris, "George Pleasures Them with Groceries," 28, 102.

32. Advertisement, *Chicago Tribune*, September 28, 1952, NW A14.

33. See, for instance, "Open National Unit in Armitage Ave. Today," *Chicago Tribune*, January 14, 1958, B8.

34. "National Tea to Open Newest Store Tomorrow," *Chicago Tribune*, January 20, 1958, C4. For a fuller discussion of supermarket operators' marketing practices, including their efforts to appeal to the senses of smell and hearing as well as sight, see Mack, "Good Things to Eat in Suburbia."

35. Brand, *Modern Supermarket Operation*, 3–4.

36. Ibid., 3.

37. For discussions of Keynesianism and its impact on American policies, see Lizabeth Cohen, *Consumers' Republic*, 54–55; and McQuaid, *Uneasy Partners*, 117–22.

38. Rockoff, *Drastic Measures*, 177–200; Lizabeth Cohen, *Consumers' Republic*, 129–30.

39. Jacobs, *Pocketbook Politics*, 246–48.

40. For an example of this line of scholarship, see Von Eschen, *Satchmo Blows Up the World*.

41. Mack, "Good Things to Eat in Suburbia," 152–53.

42. Quoted ibid., 153–54.

43. For a fuller description of the efforts of trade associations to promote supermarkets and American agriculture abroad, see Greer, Logan, and Willis, "Showcase for Democracy," in *America the Bountiful*.

44. De Grazia, *Irresistible Empire*, 389–90; Mack, "Good Things to Eat in Suburbia," 155–56.

45. "Italy Hails the Supermarket," *U.S. News and World Report*, 41 (September 1956): 88.

46. "La Méthode Américaine," Business Abroad, *Time*, November 16, 1959, 106.

47. De Grazia, *Irresistible Empire*, 387–88.

48. "Roman Matrons Fall for One-Stop Shop," *Business Week*, July 7, 1956, 87–88.

49. "Italy Hails Supermarket," *U.S. News and World Report* 41 (September 1956): 89.

50. Indeed, some scholars have suggested that the sorts of stores that were eventually built in Europe differed significantly from American supermarkets and that the first supermarkets created enormous dissonance among European women shoppers. For instance, although Victoria de Grazia sees American-style supermarkets as triumphing in Europe, she describes this process as slow and requiring tremendous changes in women's shopping and in the cultures of domesticity. See de Grazia, *Irresistible Empire*, 407–15. Adam Mack and Emanuela Scarpellini argue that there were sharp limits on the Americanization of European food retailing. Scarpellini, "Shopping American-Style," 625–68. Mack even argues for a kind of reverse-fertilization, in which U.S. retailers began looking to European models for inspiration. Mack, "Good Things to Eat in Suburbia," 158–76.

51. May, *Homeward Bound*.

52. Quoted in Harold H. Martin, "Why She Really Goes to Market," *Saturday Evening Post* 236 (September 1963): 41.

53. Blanche M. Stover, "Super Market Jubilee," *Parents' Magazine and Family Home Guide* 30 (August 1955): 64.

54. Harold H. Martin, "Why She Really Goes to Market," 41.

55. Advertisement, *Chicago Tribune*, September 28, 1952, NW A14. Lizabeth Cohen documents the increasing attention paid to male shoppers, Cohen, *Consumers' Republic*, 148. I would add, however, that the celebration of male shoppers did not translate into a decrease in women's responsibility for or supervision of food procurement. Marjorie DeVault also found that women often created the lists and were more concerned with food purchases in the early 1980s, even in families in which men "helped out" with food procurement. DeVault, *Feeding the Family*, 98–99, 117–18, 140.

56. Harris, "George Pleasures Them with Groceries," 102, 110.

57. Harold H. Martin, "Why She Really Goes to Market," 42.

58. Al Chase, "New Pattern Established in Food Shopping," *Chicago Tribune*, January 15, 1950, A7.

59. Advertisement, *Chicago Tribune*, March 12, 1952, A5. This kicked off a series called

"What Makes a Business Grow," in which each advertisement featured a different aspect of Jewel's efforts to please its customers.

60. For a lengthier discussion of surveys and consumer research in supermarkets, see Bowlby, *Carried Away*, 212–43.

61. *Life*, January 3, 1955.

62. The *Betty Crocker Picture Cookbook* sold more copies than any other nonfiction book published that year. By the next year, it had gone through seven printings. Neuhaus, *Manly Meals and Mom's Home Cooking*, 169–72.

63. Vanderbilt, *Amy Vanderbilt's Complete Cookbook*. Drawings by Andy Warhol. Indeed, production costs of large general cookbooks seemed prohibitive to some editors. See Neuhaus, *Manly Meals and Mom's Home Cooking*, 166.

64. Beard, *James Beard Cook Book*, 8.

65. Neuhaus, *Manly Meals and Mom's Home Cooking*, 219–31.

66. Neuhaus, "Joy of Sex Instruction," 109.

67. Oerke, *Mealtime*, 123–64. The quote about frozen foods is from 160. The quote about store-types is from 123. In contrast, discussions of fresh produce were marked by dozens of warnings about the dangers of spoilage and the difficulty of judging quality. The text contained the stern admonition "*Do not handle* fresh vegetables" because handing would increase the likelihood of spoilage (129). I am indebted to Shelby Balik for sharing this and many other sources on twentieth-century women's housekeeping from her personal collection.

68. Church, *Mary Meade's Kitchen Companion*, 12. See also Neuhaus, *Manly Meals and Mom's Home Cooking*, 168–69, 174–76.

69. The food editors of McCall's, *McCall's Cookbook*.

70. Marsh, *New Good Housekeeping Cookbook*, 25, 91. See also Neuhaus, *Manly Meals and Mom's Home Cooking*, 174–80.

71. *Best of the Bake-Off Collection*; Neuhaus, *Manly Meals and Mom's Home Cooking*, 169.

72. Betty Crocker, *"Honey, That's Delicious!"* 2.

73. Vanderbilt, *Amy Vanderbilt's Complete Cookbook*, x; ibid., "Casserole Meals," 153–75; ibid., "Go-Together Soups," 609–10. The paella recipe is on 452.

74. Church, *Mary Meade's Kitchen Companion*, 12.

75. Oerke, *Mealtime*, 123.

76. Nancy Crawford Wood and Jean Anderson, "Check Out Feast from the Supermarket," *Ladies' Home Journal* 79 (September 1962): 81.

77. The Women of General Foods Kitchens, *General Foods Kitchens*, 6–7.

78. Harold H. Martin, "Why She Really Goes to Market," 42.

79. James F. Ridgway, "Segregated Food at the Supermarket," *New Republic* 151 (December 1964): 6.

80. See, for instance, Morton Sonheimer, "Do You Know Your Groceries?" *Women's Home Companion* 78 (March 1951): 42; "Super Eating from Supermarket Specials," *American Home* 68 (October 1964): 62–64; "Women Sound Off about Grocery Stores," *Changing Times* (September 1968): 7–11.

81. Quoted in "Women Sound Off about Grocery Stores," *Changing Times* (December 1968): 42.

82. Vanek, "Time Spent in Housework," 117. Marjorie DeVault's ethnographic study of food procurement and preparation, *Feeding the Family*, reinforces and enriches Vanek's quantitative findings. DeVault presents evocative accounts of the time, effort, and stress involved in obtaining, supervising, and preparing for Chicago families in the 1980s. DeVault, *Feeding the Family*.

83. Julia Ahearn, "Mayhem in the Supermarket," *American Home* 54 (June 1955): 84.

84. "Women Sound Off about Grocery Stores," *Changing Times* (September 1968): 10.

85. Sontheimer, "Do You Know Your Groceries?" 48; "Women Sound Off about Grocery Stores" (December 1968), 41.

86. Weiss, *To Have and to Hold*, 39.

87. "Women Sound Off" (September 1968), 9; "Women Sound Off" (December 1968), 41.

88. A third woman explained her participation by alluding to the centrality of food shopping in her daily work: "A man enjoys talking about his vocation. When you become a housewife, this is your vocation and it's part of your life that you enjoy talking about." "Women Sound Off," (September 1968), 11.

89. Meyerowitz, "Beyond the Feminine Mystique," 229–62.

90. On the importance of food and cooking prowess in the lives of "professional" women, see Weiss, "She Also Cooks," 211–26.

91. Endrijonas, "Processed Food from Scratch," 157–73.

92. Laura Shapiro, *Something from the Oven*.

93. See, for example, Coontz, *Way We Never Were*; Breines, *Young, White, and Miserable*; and the essays collected in Meyerowitz, *Not June Cleaver*.

94. Gerson, "'Is Family Devotion Now Subversive?'"; Garrison "'Our Skirts Gave Them Courage.'"

95. Brett Harvey, *Fifties*, 122.

96. Sontheimer, "Do You Know Your Groceries?" 42.

97. Gelber, "Do-It-Yourself," 73.

98. Bureau of the Census, *1967 Census of Business*, vol. 2, *Retail Trade Area Statistics*, table 1, 1–4.

99. Hardware stores selling more than $300,000 worth of goods accounted for less than 30 percent of all sales. Ibid., vol. 1, *Retail Trade Subject Reports*, "Sales Size," 2–12; "Single Units and Multiunits," 4–9.

100. Bureau of Business Research, Northwestern University, *Margins, Expenses, and Profits in Retail Hardware Stores*, 8–9, 50. Margins represented gross—not net—earnings. Gross margins for grocery stores in the late 1920s also averaged around 26 percent. U.S. Department of Commerce, *Louisville Grocery Survey*, pt. 2, *Costs, Markets, and Methods in Grocery Retailing*, 19.

101. Bureau of Business Research, Northwestern University, *Margins, Expenses, and Profits in Retail Hardware Stores*, 46–50. One study conducted in the late 1920s put net profits for grocery stores at between 3 and 11 percent, averaging around 7 percent. However, because the study seems to have excluded stores that went out of business in the previous year and was conducted at the height of 1920s inflation, profit levels may be exaggerated. Department of Commerce, *Louisville Grocery Survey*, pt. 2, *Costs, Markets, and Methods in*

Grocery Retailing, 21. Net profits for the National Tea chain in 1928, during the time of the Louisville study, were only 3.4 percent. "National Tea Sales for 1928," *Progressive Grocer* 8 (May 1929): 88.

102. General Business Research Corporation, *Survey of Retail Hardware Business in United States, 1928*, 8.

103. "Winchester-Simmons Merger Proves Great Surprise to Hardware Trade," *Hardware Age* 110 (July 6, 1922): 69–72; "Winchester Dealers Endorse Merger," *Hardware Age* 110 (July 13, 1922): 71–74; "National Association of Winchester Clubs Meets in Chicago," *Hardware Age* 111 (July 12, 1923): 54–58; Kantowicz, *John Cotter*, 49.

104. "Chains in the Forge?" *Business Week*, September 16, 1944, 78.

105. Carpenter, *Place Is Ace*, 6–7.

106. Kantowicz, *John Cotter*, 48–49.

107. Carpenter, *Place Is Ace*, 39–49; Kantowicz, *John Cotter*, 83–85.

108. Kantowicz, *John Cotter*, 100.

109. Ibid., 144.

110. Carpenter, *Place Is Ace*, 62–63.

111. Ibid., 45.

112. "Hardware Store Takes to Supermarket Way," *Business Week*, September 8, 1956, 77. This tension between personal attention and mass retailing has remained. Home Depot, for instance, has regularly promised to boost services available in its stores and to attract more women customers, using language that could have been taken from supermarket literature of the 1930s. New stores, executives have explained, will reflect "women's" interests—with wide aisles, soft colors, and new sections on "home organization." The senior director of merchandising explained that new stores were designed to "'romance and wow the customer.'" These stores did *not*, however, feature more personal attention. That service was promised to (stereotypically) male contractors, who are urged on the company's Web site to "customize" their Home Depot experience by calling ahead so that store personnel and store goods will be available to them. "Home Depot Woos Women with a Concept Store that Exudes 'Romance,'" October 12, 2007, [http://www.foxnews.com/story/0,2933,301376,00 .html] (accessed December 20, 2007); The Home Depot, "Pro Products," [http:// contractorservices.homedepot.com/SelectStore.aspx] (accessed December 20, 2007). Both the new stores and the personalized treatment offered to contractors suggest the ongoing importance of gender ideologies to the marketing and organizational strategies of retailers, as well as the uncomfortable fit between men, male occupations, and mass retailing.

113. "Grab-It-Yourself Comes to Hardware," *Business Week*, October 18, 1952, 30.

114. "Old Time Hardware Store Turns to Glamour Trade," *Chicago Tribune*, October 23, 1955, SW A1.

115. George Schreiber, "Firms Beam at Hardware Show Sales," *Chicago Tribune*, October 8, 1961, F6.

116. "Grab It Yourself," *Business Week*, 30.

117. Gelber, "Do-It-Yourself."

118. Originating in the 1920s and 1930s with the popularization of Arts and Crafts ethos among male homeowners, the term "DIY" was first popularized in the 1950s. Gelber, "Do-It-Yourself," 94–95.

119. Ibid.; Lichtman, "Do-It-Yourself Security," 39–55.

120. The first column with this title was "Planning for the Home; Mr. Fix-It Tells How to Attach Coat Buttons," *Chicago Tribune*, October 9, 1949, SWC. The last was "Men, Women, Can Do Chair Seat Repairs," *Chicago Tribune*, April 7, 1968, NW8.

121. Gelber, "Do-It-Yourself," 97.

122. Lichtman, "Do-It-Yourself Security," 47.

123. Gelber, "Do-It-Yourself," 68–69, 101. Gelber points out that families often saved only minimal amounts of money in these pursuits.

124. Elaine Tyler May's account of post–World War II sexual discourses describes the ways that heterosexuality came to be assumed and, both because and in spite of this, encouraged in advice literature, marketing techniques, and government policy. See May, *Homeward Bound*. Later scholars have used the term "heteronormative" to refer to the development of policy, ideology, and practice that assumes that to be a citizen and to be human is to be heterosexual. For an early and useful discussion of this term, see Warner, introduction to *Fear of a Queer Planet*, xxi–xxv.

125. Gelber, "Do-It-Yourself," 99.

126. "Key Hardware Convention to Do-It-Yourself," *Chicago Tribune*, March 6, 1955, E4. For a similar sentiment, see "Firms Beam at Hardware Show Sales," *Chicago Tribune*, October 5, 1961, F6.

127. Goldstein, *Do-It-Yourself*, 48.

128. Lichtman, "Do-It-Yourself Security," 42.

129. Gelber, "Do-It-Yourself," 98.

130. "Pick Hardware to Ease Your Cabinet Work," *Chicago Tribune*, April 7, 1955, W3.

131. "Old Time Hardware Store Turns to Glamour Trade," *Chicago Tribune*, October 23, 1955, SW A1.

132. Gelber, *Hobbies*, 292–93.

133. On celebration of failures in DIY, see Gelber, "Do-It-Yourself," 101; and Gelber, *Hobbies*, 293.

134. For a rich discussion of differential evaluation of men's and women's purchases in working-class families, see Benson, "Gender, Generation, and Consumption in the United States," 223–40.

135. Packard, *Hidden Persuaders*, 107.

136. "Women Sum Up Supermarket Shopping in One Word," *Science Digest* 46 (July 1959): 25.

137. Elaine Kendall, "Open Letter to the Corner Grocer," *Harper's Magazine*, December 1960, 58.

138. Jarrell, *Sad Heart at the Supermarket*, 68–69. For a fuller discussion of the use of supermarkets in literature, including Packard's work, see Bowlby, *Carried Away*, 175–210.

The more recent U.S. success of songs like "Lost in the Supermarket" and music videos like Jane's Addiction's "Been Caught Stealing" (in which drag-wearing male band members stuffed produce and canned goods into their oversized dresses and blouses) bear testimony to the symbolic richness of supermarkets and women shoppers in critiques of consumer capitalism, alienation, and decadence. The song "Lost at the Supermarket" recounts the narrator's isolation in a consumption-driven society: "I'm all lost at the supermarket / I can no longer shop happily / Came in here for that special offer / Of guaranteed personality." Joe Strummer and Mick Jones, "Lost at the Supermarket."

139. Lizabeth Cohen, *Consumers' Republic*, 351–53.

140. Ibid., 354, 367–68. For a fuller description of the protests, see Mack, "Good Things to Eat in Suburbia," 117–42.

141. Mack, "Good Things to Eat in Suburbia," 127–31, 137–40.

142. See "Supermarkets' Newest Special; Self-Defense," *Business Week*, September 7, 1968, 34–35.

143. Ibid.

144. Lizabeth Cohen, *Consumers' Republic*, 370.

145. "Housewives' Chain Reaction," *Newsweek*, November 1966, 79.

146. Lizabeth Cohen, *Consumers' Republic*, 362–63, 368–69.

147. Chisholm, *Darlings*, 1. See also Mack, "Good Things to Eat in the Supermarket," 48–86.

148. Cross, *Supermarket Trap*, quote at 3.

149. Ibid., 8.

150. "Supermarkets' Newest Special," 34.

151. The killing of civil rights activist and Episcopal seminary student Jonathan Daniels at an Alabama grocery store makes this point especially poignantly. Daniels was shot to death by a local official who did not want him or his group of fellow activists to purchase sodas at the Cash Grocery store. "Priest Wounded," *Chicago Tribune*, August 21, 1965, 1. Daniels was later named a martyr by the Anglican Church and a lay saint by the Episcopal Church. See Eagles, *Outside Agitator*; and JonathanDaniels.org, "Celebrating Jonathan Daniels," [http://www.jonathandaniels.org/] (accessed February 15, 2009).

152. "Leaders Cite Breadbasket Success," *Chicago Tribune*, October 22, 1967, 1. Chicago's chapter of Operation Breadbasket was lead by Rev. Jesse Jackson and became the precursor to his Operation PUSH. For a longer description of the overlooked history of Operation Breadbasket, see Massoni, "Perspectives on Operation Breadbasket," 179–340.

153. "New Grocers Pact Ends Boycott," *Chicago Tribune*, November 26, 1967, SCL A2.

154. Ridgeway, "Segregated Food at the Supermarket," 6–7.

155. "How to Integrate Slum Neighborhood," *Chicago Defender*, April 11, 1966, 12.

156. See Lenwand, *Consumer*, 35–36.

157. Ridgeway, "Segregated Food at the Supermarket," 7.

158. "Supermarkets' Newest Special: Self-Defense," *Business Week*, September 7, 1968, 34.

159. Ibid., 35. Kraft Foods and the Supermarket Institute sponsored a conference for food journalists, apparently in large measure to showcase their efforts in poor neighborhoods. One speaker's presentation was called "The Riot Report and the Retail Food Industry." Ruth Ellen Church, "Candlelight Buffet in a Warehouse," *Chicago Tribune*, June 14, 1968, B1.

160. The 1968 riots were the coda to what came to be known as "long hot summer," in which northern black neighborhoods saw increasing numbers of angry confrontations between police, local politicians, and local businesses, on the one hand, and African American residents, on the other. For discussions of the riots and their effects, see Sugrue, *Origins of the Urban Crisis*, 259; and Lizabeth Cohen, *Consumers' Republic*, 356. Cohen has estimated

that there were at least "329 separate incidents in 257 American cities, involving hundreds of thousands of African Americans" between 1964 and 1968.

161. "Riots Go On," *Chicago Tribune*, April 7, 1968, 1; Donna Gill, "A Door to Nowhere Ends 22-year Dream," *Chicago Tribune*, April 9, 1968, A8.

162. Lizabeth Cohen, *Consumers' Republic*, 356–57.

163. "Bank to Aid Negro Business," *Chicago Tribune*, May 19, 1968, W1.

164. Bean, *Big Government and Affirmative Action*, 49–69.

165. Ibid., 171, 175–76. See Lizabeth Cohen, *Consumers' Republic*, 378, for a more nuanced version of this.

166. On the relationship between black women and cooking, see Williams-Forson, *Building Houses out of Chicken Legs*.

Conclusion

1. The film is based on the best-selling novel of the same name. Levin, *Stepford Wives*; *The Stepford Wives*, prod. Edgar Sherick, dir. Bryan Forbes (Culver City, Calif.: Columbia Pictures, 1975).

2. In recent years, conventional chain supermarkets have lost significant market share. There is no clear consensus on why, but alternatives to these stores range from large supercenters like Wal-Mart to smaller gourmet groceries. Although dealt with less directly by the trade press, the absence of stores in poor neighborhoods has certainly also contributed to waning sales. For studies of supermarkets' declining market share, see Paula Rosenblum, "Protecting Market Share," *Chain Store Age* (hereafter, *CSA*) 83 (July 2007): 16A; Murray Forseter, "Stories behind the Numbers," *CSA* 79 (August 2003): 10; Howard L. Davidowitz, "Supermarket Survival," *CSA* 80 (June 2004): 42–44; and Martinez and Kaufman, "Twenty Years of Competition Reshape the Food Marketing System."

3. Mari Gallagher Research and Consulting Group, *Examining the Impact of Food Deserts on Public Health in Chicago*, 7.

4. Locavores, "Locavores," [http://locavores.com] (accessed February 10, 2009).

5. "South Siders Aid Riot Victims," *Chicago Tribune*, April 14, 1968, SCL1.

6. Michael Smith, "West Side Area Rubble Is Gone but Not the Scars," *Chicago Tribune*, March 30, 1969, 3.

7. DeVault, *Feeding the Family*, 67, 178–79, 189.

8. "New Grocery Feeds Hope to Lawndale," *Chicago Tribune*, March 28, 1999, 4.

9. Block and Kouba, "Comparison of Availability and Affordability of a Market Basket."

10. As I write this, television news and the pages of newspaper food sections are full of advice about how to eat for less during the current recession. See, for example, MSNBC, "Fill Your Grocery Cart without Busting Your Budget," *MSNBC*, [http://www.msnbc.msn.com/id/24649378] (accessed May 16, 2008); "Thriftiness on Special in Aisle 5," *New York Times*, October 13, 2008, [http://www.nytimes.com/2008/10/14/business/14homeec.html?_r=1&scp=1&sq=money-saving%20groceries&st=cse] (accessed February 4, 2009); and Linda Florea, "Take Bite from Food Bill," *Orlando Sentinel*, January 28, 2009, C1.

11. Michael Pollan, "On the Table: My Letter to Whole Foods," *New York Times*, June 14, 2006, [http://pollan.blogs.nytimes.com] (accessed February 16, 2009).

12. Kingsolver, *Animal, Vegetable, Miracle*, 4.

13. Ibid., 127.

14. It is not the purpose of this book to denigrate efforts toward more just and sustainable food systems. However, potential solutions to food-related problems are unlikely to work if they reproduce resentment and inequality. In making this point, I follow the lead of many scholars who have noted that local foods proponents have a tendency to gloss over divisive social issues in relations between consumers and sellers, especially in farmers' markets. On racism in community and alternative food movements, see Slocum, "Anti-Racist Practice."

15. Rosen, *World Split Open*, 161–62, 204–5; Echols, *Daring to Be Bad*, 68, 77.

16. Two examples of this are the move to "school choice" in public school districts and the move to health savings accounts among employers, as a way to allow employees to "choose" their providers (and to cut down on employer costs). For histories of such turns toward the consumer-based model among policymakers and economists, see Lizabeth Cohen, *Consumers' Republic*; Brinkley, *End of Reform*; and Hodgson, *How Economics Forgot History*.

17. See, for instance, David Harvey, *Brief History of Neoliberalism*; and George, "Short History of Neoliberalism."

18. Duggan, *Twilight of Equality?*

19. Undergirding this argument is the understanding, first articulated by women's historians decades ago, not only that the category of "women" is treated differently in capitalism but also that its difference matters in structural ways. I have been influenced, in particular, by the work of Linda Gordon, Jeanne Boydston, and Gayle Rubin, as well as by innumerable conversations on this topic with David Chang, Jessica Simpson, M. J. Maynes, and Kevin Murphy. Much of the recent work about capitalism, although enormously welcome and useful in pointing to the social workings of business, has not directly confronted the questions raised so long ago about how gender and sexuality undergird exchange and economy more generally.

20. The possibility of consumption itself as a catalyst for radical politics has been raised sporadically in historical literature, primarily by cultural historians. See, for instance, Enstad, "Fashioning Political Identities"; and Benjamin, *Arcades Project*. I suggest that such politics emerge from and are rooted in the structures of distribution, and in people's expectation of authority over the stores in which they shop—as well as in the ideologies and subject positions suggested by Enstad and Benjamin.

Bibliography

Manuscript Collections
Chicago, Ill.
    Chicago History Museum
        Brotherhood of Sleeping Car Porters Papers
        Hyde Park Cooperative Society Papers
        Oral History Archives of Chicago Polonia
        Thelma Wheaton Papers
    Clerk of the Circuit Court of Cook County, Archives Department
    National Archives, Great Lakes Region
        National Recovery Administration. RG 9
        Office of Price Administration. RG 188
    University of Chicago Library, Special Collections Research Center
        Chicago Foreign Language Press Survey
        Ernest Watson Burgess Papers
        Hyde Park Historical Society Collection, Archives of Hyde Park Cooperative
            Society
College Park, Md.
    National Archives
        National Recovery Administration. RG 9
            National Emergency Council, Consumers' Division, County Council Files,
                1933–1935, IL, IN
            Women's Section, General Files of the Consumer Advisory Board
Hyde Park, N.Y.
    Franklin D. Roosevelt Presidential Library
        Franklin D. Roosevelt Papers, Official File
        Harry Hopkins Papers
        Carolina Ware Papers
Madison, Wis.
    Wisconsin Historical Society
        Cooperative League of the U.S.A. Papers
        Wisconsin Women during World War II Oral History Project
Mount Vernon, N.Y.
    Consumers Union Archives
        Persia Campbell Papers
Northampton, Mass.
    Smith College, Sophia Smith Collection
        Jessie Lloyd O'Connor Papers
        League of Women Shoppers Papers

Springfield, Ill.
    Abraham Lincoln Presidential Library, Manuscripts Division
        Federal Writers' Project Records
        Illinois Emergency Relief Commission Records
    Illinois State Archives
        Legislative Records, General Assembly, 600.000
        Secretary of State Records
            Dissolved Domestic Corporation Charters, 103.112
            Dissolved Foreign Corporation Charters, 103.113
Washington, D.C.
    Federal Bureau of Investigation
        "League of Women Shoppers" files (obtained by FOIA request)
    West Branch, Iowa
    Herbert Hoover Presidential Library
        Herbert Hoover Presidential Papers, Cabinet Officer Series

Journals and Newspapers
American Home
Business Week
Chain Store Age
Chain Store Age, Administration Edition
Chain Store Age, Grocery Managers Edition
Changing Times
Chicago Daily News
Chicago Defender
Chicago Journal of Commerce and LaSalle Street Journal
Chicago Realtor
Chicago Tribune
Collier's
Consumers' Cooperation (later *Cooperation*)
Co-op Magazine
Co-op News (Chicago)
Crusader
Evergreen (Chicago)
Good Housekeeping
Hardware Age
Harper's
Independent Grocergram
Ladies' Home Journal
Library Journal
Life
Look
Monthly Labor Review
New Republic

Newsweek

New York Times

Parents' Magazine and Family Home Guide

Printers' Ink

Progressive Grocer

Saturday Evening Post

Science Digest

Scientific American

Super Market Merchandising

Time

U.S. News and World Report

Women's Home Companion

Published Primary Works

Beard, James. *The James Beard Cook Book*. New York: Dell, 1959.

Best of the Bake-Off Collection: Pillsbury's Best 100 Recipes. Chicago: Consolidated Book Publishers, 1959.

Brand, Edward A. *Modern Supermarket Operation*. New York: Fairchild, 1963.

Cermak, Anton J. *Address of Hon. A. J. Cermak, mayor of the city of Chicago before the joint session of the House of Representatives and Senate, first special session . . . Tuesday, December 8, 1931*. Springfield, Ill.: Journal Print Co., 1931.

Chase, Stuart, and Frederick Schlink. *Your Money's Worth: A Study in the Waste of the Consumer's Dollar*. 1927. Reprint, New York: Macmillan, 1935.

Chicago Telephone Directory, alphabetical edition. July 1925.

Chicago Telephone Directory, classified edition. 1929, 1930, 1935, 1940, 1945, 1950, 1960, 1970.

Chisholm, Robert F. *The Darlings: The Mystique of the Supermarket*. New York: Chain Store Publishing, 1970.

Church, Ruth Ellen. *Mary Meade's Kitchen Companion: The Indispensable Guide to Modern Cooking*. Indianapolis, Ind.: Bobbs-Merrill, 1955.

Contractor Services <http://contractorservices.homedepot.com/SelectStore.aspx> (December 20, 2007).

Crocker, Betty. *Betty Crocker's Picture Cookbook*. New York: McGraw-Hill, 1950.

————. *"Honey, That's Delicious!": Husband-Pleasing Meals by Betty Crocker*. Pamphlet. N.p.: General Mills, 1965.

Cross, Jennifer. *The Supermarket Trap: The Consumer and the Food Industry*. Bloomington: Indiana University Press, 1970.

Dreiser, Theodore. *Sister Carrie*. Edited by Donald Pizer. 3rd ed. New York: Norton, 2006.

Ferber, Edna. *So Big!* Garden City, N.Y.: Doubleday, 1924.

Fischer, M. F. K. *How to Cook a Wolf*. New York: World Books, 1944.

Fitzpatrick, J. E., L. S. Edmunds, and B. A. Dennison. "Positive Effects of Family Dinner Are Undone by Television Viewing." *Journal of the American Dietetic Association* 107 (April 2007): 666–71.

The Food Editors of McCall's. *McCall's Cookbook*. New York: Random House, 1963.

Fulkerson, J. A., M. Story, A. Mellin, N. Leffert, D. Neumark-Sztainer, and S. A. French. "Family Dinner Meal Frequency and Adolescent Development: Relationships with Developmental Assets and High-Risk Behaviors." *Journal of Adolescent Health* 39 (September 2006): 337–45.

"Home Depot Woos Women with a Concept Store That Exudes 'Romance.'" October 12, 2007, <www.foxnews.com/story/0,2933,301376,00.html> (December 20, 2007).

Jarrell, Randall. *Sad Heart at the Supermarket: Essays and Fables*. New York: Atheneum, 1962.

Jane's Addiction. "Been Caught Stealing." August 21, 1990. Warner Bros. Records, Casey Niccoli, dir. <http://www.mtv.com/videos/janes-addiction/58608/been-caught-stealing.jhtml> (February 15, 2009).

Jewel Tea Company Annual Reports, 1920–1950.

Kallet, Arthur, and Frederick Schlink. *One Hundred Thousand Guinea Pigs*. New York: Vanguard, 1933.

Kingsolver, Barbara. *Animal, Vegetable, Miracle: A Year of Food Life*. New York: HarperCollins, 2007.

Levin, Ira. *The Stepford Wives*. 1972. Reprint, London: Bloomsbury Film Classics, 1998.

Lincoln, Murray D., J. Frank Grimes, Frederick C. Howe, and Joseph Mead. *Consumers' Co-operatives and Private Business*. America's Town Meeting of the Air. Ser. 2, no. 10 (January 21, 1937). New York: American Book, 1937.

Marsh, Dorothy B., ed. *The New Good Housekeeping Cookbook*. New York: Harcourt, Brace and World, 1963.

National Tea Company. *Annual Reports*, 1919–49.

———. *Historical High-Lights of National Tea Co.: Home Offices—Chicago, Ill., 1899–1955*. Chicago: n.p., 1955.

The New Settlement Cookbook. Revised and enlarged ed. New York: Simon and Schuster, 1954.

Piggly Wiggly Company Annual Reports, 1919–26.

Polacheck, Hilda Satt. *I Came a Stranger: The Story of a Hull House Girl*. Urbana: University of Illinois Press, 1989.

Shapiro, Bertha Michaels. *Memories of Lawndale*. Doris Minsky Memorial Publication, no. 1. Chicago: Chicago Jewish Historical Society, 1991.

Six Hundred Dollars a Year: A Wife's Effort at Low Living, under High Prices. Boston: Ticknor and Fields, 1867.

The Stepford Wives. Prod. Edgar Sherick, dir. Bryan Forbes. Columbia Pictures, 1975.

Strummer, Joe, and Mick Jones. "Lost at the Supermarket." *London Calling*, CBS Records, BL 36330.

Vanderbilt, Amy. *Amy Vanderbilt's Complete Cookbook*. Garden City, N.Y.: Doubleday, 1961.

Weinstein, Miriam. *The Surprising Power of Family Meals: How Eating Together Makes Us Smarter, Stronger, Healthier, and Happier*. Hanover, N.H.: Steerforth, 2006.

The Women of General Foods Kitchens. *General Foods Kitchens*. New York: Random House, 1959.

Woodsworth, Anne. "Service a la Your Neighborhood Store." *Library Journal* 121 (August 1, 1996): 49.

Government Documents

Chicago City Council. *Journal of Proceedings of the City Council of the City of Chicago.* Chicago: n.p., 1919–48.

Chicago Municipal Code of 1911. Chicago: Callaghan, 1911.

The Chicago Municipal Code of 1922. Chicago: Flood, 1922.

Illinois Commission on Taxation and Expenditures. *Report and Recommendations of the Illinois Commission on Taxation and Expenditures.* Springfield, January 24, 1933.

Illinois General Assembly. House. *Journal of the House of Representatives of the General Assembly of the State of Illinois.* Springfield, 1920–45.

———. Senate. *Journal of the Senate of the General Assembly of the State of Illinois.* Springfield, 1920–45.

Illinois Legislative Council. Research Department. *Exemption of Food under Sales Tax Statutes, Research Report on Proposals 120 and 121.* Publication no. 37. Springfield, December 1940.

———. *Major Potential Sources of State Revenue in Illinois. Research Report Proposal no. 10.* Publication no. 15. Springfield, August 1939.

Illinois Tax Commission. *Fifteenth Annual Report of the Illinois Tax Commission: Assessment Year 1933.* Springfield, 1934.

———. *Sixteenth Annual Report of the Illinois Tax Commission: Assessment Year 1934.* Springfield, 1937.

U.S. Congress. House. Committee on the District of Columbia. *Hearings before the Committee on the District of Columbia: A Bill to Amend the Code of the District of Columbia to Provide for the Organization and Regulation of Cooperative Associations and for other Purposes.* 76th Cong., 3rd sess., April 18–20, 1940. Washington, D.C.: Government Printing Office, 1940.

———. Temporary National Economic Committee. *Hearings before the Temporary National Economic Committee.* Part 8, *The Problems of the Consumer.* 76th Cong., 1st sess., May 10–12, 1939. Washington, D.C.: Government Printing Office, 1939.

U.S. Department of Commerce. Bureau of Foreign and Domestic Commerce. *Atlas of Wholesale Grocery Territories.* Domestic Commerce Series, no. 7. Washington, D.C.: Government Printing Office, 1927.

———. *Credit Extension and Business Failures: A Study of Credit Conditions and Causes of Failure among Grocery Retailers in Louisville, KY.* Trade Information Bulletin, no. 627. Washington, D.C.: Government Printing Office, 1929.

———. *Louisville Grocery Survey.* Part 1, *Census of Food Distribution.* Distribution Cost Studies, no. 6. Washington, D.C., 1930.

———. *Louisville Grocery Survey.* Part 2, *Costs, Markets, and Methods in Grocery Retailing.* Distribution Cost Studies, no. 8. Washington, D.C.: Government Printing Office, 1931.

———. *Louisville Grocery Survey.* Part 3A, *Merchandising Characteristics of Grocery Store Commodities: General Findings and Specific Results.* Distribution Cost Studies, no. 11. Washington, D.C.: Government Printing Office, 1932.

———. *The Retail Grocer's Problems.* Distribution Cost Studies, no. 5. Washington, D.C.: Government Printing Office, 1929.

————. Bureau of the Census. *Census of Business: 1935, Retail Distribution*. Vol. 1, *United States Summary*. Washington, D.C.: Government Printing Office, 1937.

————. *Census of Business: 1935, Retail Distribution*. Vol. 4, *Types of Operation*. Washington, D.C.: Government Printing Office, 1937.

————. *Fifteenth Census of the United States: 1930, Distribution*. Vol. 1, *Retail Distribution*. Pts. 1 and 2. Washington, D.C.: Government Printing Office, 1934.

————. *Sixteenth Census of the United States: 1940, Census of Business*. Vol. 1, *Retail Trade: 1939*. Washington, D.C.: Government Printing Office, 1943.

————. *U.S. Census of Business, 1948*. Vol. 1, *Retail Trade—General Statistics*. Washington, D.C.: Government Printing Office, 1952.

————. *U.S. Census of Business, 1948*. Vol. 2, *Retail Trade—Area Statistics*. Washington, D.C.: Government Printing Office, 1951.

————. *Census of Business, 1954*. Vol. 1, *Retail Trade, Summary Statistics*. Washington, D.C.: Government Printing Office, 1957.

————. *1967 Census of Business*. Vol. 1, *Retail Trade Subject Reports*. Washington, D.C.: Government Printing Office, 1971.

————. *1967 Census of Business*. Vol. 2, *Retail Trade Area Statistics*, pt 1. Washington, D.C.: Government Printing Office, 1970.

U.S. Office of Price Administration. *A Short History of OPA*, by Harvey C. Mansfield et al. Historical Reports on War Administration. General Publication, no. 15. Washington, D.C.: Government Printing Office, 1947.

————. *Volunteers in OPA*, by Imogene Putnam. Historical Reports on War Administration. General Publication, no. 14. Washington, D.C.: Government Printing Office, 1947.

————. *Chronology of the Office of Price Administration, January 1941–November 1946*, by Laurence E. Tilley. Historical Reports on War Administration. Miscellaneous Publication, no. 1. Washington, D.C.: Government Printing Office, 1946.

Secondary Sources

Abbott, Grace. "A Study of the Greeks in Chicago." *American Journal of Sociology* 15 (November 1909): 379–93.

Abelson, Elaine S. *When Ladies Go A-Thieving: Middle-Class Shoplifters in the Victorian Department Store*. New York: Oxford University Press, 1989.

Adelman, Morris. *A&P: A Study in Price-Cost Behavior and Public Policy*. Cambridge, Mass.: Harvard University Press, 1959.

Alexander, R. S. "Study of Retail Grocery Prices." *Journal of Commerce*, March 2, 1929, 9.

Allen, Frederick Lewis. *Only Yesterday: An Informal History of the 1920s*. New York: Harper and Row, 1931.

Baldwin, Davarian L. *Chicago's New Negroes: Modernity, the Great Migration, and Black Urban Life*. Chapel Hill: University of North Carolina Press, 2007.

Balkin, Steven, Alfonso Morales, and Joseph Persky. "Utilizing the Informal Economy: The Case of Chicago's Maxwell Street." Working Paper Series, no. 23. Tucson, Ariz.: Mexican American Studies and Research Center, University of Arizona, 1994.

Bartel, Andrew C. "The Politics of Food Control: The Office of Price Administration and the Dilemmas of Economic Stabilization, 1940–1946." Ph.D. diss., Johns Hopkins University, 1987.

Bayor, Ronald. *Neighbors in Conflict: The Irish, Germans, Jews, and Italians of New York City, 1929–1941*. Baltimore, Md.: Johns Hopkins University Press, 1978.

Bean, Jonathan J. *Beyond the Broker State: Federal Policies toward Small Business, 1936–1961*. Chapel Hill: University of North Carolina Press, 1996.

———. *Big Government and Affirmative Action: The Scandalous History of the Small Business Administration*. Lexington: University Press of Kentucky, 2001.

Beckert, Sven. *Monied Metropolis: New York City and the Consolidation of the American Bourgeoisie, 1850–1896*. New York: Cambridge University Press, 2001.

Behling, Laura L. *The Masculine Woman in America, 1890–1935*. Urbana: University of Illinois Press, 2001.

Beito, David T. *Taxpayers in Revolt: Tax Resistance during the Great Depression*. Chapel Hill: University of North Carolina Press, 1989.

Belasco, Warren, and Roger Horowitz, eds. *Food Chains: From Farmyard to Shopping Cart*. Hagley Perspectives on Business and Culture. Philadelphia: University of Pennsylvania Press, 2009.

Benjamin, Walter. *The Arcades Project*. Translated by Howard Eiland and Kevin McLaughlin. Cambridge, Mass.: Belknap, 1999.

Benson, Susan Porter. *Counter Cultures: Saleswomen, Managers, and Customers in American Department Stores, 1890–1940*. Urbana: University of Illinois Press, 1986.

———. "Gender, Generation, and Consumption in the United States: Working-Class Families in the Interwar Period." In Strasser, McGovern, and Judt, *Getting and Spending*, 223–40.

———. *Household Accounts: Working-Class Family Economies in the Interwar United States*. Ithaca, N.Y.: Cornell University Press, 2007.

———. "Living on the Margin: Working-Class Marriages and Family Survival Strategies in the United States, 1919–1941." In *The Sex of Things: Gender and Consumption in Historical Perspective*, edited by Victoria de Grazia with Ellen Furlough, 212–43. Berkeley: University of California Press, 1996.

Bentley, Amy. *Eating for Victory: Food Rationing and the Politics of Domesticity*. Urbana: University of Illinois Press, 1998.

Bernstein, Michael. "Why the Great Depression Was Great: Toward a New Understanding of the Interwar Economic Crisis in the United States." In Fraser and Gerstle, *Rise and Fall of the New Deal Order*, 32–54.

Biles, Roger. *Big City Boss in Depression and War: Mayor Edward J. Kelly of Chicago*. DeKalb: Northern Illinois University Press, 1984.

Bjorklund, Einar, and James L. Palmer. *A Study of the Prices of Chain and Independent Grocers in Chicago*. Studies in Business Administration. Vol. 1., no. 4. Chicago: University of Chicago Press, 1930.

Blaszczyk, Regina Lee. *Imagining Consumers: Design and Innovation from Wedgwood to Corning*. Baltimore, Md.: Johns Hopkins University Press, 2000.

Block, Daniel, and Joanna Kouba. "A Comparison of the Availability and Affordability of a Market Basket in Two Communities in the Chicago Area." *Public Health Nutrition* 9 (October 2006): 837–45.

Bowlby, Rachel. *Carried Away: The Invention of Modern Shopping.* New York: Columbia University Press, 2001.

Boyd, Robert L. "Ethnicity, Niches, and Retail Enterprise in Northern Cities, 1900." *Sociological Perspectives* 44 (Spring 2001): 89–110.

Boydston, Jeanne. *Home and Work: Housework, Wages, and the Ideology of Labor in the Early Republic.* New York: Oxford University Press, 1990.

Breines, Wini. *Young, White, and Miserable: Growing Up Female in the Fifties.* Boston: Beacon, 1992.

Brinkley, Alan. *The End of Reform: New Deal Liberalism in Recession and War.* New York: Knopf, 1995.

———. "The New Deal and the Idea of the State." In Fraser and Gerstle, *Rise and Fall of the New Deal Order,* 85–121.

Bukowski, Douglas. *Big Bill Thompson, Chicago, and the Politics of Image.* Urbana: University of Illinois Press, 1998.

Bureau of Business Research, Northwestern University. *Margins, Expenses, and Profits in Retail Hardware Stores.* Chicago: Shaw, 1928.

Burley, Orin E. *The Consumers' Cooperative as a Distributive Agency.* New York: McGraw, 1939.

Calder, Lendol G. *Financing the American Dream: A Cultural History of Consumer Credit.* Princeton, N.J.: Princeton University Press, 1999.

Campbell, D'Ann. *Women at War with America: Private Lives in a Patriotic Era.* Cambridge, Mass.: Harvard University Press, 1984.

Campbell, Persia. *Consumer Representation in the New Deal.* Studies in History, Economics, and Public Law, no. 477. New York: Columbia University Press, 1940.

Carpenter, Cheri. *The Place Is Ace: The History of Ace Hardware.* [Oak Brook, Ill.]: Ace Hardware Corporation, 1992.

Cayton, Horace, and St. Clair Drake. *Black Metropolis: A Study of Negro Life in a Northern City.* New York: Harcourt, Brace, 1945.

Celebrating Jonathan Daniels. <http://www.jonathandaniels.org/> (February 15, 2009).

Chandler, Alfred D., Jr. *The Visible Hand: The Managerial Revolution in American Business.* Cambridge, Mass.: Belknap, 1976.

Charvat, Frank J. *Supermarketing.* New York: Macmillan, 1961.

Chicago Commission on Race Relations. *The Negro in Chicago.* Chicago: University of Chicago Press, 1922.

Circle Pines Camp History <http://www.circlepinescenter.org/history.php> (July 23, 2007).

Clark-Lewis, Elizabeth. *Living In, Living Out: African American Domestics in Washington, D.C., 1910–1940.* Washington, D.C.: Smithsonian Institution Press, 1994.

Cohen, Andrew. *The Racketeer's Progress: Chicago and the Struggle for the Modern American Economy.* New York: Cambridge University Press, 2004.

Cohen, Lizabeth. *A Consumers' Republic: The Politics of Mass Consumption in Postwar America.* New York: Knopf, 2003.

————. *Making a New Deal: Industrial Workers in Chicago, 1919–1929*. New York: Cambridge University Press, 1990.

————. "The New Deal State and the Making of Citizen Consumers." In Strasser, McGovern, and Judt, *Getting and Spending*, 111–25.

Converse, Paul D. "Prices and Services of Chain and Independent Stores in Champaign-Urbana, Illinois." *National Association of Teachers of Marketing and Advertising Bulletin*. Ser. 4 (October 1931): 1–37.

Coontz, Stephanie. *The Way We Never Were: American Families and the Nostalgia Trap*. New York: Basic Books, 1992.

Cooperative League of the USA. *First Yearbook: The Cooperative League of the U.S.A.* New York: Cooperative League of New York, 1930.

————. *Third Yearbook: The Cooperative League of the U.S.A.* Minneapolis, Minn.: Northern States Cooperative League, 1936.

Cott, Nancy. *The Bonds of Womanhood: Woman's Sphere in New England, 1780–1835*. New Haven, Conn.: Yale University Press, 1977.

————. *The Grounding of Modern Feminism*. New Haven, Conn.: Yale University Press, 1987.

Cowan, Ruth Schwartz. *More Work for Mother: The Ironies of Household Technology from the Open Hearth to the Microwave*. New York: Basic Books, 1983.

Creighton, Lucy Black. *Pretenders to the Throne: The Consumer Movement in the United States*. Lexington, Mass.: Heath, 1976.

Cronon, William. *Nature's Metropolis: Chicago and the Great West*. New York: Norton, 1991.

Cruikshank, Ken, and Nancy Bouchier. "Blighted Areas and Obnoxious Industry: Constructing Environmental Inequality on an Industrial Waterfront, Hamilton, Ontario, 1890–1960." *Journal of Environmental History* 9 (July 2004): 464–96.

Cullather, Nick. "The Foreign Policy of the Calorie." *American Historical Review* 112 (April 2007): 337–64.

Cushman, Barry. *Rethinking the New Deal Court: The Structure of a Constitutional Revolution*. New York: Oxford University Press, 1998.

Davis, Belinda J. *Home Fires Burning: Food, Politics, and Everyday Life in World War I Berlin*. Chapel Hill: University of North Carolina Press, 2000.

de Grazia, Victoria. "Changing Consumption Regimes in Europe." In Strasser, McGovern, and Judt, *Getting and Spending*, 59–83.

————. *Irresistible Empire: America's Advance through Twentieth-Century Europe*. Cambridge, Mass.: Belknap, 2005.

DeVault, Marjorie. *Feeding the Family: The Social Organization of Caring as Gendered Work*. Chicago: University of Chicago Press, 1991.

————. "Women and Food: Housework and the Production of Family Life." Ph.D. diss., Northwestern University, 1984.

Douglas, Paul, Curtice N. Hitchcock, and Willard Atkins. *The Worker in Modern Economic Society*. 2nd ed. Chicago: University of Chicago Press, 1925.

DuBois, Ellen Carol, and Vicki L. Ruiz, eds. *Unequal Sisters: A Multicultural Reader in U.S. Women's History*. New York: Routledge, 1990.

Duddy, E. A. "Distribution of Perishable Commodities in the Chicago Metropolitan Area." *University Journal of Business* 4 (April 1926): 151–81.

Duggan, Lisa. *The Twilight of Equality? Neoliberalism, Cultural Politics, and the Attack on Democracy*. Boston: Beacon, 2003.

Duis, Perry. *Challenging Chicago: Coping with Everyday Life, 1837–1920*. Urbana: University of Illinois Press, 1998.

———. "No Time for Privacy: World War II and Chicago's Families." In *The War in American Culture: Society and Consciousness during World War II*, edited by Lewis A. Erenberg and Susan E. Hirsch, 17–45. Chicago: University of Chicago Press, 1996.

Dunlavy, Colleen. *Politics and Industrialization: Early Railroads in the United States and Prussia*. Princeton, N.J.: Princeton University Press, 1994.

Eagles, Charles W. *Outside Agitator: Jon Daniels and the Civil Rights Movement in Alabama*. Chapel Hill: University of North Carolina Press, 1993.

Eastwood, Carolyn. *Chicago's Jewish Street Peddlers: Toehold on the Bottom Rung*. Chicago: Chicago Jewish Historical Society, 1991.

———. "A Study of the Regulation of Chicago's Street Vendors." Ph.D. diss., University of Illinois at Chicago, 1988.

Echols, Alice. *Daring to Be Bad: Radical Feminism in America, 1967–1975*. Minneapolis: University of Minnesota Press, 1989.

Edsforth, Ronald. *The New Deal: America's Response to the Great Depression*. Malden, Mass.: Blackwell, 2000.

Einhorn, Robin. *American Taxation, American Slavery*. Chicago: University of Chicago Press, 2006.

Emery, Edwin, and Michael Emery. *The Press and America: An Interpretative History of the Mass Media*. 4th ed. Englewood Cliffs, N.J.: Prentice-Hall, 1978.

Endrijonas, Erika. "Processed Food from Scratch: Cooking for Family in the 1950s." In Inness, *Kitchen Culture in America*, 157–73.

Engel, Barbara. "Not by Bread Alone: Subsistence Riots in Russia during World War I." *Journal of Modern History* 69 (December 1997): 696–721.

Enstad, Nan. "Fashioning Political Identities: Cultural Studies and the Historical Construction of Political Subjects." *American Quarterly* 50 (December 1998): 745–82.

———. *Ladies of Labor, Girls of Adventure: Working Women, Popular Culture, and Labor Politics at the Turn of the Twentieth Century*. New York: Columbia University Press, 1999.

Farber, Lianna. *An Anatomy of Trade in Medieval Writing: Value, Consent, and Community*. Ithaca, N.Y.: Cornell University Press, 2005.

Ferguson, Roderick. *Aberrations in Black: Toward a Queer of Color Critique*. Minneapolis: University of Minnesota Press, 2004.

"Fill Your Grocery Cart without Busting Your Budget." <http://www.msnbc.msn.com/id/24649378> (May 16, 2008).

Finnegan, Margaret. *Selling Suffrage: Consumer Culture and Votes for Women*. New York: Columbia University Press, 1999.

Fischer, Claude. *America Calling: A Social History of the Telephone to 1940*. Berkeley: University of California Press, 1992.

Frank, Dana. *Buy American: The Untold Story of Economic Nationalism.* Boston: Beacon, 1999.

————. "Housewives, Socialists, and the Politics of Food: The 1917 New York Cost-of-Living Protests." *Feminist Studies* 11 (Summer 1985): 255–85.

————. *Purchasing Power: Consumer Organizing, Gender, and the Seattle Labor Movement, 1919–1929.* Cambridge: Cambridge University Press, 1994.

Fraser, Steve, and Gary Gerstle, eds. *The Rise and Fall of the New Deal Order, 1930–1980.* Princeton, N.J.: Princeton University Press, 1989.

Fridenson, Patrick. "The Impact of the War on French Workers." In *The Upheaval of War: Family, Work, and Welfare in Europe, 1914–1918,* edited by Richard Wall and Jay M. Winter, 235–48. Cambridge: Cambridge University Press, 1988.

Furlough, Ellen, and Carl Strikwerda. "Economics, Consumer Culture, and Gender: An Introduction to the Politics of Consumer Cooperation." In *Consumers against Capitalism: Consumer Cooperation in Europe, North America, and Japan, 1840–1990,* edited by Furlough and Strikwerda, 1–66. Lanham, Md.: Rowman and Littlefield, 1999.

Gabaccia, Donna R. *From Sicily to Elizabeth Street: Housing and Social Change among Italian Immigrants, 1830–1930.* Albany: State University of New York Press, 1984.

————. *We Are What We Eat: Ethnic Food and the Making of Americans.* Cambridge, Mass.: Harvard University Press, 1998.

Garrison, Dee. "'Our Skirts Gave Them Courage': The Civil Defense Protest Movement in New York City, 1955–1961." In Meyerowitz, *Not June Cleaver,* 201–26.

Gelber, Steven. "Do-It-Yourself: Constructing, Repairing, and Maintaining Domestic Masculinity." *American Quarterly* 49 (March 1997): 66–112.

————. *Hobbies: Leisure and the Culture of Work in America.* New York: Columbia University Press, 1999.

General Business Research Corporation. *Survey of Retail Hardware Business in United States, 1928.* New York: General Business Research Corporation, 1929.

George, Susan. "A Short History of Neoliberalism." Paper presented at the Conference on Economic Sovereignty in a Globalising World, Bangkok, March 24–26, 1999. <http://www.globalexchange.org/campaigns/econ101/neoliberalism.html> (7/26/2009).

Gerson, Deborah A. "'Is Family Devotion Now Subversive?': Families against McCarthyism." In Meyerowitz, *Not June Cleaver,* 151–76.

Gibson-Graham, J. K. *The End of Capitalism (As We Knew It): A Feminist Critique of Political Economy.* Cambridge, Mass.: Blackwell, 1996.

Glenn, Susan. *Daughters of the Shtetl: Life and Labor in the Immigrant Generation.* Ithaca, N.Y.: Cornell University Press, 1990.

Glickman, Lawrence B. "'Buy for the Sake of the Slave': Abolitionism and the Origins of American Consumer Activism." *American Quarterly* 56 (December 2004): 889–912.

————. *Buying Power: A History of Consumer Protest in America.* Chicago: University of Chicago Press, 2009.

————. "'Make Lisle the Style': The Politics of Fashion in the Japanese Silk Boycott." *Journal of Social History* 38 (Summer 2005): 573–608.

————. "The Strike in the Temple of Consumption: Consumer Activism and Twentieth-Century American Political Culture." *Journal of American History* 88 (June 2001): 99–128.

Goldstein, Carolyn B. *Do-It-Yourself: Home Improvement in Twentieth-Century America.* Washington, D.C.: National Building Museum, 1998.

———. "Mediating Consumption: Home Economics and American Consumers, 1900–1940." Ph.D. diss., University of Delaware, 1994.

Goluboff, Risa. *The Lost Promise of Civil Rights.* Cambridge, Mass.: Harvard University Press, 2007.

Graff, Ellen. *Stepping Left: Dance and Politics in New York City, 1928–1942.* Durham, N.C.: Duke University Press, 1997.

Grandclément, Catherine. "Wheeling One's Groceries around the Store: The Invention of the Shopping Cart, 1936–1953." In Belasco and Horowitz, *Food Chains,* 233–52.

Greenberg, Cheryl Lynn. *"Or Does It Explode?" Black Harlem in the Great Depression.* New York: Oxford University Press, 1991.

Greer, William, with John A. Logan and Paul S. Willis. *America the Bountiful: How the Supermarket Came to Main Street; An Oral History.* Washington, D.C.: Food Marketing Institute in cooperation with Beatrice Companies, 1986.

Grossman, James. *Land of Hope: Chicago, Black Southerners, and the Great Migration.* Chicago: University of Chicago Press, 1989.

Gurney, Peter. "The Battle of the Consumer in Postwar Britain." *Journal of Modern History* 77 (December 2005): 956–87.

———. *Co-operative Culture and the Politics of Consumption in England, 1870–1930.* Manchester, UK: Manchester University Press, 1996.

Guterl, Matthew. *American Mediterranean: Southern Slaveholders in the Age of Emancipation.* Cambridge, Mass.: Harvard University Press, 2008.

Haig, Robert Murray, and Carl Shoup, with the assistance of Reavis Cox, Louis Shere, Edwin H. Spengler, and staff. *The Sales Tax in the American States.* New York: Columbia University Press, 1934.

Hall, Jacqueline Dowd. "Disorderly Women: Gender and Labor Militancy in the Appalachian South." In *Unequal Sisters: A Multicultural Reader in U.S. Women's History,* 1st ed., edited by Ellen Carol DuBois and Vicki Ruiz, 293–321. New York: Routledge, 1990.

Harper, F. J. "'A New Battle on Evolution': The Anti-Chain Store Trade-at-Home Agitation of 1929–1930." *Journal of American Studies* 16 (December 1982): 407–26.

Hartmann, Heidi. "The Family as the Locus of Gender, Class, and Political Struggle: The Example of Housework." *Signs* 6 (Spring 1981): 366–94.

Hartog, Henrik. "Pigs and Positivism." *Wisconsin Law Review* (1985): 899–936.

Harvey, Brett. *The Fifties: A Women's Oral History.* New York: HarperCollins, 1993.

Harvey, David. *A Brief History of Neoliberalism.* New York: Oxford University Press, 2005.

Harvard Bureau of Business Research. *Management Problems in Retail Grocery Stores.* Bulletin no. 13. Cambridge, Mass.: Bureau of Business Research, Harvard University Press, 1919.

———. *Operating Expenses in Retail Grocery Stores in 1924.* Bulletin no. 52. Cambridge, Mass.: Bureau of Business Research, Harvard University Press, 1925.

Hatfield, Myrtle Lohner. "An Analysis of Some Grocery Store Practices from the Viewpoint of the Woman Buyer." Master's thesis, University of Chicago, 1936.

Hawley, Ellis. *The Great War and the Search for Modern Order: A History of the American People and Their Institutions, 1917–1933*. New York: St. Martin's, 1979.

———. *The New Deal and the Problem of Monopoly: A Study in Economic Ambivalence.* Princeton, N.J.: Princeton University Press, 1966.

Hayes, Joanne Lamb. *Grandma's Wartime Kitchen: World War II and the Way They Cooked.* New York: St. Martin's, 2000.

Heller Committee for Research in Social Economics, comp. *Cost of Living Studies: Quantity and Cost Estimate of the Standard of Living of the Professional Class.* California Publications in Economics, vol. 5, no. 2. Berkeley: University of California Press, 1928.

Hessler, Julie. *A Social History of Soviet Trade: Trade Policy, Retail Practice, and Consumption, 1917–1953.* Princeton, N.J.: Princeton University Press, 2004.

Hitchcock, Nevada Davis. "The Relation of the Housewife to the Food Problem." *Annals of the American Academy of Political and Social Science* 74 (November 1917): 130–40.

Hodgson, Geoffrey. *How Economics Forgot History: The Problem of Specificity in Social Science.* New York: Routledge, 2001.

Holli, Melvin G., and Peter d'A. Jones. *Ethnic Chicago: A Multicultural Portrait.* 4th ed. Grand Rapids, Mich.: Eerdmans, 1994.

Honey, Maureen. *Creating Rosie the Riveter: Class, Gender, and Propaganda during World War II.* Amherst: University of Massachusetts Press, 1984.

Hong, Grace Kyunwon. *The Ruptures of American Capital: Women of Color Feminism and the Culture of Immigrant Labor.* Minneapolis: University of Minnesota Press, 2006.

Horowitz, Daniel. *The Morality of Spending: Attitudes toward the Consumer Society in America, 1875–1940.* Baltimore, Md.: Johns Hopkins University Press, 1985.

Horowitz, David. "The Crusade against Chain Stores: Portland's Independent Merchants, 1928–1935." *Oregon Historical Quarterly* 89 (Winter 1988): 340–68.

Horowitz, Roger. *Putting Meat on the American Table: Taste, Technology, Transformation.* Baltimore, Md.: Johns Hopkins University Press, 2006.

Hounshell, David. *From the American System to Mass Production: The Development of Manufacturing Technology in the United States, 1800–1932.* Baltimore, Md.: Johns Hopkins University Press, 1985.

Hoyt, Edwin P. *That Wonderful A&P!* New York: Hawthorn Books, 1969.

Hoyt, Homer. *One Hundred Years of Land Values in Chicago.* 1933. Reprint, New York: Arno, 1970.

Hunter, Gary. "Don't Buy from Where You Can't Work: Black Urban Boycott Movements during the Depression, 1929–1941." Ph.D. diss., University of Michigan, 1977.

Hyman, Paula. "Immigrant Women and Consumer Protest: The New York City Kosher Meat Boycott of 1902." *American Jewish History* 70 (September 1980): 90–105.

Inness, Sherrie A., ed. *Kitchen Culture in America: Popular Representations of Food, Gender, and Race.* Philadelphia: University of Pennsylvania Press, 2001.

Jacobs, Meg. "'How about Some Meat?': The Office of Price Administration, Consumption Politics, and State Building from the Bottom Up, 1941–1946." *Journal of American History* 84 (December 1997): 910–41.

———. *Pocketbook Politics: Economic Citizenship in Twentieth-Century America.* Princeton, N.J.: Princeton University Press, 2005.

Jacoby, Neil H. *Retail Sales Taxation: Relation to Business and Consumers, and Administrative Problems.* New York: Commerce Clearing House, 1938.

Jaffee, David. "Peddlers of Progress and the Transformation of the Rural North, 1760–1880." *Journal of American History* 78 (September 1991): 511–35.

John, Richard. "Elaborations, Revisions, Dissents: Alfred D. Chandler, Jr.'s, 'The Visible Hand' after Twenty Years." *Business History Review* 71 (Summer 1997): 151–200.

———. "Governmental Institutions as Agents of Change: Rethinking American Political Development in the Early Republic, 1787–1835." *Studies in American Political Development* 11 (Fall 1997): 347–80.

Johnson, Walter. "The Pedestal and the Veil: Rethinking the Capitalism/Slavery Question." *Journal of the Early Republic* 24 (Summer 2004): 299–308.

———. *Soul by Soul: Life inside the Antebellum Slave Market.* Cambridge, Mass.: Harvard University Press, 1999.

Jones, Jacqueline. *Labor of Love, Labor of Sorrow: Black Women, Work, and the Family from Slavery to the Present.* New York: Vintage Books, 1986.

Joseph, Miranda. *Against the Romance of Community.* Minneapolis: University of Minnesota Press, 2002.

Kantowicz, Edward. *John Cotter: 70 Years of Hardware.* Lake Bluff, Ill.: Regnery Books, 1986.

Kessler-Harris, Alice. *In Pursuit of Equity: Women, Men, and the Quest for Economic Citizenship in 20th Century America.* New York: Oxford University Press, 2001.

Keillor, Steven J. *Cooperative Commonwealth: Co-ops in Rural Minnesota, 1859–1939.* Saint Paul: Minnesota Historical Society Press, 2000.

King, Andrew J. *Law and Land Use in Chicago: A Prehistory of Modern Zoning.* New York: Garland, 1986.

Koehn, Nancy F. *Brand New: How Entrepreneurs Earned Consumers' Trust from Wedgwood to Dell.* Boston: Harvard Business School Press, 2001.

Kornbluh, Felicia. "To Fulfill Their 'Rightly Needs': Consumerism and the National Welfare Rights Movement." *Radical History Review* 69 (Fall 1997): 76–113.

Kreskas, Amy. "Division of Domestic Work." *Journal of Family Issues* 25 (October 2004): 900–932.

Kwolek-Folland, Angel. *Engendering Business: Men and Women in the Corporate Office, 1870–1930.* Baltimore, Md.: Johns Hopkins University Press, 1994.

Laird, Pamela. *Pull: Networking and Success since Benjamin Franklin.* Cambridge, Mass.: Harvard University Press, 2006.

Laycock, George. *The Kroger Story: A Century of Innovation.* Cincinnati, Ohio: Kroger, 1983.

Leach, William. *Land of Desire: Merchants, Power, and the Rise of a New American Culture.* New York: Pantheon Books, 1993.

Lebhar, Godfrey M. *Chain Stores in America, 1859–1962.* New York: Chain Store Publishing, 1963.

Lenwand, Gerald. *The Consumer.* New York: Pocket Books, 1970.

Leuchtenburg, William Edward. *The Perils of Prosperity, 1914–32.* Chicago: University of Chicago Press, 1958.

Levenstein, Harvey A. *Revolution at the Table: The Transformation of the American Diet.* New York: Oxford University Press, 1988.

Lévi-Strauss, Claude. *Totemism.* Translated by Rodney Needham. Boston: Beacon, 1963.

Levy, Darline Gay, Harriet Branson Applewhite, and Mary Durham Johnson, eds. *Women in Revolutionary Paris, 1789–1795.* Urbana: University of Illinois Press, 1980.

Lichtman, Sarah A. "Do-It-Yourself Security: Safety, Gender, and the Home Fallout Shelter in Cold War America." *Journal of Design History* 19 (Spring 2006): 39–55.

Lipsitz, George. "Consumer Spending as State Project: Yesterday's Solutions and Today's Problems." In Strasser, McGovern, and Judt, *Getting and Spending,* 127–47.

Locavores. July 13, 2008, <http://locavores.com> (February 10, 2009).

Longstreth, Richard. *City Center to Regional Mall: Architecture, the Automobile, and Retailing in Los Angeles, 1920–1950.* Cambridge, Mass.: MIT Press, 1997.

———. *The Drive-In, the Supermarket, and the Transformation of Commercial Space.* Cambridge, Mass.: MIT Press, 1999.

Mack, Adam. "Good Things to Eat in Suburbia: Supermarkets and American Consumer Culture, 1930–1970." Ph.D. diss., University of South Carolina, 2006.

Mainardi, Pat. "The Politics of Housework," 1970. <http://www.cwluherstory.com/the-politics-of-housework.html> (February 10, 2009).

Marchand, Roland. *Advertising the American Dream: Making Way for Modernity, 1920–1940.* Berkeley: University of California Press, 1985.

Mari Gallagher Research and Consulting Group. *Examining the Impact of Food Deserts on Public Health in Chicago.* Prepared for LaSalle Bank. Chicago: n.p., 2006.

Markin, Rom J. *The Supermarket: An Analysis of Growth, Development, and Change.* Rev. ed. Pullman: Washington State University Press, 1968.

Martin, Ann Smart. *Buying into the World of Goods: Early Consumers in Backcountry Virginia.* Baltimore, Md.: Johns Hopkins University Press, 2008.

Martin, Lionel Ralph. "Grocery Chain Competition in Chicago as Reflected through Newspaper Advertising." Ph.D. diss., University of Chicago, 1931.

Martinez, Steve, and Phil Kaufman. "Twenty Years of Competition Reshape the Food Marketing System." *Amber Waves,* April 2008. <http://www.ers.usda.gov/AmberWaves/April08/Features/FoodMarketing.htm>.

Massoni, Gary. "Perspectives on Operation Breadbasket." In *Martin Luther King and the Civil Rights Movement,* edited by David Garrow, 179–340. New York: Carlson, 1989.

Matthews, Glenna. *Just a Housewife: The Rise and Fall of Domesticity in America.* New York: Oxford University Press, 1987.

May, Elaine Tyler. *Homeward Bound: American Families in the Cold War.* New York: Basic Books, 1988.

Mayo, James M. *The American Grocery Store: The Business Evolution of an Architectural Space.* Contributions in American History, no. 150. Westport, Conn.: Greenwood, 1993.

McAusland, Randolph. *Supermarkets: Fifty Years of Progress.* Washington, D.C.: Food Marketing Institute, 1980.

McCurdy, Charles. "American Law and the Marketing Structure of the Large Corporation, 1875–1890." *Journal of Economic History* 38 (September 1978): 631–49.

McDowell, Winston C. "Keeping Them 'In the Same Boat Together'? Sufi Abdul Hamid, African Americans, Jews, and the Harlem Jobs Boycotts." In *African Americans and Jews in the Twentieth Century: Studies in Convergence and Conflict*, edited by V. P. Franklin, Nancy L. Grant, Harold M. Kletnick, and Genna Rae McNeil, 208–35. Columbia: University of Missouri Press, 1998.

McGovern, Charles F. "Consumption and Citizenship in the United States, 1900–1940." In Strasser, McGovern, and Judt, *Getting and Spending*, 37–58.

————. *Sold American: Consumption and Citizenship, 1890–1945*. Chapel Hill: University of North Carolina Press, 2006.

————. "Sold American: Inventing the American Consumer, 1890–1940." Ph.D. diss., Harvard University, 1993.

McNair, Malcolm. *Expenses and Profits in the Chain Grocery Business in 1929*. Bulletin of the Bureau of Business Research, Harvard University, no. 84. Cambridge, Mass.: Harvard University Press, 1931.

McQuaid, Kim. *Uneasy Partners: Big Business in American Politics, 1945–1990*. Baltimore, Md.: Johns Hopkins University Press, 1994.

Mehrotra, Ajay. "Envisioning the Modern American Fiscal State: Progressive-Era Economists and the Intellectual Foundations of the U.S. Income Tax." *UCLA Law Review* 52 (August 2005): 1752–1866.

Merish, Lori. *Sentimental Materialism: Gender, Commodity Culture, and Nineteenth-Century American Literature*. Durham, N.C.: Duke University Press, 2000.

Meyerowitz, Joanne, ed. *Not June Cleaver: Women and Gender in Postwar America, 1945–1960*. Philadelphia: Temple University Press, 1994.

————. "Beyond the Feminine Mystique: A Reassessment of Postwar Mass Culture, 1946–1958." In Meyerowitz, *Not June Cleaver*, 229–62.

————. *Women Adrift: Independent Women Wage-Earners in Chicago, 1880–1930*. Chicago: University of Chicago Press, 1988.

Michel, Sonya, and Seth Koven, eds. *Mothers of a New World: Maternalist Politics and the Origins of Welfare States*. New York: Routledge, 1993.

Mihm, Stephen. *A Nation of Counterfeiters: Capitalists, Con Men, and the Making of the United States*. Cambridge, Mass.: Harvard University Press, 2007.

Milkman, Ruth. *Gender at Work: The Dynamics of Job Segregation by Sex during World War II*. Urbana: University of Illinois Press, 1987.

Miller, Daniel. *A Theory of Shopping*. Ithaca, N.Y.: Cornell University Press, 1998.

Mintz, Sidney. *Sweetness and Power: The Place of Sugar in Modern History*. New York: Viking, 1986.

Moskowitz, Marina. *Standard of Living: The Measure of the Middle Class in Modern America*. Baltimore, Md.: Johns Hopkins University Press, 2004.

Mueller, Willard F., and Leon Garoian. *Changes in the Market Structure of Grocery Retailing*. Madison: University of Wisconsin Press, 1961.

Murphy, Lucy Eldersveld, and Wendy Hamand Venet, eds. *Midwestern Women: Work, Women, and Community at the Crossroads*. Bloomington: Indiana University Press, 1997.

National Industrial Conference Board. *Changes in the Cost of Living, July 1914–July 1923.* New York: National Industrial Conference Board, 1923.

Neuhaus, Jessamyn. "The Joy of Sex Instruction: Women and Cooking in Marital Sex Manuals, 1920–1963." In Inness, *Kitchen Culture in America,* 95–118.

———. *Manly Meals and Mom's Home Cooking: Cookbooks and Gender in Modern America.* Baltimore, Md.: Johns Hopkins University Press, 2003.

Norling, Lisa. *Captain Ahab Had a Wife: New England Women and the Whalefishery, 1720–1870.* Chapel Hill: University of North Carolina Press, 2000.

Novak, William J. *The People's Welfare: Law and Regulation in Nineteenth-Century America.* Chapel Hill: University of North Carolina Press, 1996.

Oerke, Bess V. *Mealtime.* Peoria, Ill.: Bennett, 1960.

Orleck, Annelise. *Common Sense and a Little Fire: Women and Working-Class Politics in the United States, 1900–1965.* Chapel Hill: University of North Carolina Press, 1995.

———. "'We Are That Mythical Thing Called the Public': Consumer Organizing in the Great Depression." *Feminist Studies* 19 (Spring 1993): 147–72.

Ott, Julia. "When Wall Street Met Main Street: The Quest for an Investors' Democracy and the Emergence of the Retail Investor in the United States, 1890–1930." Ph.D. diss., Yale University, 2007.

Ownby, Ted. *American Dreams in Mississippi: Consumers, Poverty, and Culture, 1830–1998.* Chapel Hill: University of North Carolina Press, 1999.

Packard, Vance. *The Hidden Persuaders.* New York: McKay, 1957.

Palamountain, Joseph. *The Politics of Distribution.* Cambridge, Mass.: Harvard University Press, 1955.

Palmer, Phyllis. *Domesticity and Dirt: Housewives and Domestic Servants in the United States, 1920–1945.* Philadelphia: Temple University Press, 1989.

Parker, Florence. *The First 125 Years: A History of Distributive and Service Cooperation in the United States, 1829–1954.* Superior, Wis.: Cooperative Publishing Association, 1956.

Parkin, Katherine. *Food Is Love: Food Advertising in Modern America.* Philadelphia: University of Pennsylvania Press, 2006.

Payne, Charles. *I've Got the Light of Freedom: The Organizing Tradition and the Mississippi Freedom Struggle.* Berkeley: University of California Press, 1995.

Peiss, Kathy. *Cheap Amusements: Working Women and Leisure in Turn-of-the-Century New York.* Philadelphia: Temple University Press, 1986.

———. *Hope in a Jar: The Making of America's Beauty Culture.* New York: Metropolitan Books, 1998.

Pells, Richard H. *Radical Visions and American Dreams: Culture and Social Thought in the Depression Years.* Middletown, Conn.: Wesleyan University Press, 1984.

Perkins, Edwin J. *From Wall Street to Main Street: Charles Merrill and Middle-Class Investors.* New York: Cambridge University Press, 1999.

Phillips, Charles F. "The Supermarket." *Harvard Business Review* 16 (Winter 1938): 188–200.

Piven, Frances Fox, and Richard A. Cloward. *Poor People's Movements: Why They Succeed, How They Fail.* New York: Pantheon Books, 1977.

Pollak, Oliver M. "The Jewish Peddlers of Omaha." *Nebraska History* 63 (Winter 1982): 474–501.

Porter, Glenn, and Harold Livesay. *Merchants and Manufacturers: Studies in the Changing Structure of Nineteenth-Century Marketing.* Baltimore, Md.: Johns Hopkins Press, 1971.

Purvis, Martin. "Societies of Consumers and Consumer Societies: Co-operation, Consumption and Politics in Britain and Continental Europe, c. 1850–1920." *Journal of Historical Geography* 24 (April 1998): 147–69.

Ransby, Barbara. *Ella Baker and the Black Freedom Movement: A Radical Democratic Vision.* Chapel Hill: University of North Carolina Press, 2003.

Reagin, Nancy. *Sweeping the German Nation: Domesticity and National Identity.* New York: Cambridge University Press, 2007.

Rich, Melanie. "'She Would Raise Hens to Aid the War': The Contributions of Oklahoma Women during World War I." *Chronicles of Oklahoma* 81 (Fall 2003): 334–55.

Riley, Denise. *Am I That Name? Feminism and the Category of Women in History.* Minneapolis: University of Minnesota Press, 1989.

Rockoff, Hugh. *Drastic Measures: A History of Wage and Price Controls in the United States.* New York: Cambridge University Press, 1984.

Rosen, Ruth. *The World Split Open: How the Modern Women's Movement Changed America.* New York: Penguin Books, 2000.

Ross, Ellen. *Love and Toil: Motherhood in Outcast London.* New York: Oxford University Press, 1993.

Ross, Thomas W. "Winners and Losers under the Robinson-Patman Act." *Journal of Law and Economics* 28 (October 1984): 243–71.

Rubin, Gayle. "The Traffic in Women: Notes on the 'Political Economy' of Sex." In *Toward an Anthropology of Women,* edited by Rayna Reiter, 157–210. New York: Monthly Review, 1975.

Ryan, Mary. *Mysteries of Sex: Tracing Women and Men in American History.* Chapel Hill: University of North Carolina Press, 2006.

Ryant, Carl. "Kentucky and the Movement to Regulate Chain Stores, 1925–1945." *Filson Club History Quarterly* 57 (July 1983): 270–85.

Sabel, Charles, and Jonathan Zeitlin. "Historical Alternatives to Mass Production: Politics, Markets and Technology in Nineteenth-Century Industrialization." *Past and Present* 108 (August 1985): 133–76.

———, eds. *World of Possibilities: Flexibility and Mass Production in Western Industrialization.* London: Cambridge University Press, 1997.

Scarpellini, Emanuela. "Shopping American-Style: The Arrival of the Supermarket in Postwar Italy." *Enterprise and Society* 5 (December 2004): 625–68.

Schrecker, Ellen. *Many Were the Crimes: McCarthyism in America.* Boston: Little, Brown, 1998.

Scranton, Philip. *Endless Novelty: Specialty Production and American Industrialization, 1865–1925.* Princeton, N.J.: Princeton University Press, 1997.

Shapiro, Laura. *Perfection Salad: Women and Cooking at the Turn of the Century.* New York: Farrar, Straus, and Giroux, 1986.

————. *Something from the Oven: Reinventing Dinner in 1950s America*. New York: Penguin, 2005.

Shideler, Ernest Hugh. "The Chain Store: A Study of the Ecological Organization of a Modern City." Ph.D. diss., University of Chicago, 1927.

Silber, Norman Isaac. *Tests and Protest: The Influence of Consumers Union*. New York: Holmes and Meier, 1983.

Sklar, Kathryn Kish. "Two Political Cultures in the Progressive Era: The National Consumers' League and the American Association for Labor Legislation." In *U.S. History as Women's History: New Feminist Essays*, edited by Linda K. Kerber, Alice Kessler-Harris, and Kathryn Kish Sklar, 36–62. Chapel Hill: University of North Carolina Press, 1995.

Skocpol, Theda. *Protecting Soldiers and Mothers: The Political Origins of Social Policy in the United States*. Cambridge, Mass.: Belknap, 1992.

Slocum, Rachel. "Anti-Racist Practice and the Work of Community Food Organizations." *Antipode* 38 (March 2006): 327–49.

Smith, Barbara Clark. "Food Rioters and the American Revolution." *William and Mary Quarterly* 51, 3rd ser. (January 1994): 3–38.

Sparks, Cory. "Locally Owned and Operated: Opposition to Chain Stores, 1925–1940." Ph.D. diss., Louisiana State University, 2000.

Spruill, Julia Cherry. *Women's Life and Work in the Southern Colonies*. Chapel Hill: University of North Carolina Press, 1938.

Stansell, Christine. *City of Women: Sex and Class in New York, 1789–1860*. Urbana: University of Illinois Press, 1987.

Stoler, Ann, ed. *Haunted by Empire: Geographies of Intimacy in North American History*. Durham, N.C.: Duke University Press, 2006.

Storrs, Landon R. Y. *Civilizing Capitalism: The National Consumers' League, Women's Activism, and Labor Standards in the New Deal Era*. Chapel Hill: University of North Carolina Press, 2000.

————. "Left-Feminism, the Consumer Movement, and Red Scare Politics in the United States." *Journal of Women's History* 18 (Fall 2006): 40–67.

————. "Red Scare Politics and the Suppression of Popular Front Feminism: The Loyalty Investigation of Mary Dublin Keyserling." *Journal of American History* 90 (September 2003): 491–524.

Stovall, Tyler. "Du vieux et du neuf: Économie morale et militantisme ouvrier dans les luttes contre la vie chère à Paris en 1919." *Le Mouvement Social*. Translated by Colette Friedlander. No. 170 (January–March 1995): 85–113.

Strasser, Susan. *Never Done: A History of American Housework*. New York: Pantheon Books, 1982.

————. *Satisfaction Guaranteed: The Making of the American Mass Market*. New York: Basic Books, 1989.

Strasser, Susan, Charles McGovern, and Matthias Judt, eds. *Getting and Spending: European and American Consumer Societies in the Twentieth Century*. Cambridge: Cambridge University Press, 1998.

Sugrue, Thomas. *The Origins of the Urban Crisis: Race and Inequality in Postwar Detroit.* Princeton, N.J.: Princeton University Press, 1996.

Susman, Warren. *Culture as History: The Transformation of American Society in the Twentieth Century.* New York: Pantheon Books, 1984.

Tangires, Helen. *Public Markets and Civic Culture in Nineteenth-Century America.* Baltimore, Md.: Johns Hopkins University Press, 2003.

Tedlow, Richard S. *New and Improved: The Story of Mass Marketing in America.* New York: Basic Books, 1990.

Tenhoor, Meredith. "Eating by Machinery: Space, Gender, and Pleasure in the Automat." Paper presented at the 2005 annual meeting of the Society for the History of Technology, Minneapolis, Minnesota, November 4–6, 2005.

Tingley, Donald. *The Structuring of a State: The History of Illinois, 1899–1928.* Urbana: University of Illinois Press, 1981.

Tolbert, Lisa. "'The Aristocracy of the Market Basket': Self-Service Food Shopping in the New South." In Belasco and Horowitz, *Food Chains,* 179–95.

Tolliday, Steven, and Y. Yonemitsu. "Microfirms and Industrial Districts in Japan: The Dynamics of the Arita Ceramic-Ware Industry in the Twentieth Century." *Journal of Japanese Studies* 33 (Winter 2007): 29–66.

Tsing, Anna. *Friction: An Ethnography of Global Connection.* Princeton, N.J.: Princeton University Press, 2005.

Turner, Katherine L. "Buying, Not Cooking: Ready-to-Eat Food in American Urban Working-Class Neighborhoods, 1880–1930." *Food, Culture, and Society* 9 (Spring 2006): 13–39.

Tuttle, William M., Jr. *Race Riot: Chicago in the Red Summer of 1919.* New York: Atheneum, 1970.

Ulrich, Laurel Thatcher. *Good Wives: Image and Reality in the Lives of Women in Northern New England, 1650–1750.* New York: Knopf, 1982.

Vaillant, Derek. "Peddling Noise: Contesting the Civic Soundscape of Chicago, 1890–1913." *Journal of the Illinois State Historical Society* 96 (Autumn 2003): 257–87.

Vanek, Joanne. "Time Spent in Housework." *Scientific American* 231 (November 1974): 116–20.

Veit, Helen Zoe. "'We Were a Soft People': Asceticism, Self-Discipline and American Food Conservation in the First World War." *Food, Culture, and Society* 10 (Summer 2007): 167–90.

Von Eschen, Penny M. *Satchmo Blows Up the World: Jazz Ambassadors Play the Cold War.* Cambridge, Mass.: Harvard University Press, 2004.

Walton, Whitney. *France at the Crystal Palace: Bourgeois Tastes and Artisan Manufacture in the Nineteenth Century.* Berkeley: University of California Press, 1992.

Wandersee, Winifred. *Women's Work and Family Values, 1920–1940.* Cambridge, Mass.: Harvard University Press, 1981.

Warne, Colston Estey. *The Consumers' Co-operative Movement in Illinois.* Chicago: University of Chicago Press, 1926.

Warner, Michael. Social Text Collective. *Fear of a Queer Planet: Queer Politics and Social Theory.* Minneapolis: University of Minnesota Press, 1993.

Weatherford, Doris. *American Women and World War II*. New York: Facts on File, 1990.

Weinberg, Sydney Stahl. *The World of Our Mothers: The Lives of Jewish Immigrant Women*. Chapel Hill: University of North Carolina Press, 1988.

Weiss, Jessica. "She Also Cooks: Gender, Domesticity, and Public Life in Oakland, California, 1957–1959." In Inness, *Kitchen Culture in America*, 211–26.

———. *To Have and to Hold: Marriage, the Baby Boom, and Social Change*. Chicago: University of Chicago Press, 2000.

Welke, Barbara Young. *Recasting American Liberty: Gender, Race, Law, and the Railroad Revolution, 1865–1920*. New York: Cambridge University Press, 2001.

Wells, Christopher. "Car Country: Automobiles, Roads, and the Shaping of the Modern American Landscape, 1890–1929." Ph.D. diss., University of Wisconsin–Madison, 2004.

Wendt, Lloyd, and Herman Kogan. *Give the Lady What She Wants! The Story of Marshall Field and Company*. Chicago: Rand McNally, 1952.

Wiebe, Robert. *The Search for Order, 1877–1920*. New York: Hill and Wang, 1967.

Wiese, Andrew. *Places of Their Own: African American Suburbanization in the Twentieth Century*. Chicago: University of Chicago Press, 2004.

Wilk, Richard. *Home Cooking in the Global Village: Caribbean Food from Buccaneers to Ecotourists*. New York: Berg, 2006.

Williams-Forson, Psyche A. *Building Houses out of Chicken Legs: Black Women, Food, and Power*. Chapel Hill: University of North Carolina Press, 2006.

Wirth, Louis. *The Ghetto*. 1928. Reprint, Chicago: Transaction Publishers, 1997.

Wright, John R. "The Marketing History of the Jewel Tea Company." *Journal of Marketing* 22 (April 1958): 367–76.

Yanagisako, Sylvia. *Producing Culture and Capital: Family Firms in Italy*. Princeton, N.J.: Princeton University Press, 2002.

Yellin, Emily. *Our Mothers' War: American Women at Home and at the Front during World War II*. New York: Free Press, 2006.

Zelizer, Julian. *Taxing America: Wilbur D. Mills, Congress, and the State, 1945–1975*. Cambridge: Cambridge University Press, 1998.

Zelizer, Viviana. *The Purchase of Intimacy*. Princeton, N.J.: Princeton University Press, 2005.

Zimmerman, Max Mandell. *The Super Market: A Revolution in Distribution*. New York: McGraw-Hill, 1955.

Zweiniger-Bargielowska, Ina. *Austerity in Britain: Rationing, Controls, and Consumption, 1939–1955*. Oxford: Oxford University Press, 2000.

Acknowledgments

It is a pleasure to thank the many people and institutions that have contributed to the creation of this book.

I thank the Chicago Public School System for providing me with an excellent education, primarily by hiring teachers who expanded the realm of the imaginable. My decision to become an academic owes much to the teachers who made me think that my intellectual acumen was special and who gave me the skills that made me comfortable when I finally entered more elite settings. Some of these teachers stand out. Clarice Cogan taught me how to answer essay questions in fifth grade, a skill that has served me well. Jay Lee encouraged my interest in history in junior high, and in high school, Bernadette McHale changed my life one day by wearing a button that read, "Write Women Back into History." The late and much-missed Larry Minkoff made my world and my ambitions bigger. Larry Beverage pointed me in the right direction more than once, but never more so than when he mentioned that I ought to consider becoming a history professor. Dagny Bloland managed both to praise and to push me; her example of savvy, dedicated teaching continues to inspire me, and her friendship continues to reward me. For all of their years of hard work, educating me and other Chicago kids, I thank them enormously.

In addition to these teachers, I was lucky to have the encouragement of Leora Auslander, Kathleen Conzen, James Grossman, and Peter Novick at the University of Chicago and Darline Gay-Levy and Marilyn Young at New York University. At the University of Wisconsin, Colleen Dunlavy's enthusiasm and high standards guided my first research and writing on the history of capitalism; I have continued to draw on both. Jeanne Boydston's insistence on linking economic change with gender analyses has become only more important over time; Jeanne made me think not only that I *could* be a historian of capitalism and of gender but also that I would *have* to be such a scholar. It is one of the great sadnesses of my life that I was not able to give this book to her in person. My thinking about politics, consumption, and gender also benefited from the input of Rima Apple, John Coleman, John Cooper, Linda Gordon, and Jonathan Zeitlin.

This project has been aided by grants and funding from the Smithsonian Institution, Bard College at Simon's Rock, the Herbert Hoover Presidential Library, the Illinois State Historical Society, the Franklin Roosevelt Presidential Library, the Rockefeller Archives Center, the University of Wisconsin, and the Department of History and the Graduate School at the University of Minnesota. Some of my most important thinking about this book was articulated during a semester at the Institute for Advanced Study at the University of Minnesota; I remain grateful to Ann Waltner and her staff for their skillful support of intellectual exchange. I am also enormously indebted to innumerable archivists and librarians, as well as firm employees, who preserved, processed, and made accessible the documents on which this book has drawn. Special thanks go to the staffs at the Wisconsin Historical Society and the University of Minnesota Libraries.

I have been buoyed throughout this process by warm friendships and the kind of collegiality that has to be experienced to be believed. For endless potlucks, generous reads, high standards, and the refusal to let me give up many years ago, I especially thank Ellen Baker, Dorothea Browder, Sarah Fatherly, Margaret Hogan, Natasha Larimer, Eric Morser, Monica Najar, Bill Philpott, Louise Pubols, Bethel Saler, and Melissa Soto-Schwartz. I also want to thank my wonderful colleagues at the University of Minnesota for their support for this project and for a wide-ranging intellectual exchange. Some people deserve special credit for making my work life so rewarding: Susanna Blumenthal, Lianna Farber, Kirsten Fischer, Donna Garbaccia, David Good, George Henderson, Regina Kunzel, Erika Lee, Malinda Alaine Lindquist, Michael Lower, Saje Mathieu, Elaine May, Lary May, M. J. Maynes, Lisa Norling, Jeani O'Brien, Jennifer Pierce, and Barbara Welke have all been generous with advice and support. Members of the Workshop on the Comparative History of Women, Gender, and Sexuality, the members of the Markets in Time Colloquium and AgriFood Reading Group have been crucial to my growth as a scholar. All have offered advice and support along the way. Students in my graduate seminars on American capitalism and consumption have pushed my thinking in critical ways, and I thank them all.

A few people deserve special mention: Jeff Manual, Polly Reed Myers, and N'Jai-An Patters provided vital research assistance, and Caley Horan provided important editorial help. For warm friendships and homes away from home when I was doing research, I thank particularly Ellen Baker, Daniel Holt, and Rachel Baker-Holt; Debra Farkas, Moira Mcdonald, and Jonah and Naomi Farkas-McDonald; Sarah, JoAnne, and Darby Fatherly; and Jessica, Michael, Naomi, and Genna Simpson.

The encouragement of Susan Porter Benson, Lizabeth Cohen, Roger Horowitz and Philip Scranton early in the project meant a great deal to me. Pamela Laird provided support and important advice as I reframed the project. Dorothy Sue Cobble's comments on a conference paper proved enormously helpful as I wrote what became chapter 1. Ellen Baker and Monica Najar shared generous and smart comments on some crucial sections of the book, patiently reading the revisions until I got it right. Christopher Wells has helped me articulate my ideas more than once, and always with kindness and good humor. M. J. Maynes and Barbara Welke read an early draft of the entire manuscript; their characteristically astute suggestions shaped many of the revisions I made. Kevin Murphy's camaraderie enriches my thinking, my teaching, and my writing. Karen Ho and Jigna Desai helped in countless ways.

Several people helped me with the latter stages of this project. I am enormously grateful for the astute reads given this manuscript by Warren Belasco, Glenna Matthews, and several anonymous readers. Michal Safar, archivist of the Hyde Park Historical Society, located photos of the Hyde Park Co-op in the as-yet unprocessed papers of the society. Sarah Marcus has proven to be a true Chicago friend for years, most recently by helping me locate many of the wonderful photos that appear in this book. At the University of North Carolina Press, Sian Hunter has been an ideal editor; Paul Betz, a superb project editor; and Ricky Huard, an assiduous copyeditor. Their support for this project has made it better.

In addition to looking at systems (like capitalism) that make life challenging, I can't help but look at those systems that make my life and this work doable. This book would not have been written were it not for the stunning childcare provided by Debra Farkas, Hye-Jeong Moon, Erica Webb, Ann Wilner, and the staff of the University of Minnesota Child Care Center. The twin tasks of parenting and writing were also made doable by some important parental leave policies at the University of Minnesota. These policies resulted from the efforts of many dedicated people. I thank them all for their work.

I would never have written a book about grocery stores if it were not for the warm memories my family has given me. I thank my mother for taking me grocery shopping when I was a child, and both my parents, Allan and Sharon Deutsch, and my sister, Jennifer Snyder, for their longstanding support. This book is dedicated to my grandmothers who, in very different ways, taught me an enormous amount about food and Chicago. They, along with my grandfathers, my parents, and my extended family, never failed to do the hard work of sustaining family and expanding horizons; I remain very grateful to them. This book is only a small way of saying thank you.

David Chang has been with this project nearly as long as I have. I thank him for sharing his intellect, his incredible spirit, and his domestic skills with me. I am enormously grateful that we get to live our lives together.

My final words are for our children, Gabriel and Nathaniel. As a completely objective person, I can say definitively that they are great kids. I thank them for making each other laugh and for their relentless curiosity, their kindness, and their patience with this book. They give me hours of fun and, however unintentionally, remind me about the limited control a person can exert over their life and work. I look forward to teaching and learning more about the world with them.

Index

Page numbers in italics refer to illustrations